THE WEIMAR REPUBLIC AND THE YOUNGER POLETARIAT

Also by Peter D. Stachura

NAZI YOUTH IN THE WEIMAR REPUBLIC

THE WEIMAR ERA AND HITLER 1918–1933: A Critical Bibliography

THE SHAPING OF THE NAZI STATE (*editor*)

*THE GERMAN YOUTH MOVEMENT 1900–1945: An Interpretative and Documentary History

GREGOR STRASSER AND THE RISE OF NAZISM

THE NAZI *MACHTERGREIFUNG* (*editor*)

*UNEMPLOYMENT AND THE GREAT DEPRESSION IN WEIMAR GERMANY (*editor*)

The Weimar Republic and the Younger Proletariat

An Economic and Social Analysis

Peter D. Stachura, M.A., Ph.D., F.R.Hist.S.
Reader in History, University of Stirling

St. Martin's Press   New York

© Peter D. Stachura, 1989

All rights reserved. For information, write:
Scholarly and Reference Division,
St. Martin's Press, Inc., 175 Fifth Avenue, New York, N.Y. 10010

First published in the United States of America in 1989

Printed in Hong Kong

ISBN 0-312-03147-5

Library of Congress Cataloging-in-Publication Data
Stachura, Peter D.
The Weimar Republic and the younger proletariat: an economic and social analysis / Peter D. Stachura.
p.   cm.
Bibliography: p.
Includes index.
ISBN 0-312-03147-5
 1. Youth—Employment—Germany—History—20th century.
2. Unemployment—Germany—History—20th century. 3. Public welfare-
-Germany—History—20th century. 4. Juvenile delinquency—Germany-
-History—20th century. 5. Germany—Economic
conditions—1918-1945. 6. Germany—Social conditions—1918-1933.
I. Title.
HD6276.G4S725   1989
331.3'4'0943—dc19   89-30605
                                                                  CIP

For my father,

† Wladyslaw Stachura, and his Poland,
free, independent and proud

Contents

List of Tables viii
List of Abbreviations ix
Preface xi

1 Introduction 1
2 The Younger Generation in the Kaiserreich 10
3 The Weimar Sozialstaat 34
4 The Younger Generation and Welfare, 1918–1929 64
5 Youth in the Labour Market, 1918–1929 94
6 Youth Unemployment in the Great Depression, 1929–1933 115
7 Juvenile Crime, Delinquency and Correctional
   Education, 1918–1933 133
8 Conclusion: The Political Dimension 155

Notes 163
Bibliography 211
Index 230

List of Tables

3.1	Registered unemployment in Germany, 1929–33	59
3.2	Registered unemployment pattern in the regions, 1930–3	60
3.3	The percentage of registered unemployed in receipt of relief, 1930–2	63
5.1	Registered unemployed aged 14-18 years in receipt of unemployment benefit, 1926–7	99
6.1	Youth unemployment (officially registered), 30 July 1932	117
6.2	Youth unemployment (officially registered), June 1933	118
7.1	Juvenile crime figures, 1918–23	136
7.2	Juvenile crime figures, 1925–9	137
7.3	Juvenile criminals and unemployment in German cities, 1930–1	140
7.4	Number of convicted juveniles who were unemployed at the time of their offence, 1932–3	141

List of Abbreviations

ADGB	Allgemeiner Deutscher Gewerkschaftsbund
AfS	Archiv für Sozialgeschichte
AVAVG	Gesetz über Arbeitsvermittlung und Arbeitslosenversicherung
BAK	Bundesarchiv Koblenz
Bay. HStA	Bayerisches Hauptstaatsarchiv
DDP	Deutsche Demokratische Partei
DNVP	Deutschnationale Volkspartei
DVP	Deutsche Volkspartei
FAD	Freiwilliger Arbeitsdienst
FE	Fürsorgeerziehung
HASK	Historisches Archiv der Stadt Köln
HHStAW	Hessisches Hauptstaatsarchiv Wiesbaden
HStAS	Hauptstaatsarchiv Stuttgart
HZ	Historische Zeitschrift
IWK	Internationale Wissenschaftliche Korrespondenz zur Geschichte der Deutschen Arbeiterbewegung
JbADJB	Jahrbuch des Archivs der Deutschen Jugendbewegung
JGG	Jugendgerichtsgesetz
KJVD	Kommunistischer Jugendverband Deutschlands
KPD	Kommunistische Partei Deutschlands
LHAK	Landeshauptarchiv Koblenz
LJA	Landesjugendamt
NSDAP	Nationalsozialistische Deutsche Arbeiterpartei
RADA	Reichsarbeitsgemeinschaft für Deutsche Arbeitsdienstpflicht
RDI	Reichsverband der Deutschen Industrie
RGBI	Reichsgesetzblatt
RJWG	Reichsjugendwohlfahrtsgesetz
RWWA	Rheinisch–Westfälisches Wirtschaftsarchiv
SA	Sturmabteilung
SAJ	Verband der Sozialistische Arbeiterjugend Deutschlands
SAPD	Sozialistische Arbeiterpartei Deutschlands
SPD	Sozialdemokratische Partei Deutschlands

List of Abbreviations

StAB	Staatsarchiv Bremen
StAH	Staatsarchiv Hamburg
StAM	Staatsarchiv München
USPD	Unabhängige Sozialdemokratische Partei Deutschlands
VAJV	Verband der Arbeiterjugendvereine Deutschlands
VfZG	Vierteljahrshefte für Zeitgeschichte
WTB	Woytinsky (Wladimir), Tarnow (Fritz), Baade (Fritz)
ZAG	Zentralarbeitsgemeinschaft
ZBl	Zentralblatt für Jugendrecht und Jugendwohlfahrt

Preface

The theme of this study essentially constitutes for me what might be termed the 'other' or reverse side of the history of younger people in Germany during the first half of the twentieth century, for it has followed on naturally from my previous examinations of the organised youth movement. The project could not have been sustained and then completed, however, without the substantial assistance given to me, in the first instance, by the staffs of the many archives in the Federal Republic of Germany which I visited in the period 1982–8. It is a pleasure to record my gratitude to those, too numerous to name individually, whose invaluable advice and help was always freely dispensed at the Bundesarchiv and the Landeshauptarchiv in Koblenz, the Staatsarchiv Hamburg, Staatsarchiv Bremen, Hauptstaatsarchiv Stuttgart, the Hessisches Hauptstaatsarchiv in Wiesbaden, the Historisches Archiv der Stadt Köln and the Rhenisch-Westfälisches Wirtschaftsarchiv, also in Cologne, the Archiv der deutschen Jugendbewegung at Burg Ludwigstein, Staatsarchiv München and the Bayerisches Hauptstaatsarchiv in Munich.

My frequent and sometimes time-consuming enquiries about secondary and printed matter were handled with admirable efficiency by staff at the Forschungsstelle für die Geschichte des Nationalsozialismus in Hamburg, the Libraries of the Universities of Düsseldorf, Hamburg and Munich, the Bayerisches Staatsbibliothek in Munich, the Wiener Library, British Museum Library and the German Historical Institute Library – all in London – and, last but not least, at the Inter-Library Loan section of the University of Stirling Library.

My many and rather expensive researches abroad were initially made possible by a considerable grant from the Economic and Social Research Council and, latterly, by awards from the British Academy, the Twenty-Seven Foundation and the Wolfson Foundation. I am most grateful for this indispensable and generous support.

I have been the fortunate beneficiary of conversations about this project which have been conducted over the years with colleagues from a variety of disciplines in Britain and in Germany. Their views have been accorded the most serious consideration, though, of course, responsibility for what appears in the following pages, including any errors, rests entirely with me.

Preface

The University of Stirling granted me a semester's sabbatical leave in 1988 which allowed the completion of most of the manuscript. Miss Margaret Hendry is thanked for expeditiously typing the manuscript.

I much appreciate the patience and understanding displayed by my wife, Kay, and children, Gregory and Madeleine, towards my long absences from home as I scoured German archives and libraries for material, and also, later, towards my partial withdrawal from normal family life due to the exigencies of writing. My non-availability on a number of Saturday afternoons was particularly frustrating for my son as it meant forgoing the pleasure of visiting a favourite spot in the East End of Glasgow where a uniquely outstanding institution was triumphantly celebrating its Centenary Year! I hope that the sacrifice has not been totally in vain.

Munich/Bridge of Allan PETER D. STACHURA

1 Introduction

The history of the independent and tutelage youth movements in Germany has attracted extensive interest over the years, not least because of their putative connections with National Socialism. By the same token, the working-class youth movement has been the subject of considerable enquiry, partly because of its role in the socialist and labour organisations of the Weimar period and also because of the political support given to Communism by many younger members of the urban-industrial proletariat. These investigations have produced a voluminous and diverse historiography whose principal focus has been on political and organisational matters. Similarly, the Weimar Republic has been for a long time a prime area for scholarly attention, which has been directed deeply and widely into its manifold tragedies, especially in the constitutional, political, ideological, economic and international spheres. In both of these highly popular topics of study, however, social history in the broadest sense has been comparatively neglected and, in any event, centred on institutional and organisational histories.[1] In more recent times there has been a slight redressing of the balance in youth studies in so far as more concern has been trained on theories of generational conflict, the proliferation of sub-cultures, psychological response and problems of adolescence and childhood.[2] But little has been undertaken regarding the actual social experience of the young outside organised groups. The present work examines a particular group of Germany's younger generation during the period 1918–33, thus aiming to make a contribution not only to the social study of youth but also to the relatively underdeveloped social history of the Weimar Republic.

The younger working class, so defined according to the criteria of occupational and parental–social background, but representing a far from homogeneous entity, was the subject of growing discussion and examination by various middle-class interest groups from around the turn of the century onwards. There was official governmental and informed middle-class solicitude for the material, spiritual, moral and educational well-being of lower, unskilled working-class youth in particular, who were judged to be in need of remedial treatment; that is, their general conduct and life-style offended conventional bourgeois standards and had to be brought up to proper acceptable levels. These youths were increasingly regarded as dangerous nonconformists. But the remedies and policies of social welfare that were proposed and later implemented were inevitably viewed as alien to the ragged, inchoate values of the lower proletariat; considerable friction arising from this region of incomprehensibility was unavoidable in these circumstances. The predominantly bourgeois ethos of the Wilhelmine and Weimar States in social welfare could only be resented by such youths. From a broader perspective, interest in the younger proletariat followed on as a matter of course from the higher profile and more threatening posture of the industrial working class in the economic and political life of modern Germany. Accounts of their situation written after 1945 have concentrated on their political involvement and then, invariably, from a rather partisan party political or tendentious autobiographical standpoint. Only in the last few years have a number of studies sought to understand and explain the non-political, intrinsically socio-economic development of this group in a scholarly manner.

Detlev Peukert's major study, published in 1986,[3] breaks new ground in providing a detailed and comprehensive history of the social and economic environment in which the modern German State approached the problem of caring for youth that was officially deemed to be in need of protection and further education outside the parental home, with particular stress on correctional education in reformatories (*Fürsorgeerziehung*). It should be explained at this juncture that state care of the young in Germany was provided under two headings: *Jugendpflege*, in respect of the facilities and services required by or appropriate to youth in 'normal', settled family circumstances, from the age of 14 to 18 years, or to 21 years; and *Jugendfürsorge*, for the 'abnormal', from the earliest age to usually 18 years, though it could be extended also to the age of 21, encompassing orphans, the mentally retarded, physically handicapped, as well as delinquent youth. The two areas were not always strictly separated in practice which means, from an historian's point of view, that concentration on an analysis of the one to the exclusion of the other can only result in a partial, truncated assessment of overall state policy in the youth sector. Peukert's study falls into this category for he considers that part of German youth who constituted the major clientele of correctional education, the lower working class, as he calls it (*Unterschichtsarbeiterjugend*). He conducts this enquiry within a conceptual framework inspired by Marxist social theory and social pedagogy, emphasising the concepts of 'social control' and 'social disciplining'.[4] As such, his analysis is designed as a searing indict-

Introduction

ment of industrial–capitalist society and its materialistic–bourgeois system of values. A key sentence conveys the essence of his argument:

> the improvement of social care and help brings an intensification of the control mechanism, an expansion of the system of sanctions and a dissemination of prevailing norms of social relations.[5]

For the lower, younger proletariat, social policy, as practised by the state from the late nineteenth century to 1933, resulted, in Peukert's estimation, in their social disciplining and the foisting on them of coercive, class-motivated social and educational policies. In a companion volume, which is also based on his *Habilitationsschrift*,[6] Peukert attempts to reconstruct the authentic character of these youths' life-style 'from below' by using a compendium of autobiographical and contemporary investigative material.[7] But these sources are largely fragmentary and at times incoherent, so that his general depiction seems shallow; the intellectual density of the first book is regretfully absent. Both works are almost completely devoid of primary archival data.

If the arguments in *Grenzen* are presented within a wide-ranging, interesting and skilful discussion, which identifies this book as a most valuable contribution, it cannot be said that they are entirely convincing. In the first place, Peukert produces no hard evidence in support of the theory of social control from established authority except for the immediate pre-1914 and 1932/3 periods. His case ultimately reposes, therefore, on an interpretative rather than an empirically demonstrated foundation. In accentuating the concept and practice of 'social control', he makes no allowance for the different approaches of an authoritarian and a democratic government. The initiatives designed to supervise working-class youth which were introduced by the authoritarian *Kaiserreich* and later by an authoritarian Weimar Reich Chancellor (Papen, above all), were nowhere to be found during the intervening period of parliamentary democratic government. The state's policies towards the young in 1918–29 are best understood as expressions of a genuine concern to further social justice with no strings attached: a fundamental humanitarianism sought to bring about material and broadly spiritual amelioration in the situation of the young. Part of the reason for this omission from Peukert's calculations is that throughout the study he does not take sufficient account of the impetus for social change and reform supplied by an awakened youth itself, and by a variegated youth welfare lobby comprising the Social Democratic Party (SPD), trade unions, Centre Party, youth movement, professional specialists, social reformers and educationalists. They were able to mobilise effectively after 1918 to exert pressure on government to make humanitarian considerations the main priority in policy making. The broader context of a humanitarian *Sozialpolitik* dictated the nature of youth policy. There could hardly have been one set of motives behind the one, for youth, and another quite different set behind the other, for adults. It is more realistic to argue that the objective of social welfare policy across the board was to enhance material standards and not to subordinate or control anyone in the sense intimated by Peukert. If there was an 'ulterior' motive it had much more to do with constructively integrating and consolidating working-class adherence to the democratic values of the Republic.

A final point of criticism of Peukert's stimulating study is that his rigid segregation of the unskilled lumpenproletariat from the rest of the working class and Weimar society as if they were a cohesive body in splendid isolation cannot be considered valid. The lines of division between and within social classes were often hopelessly blurred by Weimar's economic upheavals, especially by the war, hyper-inflation and the Depression; thus the lines between working class and lower middle class in the cities were frequently indistinguishable. The working class undoubtedly had its deprived elements but they were not set apart by a hard and fast demarcation; divisions between employed and unemployed, irregular and permanent workers were subject to fluctuation, just as Weimar society in general passed through numerous vicissitudes, resulting in much more fluidity than Peukert suggests. Since his entire hypothesis is predicated upon the existence of this narrowly-defined, static sub-group of the proletariat, which had no basis in reality, his analysis is consequently somewhat flawed and his conclusions arbitrary. Moreover he fails to appreciate the problems that this tight class-oriented approach creates for specific parts of his survey. For example, he does not even begin to address the blatant contradiction which emerges in his account of juvenile crime because apprentices, a skilled group removed from the lumpenproletariat, were as likely to commit offences as were unskilled, lower working-class youth. It might also be said that Peukert treats the latter with a curious mixture of sympathy and denunciation, which serves to obfuscate the reality that among this group were to be found decent, law-abiding citizens whose indigence did not automatically transform them into the social misfits of his own manufacture.

In another recently completed contribution relevant to the same sphere of youth studies, Elizabeth Harvey closely follows the major contours of Peukert's conceptual approach, though perhaps not with the same degree of invigorating intellectual authority.[8] She subscribes to the view that Weimar's entire social policy was 'part of a strategy developed by political élites to organise and control an increasingly complex and unstable social and political order'.[9] Unfortunately, it is not made clear who these 'political élites' were, nor is any empirical evidence furnished for the existence of a 'strategy'. In more general terms, however, Dr Harvey's thesis makes a noteworthy statement.

The present work examines the public policies of the Weimar State towards working-class youth as a whole who were of post-school age and in the labour market. The substantial and in many ways complementary contribution in this sphere of private bodies and the Christian churches is not considered because it merits independent study, though where it is thought apposite it is touched upon for purposes of illustration and comparison. The emphasis falls on male youth, for a number of reasons. Public policy, in an age when despite advances by the feminist movement women still occupied a generally subordinate status, was devised with the needs of males primarily in mind. Female youth had a range of requirements that were peculiar to their station, and these really should be the subject of separate analysis, in the same way as it is now recognised that the female component of the German youth movement has to be treated as a distinct issue.[10] Furthermore males were much more prominent than females in a number of important areas of youth involvement – for instance, in juvenile criminality, delinquency and reformatory education. Female youth are not entirely ignored in the following pages, but their consideration is largely peripheral to the analysis and argument.

There is no absolute definition of which age groups constituted 'youth' or the 'younger generation', just as the various official bodies in Wilhelmine and Weimar Germany lacked a consensus on this point. This work adopts a flexible notion of these terms, depending on the particular sphere or activity under discussion. In relation to the labour market, the 14–25 year old group is thought legitimate to include in the review, though the emphasis is on 14–18-year-olds: apprenticeships were usually completed at age 17 or 18 years. In examining juvenile crime and delinquency, the scope is reduced to 14–18-year olds because those over 18 years were regarded and treated as adults in criminal law; in relation to institutional care, the relevant age group was 14–20 years, which corresponded to official practice. At 21 years of age, which was officially recognised as the age of majority, full legal rights as an adult in civil law were granted. For the historian, matters are further complicated by the fact that the minimum voting age in Weimar was set at 20 years. As far as most contemporary social reformers and educationalists were concerned, youth between the school-leaving age of 14 years and the usual time for call-up to military service at 19 years were crucially important and most deserving of their ministrations. Due account is taken of all these interpretations. What is very unambiguous is that the terms 'youth' and 'younger generation' do not apply to under-14-year-olds, who must be regarded as children, nor to over-25-year-olds, who are decidedly to be designated adults.

The sources consulted for this monograph since study commenced in 1982 have been rich in variety. It was thought expedient to supplement the extensive secondary material published during the inter-war years on the youth theme, which included a substantial periodical literature, with a broad base of primary archival data. By consulting collections located in different parts of the Federal Republic it was hoped to construct a representative picture of the nature and implementation of social and welfare policies at national, regional and local levels throughout the Weimar era. The State Archives in Hamburg, Koblenz and Stuttgart were particularly useful in providing detailed information on the interaction of central and regional government policies. Most of the archival material consisted of official governmental and ministerial correspondence, memoranda, regulations and directives, reports, statistical surveys and handbooks, while press reports and commentaries and sundry other printed matter added a further welcome dimension. The topics for which the documentation was significantly full included youth unemployment and relief measures, the activities of youth welfare bodies, *Jugendpflege* in the 1920s, juvenile criminality, and the situation of working youth in the industrial sector. Sources on the state's role in youth provision in Bavaria were relatively sparse, which was not unexpected in view of the dominant influence in that state of the churches and private agencies in youth welfare. Bavaria was untypical of Weimar Germany in most other respects as well, of course; consequently, the flavour of the national picture in the youth sector was more faithfully transmitted by developments within Prussia, the largest federal state by far, containing approximately two-thirds of the Reich population. The final tier of background detail and perspectives was supplied by a cross-section of the abundant post-1945 secondary literature on the youth theme and the Weimar Republic.

Since the 'youth problem' in its modern form emerged in Germany around 1900, our analysis begins with developments in the *Kaiserreich* which frequently turned out to be antecedents of concepts and policies introduced in the youth sphere by the State after 1918. This study also, at the other end, so to speak, underlines the vital importance of the Great Depression in altering the course and complexion of the state's youth policies: the contrasts between the comparatively expansive and stable mid- and late 1920s, and the early 1930s, were striking in virtually all areas of youth care. From the analysis of the economic and social situation of working-class youth in Weimar Germany that is presented here, the essential argument is that until 1929 the state's basic humanitarian concern and quest for social justice motivated its provision of youth care in all branches. While some progress was made by that date a good deal clearly remained to be accomplished. What had been achieved was obliterated by the Depression, during which certain authoritarian elements became apparent in the state's youth policies as its democratic substance was considerably reduced. In turn, the younger proletariat, suffering from mass unemployment and its devastating socio-psychological consequences, was finally alienated from the Republic and the tradition of parliamentary democracy, and ultimately, after 1933, fell victim to the false promises of National Socialism.

Chapter 2 charts the awakening and self-discovery of the younger generation before 1914 and the need of the Wilhelmine state to formulate policies to cater for their specific social and economic problems. The Prussian decree of 1911 was a landmark in this respect. Initially humanitarian, in response to the influence of the broadly-based social reformist movement and the independent youth movement, the state's approach became increasingly authoritarian and designed to control, particularly towards working-class youth who were officially regarded as a potentially disruptive, even subversive force in society. Rising juvenile crime figures seemed to offer some hard evidence for this view. But at least a platform for a more expansive social and welfare programme for youth in the future was created and their noteworthy contribution to the war effort strengthened their case. Chapter 3 establishes the necessary wider context within which this programme was pursued after 1918. The major characteristics, achievements and limitations of *Sozialpolitik* are identified, as is the virtual destruction of the welfare state as a result of the government's severe deflationary policy and reductions in public expenditure during the Depression. Prolonged mass unemployment was the most visible and deleterious manifestation of that unhappy period. How youth fared in social welfare terms in the 1920s forms the principal theme of Chapter 4. With prompting from the variegated 'youth lobby', the state's promulgation of progressive national legislation in the shape of the *Reichsjugendwohlfahrtsgesetz* and *Jugendgerichtsgesetz* in 1922/3 set up a firm basis for advance in many spheres of youth care. The state's rhetoric concerning its humanitarian quest for social justice was thus shown to contain some substance. Additional legislation was passed to safeguard the morals of young Germany as the concept of youth care became more comprehensive. By 1929 welfare provision had improved, though the results across the country were somewhat patchy, and it was clear that much work still had to be done. Above all, the material position of the younger working class in industry and in other spheres remained problematical. This is further illustrated in Chapter 5 in which their precarious situation in the labour market and the generally unsatisfactory nature of the state's relief measures for the unemployed are examined. Working conditions for youth left much to be desired, especially in relation to pay, holidays, protective legislation, apprentices' contracts, and working hours. With some minor elements of disciplining accompanying the humanitarian ethos of the state's role by the late 1920s, a certain divergence appeared between it and young workers, which only began to become unbridgeable, however, once the Depression struck.

Chapter 6 considers the nature and extent of youth unemployment in the early 1930s and its multitude of socio-psychological ramifications. As youth welfare provision disintegrated at every level as a direct result of the financial crisis, and working class youth suffered profound material and psychological deprivation, the state's humanitarianism in youth care was superseded to a certain degree by policies of social control. This became particularly apparent in 1932 under the Papen and Schleicher administrations, as exemplified by developments in the Voluntary Labour Service and other governmental initiatives *vis-à-vis* proletarian youth. One important manifestation of youth's demoralisation in the Depression was the rise in juvenile crime, which was linked to unemployment and other social maladies. Chapter 7 investigates this phenomenon which seemed to underline the severe limitations of the liberal ethos introduced into the treatment procedure of juvenile delinquency in the early 1920s. The resurgence of obstreperous, even criminalised street gangs in large cities and a major crisis in correctional education constituted further examples of the breakdown in communication between the Republic and the younger proletariat. Their alienation virtually complete by 1932, the way was wide open for these youths to become involved in radical politics. Chapter 8 discusses, in conclusion, the wider political implications of this dénouement, emphasising the essentially non-ideological orientation of unemployed proletarian youth's extremist temperament and their ultimate susceptibility to National Socialism after 1933. An overview of the development of this generation of young Germans from 1900 to 1945 might well conclude that they were a 'lost generation', an experience unfortunately shared in at least equal measure with comparable age cohorts in a number of other European countries.

2 The Younger Generation in the Kaiserreich

The prodigious expansion of Germany's economy during the last quarter of the nineteenth century following national unification established her as one of the world's foremost industrial nations. The process of rapidly accelerating if uneven industrialisation formed the backdrop to the emergence of social issues as a vital matter of concern in national life in that period. Governmental and wider public awareness of the impact of industrialisation on the social fabric of the Reich originated in embryonic form at least during the limited depression of the 1870s when the triumphant confidence of the *Gründerzeit* was badly shaken. The broad consensus in German society that the free market economy and its self-regulating mechanisms would take care of all problems was thus demonstrated in striking fashion to be untenable and that, in reality, there was a crucial role for the state to play in the general field of social welfare reform alongside the traditional agencies such as the churches and private charitable and philanthrophic organisations.

The subsequent introduction by Bismarck of an insurance system covering sickness (1883), industrial accident (1884), and old age and invalidity (1889), giving those insured a legal right to claim relief independent of any means test, was inspired by two fundamental conceptions.[1] The first related to long-standing notions of the State's paternalism towards its subjects, particularly those at the lower end of the social spectrum, while the second, more importantly, had to do with the aim of diminishing the revolutionary appeal to the lower classes of what the Iron Chancellor liked to call the 'poison of Social Democracy', which had developed by the late 1870s as a coherent political movement of the expanding industrial proletariat. Bismarck and the ruling élites in industry, agriculture and the military–bureaucratic establishment of the Reich were convinced that the Social Democratic Party posed a serious threat to the political and constitutional order of the quasi-absolutist monarchial state. Repression and persecution in the shape of the anti-socialist legislation introduced in 1878 represented one type of governmental response; the social insurance laws of the following decade were designed to show the state's caring attitude for its materially least fortunate classes and to entice them away from the allegedly dangerous, unpatriotic philosophy of international socialism.[2] The political loyalty and obedience of the workers, in other words, were to be bought through Bismarck's state socialism.

The real significance of this insurance legislation was not so much to do with the question of how far it and later extensions to it were successful in strict welfare terms, but rather the firm implanting of the social question in the public consciousness which no subsequent government in Germany could afford to ignore. This basic fact was underlined as social problems multiplied and became more complex when industrialisation advanced more and more into the economy. Although there was throughout a paternalistic humanitarianism in the attitude of the state under Bismarck and then under Kaiser Wilhelm, social policy and its accompanying legislation was regarded by the Reich's political establishment primarily as a means of maintaining the stability of an increasingly anachronistic constitutional system and staving off the threat of serious challenge and upheaval from the industrial working class. The state was not a sole operator in the social welfare sphere, of course, because at the same time concessions and reforms were granted in response to pressure exerted by the socialist and trade union movements, and by the middle-class social reformist lobby which was growing in strength and influence within a comparatively restricted context as time went on. Arising from the developing public debate about social reform was the attention directed at one particular section of the population, the younger generation, whose emergence as a factor of official and private solicitude before the First World War may be explained in a number of specific ways.

The growing recognition in Germany of the need for state intervention in defiance of *laissez-faire* liberal and stand-offish conservative attitudes to help alleviate the social ills generated by industrialisation and urbanisation demanded a sharper definition of the State's relationship with different groups in society, including youth. After all, in the case of the latter, the authorities were bound sooner or later to become alert to developments in the newer academic disciplines of social pedagogy and psychology which led to the identification of adolescence as a particular state in the life cycle with its own tensions, frustrations and needs for expression and fulfilment. The Swedish writer Ellen Key's book, *Das Jahrhundert des Kindes*, published in 1900, was notably influential in this respect, as was Heinrich Lhotzky's *Die Seele deines Kind* (1904), which refined the hypothesis of child development initially put forward in Wilhelm Preyer's *Die Seele des Kindes* in 1882, linking them to the ideas of the pedagogical reform movement. These works adduced for the first time a fresh psychological understanding of children that was located within the context of progressive theories of education.[3]

As ideas in the field of child and youth welfare were consequently developed in more sophisticated ways, social reformers and educationalists united in the belief that the younger age groups of the unskilled, urban working-class milieu were most in need of remedial action. As part of an irregular manual workforce, they were now commonly seen as requiring direction and even supervision; they were reputed to lack definite goals and orientation in life. Moreover they were increasingly understood as dangerous drifters, earning enough money to finance worthless ephemeral pleasures, often largely free of parental control, and susceptible to involvement in petty crime, street disturbances and other modes of anti-social behaviour.[4] Clemens Schultz, a Protestant clergyman, painted a vivid, convincing picture of this type of *déclassé* young unskilled worker based on his first-hand experiences of working among them in the tough docklands area of St Pauli, Hamburg, in the 1900s.[5] While the book may have shocked contemporaries, it confirmed the unflattering view of such youths held by many of the bourgeoisie.[6] Hence it did not take long for the view to be widely accepted among middle-class professionals in the welfare field that this type of working-class youth had to be 'improved' in accordance with the established and homogeneous values and standards of the reform-minded bourgeoisie. In consequence, traditional approaches and practices of youth care had to be re-examined because, as was inevitable in view of their poorer, if not deprived circumstances all round, working-class youth was its principal clientele. This applied in particular to the branch of *Jugendfürsorge*, the care of the physically and mentally handicapped, the neglected, orphaned, illegitimate and delinquent youth. From another perspective, the state was anxious to have this problem addressed as a matter of some urgency because this volatile and potentially disruptive segment of the younger generation was not subject to any form of established control. These youths had left school and were not yet settled into a regular pattern of behaviour, either through marriage or through the military discipline that came with service in the armed forces at the age of 18 or 19 years. While middle-class youth beyond the age of 14 continued to be subject to school discipline and usually also to the influence of parents and even the Church, this group of unskilled working-class youth was passing through a control-free period between the ages of 14 and 19 years which caused the state authorities to be increasingly concerned.[7] These youths were regarded as constituting a social and political risk which the State could not tolerate for an indefinite period. Thus, while youth welfare legislation before 1914 was informed to some extent by a genuine desire on the part of the state to protect and improve the situation of all young people from every type of social background, it was also enacted for the purpose of ensuring that certain sections of the younger proletariat did not become a direct threat to the *status quo*, or part of a discontented groundswell of opinion with revolutionary potential. The authoritarian yet progressively insecure Wilhelmine State thus displayed a revealing degree of nervousness here, as in other spheres.

That considerable incomprehension and friction were virtually unavoidable between two sides representing quite distinct outlooks and life-styles did not inhibit the social reformist campaign from picking up momentum from the 1890s onwards and clarifying the nature of its objectives. The major aim was to construct an educational as opposed to the traditional punitive code of assessment to the problems of youth care in general, and to the treatment of adolescent and juvenile delinquency in particular. The slogan capturing the essence of the new philosophy was '*Erziehung statt Strafe*', education in place of punishment. The reformers wanted to restore the 'proper' material and moral well-being of working-class youth. Education in the broadest sense, it was confidently asserted, held the key to eradicating the worst forms of juvenile misbehaviour and fallen standards and remoulding those concerned as solid, reliable and respectable citizens.

The increasingly defined profile of the younger generation in German society as well as the emphasis on working-class youth by social reformist circles owed something also to certain demographic trends at the end of the nineteenth century. It was not simply that the increase in the size of the industrial proletariat produced a larger pool of young workers which demanded the state's interest. While Germany's population rose substantially from 39.4 million in 1871 to 49.2 million in 1890 and then to 66.8 million in 1913, the proportion of her younger age groups (14–25 years) increased noticeably *vis-à-vis* the rest of the population, thus creating the phenomenon of a 'rejuvenation' (*Verjugendlichung*) of her population in general.[8] The youthfulness of the population, moreover, seemed to support rather conveniently the notion, which was assiduously promoted by the Kaiser on his accession, that the Reich was a 'young' country in the comity of European nations, and characterised by a youthful dynamism and vitality unmatched by any other country. Germany's birth rate reached a high level before 1900 compared with that of her rivals, including Britain and France and, although this declined sharply after that date and the process of demographic 'rejuvenation' petered out, the belief that youthfulness and the younger generation had an intrinsically wholesome and attractive value persisted. Indeed the birth cohorts in Germany of the last decade before the war were large, resulting from the above-average birth rate of the 1870s and the marked fall in the infant mortality rate in the 1900s.[9] A 'bulge' of the younger age groups was consequently produced. Also adding to the 'youthful' character of the population was the fact that by 1900 emigration from Germany, which concerned the 20–40-year-olds most of all, had tailed off so dramatically that Germany had already become a country of net immigration.[10] According to the Occupational and Population Census of 1895, there were 6.3 million in the Reich aged 14–20 years, split evenly between male and female. Some time later, in 1909, the 14–18-year-old group, male and female, numbered some 4.5 million; in the following year the 14–25-year-old male grouping constituted 20.6 per cent of the total male population, or approximately 5.9 million out of 28.5 million.[11]

Serving to further accentuate the stark visibility of youth was the propensity for the bulk of them to be concentrated in Germany's industrial cities and large towns,[12] reflecting the widespread occurrence of the movement of population from countryside to town during the last quarter of the century. As younger people migrated to towns and cities in search of better employment opportunities and higher pay, the 'rejuvenation' of the population was thus overwhelmingly urban rather than rural in character.[13] During this period cities by and large recorded a higher birth rate than country and small town districts of Germany. In 1908 there were 1.6 million male workers aged 14–21 years, mostly urban-based.[14] The congregation in cities of so many young workers, many of whom were unskilled and thus a prime target of social reformers and welfare officials, helped considerably to push the state's concern in the same direction. The formulation of welfare measures could only be pursued with increased urgency in this situation.

The process of recognising youth as a distinctive entity in German society was significantly promoted around 1900 by the manifestations of *Kulturkritik*, that nebulous but powerful anti-modernist reaction born of a middle-class cultural malaise, which other European countries also experienced at the same time. It was directly related to a period of challenging accepted ideas in many spheres, of experimentation in the arts and popular taste, which was highlighted in Germany by the conclusion of the Bismarckian era. Feelings of cultural pessimism and repudiation of modernism in the broadest sense fuelled the disaffection of various social groups, but principally the educated, professional middle class (*Bildungsbürgertum*).[15] Their uncertainties and fears had been caused by the breathtaking advance of industrialisation and the concomitant advent of mass society in Germany; they were resentful of the materialist values of that society and alarmed by a perceived threat to their social and economic position by both proletarian socialism and industrial capitalism. If only as a defensive strategy, these middle-class groups felt compelled to assert their own beliefs and traditions. Having lost confidence in the willingness of the conservative upper strata to defend their interests, they had to rely on their own efforts for survival. They saw in the ideas of Sigmund Freud in psychology, Max Weber in sociology and Albert Einstein in physics a veritable intellectual revolution which struck at the very roots of their cultural existence. Their criticism of what Germany had become in the industrial age was most vehemently and effectively articulated by writers such as Julius Langbehn, Paul de Lagarde and Friedrich Nietzsche, who denounced the supremacy of reason in favour of the irrational, spiritual approach, and the impersonal alienation of industrial society – everything, in fact, associated with modernity. Amidst the pessimism and foreboding for the future one element of hope was maintained: the younger generation. The *Kulturkritiker* added a vital dimension to the growing cult of youth in Wilhelmine society. Langbehn's *Rembrandt als Erzieher* (1890) glorified youth as the saviour of the German nation, as the embodiment of all that decadent bourgeois–industrial society was not. Nietzsche spoke grandiosely of there being a 'mission of youth', a regenerative impulse which could sweep aside all corruption and become the hope for the future on the basis of pure 'German' values emanating from the *Volkstum*.[16]

The unease of the *Bildungsbürgertum* was not simply a sign of its abhorrence of urban industrialism. It was also an expression of their inveterate disenchantment with an outdated political system which refused to countenance meaningful social or constitutional reform. The political unrest seething under the relatively ordered exterior of the Reich was also uncovered by the attempt of certain sections of the lower middle class to establish their own identity, involving the development of a new, radical *völkisch* nationalism. The profound crisis of identity in the broad range of the German bourgeoisie around 1900 was linked to emancipatory trends of which the feminist movement was a salient example. Among the younger generation from an educated middle-class background, frustration with the established order and a potent desire to assert itself as a group in its own right provided the major impetus behind the formation of the first independent youth movement in Germany, the *Wandervogel*.[17]

Officially founded in Berlin-Steglitz in 1901, the *Wandervogel* was arguably the most powerful, boldest expression of the *Kaiserreich*'s new youth culture. Drawn almost exclusively from the *Kulturkritik* social milieu in Protestant areas of northern and central Germany where, not accidentally, the impact of industrialisation had been especially marked, the *Wandervogel* was a revolt of middle-class youth against the restrictive conventions and formalities of adult society as determined by parents, school and the Church, on the one hand, and an anti-modernist impulse against the anonymous, materialist ethos of urban industrial society, on the other. In any case, the increasing fluidity and heterogeneity of modern life rendered obsolete, so it seemed, the traditional channels of socialisation of youth, including the family and the closely-knit local community. A situation where the usual conventions could no longer be validly applied gave encouragement to the younger generation to seek new paths towards understanding the world around them. For the *Wandervogel* youths Nature offered an appealing alternative to complicated, tension-laden industrial society because of its transcendent simplicity and purity, its powers of release from the dull pressures of everyday reality. They yearned for a new spiritual and moral purpose in life, believing they could be the beacon of hope for Germany as a whole. In this manner the *Wandervogel* wanted to demonstrate that youth had a mature capability of its own, that it could no longer be dismissed simply as an appendage of adult society. This was a plea for self-determination coupled with a sense of responsibility.[18]

At the beginning at least, the *Wandervogel* had a romantic–escapist character, with a proclivity for symbols, medieval images, folklore and gaudy costumes. '*Die Fahrt*' (the journey, trip), the central experience of its members, epitomised its rejection of urbanism. Subsequently, however, amidst organisational splits and personality clashes, the *Wandervogel* developed a rather more substantive persona as part of the broader neo-conservative stream of thought and action in Wilhelmine Germany. It aspired to the creation of a 'kingdom of youth' (*Jugendreich*) in which the ideals of the younger generation could be more sensitively appreciated than they were in existing society. Youth was to be much more than a mere replica of adults. More widely, the *Wandervogel* stood for the recognition and esteem of the individual, for what Lagarde had articulated:

> Youth wants to make war for concrete ideals . . . it does not want to follow in the same rut along which its grandparents travelled.[19]

The *Wandervogel* is perhaps best understood as an emancipatory–idealist movement, part of an engulfing quest for liberation which was a feature of the Wilhelmine era. In rejecting formality, authoritarianism and regimentation, and embracing spontaneity, individualism and comradeship, the *Wandervogel* struck a responsive chord in society which its relatively small membership – 25 000 in 1914 – hardly warranted. If it incorporated an undeniable element of generational conflict, it never unreservedly pitted itself against the adult world. Reformist rather than revolutionary in essence, the *Wandervogel* had by 1914 accepted part of the conservative–nationalist ethos of the Establishment without becoming overtly political. The influence of Pan-Germanism and racial anti-semitism in some sections of what had become a fragmented *Wandervogel* somehow compromised its early ideological naivety. Its overall importance as a vigorous exponent of youth's striving for autonomy and of its own individualistic youth culture, however, was underlined by the promulgation in 1913 of the Meissner Formula by which the independent youth movement pledged 'to shape its own destiny on the basis of its own initiative, on its own responsibility and with deep sincerity'. Whatever its faults, and it had many contemporary as well as later detractors, the *Wandervogel* had at least made a worthy contribution to the firm establishment of the 'youth question' on the social and political agenda of the Reich. As one of its most prominent personalities, Gustav Wyneken, remarked:

> Youth, until now a mere extension of the older generation, excluded from real participation in life and forced into a passive, frivolous negative role in society . . . is beginning to assert itself. It is now trying to shape its own future. It wants . . . to develop into a refreshing, rejuvenating element in the spiritual life of the nation.[20]

Germinating from the pervasive climate of *Kulturkritik*, and intimately allied to the *Wandervogel* was the debate over reform of Germany's secondary school (*Gymnasium*) system which the Kaiser, among many others, pronounced 'overdue'.[21] That the intense discussion which ensued attracted considerable public interest outside the ranks of the professionally engaged was a further tribute to the developing importance of the 'youth question' in Germany before the First World War. Reformist educators criticised the curricula of the *Gymnasium*, and indeed its entire ethos, as irrelevant to the new industrial age where technology and science were more crucial to the country's standing. On the other hand, the concern of conservative circles was that the schools were failing to instil in pupils an appropriate national spirit. What was really meant, and the Kaiser pointedly intervened to make the criticism explicit, was that the schools were not doing enough to combat the propagation of socialism. Following a number of changes to the curricula and to certain practices in schools during the early 1900s, the Right lost interest in the debate, as did the public at large. But the progressive educationalists continued their campaign for a more comprehensive alteration to the system and were able to advance a well-constructed programme for consideration by the school authorities and other involved parties.[22]

They sought to replace mechanical teaching methods and learning by rote, which was standard practice in the *Gymnasium*, with processes encouraging fuller intercourse between teacher and pupil, and to create more scope for freedom of expression and the development of personality. Intellectual enquiry was to be stimulated as broadly as possible, while the strict discipline and authoritarianism which dominated the everyday atmosphere in schools was to be replaced by more relaxed, flexible and personal structures. The alleged one-sided intellectualism of the *Gymnasium* was a particular bone of contention for the reformists, who aimed for a wider pedagogical approach, incorporating sports, games and the physical development of pupils. There was, in addition, and in response to the direct prompting of the *Wandervogel*, much support for co-education, music, singing, theatrical studies, and for locating schools in more natural, salubrious surroundings than was customary, in which an informal classroom atmosphere would have a better chance of prevailing. Parental involvement was encouraged as part of the desire to transform schools into more humane, satisfying institutions. While the influence of the *Wandervogel* was reflected in these ideas, it also produced a number of personalities who made their mark on the progressive educational movement: Hermann Lietz, who pioneered the archtypal reformist school in the Country Boarding Schools (*Deutsche Landerziehungsheime*), Ludwig Gurlitt, and Gustav Wyneken, the co-founder of the experimental *Freie Schulgemeinde Wickersdorf* in 1906, were all leading figures in the *Wandervogel* before the war. They were all dedicated in different ways to taking school education at the secondary level out of the pre-industrial era and structuring it above all from the viewpoint of the pupil, not the adult world. Even if the reformists constituted a minority movement in education before 1914, they succeeded in stressing the priority of meeting the needs of the younger generation in this vital area. At the same time, they made a valuable contribution to the raising of youth's profile in society as a whole.[23]

In a narrowly practical sense, the combined endeavours of the *Kulturkritiker*, the *Wandervogel* and the school reformers emphasised the situation of bourgeois youth because the thoughts and concerns which they expressed had to do mainly with areas of more relevance to middle-class anxieties. For instance, discussion about the composition of the *Gymnasium* mattered little to working-class youth who were hardly present in school education beyond the primary (*Volksschule*) level. But the needs of working-class youth were no less pressing before 1914 and, thanks to the efforts of various organisations, including the socialist and bourgeois social reformist movements, the state was eventually to display more active involvement in welfare matters. The care and protection of the younger generation demanded fresh initiatives, particularly as working-class youth were becoming an important object of official concern after 1890.

At the beginning of his reign the Kaiser subscribed to the view that the most efficacious method of repelling the threat of social revolution from the working class did not lie in their repression but in the material amelioration of their situation. To this end, he inaugurated a fresh round of welfare legislation in the 1890s which was designed to extend and improve the original Bismarckian system. Most notably, the Workmen's Protection Act (1891) regulated hours of work for various categories of worker and introduced measures aimed at reducing danger to life and health in factories.[24] But, with the Kaiser's eventual disillusionment with this approach, the pace of the Reich government's welfare programme slackened in the next decade so that whereas Germany had once been the leader in this field under Bismarck she had been overtaken before the war by the other countries, including Britain. Although improvements were made to the sickness and accident insurance schemes, resulting in 36 per cent of the Reich population being covered by 1913,[25] the tangible benefits for the German worker of state welfare remained very modest and cannot possibly be credited with preventing revolution.[26] The average worker continued to derive more substantive welfare support from the trade unions, friendly societies and private organisations such as the *Zentralstelle für Arbeiterwohlfahrt*. The churches, with their *Innere Mission* (Protestant) and *Caritas* (Catholic), were also to hand, as was the poor law for those in dire straits.[27] The limitations of the state's welfare effort were also a reflection of the restricted influence before 1914 of middle-class pressure groups, including the *Verein für Sozialpolitik* (1872) and the *Gesellschaft für Soziale Reform* (1901).

The nature and extent of welfare legislation was not the only indicator of the material condition of the working class, of course, because other factors, such as increases in real wages, especially for the skilled and semi-skilled, more or less full employment, progress in housing construction and slum clearance, improvements in public sanitation, the provision of medical care, superior dieting and less alcohol consumption, were just as important. However modest the welfare legislation of the Reich, it may have convinced sections of the working class, particularly the skilled industrial workers, that the state was genuinely committed to tackling the problem of inequality in society and consequently making it easier and more appealing for them to identify closely with the state and its value system. For the unskilled, irregular urban proletariat, however, the overall picture of their material condition was rather gloomy. They did not enjoy any real increase in wage levels and were generally bypassed by rising health standards: the incidence of serious disease such as tuberculosis in this social group remained high until 1914, and recourse to the demeaning poor relief system was too often unavoidable, especially for older and retired members of this lower working class.[28]

The state's welfare provision for the younger proletariat, and for youth in general, was brought into sharper focus after 1890 owing to economic developments, the activity of pressure groups and political calculation. It entered a field already fairly well populated by a variety of welfare organisations. In 1834 the Evangelical Church had set up in Bremen a *Hilfsverein für Jünglinge* which was soon copied in other towns, while the Catholic Church followed suit not long afterwards, in 1846, with the creation of journeymen's associations (*Gesellenvereine*) in Elberfeld by *Domvikar* Kolping. Church welfare involvement increased in response to the greater number of social problems thrown up by the industrial revolution, leading to the appearance of larger and better organised groups catering for specific categories of youth: from the Evangelical side came the likes of the *Christliche Verein Junger Männer* in 1883, the *Evangelischer Verband zur Pflege der weiblichen Jugend Deutschlands* in 1893, the *Nationalvereinigung Evangelischer Jünglingsbündnisse* in 1900, and a few years later the *Bund deutscher Jugendvereine*, which followed the innovative methods of the well-known Hamburg pastors, Clemens Schultz and Walter Classen. The Catholic Church established in 1895 the *Verband der katholischer Jünglingsvereinigung Deutschlands* and later, for female youth, the *Zentralverband katholischer Jungfrauenvereinigungen Deutschlands*. These Catholic groups had the largest memberships of all the church youth welfare bodies, with 300 000 in the male group and 500 000 in the female by 1914, comprising, unlike their Evangelical counterparts, both middle- and working-class youth. In 1904 they were joined by a private umbrella organisation, the *Deutsche Zentrale für Jugendfürsorge*, to co-ordinate the care for 'abnormal' and deviant youngsters. Many other private groups emerged in the 1900s to promote the welfare of youth inside and outside school, thus adding to the pressure on the state to become more directly involved.[29] As it was, though this kind of pressure was significant, the authorities' awareness and fear of signs of growing restlessness among the younger generation, including, in respect mainly of working-class youth, rising crime and health problems, was just as important a factor.

The state's involvement in youth welfare was three-dimensional: in the work sphere, in *Jugendpflege* and in *Jugendfürsorge*. In the first of these, the state had a long-standing if very limited interest. The Commercial Code (*Gewerbeordnung*) of 1869 in Prussia had prohibited the employment in factories of children aged under 14 years, though in practice there were numerous breaches of this law. The Imperial Commercial Code (*Reichsgewerbeordnung*) of July 1878 provided some protection for youth employed in factories in terms of strengthening the powers of factory inspectors to enforce existing laws, banning Sunday working for under-16-year-olds, laying down a maximum 10-hour day for under-16-year-olds, and prohibiting the employment of the same group in factories where there were health hazards or moral dangers.[30] To what extent these regulations were actually implemented in the era of liberal *laissez-faire* is highly questionable. In the 1890s the Prussian government issued decrees outlawing the employment of schoolchildren in factories (1891) and peddling and street-trading by under-14-year-olds (1897),[31] and in July 1900 attempted to regulate the working conditions of young workers in factories with heavy machinery.[32] The decrees were preliminary to the Children's Protection Act of March 1903 (*Reichsgesetz betr. Kinderarbeit in gewerblichen Betrieben*, or *Kinderschutzgesetz*), which sought to tighten up the rules of legislation passed since 1869. Unfortunately many abuses persisted until the war, and beyond.[33] In fact, no sooner had this law been put into effect than the authorities sanctioned a number of exemptions which simply encouraged widespread disregard for it.[34]

Where juvenile labour was concerned, the main thrust of state legislation was to improve the working environment. Clauses in the Workmen's Protection Act (1891), for instance, stipulated that young workers were to work no longer than 10 hours a day, have Sunday as a rest day, and not to be engaged in night shifts. There were attempts to provide legal safeguards, for example, in the apprenticeship contract: in 1908 it was decreed that only fully qualified craftsmen were entitled to be in charge of training apprentices (*Lehrmeisterstatus*) in the craft trades. Before 1914 also, opportunities were extended for vocational training, particularly in the Continuation Schools (*Fortbildungsschule*). This type of legislation for young workers tended, however, to be essentially by-products of laws for the adult workforce rather than part of a concerted plan for the young. The generally lax implementation and observance of such laws was reflective of a less than wholehearted commitment by government and employers, who were still attached to a large degree to the doctrine of nonintervention in industrial life.

It was probably in *Jugendpflege* in the 1900s that the state's active role in welfare provision for the young was most pronounced. It issued regulations designed to prevent alcohol abuse, the dissemination of morally pernicious literature, and other perceived evils of the modern industrial era. Something of a breakthrough occurred when the Prussian government, in response to what had become by 1900 a reasonably well-organised and vocal youth welfare lobby, acknowledged its responsibilities in a series of decrees (*Jugendpflegeerlasse*) which helped to provide a suitable framework within which the youth welfare efforts of different groups could be effectively co-ordinated. Piecemeal legislation in 1901, 1905 and 1908 paved the way for the important decree of 18 January 1911, which for the first time officially recognised *Jugendpflege* as a major concern of the State.[35]

The context in which this legislation was introduced was informed by both humanitarian and political considerations. The decree referred, with complete justification, to the many changes that had taken place in German society since unification, adding that family life had been put under especially severe strain. Pressures arising from the advent of industrialisation were said to 'have put a large part of our adolescent youth in a situation where their physical, and even more so, their moral development have been acutely endangered'. The Kaiser echoed this basic sentiment of the decree when he claimed in February 1912 to have the welfare interests of post-school youth, especially youth living in large cities, 'deep in his heart'.[36] This reference, however, is an indication of the political influences behind the decree. Against a background of increasing industrial unrest since 1907 and rising juvenile criminality, the decree was an expression of the state's concern to combat the influence of the Social Democrats on working-class youth. It was in many respects complementary to the Reich Law of Association (*Reichsvereinsgesetz*) of April 1908, which had been clearly directed against the recently formed socialist youth movement.[37]

In protest at the generally poor working conditions in factories for young workers and apprentices, inadequate legal safeguards for those aged over 16 years, the absence of holidays and, above all, the brutal ill-treatment systematically administered by many masters to apprentices[38] – and the tragic case of the 16-year-old Berlin apprentice locksmith, Paul Nähring, who committed suicide after yet another beating, was but the latest example – socialist youth groups were set up independently of each other in Berlin and Mannheim in Autumn 1904. The apathy shown by the SPD and trade unions towards the plight of young workers had also been a contributory factor in this development which, in broader perspective, was an expression of a specific, if somewhat ill-defined urban-centred proletarian youth culture. Working-class youth were seeking, like their middle-class counterparts in the *Wandervogel*, to assert their own identity through their experience of factory, neighbourhood and industrial conflict. In the passage of time, young workers were among the most militant strikers, leaders in street demonstrations (as in Hamburg in January 1906),[39] and the most radical political activists. They can be seen, therefore, as part of the broader emancipation movement in Wilhelmine Germany.

Despite the socialist youth movement's emphasis on cultural, educational and work advisory matters, the state was alarmed by its relatively successful expansion – 10 000 members by 1908 – free of any adult control or supervision, and stepped in with the Association Law to stop it.[40] Paragraph 17 prohibited everyone under 18 years of age from joining political organisations, attending political meetings or any other public assembly called for the purpose of discussing political themes. This now extended to the entire Reich restrictions on youth already in force for some years in Prussia. The socialist youth movement was declared to be a political association and was henceforth compelled to pursue non-political activities under the watching brief of the SPD's party executive committee. Indeed, the party leadership and the trade unions had regarded the youth movement with deep suspicion and annoyance and were rather pleased to have its independent existence terminated; they complied with the law without delay. In January 1909, the SPD established a Central Youth Commission to co-ordinate local branches (*Zentralstelle für die arbeitende Jugend Deutschlands*), with Friedrich Ebert, the later Reich President, as chairman.[41] Not content with this successful strike against the vitality of the working-class youth organisation, the state in the years up to 1914 subjected it to constant police harassment and persecution, and any threat it may have posed to the established order was totally eliminated. The episode, unsavoury as it was, was a lucid illustration of the German state's resolve at that time to either destroy or control any potential for revolutionary challenge to its authority.

The 1911 *Jugendpflegeerlass* was no less discriminatory of working-class youth than the Association Law, despite the innocuous appearance of its opening paragraphs: 'The State government regards youth welfare as one of the most important national tasks of the present time because of its great significance for the future of our people'. It continued:

> The task assigned to youth welfare is to cooperate in the rearing of happy, physically healthy, morally sound and public-spirited young persons, filled with the fear of God and love for their home and country . . . Its purpose is to support, supplement and extend the educational activities of parents, school, the Church, the master and the employer.

The decree, which applied only to male youth,[42] served as an example to other federal states and was widely regarded as a pacemaker in this sphere. Simultaneously, however, it blatantly sought to politicise state-sponsored *Jugendpflege* in an anti-socialist, nationalist direction. It enunciated that the facilities of cheap rail travel, overnight accommodation in barracks, and funding to the tune of one million marks in the first years alone[43] were to be given only to groups of a patriotic nature. In his speech about the decree to the Prussian *Landtag* on 26 March 1912, the Prussian Education Minister, von Trott zu Solz, left no doubts on this score when he denounced the socialist youth movement as 'led by the most radical of the radical'.[44] In a further set of regulations for the distribution of these funds in April 1913 it was announced that only those groups which were loyal to the state – based '*auf staatserhaltenden Boden*' – were allowed to benefit. Moreover groups which 'sought to educate youth in a patriotic manner without including fear of God' were likewise excluded. This reference was aimed at socialist groups which claimed to be patriotic but which could not possibly owe allegiance to traditional Christian beliefs.[45]

Though the SPD rather predictably dismissed the decree as 'dangerous dilletantism',[46] and Catholic organisations in some parts of the Rhineland refused at the behest of clergy to join forces with nationalist associations, claiming that they were 'irreligious',[47] the general public's reaction was warmly enthusiastic.[48] Representative of the consensus was the statement:

> From all circles and towns of the district there are reports of very gratifying progress in the youth welfare movement . . . men from all classes and occupations have been prepared to place themselves in the service of this cause.[49]

Since one of the principal objectives of the decree had been to combat socialist propaganda among the younger proletariat and, further, to win over as many of that group as possible to the nationalist camp, it was stressed by many local activists in youth welfare that the co-operation of masters of apprentices was vital to secure because of their weighty and direct authority over their charges. After all, working-class youth was the group most in need of welfare support, it was reasoned.[50] In the event, the class nature of the supervisory mechanism of *Jugendpflege* was underlined by the fact that those most conspicuously involved were middle-class schoolteachers and clergymen. By 1913, in Prussia, some 22 000 of them were following professional training courses in youth care.[51] The early interest in *Jugendpflege* among the public was clearly maintained until 1914, and sections of the community not initially well-disposed towards it were changing their mind and beginning to participate.[52] Even so, the achievements of the 1911 decree should not be exaggerated, for it essentially provided only some of the basic foundations for a properly organised system. In too many local areas before 1914 *Jugendpflege* amounted to little more than an insipid bureaucratic exercise.[53]

During the last few pre-war years it became obvious that the 1911 decree was a springboard for even more intensive efforts by the state to push further the politicisation of *Jugendpflege*, with the strategic objective of converting as many of the young, especially proletarian youth, to the nationalist cause as possible. Those who did not respond to the call were to be progressively marginalised in terms of state support for welfare activity: the socialists and the 'patriotic' anti-socialists were to be divided into two opposing camps. Hence nationalist sports and gymnastic associations, which were traditionally militant, received particularly strong encouragement from state patronage. But even in the Continuation Schools for post-school youth of the working class, instruction was directed towards inculcating a sense of patriotic loyalty and high Christian ideals. In this connection, many federal states went so far as to make attendance at these schools compulsory for apprentices.[54] Locked into this ever-tightening circle of nationalist drum-beating was the Boy Scout Movement, set up later in 1911 under *Reichsfeldmeister* Maximilian Bayer. With its commitment to Christian partiotism, loyalty and military drill and exercises (*Soldatenspielerei*), the Boy Scout Movement received full state support within the spirit of the 1911 decree.[55] But the most determined incursion of the state into the *Jugendpflege* field came in the shape of the *Jungdeutschlandbund*, which it established in November 1911 under the leadership of a Prussian Field-Marshal, Freiherr von der Goltz. As an umbrella organisation of right-wing nationalist youth groups, the *Jungdeutschlandbund*, with a membership of 745 000 by 1914, was the major spearhead of the state's campaign against socialism among young people. Like the 80 000 Boy Scouts, it was drawn overwhelmingly from the Protestant middle classes.[56] The extent of the state's political operation may be gauged from the fact that on the eve of the war the various youth tutelage organisations, comprising confessional, sports, political, militaristic and vocational branches, numbered some two million.[57] The degree to which the Wilhelmine State had succeeded in promoting its social control of the younger generation on the basis of *Jugendpflege* activity is even more striking when compared with the modest welfare achievement in this sphere. If the humanitarian and political impulses behind the state's involvement in *Jugendpflege* had been roughly balanced around 1900, it was patently clear by 1914 which element had asserted a dominance over the other. The authoritarianism of the *Kaiserreich* respected no boundaries. The effort to reconcile working-class youth to the *status quo* through a process of 'negative integration' was only a partial success, however, and confined to some sections of the upwardly mobile, bourgeois-aspirant skilled and semi-skilled younger proletariat.[58]

Running parallel with state-sponsored *Jugendpflege* before 1914 were important developments in the public care of disadvantaged and delinquent youth (*Jugendfürsorge*), the large majority of whom came from underprivileged groups of the unskilled urban working class. In this sphere also there is evidence of the original balance in motive on the part of authorities between humanitarianism and social control being progressively disturbed as political influences grew stronger. Accordingly, an area which until the late nineteenth century was dominated by the churches and private agencies, who administered orphanages and workhouses,[59] was caught up in the vigorous ideological battle of the 1900s. The state was not entirely responsible for this development, of course, because social reformist circles with an explicit bourgeois ethos to propagate were also very much to the fore. They stressed the need for better health care and educational training in *Jugendfürsorge*, partly in response to growing public interest in social darwinist ideas and eugenics. Social hygiene became fashionable as advances in medical science and health provision heightened awareness of the implications of health standards for the overall soundness of the population. The perceived inferior health of youth in *Jugendfürsorge* was considered a potential risk in this regard. At the same time, the more sophisticated comprehension of the needs of young people that had emerged in German society by the 1900s led to a critical scrutiny of institutional and legislative prescriptions for *Jugendfürsorge*, particularly the Prussian law of March 1878 (*Zwangserziehungsgesetz*). Pressure mounted for a more constructive contribution from the state. Despite the good intentions of reformers and the co-ordinating efforts of the private *Deutsche Zentrale für Jugendfürsorge*, progress before the war was somewhat patchy; only the more progressive-minded authorities in some of the Reich's major cities could legitimately claim advances.[60]

The branch of *Jugendfürsorge* which attracted the most concern before 1914 was juvenile crime and delinquency. From the 1880s they were clearly on the increase; for instance, in 1890 there were 40 972 convictions of 12–18-year-olds and 54 947 in 1912.[61] Explanations vary widely. It is suggested that the rise can be attributed to the greater vigilance of public authorities, who perhaps began taking a broader view of wrongdoing and misbehaviour, and to the heightened awareness of adults in general. This line of argument denies, therefore, that there was any real augmentation in juvenile misconduct.[62] More convincing, however, is the thesis, based on the Prussian experience, that socio-economic factors were to blame for the problem, which was at its zenith in Prussia during 1882–1906, with a slower rate of increase up to 1914. The prevalence of poverty, illiteracy, high mortality rates and lack of educational opportunity, which were frequently compounded by evidence of illegitimacy or family breakdown, was directly related to acts of delinquency. Periods of economic depression or of rising prices coincided with growth in juvenile crime.[63] Consequent upon these findings, little credibility can be attached to those contemporary social darwinist theories which stressed moral deficiency or hereditary faults on the part of the offender.[64]

In advocating a more humane attitude to the entire sphere of juvenile delinquency, the reformist lobby believed that more state-backed welfare support held the key to the successful treatment of offenders. The case for a progressive approach was prosecuted with vigour and skill by legal experts such as Aschrott and Appelius in the 1890s as well as by pedagogical specialists.[65] They argued for the establishment of special juvenile courts, separation of juveniles from adults in prison, and the raising of the age of legal culpability from 12 to 14 years – that is, at the school-leaving age when, it was felt, juveniles became fully appreciative of the moral difference between right and wrong. In support of their emphasis on the educational approach, these reformers could argue that the increasing rate of juvenile criminality showed that the existing system based on the concept of retribution was simply not working. Indeed, a more compelling argument in their favour was the substantial and ever-rising rate of recidivism among juvenile offenders, which in 1890–1912 lay between 12 and 17 per cent.[66] There seemed every reason, therefore, to accept the reformer's plea for the law to emphasise the individual offender, not the offence *per se*.

Juvenile courts were eventually created, in 1908, as sections of the *Amtsgerichte* (local magistrate's court) in some of the larger cities, including Berlin, Cologne and Frankfurt/Main, followed by the setting up of a rudimentary system of juvenile probation.[67] By 1914 a network of these courts existed throughout the country. But the kind of comprehensive, national legislation demanded by the reformers was delayed until the Weimar era.[68] That fundamental reform of the system could not be shelved indefinitely was underlined by the statistics concerning the number of juveniles taken into public care before 1914. Due to the rise in juvenile delinquency, and to the extension of the system of custodial education to under-18-year-olds by the Prussian law of 2 July 1900 (*Fürsorgeerziehungsgesetz*),[69] the numbers (*FE-Zöglinge*) in Prussia rose from 10 500 in 1900 to 55 229 in 1914, of whom 40 per cent were sent to institutional as opposed to foster care. Juveniles aged 12–18 years constituted the bulk of the 55 229 (70 per cent), and usually came from the poorest working-class circumstances in large cities; two-thirds were made.[70] The pressures this large increase in FE clientele had on the reformatories were not fully revealed until the well publicised difficulties of these institutions in the 1920s and early 1930s, and their efficacy as a means of reform was doubtful: it is estimated that approximately one in three of their pupils were not fully rehabilitated as a result of their time spent in care.[71]

The larger numbers of juveniles being taken into care in the 1900s stimulated much debate about the legal definition of a delinquent youth and what should be the dividing line between parental rights and the state's responsibilities. To the disappointment of reformists, the Civil Legal Code (*Bürgerliches Gesetzbuch*) of 1900 upheld and emphasised the former and set out clear limits to the state's powers of intervention, which were valid only in those cases where the parents were demonstrably cruel or negligent towards their children.[72] However the law of 1902 implementing the Civil Legal Code (*Einführungsgesetz zum BGB*) allowed more discretion in this matter to individual federal governments. They were now entitled to pass their own legislation permitting welfare agencies operating within the area of their jurisdiction to take children into care not only in cases where the parents were clearly guilty of negligence or cruelty, or where the child had broken the law, but also where it was deemed necessary to prevent the moral ruin of the child.[73] The federal governments now had that ultimate power of decision. The case for further extending the state's direct responsibility for a child's education or welfare where these were not being satisfactorily provided by parents through their clear fault, was presented by the influential Wilhelm Polligkeit in 1905 in his concept of the '*Recht des Kindes auf Erziehung*' (right of a child to education).⁷⁴ But this was yet another reformist notion destined not to reach the statute books until the 1920s.

In the meantime, the further encroachment of the conservative, authoritarian Wilhelmine State into this area of youth care showed once more the considerable extent to which the entire 'youth question' had been politicised by 1914. The small advances of reformist–humanitarian concepts were firmly within a context increasingly dominated by the political–ideological exigencies of the reactionary state whose basic aim was to discipline and control the younger generation, especially its feared working-class segment. It made strenuous efforts to predicate youth welfare in the broadest sense on a nationalist, anti-socialist ethos, with the result of permanently politicising this field. That there was such a struggle for the hearts and minds of the younger generation is ample testimony to the advance of the youth cause: the major political parties made overtures and the state established youth auxiliaries under its patronage. Clearly youth was a valuable prize to be captured. Adult society was not prepared to allow youth free rein to develop as it alone desired and, naturally, the state had certain responsibilities to shoulder towards everyone. But by 1914 the state had gone beyond a proper measure of responsibility: interference, subordination and control had become its guiding precepts. It remained to be seen if a more acceptable balance could be restored as the First World War offered a new *Spielplatz* for the youth–state symbiosis.

The advent of war appeared in Germany and other belligerent countries to offer an immediate and exhilarating release from the pressures and tedium of bourgeois society. The formalities of class and status were cast aside in favour of the pursuit of a common destiny on the basis of *Kriegerlebnis* (experience of war) and an egalitarian national community (*Volksgemeinschaft*).⁷⁵ But it would be misleading to apply the highly problematical concept of 'The Generation of 1914' to this social liberation movement because the complex society Germany had become by 1914 did not permit the rigid stratification which this notion implies.⁷⁶ No generational conflict was apparent as young Germany marched off enthusiastically with everyone else to fight an alleged defensive war for Kaiser and Fatherland. Their idealistic hopes were rudely shattered, of course, by the interminable slaughter of the trenches, of which the annihilation of the flower of the *Wandervogel* at the Battle of Langemarck in autumn 1914 was a singularly stark example. Middle-class youth discovered that, instead of the war creating a unique opportunity for a wholesale purification and restructuring of society, it merely multiplied and made more complex old problems. Their disillusionment in 1918 could hardly have been more emphatic. Even the independent youth movement, that dynamic vehicle of fresh hope before the war, lost its way, and ended up more divided and politically troubled than ever before.

The war experience of the young working class was no less traumatic. Those not enlisted in the armed services were, following a brief period of high unemployment at the beginning, sucked into the war economy in large numbers to replace adult manpower engaged at the front. Together with the new army of female workers they made an indispensable contribution to the civilian war effort in the factories. As a result of the higher wages they were able to earn, young workers, skilled and unskilled, had rarely been so well off financially; with money to spend,[77] their sense of individual independence was much enhanced. On the other hand, however, they were denied a satisfactory level of welfare care and, more ominously, were increasingly subjected to authoritarian supervision by the state, at least in theory if not always in practice. Friction between the younger proletariat and the authorities was unavoidable in these tense circumstances.[78]

In the factories, work protection measures – not extensive at the best of times – were suspended in respect of women and youth for the duration of the war.[79] Working conditions in general deteriorated noticeably as young workers were compelled to put in longer hours without additional pay and more and more frequently were obliged to forgo their day of rest on a Sunday. The promulgation of the National Auxiliary Service Law (*Vaterländische Hilfsdienstgesetz*) in December 1916 empowered the state, in return for concessions to the trade unions, to direct labour into vital areas of the war economy.[80] Young workers were inconvenienced as much as anybody by this law. Outside the factory, restrictions were placed from the earliest days on the movement of young people, including attendance at cinemas, dance halls and cafés; smoking and loitering in public places was prohibited; curfews were imposed and even compulsory savings schemes introduced[81] – all measures illustrative of the state's anxiety to assert its control. Despite some evasion and lax implementation of these regulations the intention was clear and therefore just as much resented by the young. The situation was exacerbated when food became scarcer, more expensive and of deteriorating quality. Many of the working class, young and old, found that their wages were not keeping up with food prices.[82] Chronic undernourishment was widely reported among working-class children and juveniles and the 'turnip winter' of 1916/17 heralded even grimmer times ahead. Welfare measures, which might have attenuated the harsh reality of authoritarian government and reduced the scope for conflict with the young, were drastically curtailed as an economy exercise,[83] though some authorities were fully aware of the dangers that this invited.[84] Such welfare as was still available from the state was largely reserved for the direct casualties of the conflict: was orphans, families of servicemen, illegitimate offspring of soldiers, disabled veterans and the displaced.[85] In July 1918 a draft welfare law for youth came too late from the Prussian government to improve the situation and in any case it disappeared amidst the chaos of the November Revolution.[86]

The rising anger and rebelliousness of young workers was shown by their conspicuous presence in anti-war agitation, street demonstrations against food shortages, and strikes, and they became more susceptible to radical socialist politics.[87] With fathers often at the front, mothers working in the factories, schools disrupted, church not attended, family life ceased to exist in customary form, and many working-class youngsters found themselves with free time on their hands. Welfare officials commented on 'a certain wildness about youth'.[88] One outlet was crime, and given the degree of irregularity in wartime society it is perhaps not too surprising that juvenile criminality rose to unprecedented levels: the number of youths convicted for offences increased from 47 000 in 1914 to 99 500 in 1918,[89] while the juvenile share of all crimes committed rose from approximately 10 per cent in 1913 to 27 per cent in 1917. In large cities, for example, Stuttgart, a fourfold increase was recorded.[90] Even when relevant factors such as more stringent police vigilance are taken into account, the problem had incontrovertibly reached staggering proportions, with the 16–18-year-olds most heavily implicated. Adults and officials joined in loudly condemning the ill discipline of the young, while the immorality of working-class youth, in particular, was the subject of persistent complaints.[91] But it was not sufficiently realised that a good deal of juvenile crime was motivated by material hardship; despite a trend towards more serious offences, petty theft was easily still the most prevalent type of crime. The youth gangs which sprang up in proletarian districts of large cities during the war were more a manifestation of frustration and material want than of intrinsic criminal proclivities.[92] Increasingly defiant of authority in any form, and more radically-minded in political persuasion than previously, the young working class, especially its lower, unskilled members, was bound to pose a serious challenge to whatever form of state emerged from defeat in Germany after 1918.

Paradoxically, from the vacuum brought about by the collapse of the Reich, a favourable environment emerged for the constructive progression of two important developments which had their genesis in the pre-war period: the extension of welfare legislation for all Germans within the framework of the new Weimar welfare state and, closely associated with this, the promotion of official recognition of the younger generation as a social grouping in its own right and entitled to special treatment. The two major imperatives of the state's welfare philosophy towards the young, humanitarianism and social control, were in 1918 confronted by new challenges in a new setting. The wartime experience had witnessed the further extension of supervision over the young to the detriment of welfare provision, but the democratic–parliamentary political system of the Weimar Republic offered an opportunity for the original balance in this sphere to be restored.

3 The Weimar Sozialstaat

The *Kaiserreich* collapsed in autumn 1918 as a result of Germany's unexpected but decisive military defeat. The army command came to the reluctant conclusion that an armistice was needed and advised the government to accept the Allies' terms. The generals also believed that the Allies would be prepared to deal more sympathetically with a representative rather than the autocratic government headed by the Kaiser. In any event, labour unrest in October 1918 became serious and intimated a clear political message that the monarchy was no longer acceptable in any circumstances and should be abolished. The naval mutinies at Kiel and Wilhelmshaven and disruption in the ranks of the army underlined that position. On the further advice of the army leadership the Kaiser abdicated and the Weimar Republic was proclaimed on 9 November 1918 under the guidance of a new Chancellor, the Social Democrat, Friedrich Ebert. The task of the Social Democratic Party (SPD) was clearly to fill the political vacuum created by the disintegration of the old order and establish the parliamentary democratic system of government on a sound footing. The former leading 'enemy of the Reich' was charged, in effect, with making the transition from a party of opposition to a party of government. But immediately the SPD's authority was challenged by the November Revolution.

The SPD's determination to oppose radical change of any kind was the principal influence on the course of the Revolution. The party, after all, had effectively repudiated some time before 1914 the revolutionary path to the attainment of the socialist state and society as the spirit and practice of reformism permeated its leadership cadres and a large section of the rank and file party members. The movement towards moderation and adoption of an evolutionary approach was taken up by the SPD in response also to broader social and economic developments in Wilhelmine Germany which had improved to some extent the material status of its main sources of support among the urban industrial proletariat, the skilled and semi-skilled workers. They had forged a closer identity with the capitalist state despite being officially regarded with deep suspicion as potential subversives of the *status quo*. The pragmatic, conservative-minded trade union movement also played a not unimportant part in the abandonment of what might loosely be called 'full-bloodied' socialism by placing a non-ideological emphasis on ameliorating the working conditions of its membership. The committed Marxist revolutionaries in the SPD were a minority of declining significance, in substantial retreat before the advance of reformism. They were even less well-positioned to press their views, of course, once they had seceded in 1917 to set up the Independent Social Democratic Party (USPD). Confronted by revolution in 1918 it is hardly surprising, therefore, that the SPD should seek, in conformity with its moderate brand of socialism, to establish law and order without delay and, given its belief in the virtues of democratic parliamentarianism, to fend off the violent opposition of the extreme Left, including the Spartacists around Rosa Luxemburg and Karl Liebknecht, and be unwilling to tolerate thoroughgoing, disruptive change. The cautious party leaders identified the elimination of the radicals as their first priority and to this end were prepared to form the infamous alliance with their one-time keenest adversary, the army. The Ebert–Groener Pact became the hallmark of the Revolution. In perfectly complementary fashion followed the restrained attitude towards all major social, economic and political affairs: the capitalist economy and the feudalistic landed estates east of the Elbe were left undisturbed, the major institutions in national life unreformed and the élitist groups virtually unchallenged in their authority. The overall consequence was a parliamentary republic in the mirror image of a conservative Social Democracy. By its own terms and criteria the SPD had a good revolution.

While the SPD's fears of Bolshevism and the threat of radical change were exaggerated in 1918/19, there is no denying that there was not a substantial popular will among either the working classes or the broad range of the bourgeoisie in favour of the type of Soviet–Bolshevik state advocated by the radical left. Most of the Workers' and Soldiers' Councils eventually took a moderate line, and only a minority of the working class drawn predominantly from younger unskilled and irregular workers were disillusioned and alienated by the SPD's strategy. But, while the objective scope for fundamental initiatives in any sphere was very limited, the SPD might still have been rather more flexible and even adventurous in its vision of the society to emerge from the chaos of that period without necessarily running the risk of outright revolution. A more viable democratic republican infrastructure might have been created in the long-term interests of the Weimar state. As it transpired, the SPD took the view that the Republic's survival was initially dependent on not provoking a counter-revolution from the Right and, more positively, on taking appropriate measures to bring its natural constituency, the working class, into muscular support by giving it a major influence in government at national, federal and local levels for the first time in German history, supplementing this by promoting its material position. The creation of a *Sozialstaat*, or social welfare state, in other words, was regarded by the SPD as crucial to the credibility of the Republic in the eyes of the working class, who would be the principal beneficiaries. Ideas of basic humanitarianism but also of political expediency thus motivated the SPD's policy on social welfare, which consequently became a vital and controversial element in Weimar's development. In the immediate context of the lost war and the November Revolution, meaningful social reform was deemed necessary to dissipate what residual revolutionary animus remained among the workers.[1]

The early postwar years in Germany, stretching from the Revolution to the hyperinflation and currency crisis of late 1923, were characterised by profound economic upheaval and political instability. Yet against such an inauspicious background, during which the Republic had to endure the consequences of the Versailles Peace Treaty, secessionist revolt and challenges from the extreme Left and Right, not only the foundations but also much of the substance of the *Sozialstaat* were put in place. Thus, paradoxically, while the Republic was a failure on so many other fronts, to the extent that its very existence was in serious question, it made remarkable progress in the field of social reform. Large-scale state intervention in welfare, in fact, contributed significantly to keeping the Republic afloat and to its relative stabilisation in unfavourable circumstances in 1923/4. Naturally the impetus and support for social legislation did not come exclusively from the SPD and its trade union allies:[2] the other constituents of the so-called 'Weimar Coalition', the German Democratic Party (DDP) and, more especially, the Centre Party, which had a strong left wing with a traditional interest in social affairs, lent powerful backing for the enterprise of a *Sozialstaat*. The first seven Reich Cabinets of the Republic, from February 1919 to November 1922, were headed by chancellors from the SPD or Centre Party, which at least guaranteed sympathetic guidance from the top for the advance of welfare provision. In the country at large, a whole galaxy of professionals and specialists in the broad social reform movement dramatically extended from their pre-war base to participate in a most telling, activist fashion. Their belief in improving the lower classes by way of welfare benefits and broadening acceptance of 'proper' middle-class values remained firmer than ever before. Specific organisations were established alongside these interested groups to promote the welfare objective including, most notably, the socialist *Hauptausschuss der Arbeiterwohlfahrt*, in 1919. This diversified but formidable alliance of politicians, trade unionists and social workers combined to make the concept of the *Sozialtaat* an unmistakable reality.

Even before the introduction of the Weimar Constitution with clauses relating to labour in 1919, the groundwork for a new era of social reform in Germany had been laid by an ostensible outbreak of peace in capital–labour relations. The historic Stinnes-Legien Agreement of 15 November 1918 signified in theory at least an era of class compromise and partnership which was given institutional recognition shortly afterwards by the formation, as a result of the Agreement, of the Joint Industrial Alliance (*Zentralarbeitsgemeinschaft* or ZAG). The reformist optimism of union leaders and the pragmatism of the employers made ZAG possible. It guaranteed for the time being non-socialisation of the economy and protection of property, and conveyed the unions' belief in an empirical, evolutionary road to socialism in the manner of the SPD. For their part, the employers, who may have simply seen ZAG as a temporary expedient to be discarded when the time and circumstances in politics and the economy were more propitious, granted the major concession of an eight-hour day, which was at once hailed by the SPD as convincing evidence for the success of its social welfare strategy. Only the passage of some years would tell that ZAG was built on essentially insecure foundations because each side ultimately saw different possibilities in it.

The Weimar Constitution acknowledged that the state had important responsibilities towards the working-class and labour movement by incorporating a series of undertakings designed to protect and further their social and economic well-being. Besides extending the franchise to women, which meant the creation of a substantial female, working-class electoral constituency as an influential factor in national politics, the Constitution recognised, fundamentally, the right of every German to have work (Article 163, paragraph 2):

> Every German has, without prejudice to his personal liberty, the moral duty to use his intellectual and physical powers as is demanded by the welfare of the community. Every German shall have the opportunity to earn his living by labour.

And in the same clause the state pledged to provide for those unable to secure employment: 'Where suitable employment cannot be found for him, his maintenance will be provided for. Details will be regulated by special national laws'. Moreover it was asserted (Articles 157, 158) that 'labour stands under the special protection of the Reich'. The trade unions gained legal recognition as the occupational representatives of labour (Article 159), and parity was accorded to capital and labour in the determination of economic policy (Article 165). The unions had already gained in status in connection with the National Auxiliary Service Law of December 1916, of course, when boards composed equally of representatives of employers and unions were introduced under the presidency of a state-appointed chairman to arbitrate on wage claims. Now, after 1918, the unions broadened their advantages to include the legal right to organise (*Koalitionsfreiheit*), the validity of wage agreements (*Tarifverträge*) arising from collective bargaining procedures granted by the Labour Law, and the creation of new forms of unemployment benefit. In addition, new work protection measures included regulations that workers could not be dismissed on grounds of sex, religion or political persuasion and that workers could be laid off only after consultation with the factory council had taken place. The Factory Councils Act (*Betriebsrätegesetz*) of 4 February 1920 provided for full worker representation and workers' limited rights of co-determination (*Mitbestimmung*) in large companies within the framework of committees, which was a considerable departure, on paper at least, from the prewar '*Herr-im-Haus*' attitude of employers.[3] In practice, unfortunately, the factory councils suffered from persistent employer suspicion and the inadequate training of workers, and seemed too often caught between two stools: protecting workers' rights and promoting the company's interests at the same time. A National Factory Council, as envisaged in the Weimar Constitution, and which might have been able to reconcile these inherent differences, never materialised, for a variety of political and financial reasons. While the implementation of these reforms inevitably left something to be desired, their established fact exercised an important influence on the trade unions in March 1920 when they were moved to call a general strike which was decisive in defeating the reactionary Kapp Putsch; the unions and the working class in general reacted to this episode as an attack on *their* Republic. Their integration into and identification with the state was thus strikingly demonstrated. The reform of labour legislation in these early years of the Republic was completed by the establishment on 30 October 1923 of a state arbitration system, under the supervision of the Reich Labour Ministry, to deal with disputes over wages and working conditions (*Schlichtungsverordnung*). The chairman of the arbitration committee was empowered to impose an award, even if the employers or the unions rejected its terms. Moreover the Reich Labour Minister, who at this time was the Centre Party politician Heinrich Brauns, known to be sympathetic to the Catholic concept of a 'just wage' and to improving the position of labour overall within the context of *Sozialpolitik*, could make such an award legally binding. This system of arbitration, which remained in force until suspended by von Papen in July 1932, gave the unions a vital role in negotiations and it formed the basis of wage advances in the mid-1920s. Its introduction by way of an emergency decree during the height of the hyperinflation crisis was designed to eliminate any mood of incipient revolutionism in the workers as well as to complement other important legislation in this sphere.[4]

State intervention in the welfare sphere after 1919 was by no means confined to the unions and work protection. Every form of social activity was brought under official scrutiny and significant reforms resulted. Many of these were rooted in wartime or even in pre-war developments but now the Republic was concerned to expand what had been merely embryonic practice and experimentation into wholesale achievement. A new state-funded housing programme was launched in response to the pledge in the Constitution to provide every German with a sound home (Article 155), and between 1919 and 1923 444 794 new homes were built and a start made on slum clearance, which was a major problem in large cities.[5] Tenants in rented accommodation, who had been given a measure of legislative protection during the First World War, received further help. Most federal governments issued rent and tenancy regulations after 1919 and rent levels were generally pegged at wartime levels until 1923; in some areas rents declined by as much as 20 per cent compared with pre-war levels. The Reich government capped these developments with the Tenants' Protection Act in 1923 which conferred rights as well as responsibilities, bringing clarity and order to what had once been an uninviting area of social policy.[6] In the related area of health, the state also expressed unprecedented commitment, with large sums of money provided to increase the number of hospitals, doctors, nurses and paramedical staff. Thanks also to advances in medical science, the incidence of diseases such as tuberculosis and pneumonia was reduced. Social spending by federal and local municipal authorities also rose considerably after the war.[7] One of the few areas not to record noticeable improvement was the social insurance system covering accident, sickness, invalidity and old age. Its financial basis had been destroyed by the war and revolution, and pensions, despite their meagre level, continued to be paid only by means of a subsidy from the Reich government.[8]

While these welfare reforms were of substantial benefit to the working classes, in particular, their material situation was improved from another direction during the early postwar years. They derived advantage from the redistribution of national wealth brought on by the dislocation of war. The cost of the war and the losses exacted by the Treaty of Versailles resulted in an important reduction of Germany's economic substance, and differentials in income and wealth in the population were narrowed in favour of the lower groups. After taking into account price and wage movements, their real income increased between 1918 and 1922 until overtaken by hyperinflation in 1923.[9] Once the currency had been reformed and the economy relatively stabilised after 1924, the distribution of income continued to shift in favour of workers and employees at the expense of middle-class groups, including the self-employed, property owners and small farmers.[10] In total, there is a strong case for arguing that the working class and the labour movement were 'winners' in respect of their political, social and financial gains in 1918–23.

The currency stabilisation crisis of 1923/4 gave employers their first significant opportunity to launch a campaign against the achievements of the *Sozialstaat*. They emerged strengthened, labour and the unions weakened by that traumatic episode. Membership of the unions, which had been in some decline since 1920, was shattered by the impact of hyperinflation, and was reduced from its postwar peak of over eight million members to four million. In no position to resist the onslaught from the employers, the unions were forced to accept an extension of working hours without additional pay, a relaxation of work protection measures, abrogation of wage agreements and, above all, the loss of the eight-hour day. The ZAG, already languishing uneasily before 1923, was finally swept aside in January 1924.[11] However the employers' *Blitzkrieg* was a temporary phenomenon and although somewhat battered the *Sozialstaat* not only survived with many of its reforms intact but was in a position to take advantage of the relative economic and political normality of the mid-1920s to expand further. What had been an undoubted setback in 1923/4 was quickly reversed in a more determined climate of welfare reform than before.

The extension of reform in the mid-1920s took place despite the fact that the SPD withdrew from participation in national government. Its 'flight from responsibility' (Bracher), which was intrinsically motivated by narrow party considerations, thus making a mockery of the party's pretensions to being a *Volkspartei* with a truly national vision, was at least partly attenuated by its continued domination of the Prussian government and involvement in numerous local authority bodies throughout the country. This gave the SPD some kind of coherent base from which to exert influence on national decision making, albeit from the periphery. The *modus vivendi* it established with the middle-class Reich cabinets in 1924–8 meant that, in return for its general support, the SPD was given in exchange the opportunity to extend social welfare provision and legislation. But this was less than could have been achieved for the Republic as a whole. With its radical enemies temporarily silenced and the economy on a relatively even keel, the mid-1920s offered a unique opening for a rallying of all pro-democratic supporters behind the aim of consolidating their state on sound foundations. The election of an authoritarian-minded, conservative monarchist, Field-Marshal Paul von Hindenburg, to the Presidency of the Republic in 1925 ought to have reminded republicans of the precariousness of their situation. The SPD, as the largest political party and, in the words of Friedrich Stampfer, Editor-in-Chief of *Vorwärts*, the 'Party of State' mainly responsible in the first place for and most closely identified with the Republic, ought to have taken the lead in bolstering support for it. That was its duty and responsibility. But the ageing, circumspect leadership of the party proved incapable of acting decisively in the national interest at this critical juncture. Its fear of losing votes to the Communist Party (KPD) by being associated with the policies of the bourgeois parties in government transcended all other factors. Indeed, the SPD withdrew even further into itself by further developing in this period the socialist sub-culture through a host of ancillary organisations. Its ghetto-like appearance, character and mentality were strengthened not diminished, as they should have been in the national interest. The Republic was denied an important source of support at the very centre of its governmental and constitutional apparatus and consequently failed to establish the kind of substance and self-confidence which might have allowed it to overcome the storms that lay ahead.[12] If its achievements in social welfare reform in the 'Golden Twenties' were less impressive and durable than they might have been, it is none the less legitimate to acknowledge the further progress made by the Republic in this increasingly contentious area.

The influx of mainly American investment capital into Germany following the currency reform (*Rentenmark*) and the regulation of reparations by the Dawes Plan allowed virtually unrestricted growth of the public deficit. Between 1925 and 1928 the state's social spending rose by 25 per cent, from eight billion to ten billion marks, and by 1928 it had doubled the level of expenditure in 1913.[13] Altogether public sector expenditure as a proportion of national income rose from 14.5 per cent in 1910/13 to 24 per cent in 1925/9.[14] Reich, federal and local authorities went on a spending bonanza on a wide range of civic and social amenities, including parks, libraries, swimming pools, sports complexes and exhibition centres.[15] Cologne, whose *Oberbürgermeister* since 1917 had been Konrad Adenauer, was among the most profligate of city authorities.[16] There was substantial state funding for public education, as demanded by the SPD and unions, and public-funded housing construction received a further boost. Just under two million new homes were built between 1924 and the collapse of the construction industry in 1931, and during the same period 195 000 homes were modernised.[17] Although Weimar's chronic housing shortage, which in 1927 alone amounted to 800 000 homes,[18] was by no means solved it had been considerably alleviated. The quality of the new housing was generally superior, moreover, to that of older homes. A further indication of improved social conditions is perhaps provided by the sharp fall in emigration from Germany. It had reached a postwar peak in 1923 when 115 431 left, but dropped consistently throughout the remainder of the decade.[19] Behind the administration of welfare progress lay an updated, more unified and rational structure which was introduced by a new public welfare law on 4 December 1924.[20]

The most important advances in the mid-1920s were made by the labour movement. While the cost of living rose modestly, real wages increased by 9 per cent in 1927 on average and by a further 12 per cent in 1928, making the German labour force the highest-paid industrial workers in Europe. The change in the balance of power in industry was also illustrated by the Labour Courts Act of 23 December 1926 (*Arbeitsgerichtsgesetz*). It regulated contracting out and piecework and incorporated both into collective wage-bargaining machinery. Work protection measures were reinstated, and in some cases, improved. In April 1927 a Working Hours Act (*Arbeitszeitgesetz*) effectively restored the eight-hour day in many large plants and provided for substantial wage supplements for hours worked in excess of eight hours per day, or 48 hours per week, thus retrieving for labour the position lost in 1923/4. Furthermore an amendment to a 1924 regulation obliged factories operating a 24-hour per day system to switch to a three-shift arrangement. On the debit side for labour, a general reduction in hours to compensate for progress in rationalisation and to relieve unemployment did not materialise.[21] The balance of power did swing towards labour in many ways but it was a far from absolute triumph.

As the end of the decade drew closer, the expensive labour force was increasingly resented by employers, particularly in heavy industry, who claimed that wage rises were often politically inspired and calculated to damage their interests. The particular target of the employers' enmity was the state arbitration system and its legally binding decisions. Statistics show that between 1924 and 1932 there were no fewer than 77 224 cases of arbitration of which 4000 required binding arbitration decisions by the Reich Labour Ministry. Until at least 1928/9 a majority of these decisions favoured the workers, while during the Depression this ceased to be the case.[22] The Reich Labour Ministry, headed by Heinrich Brauns up to 1928 and from then until 1930 by the Social Democrat Rudolf Wissell, was a particular source of employers' criticism, which before long carried serious political implications. The general practical effect of wages policy before 1929, to which the arbitration system made a notable contribution, was to diminish differentials between skilled and unskilled workers and between workers and certain middle-class groups, including civil servants and white-collar employees (*Angestellte*).[23]

The mid-1920s witnessed, therefore, undeniable victories for *Sozialpolitik* in terms of real wage gains, housing construction, provision of civic amenities, and others, all to the substantial material advantage of large sections of the industrial proletariat. The Republic had unequivocally demonstrated its genuine commitment to improving the living standards of its least priviledged classes, and in the process had effected something of a social revolution. The political pay-off for the SPD in a short-term perspective was its convincing triumph in the Reichstag Election of May 1928, where it consolidated and enhanced its status as the party of a majority of the working class. But the SPD would have cause to regret that its standing and that of the Republic did not rest on a more solid platform as the Depression loomed, with its spectre of mass unemployment.

For much of the nineteenth century, unemployment was seen in Germany and the rest of Europe as an entirely personal and self-induced condition. It was widely accepted that a jobless worker had inherent personal failings which accounted for his unhappy state: natural indolence, lack of character, low self-esteem and morals were all generally considered to lie at the root of the problem, and the unemployed were castigated in the same manner as other social misfits such as vagabonds, paupers, ruffians, gypsies, even criminals, who were despised as an underclass of no-gooders.[24] Until the 1890s in Germany, the work-shy were liable to criminal prosecution according to paragraph 361 of the Criminal Code (*Strafgesetzbuch*) along with vagrants, the homeless and drunkards, if they became a burden on charity organisations.[25] This severe attitude had been strengthened by the connection between unemployment and revolutionary upheavals for, politically, unemployment seemed to form part of the essential background to periodic affronts to established authority. For the material deprivation that was invariably the misfortune of the unemployed, officialdom had little sympathy. Such ignorance only began to be dispelled and a more compassionate view taken later in the century when it was more widely recognised that the vagaries of the business cycle in the age of industrialisation might have something to do with disturbances in the labour market over which an individual could not exercise control.[26] Before 1914 everyone was in theory vulnerable to the vicissitudes of the capitalist system, though in practice it was almost exclusively the industrial working class that was affected. Large-scale social problems resulting from the development of urban industrial society, of which unemployment was only one, of course, also helped to change attitudes for the better, prompting the formation of an increasingly vocal social reformist movement. The socialist and labour movement also began to act as a pressure group for official remedial action.

Oddly, in most European countries until a relatively late date in the nineteenth century, there was little agreement on the definition of who should be regarded as an authentically unemployed person. Certain basic criteria only emerged slowly: the individual concerned had to be financially in need of a job, to be willing to work and actively looking for regular employment. He had also to be able-bodied and genuinely unable to find a job. Often, too, he had to be able to demonstrate a record of previous regular working. Those entering the labour market for the first time and those returning to it after a prolonged absence could also be included in the unemployed category, as were workers dismissed by their employer, for whatever reason, and seeking another position.

The first spur to changing attitudes about unemployment and the unemployed in Germany was given by the depression of the 1870s, but it was some time yet before any substantive action was taken by anyone. Bismarck's social legislation in the following decade, for instance, made no provision for the unemployed and right up to 1914 this problem remained the least developed area of the state's social policy. The only public measures of alleviation were workhouses, community work schemes and work camps, or labour colonies, from the 1880s, in which manual labour in agriculture and forestry was provided. The numbers of jobless involved, however, were exiguous.[27] Those campaigning for the inclusion of unemployment insurance in the state's social security framework were confronted by formidable opposition from the traditional liberal view of self-help and non-interventionism by the state, and from the cruder proponents of social darwinist philosophy who stressed the 'survival of the fittest' ethos.[28] However, perhaps the principal obstacle to state initiative in this field was the simple fact that at no time before the First World War was unemployment a problem of serious proportions in Germany.

There are no reliable statistics available as to the precise extent of unemployment because the requisite data-collecting mechanisms had not yet been created and what information was to hand was taken before 1914 from trade union and labour exchange records. There were clear limitations to this provenance because trade unions represented a minority of German workers before 1914, a total of only 2.5 million; the socialist unions represented a mere 15 per cent of workers in 1914, drawn largely not from large concerns but from the craft-based, medium-sized companies.[29] Few unskilled workers, the group mainly affected by unemployment, belonged to any union. The unions recorded only those of their members out of work. Even so, publication of unemployment figures in a systematic fashion was not undertaken by the unions until 1903, when they appeared in the *Reichsarbeitsblatt*. Until the creation of the *Reichsanstalt* (National Board) by the Unemployment Insurance Act of 1927, fully comprehensive and accurate statistics on unemployment were unavailable. The *Reichsanstalt* was the first body equipped to overcome deficiencies in methodology and compilation and to carry out regular, nationwide surveys on the basis of uniform criteria.[30]

Before 1890, as the industrial economy expanded, unemployment in Germany was hardly an issue. But thereafter conditions in the labour market became less tranquil in response to the often abrupt and significant fluctuations in the business and trade cycles; unemployment became a more visible phenomenon. The Occupational Census of 14 June 1895 and Population Census of 2 December the same year (*Berufs-und Volkszählung*), the only large-scale survey of the German working population before 1914,[31] revealed an unemployment figure of just under 300 000, or 1.35 per cent of a working population of 22 million, in June 1895, and 771 000, representing 3.46 per cent, at the end of the year. A large majority of the jobless were unskilled and seasonally idle workers in agriculture, forestry and construction. These figures, however, should be taken as general indicators only rather than precise calculations. Only those out of work who fulfilled certain rigid criteria were included in the Census, that is, workers who were physically fit, in need, and in active pursuit of employment. Excluded from the statistics were whole categories of jobless, including those seeking their first employment, those returning to the labour market after a prolonged absence, and those between jobs which involved a time-lag. Those in 'hidden' unemployment (for example, agricultural and building workers) and in 'underemployment', including short-time workers, were also omitted.[32] Taking all relevant factors into account, the best-informed estimate of the average rate of unemployment in Germany between 1890 and 1913 is just under 3 per cent.[33] During periods of cyclical depression, as in 1892/3, 1901/2 and 1908/9, the average rate was probably closer to 6 or 7 per cent. In most normal years the rate could easily be zero or around 1 per cent. Apart from agriculture, forestry and construction, the industries most regularly visited by unemployment were textiles and the metal trades.[34] The embryonic network of labour exchanges (*Arbeitsnachweise*), which expanded after 1890 under trade union and employer supervision in most towns and cities, facilitated the placement of labour and made available reasonably up-to-date information about vacancies and training opportunities.[35] A Prussian government decree in 1894 required towns with a population of 10 000 or more to establish a labour exchange.[36] When an umbrella agency, the *Verband deutscher Arbeitsnachweise*, was set up in 1898 under the chairmanship of Dr Richard Freund, this area of activity in the labour market was given the means for more effective national co-ordination. By 1910 almost half of the 450 local exchanges throughout the country were associate members of this central body based in Berlin.[37]

A number of trade unions instituted unemployment relief schemes for their members before the war – the German Bookbinders' Association was the first to have such a scheme in 1879 – but the large majority of the unemployed who were not unionised had to look for assistance in their plight from other sources. By 1913 there had developed an extensive system of municipal unemployment insurance, but it was rather limited in scope and covered relatively few workers. Some local authorities took initiatives in other ways. In 1893, for instance, Cologne and Leipzig set up a *Winterhilfekasse* for unemployed construction workers, and from 1902 Cologne supported an annual winter unemployment fund.[38] Otherwise, for many unemployed, particularly if there were dependants, recourse had to be had to private and Church charities, or to the locally-administered and demeaning poor relief service (*Armenfürsorge*). The poor law stripped the unemployed of their civil rights, including the right to vote. Fortunately, even for this most underprivileged section of the proletariat, there was no long-term unemployment before 1914. That it remained an ephemeral experience for workers partly explains the SPD's somewhat hesitant, if not ambivalent, attitude towards the whole idea of relief. The fact that unemployment was largely confined to those unskilled groups of the male working class considerably under-represented in its membership and thus unable to exert any pressure on the party leadership to adopt a more positive attitude is also very relevant to the SPD's stance. Elderly workers, young, unskilled, unmarried and low-paid workers, itinerant and seasonal workers, and the small number of congenital work-shy and unfit constituted the bulk of the unemployed – in other words, the poorer, rougher lumpenproletariat of the larger cities and heavily industrialised areas.[39] The 'labour aristocracy' was only marginally affected by unemployment at that time. Consequently, unemployment was not a particularly urgent concern for any established vested interest in Germany, let alone the SPD. Those middle-class groups who feared the unemployed would form the vanguard of a revolutionary army were justifiably not taken seriously. Their perceptions were a reflection not of reality but of their own exaggerated apprehensions of the disruptive influence of modern industrial society.

The reluctance of the Wilhelmine State to become too involved in the debate over provision for the unemployed is perhaps politically understandable in these circumstances. The general ignorance and lack of information about unemployment militated against the taking of any energetic steps to devise a state-sponsored national insurance scheme, as some trade unionists were demanding. Unemployment simply was not a big enough problem before 1914. In 1902 the Reichstag did establish a specialist commission to investigate this proposal but some time before the war it lost its way as discussion among the political parties became bogged down in detail and, more usually, in disagreement about how such a scheme should be organised and financed.[40] Not until the theme of unemployment was given a sharper profile by the impact of the First World War was impetus injected into this debate. The catastrophic increase in the number of jobless during the early months of the conflict was ample confirmation, if any more were needed, that unemployment could no longer be dismissed as a self-induced misfortune of the few, that it could happen to any conscientious worker caught up involuntarily in economic upheaval. Although the labour market had settled to its customary levels of employment by April 1915 and continued like this until 1918, the state was becoming more aware of its responsibilities in this fundamental sphere and could no longer avoid taking meaningful action In 1915 the Reichstag considered the establishment of a National Labour Office (*Reichsarbeitsamt*), but this struggled into existence only two years later and then in reduced form under military control. From June 1917 the army also took over supervision of the labour exchanges to help with the direction of manpower into vital war industries.[41]

The advent of the Weimar Republic, accompanied by the SPD's commitment to the forging of a *Sozialstaat*, was bound to have the most important implications for the unemployment question as it finally moved to near the top of the political agenda. What left no doubt about such an order of priorities was the massive unemployment in late 1918 and early 1919 occasioned by the transition from a wartime to peacetime economy and the impact of military demobilisation. State intervention was necessary to regulate the labour market in a manner consistent with the imperatives of the National Auxiliary Service Law of 1916 and, of course, government was alarmed at a time of deep political ferment by the extent of social unrest arising from unemployment affecting millions.[42] The Reich government allocated considerable sums to industry for work creation and incentive schemes for the re-employment of returning soldiers. Its efforts to overcome unemployment and to maintain normal levels of employment were assisted in the early 1920s by the inflationary trend. Success was quick and stunning. The numbers of jobless fell to 620 000 in June 1919, to 370 000 in March 1920 and to a mere 150 000 in late 1921. Throughout 1920–2 the official rate of unemployment averaged under 3 per cent, thereby reflecting prewar levels of employment. However these statistics do not expose the extent of female unemployment or the substantial amount of short-time working at the same time. There was, in addition, considerable 'veiled stretching' and other forms of unproductive and inefficient practice. Nor do the statistics reveal the existence of a number of unemployment blackspots, for example, in Greater Berlin, Hamburg and Saxony.[43]

The postwar intervention of the state in unemployment relief was initiated within the framework of the demobilisation scheme. An ordinance of 13 November 1918 (*Erwerbsloserfürsorge der Kriegswohlfahrtspflege*) created relief for all those aged 14 years and over who were in need, able-bodied and willing to work, and where their unemployment was deemed, quaintly, 'a consequence of the war'. Home ownership and savings disqualified the applicant. Benefits were extremely modest and varied according to the age and sex of the claimant.[44] In February 1919, just over one million were in receipt of relief.[45] But operation of the system caused many practical problems: who or what was to decide whether unemployment had been caused by the war or not? The scheme created financial problems also because local authorities were able to pay benefit rates that exceeded local wage levels and thus were a disincentive to find work. Inevitably complaints mounted that the jobless were better off than many in jobs, but attempts to close the loopholes were not entirely successful.[46] The view that the legislation aimed to push female workers out of the market was also aired with annoyance.[47] The government, aware of the imperfections of what had always been regarded as a temporary measure anyway, sought to put unemployment relief on a more orderly basis in a new decree of 6 May 1920, which allowed benefit on the same criteria as before for a maximum of 26 weeks, in exceptional cases for 52 weeks. The modesty of the scheme and of the level of unemployment in the early postwar period is illustrated by the number of recipients: in 1921 150 000 and in 1922 only 12 000 were principal beneficiaries (*Hauptunterstützungsempfänger*).[48] If nothing else, however, this early, somewhat tentative legislation was a step in the right direction of a state-sponsored national unemployment insurance scheme. The costs of these early initiatives were borne mainly by the Reich government, thus adding yet another component to the accumulating public deficit, but the federal states and local or district authorities, who administered the relief on a day-to-day basis, contributed one-third and one-sixth, respectively.

Large-scale unemployment did not return to Germany until the economic and financial crises of late 1923. The proportion of trade unionists out of work rose from 2 per cent in November 1922 to a peak of 28.2 per cent in December 1923, while a sizable proportion were put on short time.[49] In January 1924 the jobless figure had fallen slightly to 26.5 per cent.[50] Once the stabilisation of the currency had been effected, unemployment fell consistently throughout that year to reach 8.1 per cent in December.[51] None the less the crisis prompted a fresh look by government at the unemployment relief scheme which was patently inadequate to cope with the demands made on it in this highly disturbed period: no fewer than 1.5 million were in receipt of benefit at the height of the crisis.[52] In some parts of the country there was clear evidence of the system breaking down altogether and a tendency for unemployment relief to degenerate into poor relief because of the Reich's financial embarrassment. As part of its currency reform the Stresemann government had to bring the public deficit under control and put the financing of unemployment relief on a fresh basis.

New legislation introduced on 13 February 1924 (*Verordnung über Erwerbslosenfürsorge*) restricted the award of benefit to those who had taken out a state sickness insurance policy for a minimum of 13 weeks in the previous year. Alongside the introduction of the principle of insurance, the ordinance effectively excluded certain large categories of workers from participating in the scheme, including poorly-paid workers and long-term unemployed who were unable to fulfil the condition of three months' continuous employment, and many white-collar staff and the self-employed who did not enrol in the health insurance scheme. The legislation decreed that the new arrangements were to be financed by a statutory requirement of employers and workers to pay a 20 per cent surcharge on their health insurance contributions: the Reich and federal authorities were exempted from all financial responsibility in this respect. As had been the case in unemployment relief since 1918, a stringent means test still applied to claimants, as did the nonsensical stipulation that a worker's unemployment was to be a result of the war. The maximum period of eligibility for receipt of benefit was retained at 26 weeks, but the possible extended period was reduced from 52 to 39 weeks. The rate of benefit was still very modest, and different rates were set for men, women and youth.[53] The final reform introduced by this legislation concerned the institutional arrangements for operating the relief scheme. In 1919 the government had taken over the network of local labour exchanges and in May 1920 put them under a central co-ordinating body, the National Office for Labour Exchange

(*Reichsamt für Arbeitsvermittlung*). Later, in 1922, the Labour Exchanges Act (*Arbeitsnachweisegesetz*) led to the creation of labour exchanges under public control in all localities. They were to exercise their functions in a neutral, non-partisan fashion, and in 1924 seemed perfectly placed to administer the new unemployment relief scheme. The local welfare committees for demobilisation, which had administered the system hitherto, were dissolved, saving the government some money into the bargain. In practice, however, the labour exchanges did not administer the scheme wholly satisfactorily. They tended to be too bureaucratic and staffed by untrained personnel. More importantly, the continuing modesty of the scheme was not likely to meet the growing demands of the broad social reform lobby for more thoroughgoing and sympathetic state treatment of the unemployed, particularly as there were clear signs of the problem becoming worse.

The fundamental reasons why legislation had been piecemeal in the early 1920s were the financial, economic and political uncertainties of the Republic and the fact that the whole question of unemployment relief was locked into the sensitive capital–labour relationship. Many employers still clung to the reactionary view that any kind of relief system undermined the will to work, though further developments in the mid-1920s, which saw the unions able to gain considerable ground in welfare provision, ensured that such attitudes would not prevail against those of the social reformers who were engaged in the business of extending the parameters of *Sozialpolitik*.

Although officially recorded levels of unemployment were low during most of 1925 (3.5 per cent in June),[54] these did not reveal the not inconsiderable disguised unemployment in agriculture or, more worryingly, the existence for the first time in German history of a permanent and sizable pool of able-bodied, long-term unemployed, who numbered some 195 000 in late 1925 and who were destined to grow as a proportion of the jobless in the years ahead.[55] For them, in particular, unemployment signified a protracted period of real need, for even the traditional personal and family support systems could not compensate for the deficiencies of the public relief scheme. Growing awareness of the predicament of the long-term jobless could only add further impetus to the campaign for a modern, properly funded scheme in keeping with the proclaimed virtues of the Weimar welfare state. That proposition was also advanced by the mass unemployment in 1925/6 arising from the process of intensive and rapid rationalisation in industry. The amalgamation of giant companies, the widespread adoption of American management and mass production methods, and the elimination of uneconomic plant produced, despite a rising demand for cheap, unskilled female labour, structural unemployment on a large scale, not only among unskilled manual workers but also among the artisan and white-collar classes.[56] Together with normal seasonal influences on the labour market, this shake-out resulted in 2.27 million unemployed in February 1926. The unemployment rate among trade unionists in December 1925 was 19.4 per cent, rising to 22.6 per cent in January 1926, and holding at 22.0 per cent in February. Even with the ending of winter, the rate was still 18.6 per cent in April and remained at a high level for the remainder of 1926 (14.2 per cent in November). During the following winter, the situation showed improvement but still there were rates of 16.7 per cent in December 1926 and 16.5 per cent in January 1927.[57] Although the SPD and trade unions generally welcomed rationalisation, believing that it could lead to higher wages and accepting the argument of employers that a trimming of the workforce was a necessary prerequisite for Germany maintaining her competitiveness in world markets,[58] a wider public was shaken by the social consequences of so much unemployment. A consensus along the same lines was forming in government circles, and a greater sense of urgency informed their deliberations.

Draft plans for a comprehensive national scheme of unemployment relief had been in desultory preparation by government since 1919. At last, against a background of industrial rationalisation and its attendant labour problems, and growing optimism about future prospects for the economy in a period of relative political peace, the Reich Labour Ministry produced in late 1925 the blueprint of a scheme which essentially formed the basis of legislation two years later. Also the creation of a scheme of Emergency Aid (*Krisenfürsorge*) on 20 November 1926 helped pave the way for fundamental reform. Emergency Aid was designed to give additional relief to those long-term unemployed whose entitlement to unemployment relief had run out, for a period to be determined by occupation or trade and place of residence, and subject to a means test. The Reich government provided most of the funding (75 per cent) and local authorities the remainder. Subsequently it was decreed that this form of standby aid could be awarded for those who qualified for a maximum of 26 weeks; white-collar workers aged over 40 years could receive benefit for 45 weeks.[59] The new era of state-sponsored unemployment relief was totally fulfilled, or so it seemed, on 16 July 1927 when the Reichstag approved by a large majority (excluding the KPD and National Socialists (NSDAP)) the Law on Labour Exchanges and Unemployment Insurance (*Gesetz über Arbeitsvermittlung und Arbeitslosenversicherung*, abbreviated to AVAVG), which was immediately acclaimed by a wide cross-section of society as the crowning glory of the *Sozialstaat*.[60]

AVAVG, which took effect on 1 October 1927, combined a series of innovations with elements already established by previous legislation.[61] Thus, while the Act linked compulsory contributions (payable by those already insured against sickness) by employers and workers to unemployment insurance and the legal entitlement to automatic benefit irrespective of any other means of support, provided the claimant was able and willing to work, had been made redundant through no fault of his own and had worked for 52 weeks in the previous two years, he had to have made contributions for at least 26 weeks during the preceding year. Employers and workers contributed equally to the insurance fund – about 3 per cent of the average industrial wage in 1927. The weekly-paid benefit (*Arbeitslosenunterstützung*), which was given out after a waiting period of between three and 14 days following application, depending on the claimant's age and family circumstances, was granted for a maximum of 26 weeks, with further extension possible in exceptional circumstances to workers over 40 years of age to 39 weeks, thus replacing the 52 weeks allowed under earlier legislation. The level of benefit was not calculated as before as a flat rate for men, women and youth,[62] but was determined for each worker according to a complicated system of eleven wage categories, his average wage over the last six weeks of employment, number and age of dependants, marital status, gender and type of locality in which resident. On average, between 35 and 75 per cent of a claimant's previous wage was paid, plus, if appropriate, a small supplement for each dependant. In practice, a higher percentage of normal earnings was given to non-skilled than to skilled workers. Some 17 million workers were immediately covered by the scheme,[63] but excluded were agricultural, forestry, fishing and casual workers who were employed for not more than 30 hours per week and earning no more than 10 marks per week, domestic piece-time workers, domestic servants in agriculture, and certain categories of apprentices.[64] When applying for benefit an applicant was obliged to produce a certain amount of documentation, to include a police certificate of residence, a report from his previous employer about his work performance, a statement of earnings, a certificate of sickness insurance and, if relevant, a marriage certificate and the birth certificates of children. Finally, the Act established an independent, central agency, the *Reichsanstalt für Arbeitsvermittlung und Arbeitslosenversicherung* (National Board for Labour Exchanges and Unemployment Insurance), to co-ordinate the nationwide system of local labour exchanges, now renamed Labour Offices (*Arbeitsämter*) and grouped into 13 districts corresponding to economically determined geographical areas rather than to existing administrative units. This development was a logical extension of the 1922 Labour Exchanges Act.

The new scheme was meant to accommodate a maximum of 800 000 unemployed on average per year – a not unreasonable figure at a time when the rate of unemployment had fallen to 4.5 per cent of trade unionists (October 1927). When the jobless worker had exhausted his period of benefit and he was still without work he could turn to Emergency Aid, which was included in AVAVG and then given a firm structure by a decree of 28 September 1927 (updated on 6 November 1928). Those who had not fulfilled the qualifying period for unemployment insurance benefit but had worked for at least 13 weeks in the previous two years in an insured occupation were also now eligible. Benefits were paid, still subject to a means test, at a lower level than unemployment relief and, in practice, following further changes to the regulations in June 1929, were directed largely at skilled workers from particular branches of industry, and white-collar workers.[65] When the benefits under both these schemes had run out for an unemployed worker, he had recourse to a third tier of support, the locally-administered and financed welfare relief (*Wohlfahrtserwerbsloser-pflege*). Benefit was paid at a level regardless of former wages or occupation and was designed simply to provide what officials regarded as the bare essentials to keep body and soul together. In some parts of the country, the able-bodied recipients of this form of support – known as the 'welfare unemployed' – were required to perform work of a communal nature in exchange for the meagre assistance. They were mainly unskilled workers of all age groups whose numbers increased dramatically during the Depression. All payments made under this scheme had to be repaid in time by the 'welfare unemployed' (*Rückzahlungspflicht*).[66]

Although the scales of benefits in all three schemes were relatively insubstantial, the entire package was considered an important step forward for the cause of social justice. Ironically, however, while AVAVG may have been the jewel in the crown of the welfare state, it also represented the beginning of its demise, thus before the onset of the Depression. AVAVG had hardly become operational when it was overtaken by a hostile amalgam of economic and political developments.

In winter 1927/8, the jobless figures, which were exacerbated as usual by seasonal factors, rose to 1 896 274 officially out of work, representing 12.9 per cent of trade unionists.[67] Most of them were eligible to claim and to receive unemployment insurance benefit, which at once put AVAVG under the kind of pressure it was not designed to cope with. It fell into a substantial financial deficit, for the level of contributions, on which it was exclusively dependent, was palpably insufficient to meet its legal obligations. The *Reichsanstalt*, the scheme's administrator, had to apply to the Reich government for additional funding at a time when the central budget was overextended and causing political acrimony. Nor did the situation confronting AVAVG in 1927/8 prove to be exceptional, as officials had hoped, because in the following winter even more pressure was exerted on the scheme when the official unemployment rate escalated to unprecedented heights: in December 1928 it was 16.7 per cent, in January 1929 19.4 per cent and in February 1929 it reached a peak of 22.3 per cent, or three million workers.[68] In March of that year the scheme needed a loan from the Reich of 288 million marks. The financially embarrassed government felt compelled, in turn, to undercut its debts in respect of AVAVG by changing some of the regulations. Amendments to AVAVG were passed on 18 December 1928 and 12 October 1929 – ironically, by the socialist Müller-led cabinet – which curtailed the period of benefit support for workers in occupations badly affected by seasonal unemployment, and reorganised the *Reichsanstalt*'s organisational machinery in a bid to promote efficiency and save running costs.[69] But even if these changes had been efficacious, which they were not, AVAVG's relationship with the labour market was being strained further in the late 1920s by the growing number of women entering employment and by demographic factors which were adding younger workers to the pool of labour. AVAVG, in fact, had been the product of official thinking governed by the relatively stable conditions in the labour market prevailing between 1920 and 1922. It was increasingly to be exposed as unequipped to deal with the volatile situation that had emerged prior to the Depression and, naturally, it was bound to flounder altogether in the mass unemployment scenario of the early 1930s.

From another, equally damaging direction, AVAVG was criticised by many employers who regarded it as just about the final straw in terms of their opposition to government expenditure on welfare. Indeed, AVAVG epitomised all that the same employers detested of the entire *Sozialstaat*. They claimed that the high taxes levied on them by a state hostile to business provided the financial underpinning of a system to which they had deep-rooted ideological and political objections. Money that should have gone into investment in industry went instead into welfare, mainly for the benefit of labour. Reduced profit margins caused by advances in real average wages and reductions in working hours in the mid-1920s removed the incentive to invest, it was alleged. The massive pay increase given to civil servants in 1927 by Reich Finance Minister Heinrich Köhler 'in the interests of social justice', as he put it, was greeted with dismay by employers. High labour costs – and by the late 1920s the German worker had become very expensive in comparison with his counterparts in other major industrial countries – weakened Germany's crucial export performance by increasing prices of goods sold abroad, and at the same time led to an augmentation in imports because of the larger consumer demand from workers with money to spend. The consequent balance of trade problem was thus attributed by employers to the condition of the labour market. The accumulating public deficit, which by 1929 was making the Reich government non-creditworthy, can also be explained, however, by the costs of maintaining an overblown bureaucracy at national, federal and local level and by huge subsidies to crisis-laden agriculture.[70]

The SPD's victory in the Reichstag election of May 1928, the ensuing installation of a socialist Chancellor and the appointment of the same party's Rudolf Wissell to the Reich Labour Ministry confirmed the worst fears of many in industry that they were operating in an environment loaded against them. The system of state arbitration in wage disputes, with its legally binding awards, was another particular object of their hatred at this time. Reinforcing this attitude, also, was the advocation of theories of 'economic democracy' (*Wirtschaftsdemokratie*) in 1928 by Fritz Naphtali, Fritz Tarnow and Hugo Sinzheimer, which envisaged the capture of the means of production by labour not through socialisation from above but through 'cold', or 'creeping' socialisation from below on the basis of factory councils and union pressure.[71] Heavy industry, in particular, took fright and began promoting in response an antithetical *Werksgemeinschaft* (work community) ideology directed against the unions and the practice of collective bargaining. Locked into such calculations on capital–labour relations were conservative–nationalist, anti-democratic attitudes which identified the entire spectrum of left-wing politics as an enemy that had to be extirpated. The decisive alienation of many employers (and large agrarian interests) from the parliamentary Republic took place, therefore, in advance of the Depression, and was spearheaded by their major organisation, the *Reichsverband der Deutschen Industrie (RDI)*, supported by smaller pressure groups such as the *Ruhrlade*.[72] The most obvious example of the employers' resolve to counter-attack came with the lock-out of Ruhr miners in October 1928, which was an attempt by iron and steel magnates to undermine *Sozialpolitik* by preventing a fresh round of large wage demands and intervention by the state's arbitration machinery. Although the bitter episode ended in a compromise which pleased neither side the employers had given notice of their future intentions: the democratic, pro-labour *Sozialstaat* had to go, to be replaced by an acceptable form of authoritarian government sympathetic to capital and committed to eliminating the preponderant profile of labour. This is not to say, of course, that many employers were edging towards National Socialism at this time, or that they would support Hitler later. The Nazi – capital symbiosis is not so easily explained.

For nearly a decade since the establishment of the Republic there had been steady, in some respects impressive, advances on the social welfare front, chiefly to the advantage of the working class. Although, inevitably, some workers thought reform had not gone far enough and had turned to the revolutionary KPD, the majority of the working class and trade unionists took satisfaction from the reality of the welfare state, which had been achieved against formidable economic and political odds. It forged an indispensable link in the identification of most of the workers with the Weimar Republic and under normal circumstances that link would assuredly have been strengthened with the passage of time. From the outset, however, the Grand Coalition government was disturbed by disagreements over financial policy, arising from the conflicting economic and political priorities of its constituent members, which had grave implications for the welfare edifice.[73] When unemployment soared over three million in the winter of 1929/30, the additional burden on a Reich budget already in profound difficulties focused attention on the unemployment insurance scheme and its future funding. There was almost unanimous support in the cabinet for restructuring its financial base in such a way as to reduce its dependence on subsidies from the hard-pressed Reich, but widely differing opinions as to who should pick up the bill. An unbridgeable impasse was reached in early 1930 between the German People's Party (DVP), now heavily influenced by a determined employers' lobby in the absence of the recently deceased Gustav Stresemann, and the SPD, desperately trying to uphold its commitment to the welfare ideal: one side wanted to reduce the level of benefits payable under AVAVG, the other wanted to increase marginally employers' contributions to the scheme.[74] The collapse of the Müller government as the Depression began to bite emphasised the precarious situation of the *Sozialstaat*. The accession to power of a cabinet whose viable options for manœuvre in economic matters hardly existed, and whose authority came to rest on presidential emergency decrees, could not have been more ominous. The era of political authoritarianism in Germany set the scene for the virtual wholesale destruction of the welfare state.

The Great Depression was the severest economic crisis ever experienced by modern capitalist society, and in no other European country were its wider social and political consequences more devastating than in Germany.[75] A three-dimensional catastrophe of epic proportions was occasioned by a long-standing sluggishness and inherent weakness in the industrial economy, causing a rapid contraction of production after 1930, and compounded by a deep agricultural crisis since 1927 and then by the near-collapse of financial and banking institutions in 1931.[76] All three sectors of the economy interlocked in a rapidly accelerating downward spiral, coinciding with an equally shattering political and social crisis. Mass unemployment was at the one time the centrepiece and tragic symbol of the Depression, and in Germany was more extensive, of longer duration and more penetrative of the social fabric than in any other country, except the United States. This was owing not only to the unique features of the Depression in Germany, but also to a series of factors peculiar to her labour market in the 1920s, including substantial rates of seasonal and structural unemployment and the expansion of the pool of labour through high female participation and the heavy birth cohorts of the pre-war period.

The registered number of unemployed rose from 1.6 million in October 1929 to 6.1 million at its peak in February 1932. Table 3.1 provides full details. The numbers in full-time employment fell from 20 million in June 1929 to 11.4 million in January 1933; thus two out of every five Germans employed in 1929 were out of work in winter 1932/3. The percentage of trade unionists who were jobless was 8.5 per cent in June 1929, 31.7 per cent in December 1930, 42.2 per cent

Table 3.1 Registered unemployment in Germany, 1929–33 (in millions)

Month	1929	1930	1931	1932	1933
January	2 850	3 217	4 886	6 041	6 013
February	3 069	3 365	4 971	6 128	—
March	2 483	3 040	4 743	6 034	—
April	1 711	2 786	4 358	5 739	—
May	1 349	2 634	4 052	5 582	—
June	1 260	2 640	3 953	5 475	—
July	1 251	2 765	3 989	5 392	—
August	1 271	2 882	4 214	5 223	—
September	1 323	3 004	4 354	5 102	—
October	1 557	3 252	4 623	5 109	—
November	2 035	3 698	5 059	5 355	—
December	2 850	4 383	5 668	5 772	—

Source: Statistisches Jahrbuch für das Deutsche Reich, vols 49–53 (Berlin, 1930–4) pp. 316, 301, 291, 291, 309, respectively.

in December 1931 and 45.1 per cent in December 1932.[77] To these figures must be added the so-called 'invisible' unemployed, for whom the most reliable estimate is 640 000 in early 1929, 500 000 in early 1930, 860 000 in early 1931 and 1 330 000 in early 1932, reaching a peak of 1 580 000 in the third quarter of that year,[78] and substantial numbers either underemployed or on short time: in January 1933, 23.7 per cent of trade unionists alone were in the latter category.[79] Clearly employers were operating in what was from their standpoint an extremely favourable labour market, allowing them decisively to gain the upper hand in their confrontational strategy with a debilitated trade union movement unable even to look to the static and unnerved SPD for assistance. In the 1931–2 period especially, employers were able to extend working hours without additional pay, abolish bonus schemes, reduce wages below the legal minimum, neglect working conditions and ignore legislation designed to protect workers from unfair dismissal. They often picked out trade union or leftist militants as the first to go.[80] A remarkable reflection of the new reality was the steep decline in the number of workers involved in strikes, despite an increase in the number of stoppages, from 342 in 1930 to 643 in 1932: in 1931, only 178 000 workers and in 1932, 128 000 went on strike.[81]

As in other industrial countries, the extent and impact of unemployment was very diversified in terms of geographical area, econ-

Table 3.2 Registered unemployment pattern in the regions, 1930–3 (in percentage terms)

Region	July 1930	July 1932	January 1933
1. East Prussia	7.6	18.6	35.5
2. Silesia	17.0	43.1	63.5
3. Brandenburg	18.7	46.1	57.0
4. Pomerania	9.0	24.9	41.7
5. Nordmark (i.e. Schleswig-Holstein and Hamburg)	11.2	41.3	51.2
6. Lower Saxony	9.1	37.0	49.4
7. Westphalia	12.9	48.3	51.3
8. Rhineland	17.7	51.5	56.2
9. Hesse	17.0	47.0	56.9
10. Central Germany (i.e. Magdeburg, Thuringia, Merseburg)	13.7	43.7	54.2
11. Saxony	19.2	57.3	65.6
12. Bavaria	12.7	34.3	45.1
13. Baden & Württemberg	8.7	27.0	33.5
National (Reich) average	14.4	42.3	52.4

Source: The percentages have been calculated from data included in the *Statistisches Jahrbuch für das Deutsche Reich*, vols 50–3 (Berlin, 1931–4) pp. 300f, 290f, 290f, 297, respectively.

omic branch and social class. Although the percentage of white-collar workers out of work increased from a mere 2.4 in 1927 to 13.6 (on average) in 1932,[82] it was the urban proletariat in the most heavily industrialised areas in the Ruhr, Rhineland, Berlin, Brandenburg, Westphalia, Saxony, Thuringia and Silesia who were the major casualties.[83] (See Table 3.2 above.) In 1930 92.3 per cent of the unemployed were blue-collar workers and only 7.6 per cent white-collar workers; in 1931 the figures were 91.9 per cent and 8.1 per cent, and the following year, 88.7 per cent and 11.3 per cent.[84] In 1932, 44.3 per cent of the registered unemployed lived in the 50 largest cities and towns.[85] The metal, mining, timber, textile and construction industries were the worst-hit in the economy: in February 1932, 90 per cent of unionised construction workers, 64 per cent of timber workers and 42 per cent of metal workers were unemployed or on short time.[86] A large majority of the jobless were male, drawn principally from the unskilled at opposite ends of the age spectrum.

The comprehensive immiseration of the industrial proletariat, and especially of the unemployed within its ranks, extended also to millions of family dependants. Although there was an overall downward movement of prices of consumer goods, wage levels fell even more, so that the average drop in the real value of wages between 1928 and 1932 was 14 per cent. Food and clothing consumption declined markedly in 1932, while malnutrition increased, as did levels of indebtedness and divorce. Psychological anguish was liberally added to the material distress. Suicide, which for most of the Depression years was mainly confined to the middle and upper classes, spread in 1932 to the long-term unemployed of the working class.[87] Foreign observers were shocked by what they saw around them[88] and a contemporary German was no less poignant when recording his experience of visiting proletarian districts throughout the country in 1930: 'increasing misery, increasing bitterness, increasing despair. A world of poverty, hunger and exploitation'.[89]

The vast scale of unemployment and social misery can be partly attributed to Chancellor Heinrich Brüning's severe deflationary strategy.[90] He applied a Prussian-type austerity in pursuing the central objective in domestic policy of reducing the Reich deficit and balancing the budget, which was intimately linked to his aim in foreign policy of finally having reparations cancelled. Indeed the primacy accorded this priority abroad largely accounts for the inflexibility of Brüning's economic and fiscal policies at home. He was convinced that public finances could only be restored by sweeping expenditure cuts and parsimony at all levels of society.[91] In a series of emergency decrees he imposed wage cuts of up to 23 per cent, salary reductions in the civil service and dismissal of non-permanent staff in public service, higher taxes and social insurance contributions, and savage curtailment of welfare provision. Ever conscious of the 1923 hyperinflation,[92] Brüning would not countenance any sizable deficit-financed schemes of public works for job creation for fear of bringing on a renewed currency crisis. In any event, he took the firm view that the economy would be revived by the private sector and remained highly sceptical of the efficacy of direct governmental intervention. Even the SPD accepted quite readily the argument about budget balance and supported the chancellor's fiscal rigour and pro-capital tax programmes.[93] The party failed, to its discredit, to produce an agenda for combating unemployment and was an ineffectual discussant in the emerging debate about the possibilities of an anti-cyclical economic policy. It rejected the Woytinsky,Tarnow, Baade (WTB)-Plan put forward by the socialist trade union movement in April 1932 because its requirement of two billion marks from public funds for job creation was considered potentially inflationary.[94] Given these attitudes of the SPD, it is hardly unexpected to find the *Sozialstaat* being dismantled root and branch by 1932.

Total government expenditure on social welfare dropped by 15 per cent between 1929 and 1932,[95] and the principal casualty was the unemployment insurance scheme. It was scaled down by successive emergency decrees in relation to levels of benefit, conditions of eligibility, social groups entitled to support and period of assistance. Worse still was the reintroduction by the emergency decree of 5 June 1931 of means assessment (*Hilfsbedürfigkeit*) for claimants who were married women in place of the legally guaranteed right to benefit. Thus the fundamental principle, indeed the very *raison d'être* on which AVAVG was based, was abandoned.[96] The authoritarian von Papen government's even tougher line on welfare resulted in the infamous decree of 14 June 1932 which not only reduced the period for receipt of benefit from 20 to six weeks as well as the rate of benefit by up to 23 per cent, but also made payment of support after the six weeks had elapsed subject to a means test for all claimants.[97] This legislation signalled the end of social welfare as the Republic had known it, notwithstanding General Kurt von Schleicher's brief and unsuccessful flirtation with some aspects of *Sozialpolitik* when he took over as chancellor in December 1932.[98]

As the Depression deepened in 1932 more and more of the unemployed, having exhausted their entitlement to unemployment insurance benefit, were compelled when still out of work to turn to Emergency Aid and thereafter to welfare relief, for which the eligibility and other criteria were also progressively tightened in order to cut the number of claimants and recipients of their derisory benefits. For example, Emergency Aid benefit fell by 33 per cent between 1928 and 1932. By late 1932 the three-tier unemployment support system had been turned on its head as the financial burden of providing relief had moved inexorably from unemployment insurance to welfare relief. The unfortunates thrown onto the latter were discriminated against by the law and suffered most from material want and loss of self-esteem. They constituted a vast army of sullen, demoralised, unskilled workers banished to the margins of Weimar society.[99] By the same time, moreover, a substantial percentage of the total unemployed, including the 'invisibles', were devoid of any kind of public support: 37.6 per cent, or 2 520 000 workers, according to the best estimate. Table 3.3 illustrates this overall movement for registered unemployed.

In January 1933 Schleicher's fanciful notion of a collaborationist

Table 3.3 The percentage of registered unemployed in receipt of relief, 1930–2

Scheme	August 1930	December 1932
1. Unemployment insurance	52.3	13.7
2. Emergency aid	15.3	22.2
3. Welfare relief	15.7	41.7
4. No support	16.7	22.4

Sources: *Statistisches Jahrbuch für das Deutsche Reich*, vols 50–2 (Berlin, 1931–3); Wladimir Woytinsky, *The Social Consequences of the Economic Depression* (Geneva, 1936) pp. 175–9; Willi Hemmer, *Die 'unsichtbaren' Arbeitslosen. Statistische Methoden-soziale Tatsachen.* (Zeulenroda, 1935), pp. 101f, 184f.

front with the unions and that element in the National Socialist Party erroneously perceived as 'socialist' was regarded with anathema by influential groups of heavy industry. Any suggestion, however faint, of a revival, even in emasculated form, of the *Sozialstaat* and what that implied for the balance of economic and political power, was to be strenuously resisted. Hjalmar Schacht and his associates finally saw in National Socialism the soundest guarantee that the unthinkable would not happen. Hitler's accession to the chancellorship ensured that after 1933 a rather different welfare ethos would prevail in Germany. The basic humanitarianism, regard for social justice and wholesome political expediency that had inspired so much of the Republic's approach until the late 1920s disappeared amidst the detritus of the democratic state.

4 The Younger Generation and Welfare, 1918–1929

The collapse of the Reich accelerated recognition in German society of the desirability of further promoting what was broadly perceived as the major hope for the future – the younger generation. While defeat in the First World War was seen, somewhat facilely perhaps, as confirming the bankruptcy of the old ideas and of the older generation itself, the advent of the Weimar Republic heralded the beginning of a new era for youth in terms of their status in the social order and also in relation to what was now expected of them. If before the war there had been in some quarters grudging, limited acceptance of the 'youth factor', the political and military events of 1918/19 swept away most reservations. Influential circles united in propagating the theme that only youth could lead Germany out of the shame and humiliation that was the price of a lost war to a better, honourable future. Reinhold Wulle, the *völkisch* writer and propagandist, coined in 1919 the phrase which was to ring throughout the Weimar era as a kind of battle-cry, 'Who has youth, has the future'.[1] A veritable 'youth myth' was created and relentlessly disseminated, supported by new theories of generational conflict formulated by sociologists, psychologists and others in related fields. Most influential in this regard was Eduard Spranger's *Psychologie des Jugendalters* (1924). What had begun before 1914, therefore, was consummated and further extended in the 1920s.

Helping also to excite public interest in the possibilities of the younger generation was the debate in Germany after the war about the 'crisis of the family' which, following the disruptive impact of industrialisation and urbanisation on normal processes of socialisation, particularly of children and younger people, was deemed to be in dire need of remedial assistance through more substantial welfare provision.[2] In the eyes of some observers this case was made by the sight of the involvement of many youths, especially from the urban working class, in the November Revolution and subsequent disorders. The state authorities may also have taken fright and concluded that the anger of these youthful revolutionaries could at least be assuaged by material improvements created by welfare reform. The ending of military conscription in 1918, it may be suggested, left a gap in the state's ability to influence or even direct the socialisation of working-class youth at a critical stage of their development. This awareness may have helped formulate the outlook of the state regarding the 'youth question', though there is no convincing empirical evidence to show that this was the most important element in its deliberations. The democratic Republic might reasonably be expected to operate according to more wholesome criteria than the reactionary, authoritarian state it replaced.

When the initial euphoria about the younger generation's 'mission' had at least subsided, the more practical questions of how it was to provide a lead in the new state and what kind of youth was to be entrusted with leadership responsibilities were not so easily answered. Many different responses emerged, and were invariably conditioned by ideological, political and other vested interests. Every major political party had its own thoughts on the matter, though all of them recognised the importance of capitalising on the enhanced status of youth by enlisting their organised support, and thus creating for themselves a ready-made nucleus of dependable loyalty. On the other hand, the rapid postwar politicisation of youth, their quest for a new identity and need to find a cause, facilitated this process of approximation to the political parties. Now that young people were more confident and self-assertive than at any previous period in German history, and appeared willing to accept the formidable challenges posed by defeat and revolution, their help was easily to hand. For many of the young the prospect of participating in the postwar reconstruction of their country was thrilling; everything and anything seemed possible to them. To this challenge they were equipped to bring a sense of purpose, commitment and idealism. The political parties eagerly established youth affiliates to satisfy their needs and those of youth in this respect.

The two leading democratic parties, the SPD and the Centre Party, had already something to build on in 1918 for both had youth groups under their wing before the war. In 1895 the Centre Party had organised the *Windthorstbünde* (named after one of its most prominent political figures, Ludwig Windthorst 1812–91), and in 1920 formally set up the *Reichsverband der deutschen Windthorstbünde*, also known more simply as '*Jung-Zentrum*'. The main weight in Catholic youth work still lay in the large confessional groups because the membership of the political youth association remained rather modest. The reconstituted socialist youth movement which developed after the war took shape in 1919 as the *Verband der Arbeiterjugend-*

vereine Deutschlands (VAJV), which sought to combine socialism with the ideals of the independent youth movement and was not officially part of the SPD. In late 1922, the VAJV joined with parts of the dissolved *Sozialistische Proletarierjugend*, the youth group of the Independent Social Democratic Party (USPD), to form a new organisation, the *Verband der Sozialistische Arbeiterjugend Deutschlands* (SAJ), which acknowledged the SPD as before as its political guardian without being organisationally bound to it. On the far Left, the KPD enjoyed the early allegiance of the *Freie Sozialistische Jugend*, the forerunner of its later principal youth groups, the *Kommunistischer Jugendverband Deutschlands (KJVD)* and *Rote Jungfront*. In 1918 the German Democratic Party (DDP), the third member of the so-called 'Weimar Coalition', established the *Reichsverband deutscher demokratischer Jugendvereine*, and in the following year a *Reichsjugendbewegung*, renamed the *Hindenburg-Jugend* in 1929, appeared for the German People's Party (DVP). The parties on the Right were rather slower to organise in this field, which was ironic in view of their subsequent propaganda about constituting the authentic voice of young Germany: the German National People's Party (DNVP) set up in 1922 the *Reichsverband der deutsch-nationalen Parteijugendgruppen*, from which evolved shortly afterwards the *Bismarckjugend*. The NSDAP had a *Jugendbund* in 1922 before the emergence of the Hitler Youth four years later.[3]

The reality of the political parties' relationship with their own youth groups, however, never quite matched the early promise. The influence of youth on the policy-making decisions of the parties was insignificant, and none more so than in the SPD, which was the outstanding failure of Weimar politics in this sphere. Its entrenched but ageing leadership, its ponderous style and highly centralised governing machinery produced a dead weight of a party, making it unattractive to many of working-class youth.[4] The SPD did not seriously compete for the attention of youth, partly because it traditionally harboured suspicion and distrust of younger activists in its ranks, dating back to the pre-war era. It failed to make a credible appeal to the spirit of ebullient idealism which was evinced by many of the younger Weimar generation, and was easily overshadowed long before the Depression struck by the rumbustious KPD, a successfully self-styled 'party of youth'.[5] It was scarcely surprising, therefore, that the SAJ experienced only modest growth in the 1920s (105 000 members in 1925) and then virtual stagnation in the early 1930s, or that young activists in the SPD should demonstrate their frustration by seceding in 1931 to form the Socialist Workers' Party (SAPD).[6] The SPD's failure during the Depression to find a formula for combating unemployment, its obdurate 'toleration' of Brüning's deflationary policies and passive reaction to manifestations of political authoritarianism and the rise of National Socialism, was bound to alienate the younger proletariat. The free trade unions were just as culpable of neglecting to forge direct, meaningful links with their younger members. Their inherent pragmatism could not capture the imagination of the young and, in any case, the interests of adult workers were always put first. Although the unions made certain provisions for educational and vocational training for their young members, they were not interested in constructing a vigorous proletarian youth crusade on behalf of the democratic state. At the same time, concern for the material improvement of the working class, which both the SPD and unions shared, did produce considerable tangible benefits for youth, especially working-class youth, as a consequence of welfare reform.[7] The SPD and unions were perhaps the most energetic political agencies after 1918 in the campaign for a welfare state, a vital component of which was enhanced provision for the young.[8] They were given powerful backing in most respects by the Centre Party, with its long-standing commitment to a coherent concept of social justice.

At a less politically influential but more approximate level to the interests of the young was the multifarious 'youth lobby', which arose very quickly in the early postwar period. Many of the organisations active in the youth field had their origins in Wilhelmine Germany, of course, but the radically altered political and social landscape after 1918 demanded that they reorganise on a more streamlined, professional basis. The generally *ad hoc*, loosely co-ordinated earlier approach of the youth welfare groups would not suffice in the more intense, competitive atmosphere of the Republic; they realised that their efforts on behalf of youth had to be presented in a more systematic manner.[9] However well-intentioned and more carefully directed their involvement was, none the less, the youth welfare organisations would have been unlikely to meet with success had they not enjoyed further backing from other vital components of the 'youth lobby', including, most notably, the social reformers and the youth movement.

The middle-class social reformers, who included in their ranks child psychologists, paediatricians, educationalists and other professional specialists in the youth field, combined after 1918 to press for direct state intervention with the aim of ameliorating the overall material situation of young people, particularly its most underprivileged sections in the industrial-urban working class. The enactment and full implementation of a range of welfare measures was the central objective of the social reformers whose motivation was supplied fundamentally by their humanitarianism and commitment to social improvement. There were some who attached to their welfare aims certain ideological or political notions relating, for example, to social darwinist precepts on a biologically sound or 'healthy' population, but they constituted a mere minority. Besides striving for welfare legislation, the social reformers were convinced of the need for accompanying educational reform, thus to extend in the 1920s what they had been campaigning for since the late nineteenth century with some success. The movement for reform in education, involving an emphasis on the requirements of the individual, on a more humane, compassionate ethos and on a more relaxed and mutually respectful relationship between teacher and pupil, developed a new dynamism after 1918.[10] Experiments in education, such as those carried out by the Country Boarding Schools, served as inspiring examples of what might be achieved on a broader front involving greater numbers. The importance of the individual pupil and his needs formed the very centrepiece of the reformers' solicitude, which required further support from the state.

The movement for social reform, and particularly those within it who took a special interest in educational reform, had a major ally in the independent youth movement, which after 1918 saw the replacement of the *Wandervogel* with the *Bündische* Youth. Although small in comparison with the total numbers of young Germans in the broader Weimer youth movement, the overwhelmingly middle-class *Bündische* Youth was the most influential sector by far. It was itself split into many different kinds of groups and factions, but still contrived to maintain a collective identity and purpose which allowed it a special role in Weimar's youth culture. The concept of a 'new person' (*Neue Mensch*), who was to be created by educational means on the basis of wholesome elements such as trust, honesty, comradeship and positive endeavour, represented the essence of the *Bündische* perspective, that is, the development of a type who embodied all the virtues and none of the vices of the human condition. On this type the new Germany would be constructed.[11] In their own peculiar ways, many other parts of the German youth movement subscribed to this ideal. For instance, the SAJ was dedicated to the creation of the 'new socialist man' as the prototype of future German society.[12] On a more practical level, *Bündische* Youth sought to extend its ideas by contributing to the process of broader educational reform in the same way as the *Wandervogel* had done before the war. In spheres as far apart as adult education and the small rural communities based on a simplistic philosophy of humanity,[13] *Bündische* Youth made a significant mark. The *Deutsche Freischar*, usually regarded as the quintessential *Bündische* group, practised many of the new educational concepts.[14] Distinguished pedagogical theorists, including Herman Nohl, Paul Natorp and Theodor Litt, drew inspiration from their background in the independent youth movement. *Bündische* Youth's participation in the social welfare reform campaign was much less direct and substantial, though many of its members eventually took up positions in the welfare services. The *Bündische* groups which were concerned above all with social welfare issues were restricted to a few with very small memberships, most notably, the *Zugscharen*, the *Gildenschaft Soziale Arbeit* and the *Soziale Arbeitsgemeinschaft Berlin-Ost*, which was led by Friedrich Siegmund-Schultze.[15] Even they, however, drew considerable admiration for their commitment and pioneering methods from many observers, among whom were government officials involved in constructing youth welfare as a part of Weimar *Sozialpolitik*. At a meeting of a youth agency set up by the Prussian government an official, *Oberstudiendirektor* Schleunner, remarked that 'we who are involved in youth welfare must ourselves become good people in the sense of the new youth movement'.[16] It was a telling tribute. The bulk of the broader youth movement was mostly interested in matters divorced from social welfare: sports, politics, education in the widest sense and vocational training constituted the major preoccupations.

The central umbrella body of the youth movement, the *Reichsausschuss der deutschen Jugendverbände*, representing in 1926 some 4 353 050 members aged 14–21 years drawn from 76 separate groups, devoted most of its energy to promoting authentic youth movement activities such as hiking, and did relatively little on the social welfare front.[17] It did issue statements from time to time on the need to improve conditions for young workers and apprentices in factories and was concerned about the plight of unemployed young people in the Depression, but its predominantly bourgeois membership and outlook precluded more direct involvement in that sphere. In view of its considerable size and status, however, the *Reichsausschuss* was of undeniable benefit to the general cause of the younger generation in the Republic. Its high profile was evidence for the enhanced standing of young people in German society at large and acted as a constant reminder to government and politicians of their obligations in this direction.

The broadly-based youth welfare lobby generated a sustained momentum in the 1920s and was further encouraged by the practice of *Sozialpolitik* at the national, regional and local levels by government. The younger generation were beneficiaries of the political commitment to welfare reform, which was seen as essential to the consolidation of the democratic system of government. The combined efforts of the youth lobby and of the state ensured a meaningful attempt at social and welfare achievement for young people during the pre-Depression period.

As early as 17 December 1918 the Provisional Government indicated the importance it attached to the position of youth when it emphasised that *Jugendpflege* 'would contribute to the establishment of the internal unity of our nation and towards this end [it] would seek to foster a broad brotherly spirit among the rising generation'.[18] In August 1919, the new Weimar Constitution provided a set of pledges which formed a useful basis for youth welfare work. Articles 119–22 made specific reference to the needs of the young and intimated the duties of the state to them and to families:[19] '. . . the maintenance of the purity, health and social advancement of the family is the task of the State and local authorities . . .' (Article 119). Article 120 addressed the parental role: 'The physical, mental and moral education of their offspring is the highest duty and the natural right of parents, whose activities are supervised by the political community'. Perhaps the most important statement on youth was given in Article 122: 'Youth shall be protected against exploitation as well as against neglect of their moral, mental and physical welfare. The necessary arrangements shall be made by the State and local authorities'.

There was widespread official awareness after 1918 of the extent to which the material situation as well as the wider socialisation of the young had been compromised by the experience of the First World War, and a consequent acceptance of the state's responsibility to become more seriously engaged in welfare provision than ever before. If youth was the hope for the future that almost everyone said it was, then there had to be appropriate action to reconstitute its material and moral situation on a firm basis. The breakdown of *Jugendpflege* during the war was officially acknowledged,[20] and statistical evidence was produced to show just how far health standards, especially of working-class youth, had deteriorated.[21] The Prussian authorities gave a sober assessment:[22]

> The situation into which our nation has fallen as a result of the unfortunate outcome of the war is quite appalling . . . but it would be unworthy of a great nation to retreat in despair into idle mourning. What is needed instead is the unbroken courage to begin work again as soon as possible to lay the foundations for a happy future for Germany. In this respect, the sphere of Jugendpflege is also called upon to contribute because a physically and mentally strong, creative youth constitutes the first foundation for renewal.

In an important statement in November 1919, the Prussian Minister of Welfare, Adam Stegerwald, of the Centre Party, underlined the priority to be given youth care by government:[23] '*Jugendpflege* is designed, above all, to preserve love and loyalty for the Fatherland in its present profound misfortune and to maintain intrinsic German values'. It was to develop a spirit of comradeship in the New Germany and to cultivate a basic feeling of humanity among all Germans: 'Youth must be willing and capable of fulfilling their responsibilities to the nation as a whole in a conscientious and selfless manner'. Stegerwald added that it was imperative for *Jugendpflege* to be totally free of party politics: it was a national undertaking for the benefit of the entire community. He followed up this ringing declaration by organising a top-level conference on the subject in Berlin on 18 and 19 December 1919 at which future policy guidelines and the organisational structure of *Jugendpflege* were fully discussed.[24] Shortly afterwards, and once again stressing 'the major importance of *Jugendpflege* at the present time', Stegerwald advised local and regional authorities to develop constructive practices,[25] particularly as it appeared that too many parents were incapable of bringing up their children according to proper principles. As one regional official complained:[26]

> In many cases, they [the parents] no longer exercise any control over the children or they do not want to . . . Through the Church, School, youth associations and so on, awareness of what is decent and good must be awakened and cherished. All serious-minded men and women who have the cause of the rising generation at heart must join hand in hand with the clergy, teachers and parents in serving this noble task. Only by working together and by giving

powerful support through State means can really effective work for youth be achieved.

These sentiments were representative of local authority views, and the *Oberbürgermeister* of Cologne, Konrad Adenauer, stressed that a primary task among youth 'in these disturbed times' was 'to maintain and cultivate German feeling', and he singled out sports and athletics organisations 'in which an absolute national spirit prevailed' as particularly worthy of official backing.[27] In the early postwar period the advantages of youth involvement in sports were constantly urged by officials not only as a way of restoring the physical well-being of young people but also their spiritual and moral strength.[28] Sports associations proved very popular, with their membership growing at a substantial rate.[29] Umbrella organisations such as the *Zentralausschuss für Volks-und Jugendspiele in Deutschland*, based in Hanover, took every opportunity to encourage participation. From 1920, a *Reichsbeirat für körperliche Erziehung* was attached to the Reich Interior Ministry, partly for the same purpose,[30] and during the 1920s a flourishing youth hostel movement promoted hiking and hill-walking on a large scale.[31] An expanding *Jugendpflege* needed more trained personnel, of course, and government sought to increase the size of what was a new profession by funding specialist courses of instruction and encouraging unemployed young teachers to change the direction of their careers into a related discipline.[32]

The scale of the task confronting all those involved in *Jugendpflege* was further extended by what many observers regarded as unhelpful attitudes being displayed by youth. The *Jugendpflege* office in Cassel, for instance, lamented:[33]

> Anxiety is created among many people on observing today's youth. Can our salvation be expected from them – our only hope for the reconstruction of our Fatherland? Who would deny that the thoughts of many youths nowadays are directed exclusively towards the material, that self-discipline, obedience to authority, loyalty . . . are for many of them associated with a past that has disappeared? In these unhappy circumstances . . . *Jugendpflege* needs to strengthen youth and encourage its idealism . . .

Most federal governments were more than ready to take up the challenge. Württemberg quickly created machinery to co-ordinate youth welfare after introducing a *Jugendamtsgesetz* on 8 October

1919, and officials were willing to involve all sections of society in the enterprise.[34] A request from the Socialist Youth Movement that the *Jugendamt* in Stuttgart be staffed 'from the circles of the working population' was granted.[35] The example set in Württemberg in organising these offices was carefully noted by the Reich government which was contemplating national legislation on this matter. In Hesse, it was recognised that, while a part of the younger generation remained committed to high ideals, another part 'had had their sense of morality blunted by wartime and postwar conditions', which it was the task of youth care to make good.[36]

The first prerequisite for encouraging a correct sense of responsibility to the wider community on the part of the younger generation was an improvement of its general standard of health. Against a background of food shortages during and after the war, there was substantial evidence from many areas of Germany of poor health, malnutrition and disease among young people, particularly those living in large cities and urban industrial districts, which often persisted until the mid-1920s. Industrial parts of Württemberg had a major problem with tuberculosis.[37] From Hamburg came reports of the poor health of many schoolchildren, 'so that preventive measures are absolutely necessary', which included a programme of municipally-organised holidays.[38] In the same city, in 1922, 46 per cent of male youths attending vocational classes were physically unfit to pursue their chosen trade.[39] Some two years previously, officials urged that youths who were weak should not be apprenticed to trades which demanded physical strength, and regulations were issued insisting that every applicant for an apprenticeship have a medical examination.[40] In Hamburg's working-class areas undernourishment among children and youths was commonplace in the early 1920s, particularly during the harsh winter of 1921/2.[41] The city's troubles with providing sufficient care were compounded by the fact that it was a haven for runaway and vagrant youth from all over Germany and even from abroad who were invariably poorly educated and unskilled in a trade. Without employment or shelter, they put considerable pressure on Hamburg's already stretched youth welfare budget. The females among them were particularly vulnerable to prostitution.[42]

Other cities were hardly better off. In Frankfurt/Main in 1922, 31 per cent of school-leavers were unable because of ill health to take up a job or an apprenticeship without a course of medical treatment, a situation also experienced to more or less the same degree in Düsseldorf and Elberfeld.[43] In Saxony in 1921, of 3000 youths seeking work,

600 were physically unfit or too small to handle machinery, and the Prussian authorities found that in a survey of 3110 vocational college pupils, 71.5 per cent were poorly nourished, 25.2 per cent were physically ill-developed and only 2.2 per cent enjoyed sound health.[44] The overall situation was not hidden in dry official statistics, for contemporary press coverage of the plight of younger people was extensive, and it was estimated that up to 40 per cent of children and youths in towns and nearly half of those in large cities in 1921/2 suffered from malnutrition.[45] The housing shortage, cramped living space, inadequate clothing and the spread of disease completed the miserable picture and stressed the enormity of the remedial task of *Jugendpflege*. As one journalist wrote:[46] 'Instead of an economically secure and morally strong generation, Germany's youth is growing up as a cohort of cripples eligible for welfare support'.

State funding for social welfare is a perennially contentious subject because essentially there is never enough for everything that those in the field would like to accomplish. With this proviso, it may be said that in 1919/20 there appears to have been, with a few notable exceptions such as Württemberg,[47] a relative shortage of official funding for *Jugendpflege*, despite the lofty sentiments about its importance that government spokesmen expressed.[48] In 1921/2, however, the situation eased considerably, until overtaken by hyperinflation. Thus, in 1920/1 the Rhineland had a youth welfare budget of 82 500 marks, nearly a sixfold increase on the allowance two years previously, and in 1921/2 a total of 100 000 marks, which dropped to 22 300 marks in 1922/3.[49] The Prussian Ministry of Welfare gave six million marks in 1921/2, compared with only 3.5 million in 1913/14. This large sum was allotted 'despite the overall difficult financial situation . . . and because the State government, along with broad circles of the population, is convinced that *Jugendpflege* . . . must be given stronger support in the interests of Germany's future'.[50] The additional resources and sanguine statements by the Prussian Minister of Welfare that '*Jugendpflege* had made good progress in most administrative districts' (in 1922) and that there had been since the war 'substantial achievement' in this sphere, could not conceal the reality of the deteriorating situation from the beginning of 1923 as the inflationary crisis began to bite.[51] The Reichstag began to hear about health standards being once again in serious decline, owing to food shortages, poor dieting and inadequate conditions of hygiene in many working-class homes, in which the rate of infant mortality was also increasing. Children and youths begging in the streets became a common sight in large cities like Cologne and Berlin.[52] Not only was welfare funding severely reduced by government during that year, but the crisis revealed that a good deal of the machinery of *Jugendpflege* was deficient: there was, for one thing, a serious lack of co-ordination between local and regional authorities. In an attempt to make good this weakness the Prussian Ministry of Welfare created a special section (*Landesbeirat*) for *Jugendpflege* under Dr Hinse, with six sub-divisions, with a remit to streamline the organisation and channel funds more efficiently.[53]

Throughout the country in 1923 local authorities found their budgets inadequate for their responsibilities in *Jugendpflege*. The response in Duisburg was fairly typical:

> Despite fully recognising the need for *Jugendpflege*, we must state that in the current emergency there are more pressing matters for us to deal with than *Jugendpflege*. We cannot therefore maintain *Jugendpflege* any longer on the basis of our own resources.[54]

In Trier, provision for youth virtually came to a standstill 'because of numerous obstacles' in 1923,[55] and in many rural areas of Prussia where there had been only very limited development of *Jugendpflege* since the end of the war, matters reached a critical stage, notwithstanding the efforts of the *Arbeitsgemeinschaft für ländliche Jugendpflege*.[56] In vocational schools, where provision was also ill-developed, the situation in 1923 could hardly have been any worse.[57]

The Prussian welfare authorities were forced to admit that by Autumn 1923 *Jugendpflege* was hardly functioning and that the consequences for the younger generation in terms of their health and morals could be catastrophic. But they complained at the same time that not everyone in government appreciated how serious the situation had become: the state's acknowledged responsibilities were being worn too lightly for comfort.[58] Disregarding this criticism from one of its most important ministries, however, the Prussian government instituted a tough programme of retrenchment which decimated *Jugendpflege* provision.[59] The juvenile suicide rate increased alarmingly, claiming no fewer than 104 under-15-year-olds by early 1924.[60] Although the Prussian Welfare Minister spoke of 'these deplorable abuses which . . . threaten to endanger the much longed for reconstruction of the Fatherland', the best he could offer in these circumstances was agricultural work for jobless school-leavers and an extension of the school year, which no one wanted.[61] Only once the

Republic had overcome the currency crisis and the reparations issue had been dealt with through the Dawes Plan could the state begin to take a further constructive view of *Jugendpflege*. By 1924, also, the major legislation in this field that had been enacted in 1922/3 was being implemented, which meant, above all, that *Jugendpflege* was finally provided with what appeared to be a secure base for its future development. After the trauma of 1923/4, the Prussian Minister of Welfare, once again equipped with a reasonable budget, began to express cautious optimism.[62]

In keeping with the more pronounced interest in the younger generation shown by officialdom at every level after 1918, the Republic lost little time in devoting serious thought to the idea of comprehensive national legislation for youth welfare. Private discussion took place in 1919 in interested circles, which included welfare workers, educationalists, lawyers, accountants and government ministers,[63] resulting in the formulation of a draft law for 14–18 year olds (*Entwurf eines Reichsjugendwohlfahrtsgesetz*) by the Reich Interior Minister in January 1920. The draft, which was a mixture of established and new concepts and practices, was extensively circulated for comment.[64] The initial reception was somewhat varied but generally welcoming. The Prussian Welfare Minister, Stegerwald, praised it for highlighting 'the great importance' of *Jugendpflege*,[65] but the Reich Finance Minister immediately raised searching questions about the one fundamental theme which was to haunt the progress of the legislation, namely, its financing. Where were adequate resources to be found for what was accepted as a laudable initiative? He agreed with the proposal that *Jugendämter* (Youth Offices) be created as the responsible local agency for the law's implementation, but stressed the importance of providing proper levels of funding so as to avoid the danger of them becoming mere administrative organs of dubious value.[66] Similar fears about funding were expressed by many welfare workers in the field. One wrote that 'the plan is generous but its implementation requires large-scale finance. The Reich government must participate fully in the costs involved in setting up and administering the law'; otherwise, he was certain local authorities, while eager to co-operate, would find themselves in immediate difficulties.[67] Much concern was also expressed about the draft's failure to state unambiguously what the precise function and executive role of the *Jugendämter* was to be, particularly as their area of jurisdiction appeared to conflict to some degree with the existing powers of local authorities.[68] The Reich Minister of Justice also took up this point and felt it simply illustrated the unhappy circumstance that the draft had not been drawn up by legal experts and was likely, therefore, to run into difficulties of a legal, technical nature alone.[69]

The churches, who were heavily involved in youth welfare, were displeased by the prospect of extensive intervention by the state because they felt their activities would be threatened and eventually eliminated altogether. Their added reservations about 'the bureaucratisation' of youth welfare perhaps failed to appreciate that, in view of escalating social problems, welfare in any field could no longer be a largely private domain. The government made strenuous efforts to reassure the churches that their fears were groundless and that they still had a valuable contribution to make.[70] Of the views of the federal governments to the draft, the Bavarian response was perhaps the most guarded. While declaring itself 'fully in agreement with the motives and the general aims of the draft', the Bavarian government wondered whether it was entirely compatible with the Reich Constitution, bearing in mind the powers of the various bodies already engaged in youth work. It welcomed the notion of placing youth welfare provision in Germany on a national, unified basis for the first time, but warned of practical difficulties that might easily arise from the different traditions and practices of the federal states. This was, of course, the essence of Bavarian concern: to ensure that the prerogatives of the federal government would not be undermined by new powers conferred on the Reich government. Bavaria wanted the principle of decentralisation firmly enshrined in the legislation as it played out its customary role as the champion of federal rights. As it was, there was comparatively little public provision for youth in Bavaria. Private bodies, mainly controlled by the Catholic Church, exercised a dominant influence. The Bavarian authorities, however, did not wish to appear over-critical of the draft and pledged their co-operation because 'German youth . . . had never before been in such danger; never before had it been as urgent to develop welfare for them'.[71]

Professional youth welfare executives gave the draft emphatic support. Dr P. Riebesell, Deputy Director of public youth welfare in Hamburg, expressed the feeling of most when he commented that 'all friends of youth will greet the new law with joy, as it will put youth care on an organisationally sound uniform basis' Everything must be done, he added, to make the law as effective and durable as humanly possible.[72] One of his colleagues, Dr Wilhelm Hertz, a lawyer in the city's public service and soon to be in charge of youth welfare provision, also responded enthusiastically:[73]

> It is very clear that, compared with the almost intolerable situation with existing legislation, the draft signifies an extraordinary advance, which we friends of youth must welcome with the utmost delight, even if it does not fully correspond to all our wishes.

As a lawyer he praised most of the provisions for improving the legal treatment of juvenile offenders because they were based on enlightened educational precepts rather than the old punitive ethos. He stressed in a further commentary that it was essential for the successful operation of the law to bring working-class representatives into the system for their own interests and those of the community as a whole. If that came about 'then this law will prove itself a secure cornerstone in the reconstruction of our national life'.[74] However a complicating factor arose from proposals for a new juvenile courts law (*Jugendgerichtsgesetz*) which began to circulate in 1920. Dr Riebesell's anxiety was widely shared, as he wrote with some sarcasm:

> The German people will be blessed in the near future with two laws which will be in insoluble contradiction of one another. On the one hand, the Juvenile Courts Law makes the education of youth a task of the courts, while the other, the Youth Welfare Law, introduces special educational authorities who are to operate alongside the school authorities in Germany.

He accused the Reich Justice and Interior Ministries of not working together on the drafting of the laws, which was taking place almost simultaneously, and listed a series of contradictions. He was especially worried that the *Jugendämter*, to be created by the welfare law, would have its powers usurped by the courts and thus be reduced to the status of 'beadles' (*Büttelbehörde*).[75] Fortunately a revised draft of the Juvenile Courts Law which was released for circulation on 27 April 1921, took account of the contradictions exposed by Riebesell and others,[76] and the draft which reached the Reichstag the following year was much more acceptable to youth welfare circles.[77]

Finally, the draft youth welfare law was warmly received by both educational reformers, who saw it as the new centrepiece of the state's policy for education, and the medical profession, who were impressed by the enlarged scope it seemed to promise for combating serious problems among the young, particularly tuberculosis, rickets and sexual disease.[78]

The momentum in favour of the youth welfare law gathered pace throughout 1921, greatly assisted by the activities of interested bodies, most noticeably the *Deutsche Zentrale für Jugendfürsorge*. At a specially convened meeting in Berlin in March 1921 to co-ordinate the campaign across the country, it established a specialist advisory group (*Sachverständigenkommission zur Beratung des RJWG*) whose primary task was to liaise with the committee set up under the chairmanship of the Centre Party politician Wilhelm Marx by the Reichstag following the introduction of the draft law to parliament in March 1921.[79] Local authorities began making necessary preparations in the expectation that the draft would become law in the near future, though not all by any means were convinced that they could deal adequately with the new demands. In Cologne, fears were expressed that staff, particularly older ones, were not fully trained to cope with the full legal and administrative responsibilities they would have to bear, while there was concern that insufficient numbers of staff would be available.[80] Many authorities laid on special training courses, for which welfare budgets had to be stretched. Concern about proper funding levels for the law had not subsided since it was originally mooted.[81]

When the final version of the draft reached the Reichstag in June 1922 there was intense debate from all sides. The advocates of the bill, who included the three Weimar coalition parties, spoke of it as being designed 'for the resurrection of our Fatherland'.[82] But there were important hurdles to be overcome before approval was secured. It was feared that the law would lead to 'state nationalisation' (*Verstaatlichung*) of what had been traditionally a private, voluntary undertaking, and that this would be accompanied by a huge, unwieldy bureaucracy which would reduce welfare to an anonymous, impersonal exercise, as the churches had argued. More seriously, many feared that the result of the state's large-scale involvement would be a politicisation of youth welfare. The answer was that, while such a danger certainly existed, the best means of avoiding it was to encourage all political parties, regardless of ideological commitment, to shoulder an equal part of the burden of welfare for the good of the younger generation.[83] But this unanimity, it soon was made clear, would not materialise. The USPD, which had not much longer as an independent entity, criticised the law's 'general inadequacy', but specifically its alleged delivery of the *Jugendämter* into the hands of the churches – which was patently not true – and its need of better funding – which was a valid point.[84] The most vehement, comprehensive critique, however, was issued by the KPD. It found the law wanting because it retained the 'immoral difference' between legitimate and illegitimate children, for its continued separation of *Jugendpflege* and *Jugendfürsorge*, for giving no protection to children of foreigners living in Germany and for not providing long-term protection for German youth. The KPD also denounced the law as a product of the political machinations and interests of the SPD and Centre Party, and deplored the influence the churches would be able to exert on welfare and education of the young in general. As regards *Jugendfürsorge* in particular, the law was dismissed as a blatant piece of class legislation because middle class policy makers brought their ideas to bear on a sphere which was virtually the exclusive preserve of the poorer sections of working-class youth. Altogether, the KPD rejected the basic principles and ethos of the law, and for good measure declared that it would not work in any case because, as others had already indicated, it was not guaranteed adequate funding.[85]

Some deputies were disquieted about how the law would be implemented by certain federal governments, and Marie Juchacz of the SPD singled out Bavaria for special mention in this respect. There was always the danger that with so much power given to federal authorities implementation of the law might be in a spirit contrary to what the framers had intended.[86] Outside the Reichstag, public opinion was generally positive, though there were some who remained unconvinced that the law really did mark a significant advance in youth welfare provision. One critic identified a number of weaknesses which supporters of the law might have admitted privately: 'It is not really one law, but rather a disorganised mass of a series of laws, which will be disfigured more and more by often far-fetched regulations'. The same critic pointed out that apparently there was not a logical plan behind the creation of the *Jugendämter*, even for its financing. The very language of the law he excoriated as 'bad German', while its overall mode of expression lacked clarity and precision.[87] Another outspoken critic was Dr Heinz Dähnhardt, a well-known personality in youth movement circles and later chairman of the *Reichsausschuss der deutschen Jugendverbände*, who believed with others in the youth movement that the entire field of youth welfare was failing into the hands of soulless bureaucrats whom he accused of being more concerned about their own position and careers than they were about the needs of young people.[88]

Despite the criticisms and objections the National Youth Welfare Law (*Reichsgesetz für Jugendwohlfahrt, or RJWG*) was passed on 9 July 1922, placing youth care in the broadest sense on a unified legal and administrative basis. The Law's first paragraph, which was based on Articles 120 and 122 of the Reich Constitution, enunciated the new ethos of youth welfare: 'Every German child has a right to a sound physical, moral and social education'.[89] The state was required to intervene in fulfilment of this pledge when a child's education was not being adequately attended to by its family. The worth of the individual was recognised as paramount,[90] but the rights of parents were not overlooked. By accepting its responsibility to ensure the care and protection of the young expected of a civilised, humane and liberal society, the law was a shining example, on paper at least, of the principles underlying the Weimar *Sozialstaat*. It represented nothing less than a new enlightened conception of state guardianship of the young. On a practical level, due to further political wrangling and the currency and hyperinflationary crises, the law was not put into effect as intended in April 1923 but on 1 April of the following year.[91]

The RJWG, which provided for both *Jugendpflege* and *Jugendfürsorge*,[92] represented in some respects a compromise of a number of its earliest proposals.[93] In other words, it went through the same process as almost all Weimar parliamentary legislation and inevitably did not go quite as far in certain areas as may have been originally hoped. Indeed, as late as February 1924, government imposed further restrictions on its practical implementation, including changing the legal requirement to set up independent youth welfare offices, which resulted to some degree in an emphasis on the organisational rather than the educational side of their operation.[94] Moreover, in allowing private youth welfare groups to continue beside public bodies, in an attempt to reconcile the interests of the SPD and Centre Party, the objective of a totally public system as envisaged by the socialists in 1918 was lost forever. None the less, the RJWG was a most worthwhile and significant piece of legislation, inspired by humanitarian idealism, and demonstrating that at least in the early 1920s the Republic recognised the need to build concrete bonds with young Germany.[95] But what of the law in practice?

The goodwill of youth welfare officials was the only secure basis that existed in 1924/5 for the successful application of the RJWG.

Once the financial and economic crises of 1923/4 subsided, the situation regarding the level of funding for the legislation appeared more promising, though the Reich Finance Ministry cautioned in early 1924 that it could provide resources 'only within the framework of the general economy measures decided by Cabinet'.[96] A small amount of additional funding was made available at the end of that year but the grave uncertainty about this issue continued for some time, thus circumscribing the short-term efficacy of the law.[97] Almost a year after its activation, the RJWG remained something of a dead letter as the Reich authorities and federal states were locked in discussion about funding and also about the organisation and powers of the *Jugendämter*, the executive arm of the RJWG in the country.[98] Prussia, Baden and Bavaria were among the states experiencing great difficulty on these fronts,[99] even though there was considerable enthusiasm for the law.[100] In an attempt to break the deadlock and get things moving, the Reich Interior Minister intervened and held further negotiations with individual federal states.[101] Although the *Jugendämter* continued to attract criticism for not being prepared to cooperate in good faith with other welfare bodies,[102] the situation regarding the implementation of the RJWG settled, allowing youth welfare provision to enter a relatively positive and fruitful phase of development in the mid-1920s.

The successful passage of the RJWG in the Reichstag in 1922 facilitated parliamentary approval for the proposed Juvenile Courts Law (JGG), which was its perfect complement in many ways. The JGG of 16 February 1923 incorporated in principle the progressive educational ethos (*Erziehung statt Strafe*) and the basic humanitarianism of Weimar's welfare policy.[103] It put the emphasis in handling juvenile offenders on educational and rehabilitative measures instead of the existing retributive approach (*Vergeltungstheorie*). The leading purpose was to adjust the delinquent child and to assist him in becoming a useful member of society. The understanding of the psychology of childhood and adolescence, and faith in effective education, were the concepts underpinning the law. Punishment was to be given only if it was decided that the offender had the moral and intellectual capacity to recognise his wrongdoing. The educational means now to be introduced included warnings by the courts, suspended sentences and a system of probation. Capital punishment, life imprisonment and confinement to hard labour were prohibited for young offenders. A supplementary and important step was the raising of the age of criminal culpability from 12 to 14 years, while the upper boundary of the age of limited responsibility was set at 18 years. Youths who were older than this at the time of committing an offence were still to be tried before the ordinary criminal courts; offenders under 14 years of age were dealt with by the *Jugendamt* and the Guardianship Court. The law also placed the administrative legal machinery for dealing with juvenile crime on a more realistic and modern foundation. Recognition was not only extended to youth as a separate legal category entitled to its own rights, but also substantive meaning was directed to this status by the reorganisation and extension of the system of juvenile courts as a special division of the criminal courts that had existed in many parts of Germany since before the First World War. The central role allotted to the new juvenile courts, which had jurisdiction over all offences committed by juveniles aged 14–18 years, ensured that the individual and his circumstances were pushed to the forefront of legal deliberation. At the same time, juvenile detention centres and independent wings in prisons for youths were brought into being by the JGG.[104]

Lawyers were not quite as pleased with the legislation as were educationalists and welfare officials, and argument about certain aspects of the law continued in legal circles throughout the 1920s.[105] The *Jugendämter*, which were charged with implementing the new legal code, inevitably attracted hostile comment from some traditionalist lawyers. Others complained that the law, far from simplifying procedures and reducing costs, as intended, actually produced from an organisational viewpoint unnecessary duplication of effort and additional expenditure. Whereas in ordinary criminal court proceedings serious offences were dealt with by only one judge, in the case of youthful offenders, even in the simplest, petty matters, two courts were engaged. One expert rightly observed that 'the involvement of the courts and the *Jugendämter* in all cases of law-breaking gave the matter in hand an importance which it should not have, in the interests of youth'.[106] Confusion also arose about which courts were responsible for dealing with particular categories of juvenile offenders – an issue which persisted right up to 1933.[107] But, while a majority of lawyers could agree that the JGG had shortcomings which needed to be addressed as urgently as possible, they also acknowledged that the fundamental concepts of the law had been proved valid.[108] They were able to concur with youth welfare officials, in particular, in hailing it as 'representing for the friends of youth . . . a victorious ending to a long, hard struggle' for much-needed reform.[109] Both sides were generally eager to co-operate with one another as constructively as possible, confident in the belief that the many positive features of the legislation would enhance the quality and effectiveness of youth welfare provision.[110] The only thoroughly displeased commentators were of the extreme Left who were upset that despite the new emphasis on the individual child and its needs the family remained a significant, and in some respects, primary factor in education. They had also been looking for the removal of church influence – what was termed the 'deconfessionalisation' – from youth welfare altogether, and its replacement by a communal system of administration.[111] But tendentious dogma of this type had its limitations in the reality of Weimar society.

The national legislation for youth in 1922–23 was used as a basis by would-be reformers in other spheres of youthful activity for further protective measures, most notably in the thorny question of morality. Where the moral standing of young people was considered to be at risk, a whole range of political, ideological and even philosophical perspectives regarding intervention by the state or anyone else are bound to arise. Particularly in a democratic, parliamentary state like the Weimar Republic the boundaries between personal freedom and civil liberties, on the one hand, and the rights and duties of the established authorities to extend protection for the benefit or control of certain groups and for the community as a whole, can never be created to everyone's satisfaction. In authoritarian states the motivation of social control is more easily demonstrated. Marxist theorists argue that the element of state control is implicit in bourgeois–industrial–capitalist society. As regards the Weimar Republic, the overriding concern of government – at least until 1930 – in the field of welfare, including youth welfare, was to improve material conditions from the standpoint of a wholesome humanitarianism. This applied, in consequence, to the Republic's intervention in moral questions pertaining to youth.

In the early postwar era, public authorities repeatedly voiced their consternation at certain trends and influences which were considered to be inimical to the interests of a healthy, morally sound younger generation on whose shoulders so much responsibility and expectation for the revival of Germany's fortunes in the world were placed. It was thought vital for the resources of *Jugendpflege* to be deployed against such influences, backed up if necessary by appropriate parliamentary legislation. The perceived creeping waywardness of sections of youth (*Jugendverwahrlosung*) had to be stopped. Particular official hostility was directed at the growth in alcohol consumption, cigarette smoking, and a youthful liking for dancing, cinema-going, sex, dubious literature and other transient pleasures which, in retrospect, seem innocuous enough but which when taken together were regarded as unacceptable by the guardians of young people at that time.

Across the country the flavour of official sentiment was fairly uniform on this issue, with the First World War and its aftermath invariably blamed for creating the problem on a large scale. Typical was the reaction of authorities in Koblenz:[112]

> The present sad appearance of the young, their debasement on the streets, in pubs and dance halls results from the absence of firm authority by fathers and by schools during the war. The children of that time are today's young people who have little sense of authority and discipline.

A clear reference was made to the social background of those mostly giving rising for concern:

> It is also the case that in the years after the war youths have been able to earn a relatively high wage. Unfortunately, parents permit the youngsters to spend too much on pleasures . . . a sense of what is good and honest must be stimulated and cultivated in them . . . only through co-operation and strong support from the State can truly beneficial work with the youth be achieved.

From Cologne the authorities reported:[113]

> It was inevitable that during the war and afterwards, in town and countryside, there would be as a consequence of a neglected education, unsatisfactory supervision and poor employment prospects, a waywardness, unruliness and licentiousness among youth which was expressed, for example, in visits to pubs, excessive drinking and dancing . . . It all followed on from a fundamental, violent revolution affecting the State.

From Trier it was stated that 'smoking among young persons under 16 years of age has substantially increased during the last few years, especially among those from a working-class background'. The explanation lay 'in the higher wages which allow these youths to satisfy their extraordinary desire for self-gratification' (sic), which had produced 'a nadir of morality'.[114]

Youth welfare workers fully shared these views. The *Kreisjugendpfleger* in Montabaur in the Rhineland wrote that 'recently, abuse of alcohol among youth has considerably increased and the dance craze has long since become a real danger to our youth. Decisive measures must be taken'.[115] In Wiesbaden, youth officials ascribed youth's excessive drinking and love of dancing to 'many years of deprivation . . . and episodes of major national upheaval'. Prohibition of alcohol to youth would be worthwhile, it was further remarked, 'only if rigorously enforced, and previous experience, as in relation to the wartime ban on youths smoking in public, has been far from encouraging'. The answer had to be rather more draconian: the closure of pubs and bars which served drink to youths and of cinemas which showed questionable films. More positively, youth should be encouraged to become active participants in sports and athletics, a measure widely favoured at that time, just after the war.[116]

Government was fully prepared to do what it could to help the situation. In August 1920 the Reich Interior Ministry stressed the importance of discouraging smoking by youth when it gave support to the campaign organised by the League of German Opposition to Smoking (*Bund deutscher Tabakgegner*).[117] The Prussian government was also sympathetic:

> There are repeated loud complaints about the attitude of broad sections of the younger generation, especially concerning their growing abuse of alcohol and fondness for dancing. In so far as these complaints are justified, matters can be improved . . . above all, by deepening and extending positive care among youth.[118]

The Minister issued a decree on 16 November 1920 which, in effect, extended the wartime measure banning the sale of tobacco to under-16-year-olds, though it proved no more successful than the earlier decree.[119] He also threatened action against pub-owners who allowed young people on their premises unaccompanied by an adult. Rather more unrealistically, however, he advised that the best way to combat the dance epidemic was 'to encourage good folk dances, which can satisfy youth's exuberance without running the danger of being morally detrimental'.[120] A later Prussian Welfare Minister, Heinrich Hirtsiefer, acknowledged that the deeply unsettled period after the war created many 'spiritual and moral dangers for youth' which government had a responsibility to challenge.[121] The law regulating cinemas (*Lichtspielgesetz*) was introduced in 1920, and in 1923, when the economic crisis intensified fears of youth's morals being in danger, legislation made it illegal for alcohol and tobacco to be sold to under-16-year-olds and for 16–18-year-olds to attend dance halls after 8 p.m.[122] At the same time, government continued to exhort youth to abandon drinking, smoking and immoral behaviour and to adopt instead 'a decent, healthy life-style'.[123] An attempt to legislate for youth's attendance at places of amusement (*Entwurf eines Gesetzes über den Schutz der Jugend bei Lustbarkeiten* of 21 April 1923), however, finally floundered.[124] The most contentious legislation focused on the literary field where disquiet about 'trashy' and 'dirty' literature circulating among youth prompted a decree from the Prussian Welfare Minister in September 1925.[125] which paved the way for the promulgation by the Reich government on 18 December 1926 of the Law for the Protection of Youth from Trashy and Erotic Literature (*Gezetz zur Bewahrung der Jugend vor Schund-und Schmutzschriften*).[126] It thus fulfilled the pledge in the Weimar Constitution (Article 118, paragraph 2) to combat such literature, but it caused an immediate political storm with the SPD and KPD uniting for once to denounce the law as an example of reactionary cultural attitudes, while the right-wing parties vigorously applauded it.[127] The issue has to be situated within the broader context of an age of permissiveness in Weimar culture generally which, of course, produced many brilliant innovations and advances. But whether the law is assessed from a liberal or conservative moral standpoint, it is surely untenable to argue that it had 'regimenteering tendencies',[128] because the state genuinely wanted to protect a vulnerable section of society. There is no evidence to support the view that the state's intervention was a kind of evil conspiracy against youth. Even more absurd is the contention that the law was a right-wing plot by the DNVP and Centre Party to oppress working-class youth and promote allegedly authoritarian concepts such as patriotism and militarism as a means of reasserting a controlling influence apparently lost in 1918![129] To depict the law as a squalid exercise in repression and social discipline is simply to distort historical reality beyond all limits. The motivation behind it was entirely consistent with the fundamental humanitarianism of Weimar *Sozialpolitik*.

A central office (*Oberprüfstelle*) was established to supervise the application of the law in Leipzig in May 1927 which had branches or representatives in all the federal states. The government stressed the importance of appointing the 'right' people to the offices, which resulted in personnel drawn from broadly cultural and literary circles, the teaching profession and from youth welfare and youth movement officials; specifically excluded from appointment were, significantly, representatives of political and nationalist associations. Marie Juchacz joined from the Workers' Welfare organisation (*Arbeiterwohlfahrt*) despite the negative stance of her party, the SPD, to the law, and Max Westphal, also a Social Democrat, represented the *Reichsausschuss der deutschen Jugendverbände*.[130] Unable to appoint 'a famous literary figure' to head the central office, as planned by the Reich Interior Ministry, the government gave the sensitive position to one of its own employees, *Ministerialrat* Dr von Zahn, in May 1927. He was given a staff of six colleagues, who included the highly regarded Director of the Hamburg *Landesjugendamt*, Dr Hertz.[131]

To meet the immediately obvious definitional problem of what exactly constituted 'trashy' and 'erotic' literature which Dr von Zahn and his staff were confronted with, the youth welfare authorities in Trier produced a colourful answer which could be employed as a rough guide:[132]

> The bad book. Its distribution in millions upon millions of copies every year is testimony to this more loathesome business enterprise. Its external features are: sensational titles and pictures, poor quality paper, inferior printing, distribution on a door-to-door basis and through low-grade shops. Its content is characterised by bad style, a poverty of ideas, and preference in subject matter for the sentimental, adventurous, sensuous and criminal.

The Prussian government subsequently attempted to standardise the criteria whereby juvenile literature could be judged and from June 1929 issued the *Nachrichtendienst zur Bekämpfung von Schund-und Schmutzschriften* to help co-ordinate efforts. A united front never quite materialised, but, despite manifold legal, political and other problems, many local and regional youth welfare officials sought to make the law effective. The *Landesjugendamt* of the Rhineland, for example, gave its campaign a high priority on its budget and created a specialist unit to co-ordinate action throughout the area.[133] But it is highly questionable how far the law surmounted formidable obstacles, even before the Depression struck and drastically reduced the resources available.[134] It became clear that the law was not being strictly enforced nor were violations of it heavily punished, as many of its critics had predicted.[135] In 1928 the Catholic press, among the law's most vociferous backers, conceded that it had failed to serve its intended purpose, though this pessimism did not stop those areas of the Reich with a predominantly Catholic influence from maintaining vigilance.[136] As with a fair amount of Weimar's social welfare legislation it was not the motivation that was suspect or deficient, but the application and operational process.

The relative stabilisation of the Republic in 1924–9 augured well for the situation of young people as the parameters of the state's social and welfare programme were extended once again following the economic and political crises of 1923/4. The proliferation of *Jugendämter* opened up careers for a new generation of professional youth welfare workers: by 1928 the 1251 offices in the Reich employed 11 705 paid officials.[137] Of particular note was the pioneering work of Walter Friedländer, leader of the *Bezirksjugendamt* Prenzlauer Berg, one of the poorest working-class districts of Berlin. He drew around him colleagues from a background in either the Youth Movement or the working-class movement who shared his political commitment to the moderate Left.[138] After the initial uncertainty over funding for the RJWG, grants and subsidies for *Jugendpflege* increased quite substantially as local authorities and other bodies throughout the country went on a spending spree. Youth hostels, sports arenas and swimming pools were among the wide range of civic amenities laid on.[139] Cologne, which had established since 1918 a strong reputation for generous youth welfare provision, having accepted that families could not be reasonably expected to cater for all needs of their children, spent conspicuously on youth at this time,[140] while the *Landesjugendamt* (LJA) of the Rhineland increased its budget every year to 1929.[141] 'Good progress' was recorded in Hesse[142] and in Württemberg the introduction of the *Landesjugendwohlfahrtsgesetz* on 23 November 1927 produced excellent results.[143] In contrast, public provision for youth in Bavaria continued to be rather half-hearted, with an exiguous 123 155 marks allocated in 1925. Moreover, a LJA did not become operational until January 1928, making Bavaria one of the last federal states to create this new-styled machinery.[144] Mecklenburg-Schwerin and Mecklenburg-Strelitz were also among the least generous in their provision of the federal states, while Saxony, Thuringia, Brunswick and Schaumburg-Lippe were among the leading providers. In northern Germany, the cities with the largest expenditure on youth were Altona, Kiel, Magdeburg and Hamburg.[145] By 1928, in fact, the youth authorities in Hamburg were being called to account for their rising levels of expenditure by the city government. The explanation centred on the high living costs in Hamburg, the extremely difficult postwar economic circumstances which left a major social legacy, an increase in population and, finally, a determination to fully implement the RJWG. It was pointed out, in reply, that since 1927 alone there had been an increase in the youth welfare budget of 21.5 per cent while the increase in population in 1927–9 had been only 3 per cent and the cost of living 3.5 per cent. The finance officials advised caution on future expenditure.[146]

The Prussian government's view in mid-1925 that *Jugendpflege* had largely surmounted recent problems and could look forward to a period of unprecedented growth[147] was at least partly vindicated not only by rising levels of expenditure but also by achievements in the general area of health. There was a broadly-based endeavour to raise the health standards of young people, particularly of the working class, following years of want during and after the war. In many urban areas of Germany in 1925 a substantial section of proletarian youth was still living in sub-standard housing and too easily prone to disease and undernourishment.[148] Improvement was likely to be a formidable and long-term task requiring the injection of very considerable amounts of time, energy and funding. The root problem was that the socialisation process of many of these youths was uneven and insecure both in the workplace and at home, where the atmosphere was too often emotionally unsympathetic, aggressive and even violent. Working-class parents, including those schooled apparently in the fraternal ethos of the socialist and labour movements, exercised an authoritarian overlordship. Together with the alien, middle-class atmosphere in many schools which may have created feelings of inferiority among working-class pupils, this situation tended to breed a suspicious, resentful attitude of anti-authoritarianism that was displayed towards teachers, clergy and all types of officials, including those in welfare. Children of the unemployed and unskilled working class of the cities were probably the most disadvantaged in these respects.[149] These were barriers that could not be overcome by welfare alone, but at least it could make a start.

Provision of subsidised holidays in the countryside, mountains and seaside for the urban underprivileged (*Erholungs-und Heilfürsorge*) became an important part of this campaign after 1925. Commendable initiative was shown by welfare authorities in organising large-scale programmes of vacations in specially constructed camps, hostels and homes. In the Rhineland, generous funding for the venture allowed most of the 20 per cent of children and youths who were eligible for a holiday to be taken in 1928/9,[150] and Hamburg, which had been to the forefront of developments in this sphere since the end of the war, was able to accommodate some 56.6 per cent, or 98 000 of its pupils in state schools in 1929.[151] Particular emphasis was put on youth's participation in the scheme because, as one official remarked, 'all medical opinion agrees . . . that the health of youths is considerably worse than that of schoolchildren because of the experience of war and the inflation years'.[152] The holiday programme nationwide was put on a more secure foundation in May 1928 when the *Reichsarbeitsgemeinschaft für Jugenderholungs-und Heilfürsorge* was set up with government backing. Dr Ruth Weiland, the well-known writer on youth welfare problems, was appointed its secretary and, despite a degree of initial opposition to the organisation from some federal states, it was fully operational by late 1929.[153]

The organisation of medical supervision in schools expanded along more efficient lines after 1925 with assistance from the *Deutscher Verein für Schulgesundheitspflege*. More doctors were recruited, more equipment and support services made available, enabling more frequent and stringent testing of children.[154] School dental care also improved with prompting from the *Deutsches Zentralkomitee für Zahnpflege in den Schulen*, though initially there were problems of recruitment because some dentists feared the socialisation of their speciality within the framework of the welfare state.[155] Government continued to stress the 'moral and cultural advantages' to youth of sports and hiking,[156] both of which showed substantial growth, helped no doubt by the generous fare reductions and discounts offered youth groups on the railway network. The state took the view that the realisation of *Jugendpflege*'s potential was not only good in itself, which was the primary consideration, but also in terms of increasing respect and loyalty to the democratic system. The Prussian Ministry of Welfare frequently stressed that youth welfare officials were representatives of the state and should always conduct their duties in such a manner as to enhance its standing, even to the point of insisting that the Republic's *Reichsflagge*, and not the imperial colours, was displayed at public meetings and on official buildings.[157]

By 1929, health authorities throughout Germany, including large cities such as Hamburg which had extensive degrees of deprivation to contend with, were reporting a decided amelioration in the general health standard of young people, who were described as being taller and weightier than in the early 1920s.[158] The sterling efforts of dedicated youth welfare officials, supported by relatively considerate funding from the state,[159] must take much credit for this progress, though wider improvements in health care, hygiene and medical science, and the broader expansion of the Republic's social welfare programme also played an indispensable role. Naturally, a great deal still remained to be done and areas where developments were not fully satisfactory are readily identifiable. Though the incidence of disease had declined, tuberculosis remained a matter for concern in many cities and would require longer to be conquered, while there was an upward movement in sexual diseases.[160] A number of welfare areas needing specialist involvement on a large scale, including the care of orphans, displaced, illegitimate and vagrant youth, had not shown the progress pledged in the RJWG. The essential dilemma was that resources could never match the scale of these problems which increased throughout the 1920s.[161] For instance, while in 1914 98 of every 1 000 births in Germany were illegitimate, that figure had risen to 123 of every 1 000 in 1927.[162] In the case of vagrant youth, who in 1924 numbered about 200 000, welfare officials took a generally sympathetic attitude but could offer only token relief in the form of short-term accommodation and agricultural work because their resources were inevitably channelled into the mainstream of *Jugendpflege*.[163] Supplementary assistance was provided by various bodies such as the *Reichsverband für deutsche Jugendherbergen* which on occasion allowed free accommodation,[164] and some trade unions which had by 1929 given some 19 million marks in '*Wanderhilfe*'.[165] All these efforts, however laudable, only scratched at the surface of the problem which, of course, grew out of all bounds during the Depression.

A sizable and persistent constraint on welfare progress was supplied by the problematic situation of working-class youth, especially those resident in large urban and industrial areas and with a background of personal or family unemployment and unskilled, irregular labour. By 1929 they still unequivocally constituted a deprived, underprivileged minority. Their material and health standards had not appreciably improved and, together with continuing deficiencies in their schooling and employment situation, it is clear that a certain credibility gap existed between them and the Republic. Evidence of cutbacks in youth welfare expenditure because of the budgetary difficulties of the Grand Coalition government in early 1929 could only have exacerbated this feeling of alienation. But the reaction of these poorer sections of proletarian youth was not representative of a majority of their class comrades who could acknowledge that, although the RJWG had not fully realised its pledges, and there were clear limitations to Weimar's social welfare reform, they did have for the first time in German history a state which exercised a powerful, benevolent interest in them.

The constructive development of *Sozialpolitik* during the 'Golden Twenties' in respect of youth did not mean, however, that all was well in the state's overall relationship with them or in the way the position of younger people was viewed by the public at large. Many middle-class youths were by 1929 unsympathetic to the Republic for specifically political reasons and were already displaying an unhealthy interest in the extremist parties of the Right whose objective was the wholesale destruction of the democratic system and its welfare programme. The general public seemed not to be entirely convinced that welfare provision was having a salutary effect on the young after all. There was widespread unease about the perceived fecklessness and unreliability of sections of the younger generation of all classes. The notorious murder trial of an 18-year-old, Paul Krantz, in Berlin-Steglitz in early 1928, was seen by a large number of adults as confirmation of their view that the 'crisis of youth' phenomenon had not been diminished, because it revealed a younger age group in revolt against all conventional social and moral values and engaged instead in an alternative culture which was self-indulgent, rather seedy and susceptible to sexual indiscretion.[166] In other words, a picture emerged that stood in sharp contrast to the idealistic and self-sacrificial ethos portrayed by the Youth Movement and the youth lobby as a whole. Where now the lofty hopes placed on youth in 1918? Even some prominent social reformers were voicing misgivings,[167] while the still comparatively high suicide rate among youths in the mid-1920s added to the public's concern as it appeared to be another indication of someting fundamentally amiss despite the welfare effort.[168]

The provision of welfare was never designed to solve all the deeply embedded problems of youth, and given the very brief time-span of relative stability in Weimar Germany ambitions for advance had to be necessarily circumscribed. The Depression, of course, furnished decisive, wholly negative answers to all welfare concerns as everyone's hopes for progress were then irrevocably shattered.

5 Youth in the Labour Market, 1918–1929

The Weimar Constitution had made clear the Republic's intentions in the labour sphere, and pledges to provide employment and protection for the working population were meant to encompass younger workers as well as adults. The state's labour market strategy for youth in the pre-Depression era was, therefore, clear-cut and unambiguous: provision of work for all able-bodied workers, protective measures relating to conditions and wages in the factory, and sufficient numbers of trained, skilled personnel for industry and commerce.[1] These objectives implicitly recognised the fundamental importance of the labour market and material situation to the overall socialisation process of proletarian youth. The Republic acknowledged a basic humanitarian obligation to make sure that the younger workforce's needs and aspirations were accommodated within that kind of framework. To this extent the Republic's approach was pragmatic. At the same time, the concern of the democratic state to 'control' or 'discipline' the younger working class, which had been a major feature of the authoritarian Kaiserreich's policy during the last years before the First World War, was not in clear evidence until the early 1930s when parliamentary government was replaced by increasingly right-wing and quasi-dictatorial administrations. The political emphasis in the Republic's policy throughout the 1920s lay in constructing as far as was possible a satisfactory life for the younger proletariat and in encouraging positive conversion to democratic ideals. The Great Depression generated a new set of imperatives on the part of government, however, when coercion in certain forms of the young workforce returned in a development reminiscent of the late 1900s.

In 1918/19 the Republic could never have expected that its reasonable, constructive aims in the labour market for the younger generation would have been immediately put at risk or, arguably, irreparably undermined because of the violent vicissitudes of the economy: the trauma of the massive exercise in demobilisation at the end of a lost war, which had gravely weakened the country, followed by the substantial losses inflicted by the Treaty of Versailles, the hyperinflation crisis of 1922/3, and finally, worst of all, the unprecedented scale of the Depression. Before that last decisive crisis presented itself, the position of youth in the labour market had already been severely tested. Above all, young workers were shown even before 1929 to be particularly vulnerable to unemployment.

The character of the Weimar labour market was distinguished by a number of interrelated demographic and social features which added to the difficulties confronting younger people in it. The increase in the population of the Reich (despite territorial losses in 1919) by 13.2 per cent between 1910 and 1933[2] resulted in a large working population at a time of relative economic stagnation which by itself would have produced a situation where too many workers were chasing too few jobs. But, in addition, the heavy birth cohorts of the pre-war years were beginning to join the labour pool in the 1920s, so that there were more people aged 14–25 years than ever before in Germany's history looking for employment. The numbers of young people increased in absolute and relative terms during the 1920s. In 1910 males aged 14–20 years constituted 11.9 per cent of the total male population but 12.9 per cent in 1925; the 20–25-year-old male group was 8.7 per cent of the total male population in 1910 and 10.1 per cent in 1925.[3] The census of 16 June 1925 recorded that 14–21 year olds, male and female, accounted for 14.5 per cent of the Reich population, or 9 068 668, of whom 5 247 055 were aged 14–18 years and 3 821 613, aged 18–21 years;[4] the total of 9.0 million was 1.2 million more than in 1910. Also, in 1925 the total child and youth population was 14 491 889 males aged under 25 years and 14 273 605 females. In each category of gender approximately half were aged 14–25 years: the groups looking for or in work.[5] Of 7.8 million 14–20-year-olds, 6.1 million were in employment, including 3.3 million of the 3.9 million males.[6] The ultimate result was the largest-ever generation of young people in Germany competing in an already overcrowded labour market, a problem compounded by the substantial increase during the 1920s of the female labour force. Particularly during the period of rationalisation in industry in the mid-1920s cheap, unskilled female labour was in high demand and thus helping to make superfluous more expensive unskilled male workers. Overall, despite the war losses of 2.3 million, and the fuller consequences of these losses for the birth rate, there were five million more in the labour pool in 1925 than there had been in 1907, a considerable proportion of which was young labour. Limited relief on this front came only after 1930/1 when the relatively low birth rates of the war and early postwar years worked their way through to the labour market. While the proportion of 14–20-year-olds in the male population of the Reich rose from 11.9 per cent in 1910 to

12.9 percent in 1925, it sank to 8.1 per cent by 1933; 14–18-year-olds dropped in number from 1925 to 1933, by over two million.[7]

The tightness of the labour market in a period of economic sluggishness and fluctuation meant that, prior to the era of mass unemployment after 1929, younger workers experienced particular susceptibility to joblessness, short-time working and restricted career prospects. Younger workers had fewer safeguards against the ups and downs of the market than adult workers, including female workers. The impressive labour legislation of the early 1920s proved disappointing for youth. Thus, the rigours of the Weimar labour market stood out in sharp contrast to the propitious war years when young workers generally enjoyed a period of full, well-paid employment. That a new era for them had begun in 1918 was swiftly demonstrated by the impact of demobilisation when the government moved to reintegrate into the economy as quickly as possible millions of former servicemen. In these circumstances, young workers and all types of female workers were expendable, particularly unskilled workers in industry and, to a lesser extent, in commerce and transport. The government admitted openly that 'numerous youths and girls will lose their jobs. For many a long or short period of unemployment will result'. It warned of the material and moral dangers of the situation and appealed:

> In order to avoid or to minimise such and similar unfortunate circumstances, it is the duty of all patriotically-minded people to give the young advice and assistance . . . it is especially important for new employers in the countryside and in towns to be sympathetic to the difficult situation of youth . . .[8]

Although the large-scale unemployment associated with demobilisation was ephemeral, it gave a shock to the youthful labour force which it could hardly have anticipated. Apprenticeships, which traditionally were taken up by a large percentage of German youth, were in those sombre early postwar days in comparatively short supply, allowing employers to pick and choose more or less as they wanted from the cascade of job applications flooding into their offices. The situation was so competitive that anxious parents frequently sent in to prospective employers supplementary statements in support of a son's or daughter's application for a position.[9] This no longer applied after a few years, however, as many youths then rejected the idea of a three- or four-year apprenticeship because of the uncertainty of the economy and also because in an increasingly materialistic age the earning of quick money in an unskilled job was more of an attraction. In any case, wage differentials between skilled and unskilled workers had virtually disappeared by 1923 in many branches of the economy.[10] The short-term outlook of many youths in this respect was seen to be misplaced in the periods of substantial unemployment that lay ahead, for the unskilled were among the first to be made redundant.

The precise degree of youth unemployment in the 1920s is impossible to ascertain because no comprehensive or systematically collated statistics were kept by any authority until after the establishment of the *Reichsanstalt* in 1927. Even then there were still certain difficulties in establishing the situation of youth. Local authorities had a record of the numbers claiming unemployment benefit, which were only a percentage of the total number of young jobless. School-leavers unable to find a job and ineligible for benefit were simply not picked up in the statistics. Unemployed young workers who were not in a union would not show up in official trade union data on unemployment, while unemployed female workers, even if eligible for benefit, had a record of not consistently registering with the authorities. Consequently the statistics which are available for the young unemployed in the 1920s do not convey the exact or whole story and undoubtedly represent a rate of unemployment that was below the real but unknown figure.

The high youth unemployment rate of 1918/19 did not reappear until the hyperinflation crisis reached its zenith in autumn 1923, for the 1920–2 period saw Germany as a whole return to more or less full employment, which was assisted by an inflationary cycle still not in an uncontrollable phase. In the last months of 1923 and at least until the spring of the following year, youth unemployment reached heights which were distressing to those directly affected and disturbing to the government who intimated acute awareness of the physical, psychological and moral dangers accompanying the situation.[11] Unskilled industrial workers aged under 25 years and who were single and without wider family responsibilities were the worst affected, even though there were examples of older, married but highly-paid workers being replaced by cheaper, younger unskilled personnel.[12] Very often, and a pattern which intensified in the Depression, the trade unions agreed or even suggested that young workers be dismissed to save the jobs of older workers with families to maintain.[13]

Following the currency stabilisation and Dawes Plan, especially in relation to easing reparations payments and attracting foreign investment, the German labour market regained superficial, transient equilibrium which allowed a return to fuller employment. As regards youth employment however, there were marked regional variations.[14] But the basic insecurity in the position of the entire workforce was revealed shortly afterwards as the rationalisation process swept through industry. As technological progress pushed mechanisation and high-speed production and finishing procedures to new levels of efficiency labour, especially unskilled male workers in heavily industrialised areas, was put increasingly on the defensive. School-leavers found it more difficult than ever before to find a first job. Apprentices now discovered for the first time that in periods of economic crisis they could be as expendable as anyone else, particularly as written contracts (*Lehrvertrag*) in the early 1920s had not been common in industry. Apprentices who had just completed their training and were ready to be employed as journeymen at higher wage rates were frequently among the first to face dismissal. Mechanisation reduced demand for skilled workers and at the same time eliminated large numbers of unskilled ancillary jobs. In the mid-1920s, male youth unemployment was heaviest in the metal and machine-making industries, and female unemployment in textiles, food and clothing.[15] The numbing experience of losing his job for the first time was poignantly expressed by one youth thus: 'This horrible uncertainty kills people . . . with no prospect of improvement, no prospect of further training, one had the terrible feeling of being superfluous'[16]

It was estimated that in 1925 some 200 000 under-21-year-olds were unemployed throughout the Reich,[17] but the impact of rationalisation was dramatically revealed in the jobless figures for winter 1925/6, when the usual seasonal factors also made a contribution. Unemployment among the young rose disproportionately against the overall total, which was substantial. The numbers of registered unemployed aged 14–18 years of age, male and female, who were in receipt of unemployment benefit (*Erwerbslosenhauptunterstützungsempfänger*) are shown in Table 5.1.[18] The bulk of youth unemployment in 1925/6 was provided by the older age group of 18–25 years. In July 1926 there were 185 605 male and 59 381 female workers (*Arbeiter*) out of work who were aged 14–21 years, a total of 244 986, or 16.9

Table 5.1 Registered unemployed aged 14–18 years in receipt of unemployment benefit, 1926–7

Date	14–18-year-olds	As a % of total registered unemployed
15 January 1926	39 973	2.3
15 March 1926	52 228	n.a.
15 June 1926	45 193	2.6
15 September 1926	34 448	n.a.
15 December 1926	29 958	2.0
15 March 1927	26 243	n.a.
15 June 1927	8 257	1.4
15 September 1927	2 841	0.7

per cent of the total registered unemployed of 1 450 110 workers. Although an overwhelming majority of the youth unemployed were working-class, not to be ignored are the 27 151 white-collar employees (*Angestellte*) aged 14–21 years out of a total of 144 190 registered white-collar jobless. Altogether, of a total of 1 594 300 registered jobless (workers and *Angestellte*) in July 1926, there were 272 137 male and female 14–21-year-olds, or 17.1 per cent of the total: 75 per cent of the youth unemployed were male, most of them concentrated in the 18–21-year-old group.[19] Berlin had a particularly serious problem of youth unemployment at the same time when, of 112 000 male jobless who were registered, nearly 15 000 were aged 14–21 years.[20] Other large cities, such as Essen, were also badly affected in this respect.[21] Throughout 1925–7 the under-18-year-old unemployed were a modest 2.6 per cent on average of the registered unemployed total, and 5 per cent of all youth in employment.[22] When the 21–25-year-olds are added the final numbers of youth unemployed were considerably higher. It is not surprising that in early 1926 large numbers of jobless youths took to the roads in search of work and invariably ended up destitute in large cities.[23]

While for all categories of worker the labour market once again achieved an ostensible balance during the second half of 1926, which was sustained throughout the following year in most parts of the country, the winter of 1927/8 saw a familiar pattern re-emerging whereby increased unemployment figures contained a sizable proportion of younger workers.[24] On 31 January 1928, under-21-year-olds were 13.4 per cent of the total registered unemployed, or 178 753 of

1 333 115. With the abeyance of seasonal factors and an absence of crises, the economy absorbed many of the jobless in the second half of 1928, until the winter months once again uncovered the inherent volatility of the economy. Unemployment levels then attained heights which put the recently introduced unemployment insurance system (AVAVG) into immediate, dire trouble. On 31 December 1928, under-21-year-olds were 14.7 per cent of the total official jobless figure, or 250 774 out of 1 702 342. Even in the early summer of 1929 this 'crisis before the crisis' was showing respective figures of 14.2 per cent, or 115 026 out of 807 882.[25] The impact of the Depression on the youth labour market was such that already by December 1929 officials were talking about 'an emergency situation' prevailing.[26] Whereas in March 1929 there were 245 888 registered jobless aged 14–20 years, representing 12 per cent of the total, and 465 398 aged 20–25 years, which was 22.5 of the total, these figures had climbed by the end of the year to levels which finally destroyed what remained of the Republic's original labour strategy, particularly that relating to the younger generation. On 31 December 1929, the under-21-year-olds alone constituted 13.3 per cent of the total official unemployed, some 237 367 of 1 774 571.[27]

Both the magnitude and underlying persistence of youth unemployment compelled the state to consider various relief and support measures. There was clear recognition, encouraged by the large, professional youth lobby in the Republic, of the many dangerous repercussions of unemployment on the life of youth, material and non-material.[28] A number of early studies, including that by Lau and Kelchner,[29] had produced convincing evidence for the psychological harm that could be caused, especially by long periods of unemployment. The threat to the moral standing of young people and links between unemployment and crime were also acutely appreciated.[30] However, in the sphere where material assistance at least might have been most obviously and immediately provided for the young unemployed – the unemployment benefit system – the state's response was largely disappointing.

The national system of unemployment benefit based on a means test which was introduced on 13 November 1918 was meant to cater also for younger workers, but in fact they were treated less well than adult workers – a pattern that continued until AVAVG in 1927 and beyond that to 1933. The 1918 decree laid down that those aged 14 years and over were eligible to receive benefit if out of work, provided they could prove a need and be able and willing to work, in return for which they were required to attend prescribed training courses of a vocational or manual type. The level of benefit depended on the age, sex and circumstances of the applicant, but as a general rule men received more than women who, in turn, received more than youths. In January 1920, however, an important restriction – the first of many to be imposed – was made when the minimum age for entitlement was raised from 14 to 16 years (*Verordnung über Erwerbslosenfürsorge*). School-leavers unable to locate an opening were thus barred for perhaps two years from receiving relief and had instead to look to their own family for support, or worse. The decree made clear that the unemployment relief system was not in any way designed to give the unemployed and their dependants a better economic standing than that enjoyed before the loss of a job.[31] Subsequent legislation in October 1923 and particularly on 16 February 1924 only made matters worse for the young unemployed. The 14–16-year-olds were still excluded from receiving benefit but they could now, as an exception, and at the discretion of their local authority, be permitted to join compulsory labour schemes; in return, they would qualify for the still means-tested benefit. This was the way open for school-leavers to obtain support if out of work. The 16–18-years-old group were now entitled to receive benefit only with the sanction of their federal state authority, who would make a decision according to the condition of the labour market in their state; only if deemed 'unfavourable' would benefit be allowed, and then on the further condition of the youth performing unpaid *Pflichtarbeit*. This clause relating to compulsory labour was regarded by the state as an effective way of protecting youth from the demoralising consequences of long-term unemployment. Alternatively, attendance was made compulsory at vocational training courses.[32] If either option was rejected without good reason by the unemployed youth, his benefit was stopped for a period not exceeding six weeks. Particularly following the legislation in 1927, the compulsion to work was rarely enforced and applied only in cases where it was suspected that a youth was really unwilling to work.[33] Finally, the 1924 legislation reiterated that all applicants for relief had to be willing and able to work and stipulated further that they now had to have worked for 13 weeks in a health-insured occupation in the previous year prior to loss of job. With so much discretion given to federal state authorities, the practical implementation of the 1924 legislation inevitably varied across the Reich, and it was only by 1926 that a clear majority of them granted benefit to 16–18-year-olds under the stated qualifying conditions.[34] Even so, there is no denying that the young unemployed were dealt with rather harshly by this system. Indeed their treatment was incompatible with the more beneficent general tenor of Weimar's *Sozialpolitik*.[35] The explanation may not lie in any desire on the part of the state deliberately to penalise young people as such, but rather in a mistaken belief that the jobless young did not need much money to support themselves and that they could be expected to keep body and soul together within a supportive family network. Given the material reality of working-class families, however, such assumptions were too often ill-founded, at considerable cost to the young people affected.

In 1927, AVAVG, the modernised and comprehensive unemployment benefit scheme, changed the rules yet again in respect of the young unemployed's claims to benefit. As before, unfortunately, the young were treated less sympathetically than adult male and female workers.[36] In only one aspect did the new law represent an advance for the young, in that it did not specify a minimum age for entitlement: all workers over 14 years of age, in practice, were legally entitled to benefit, if they had paid the requisite number of insurance contributions and fulfilled the customary basic criteria. On the other hand, the law imposed various restrictions which put the young at a peculiar disadvantage. Firstly, paragraph 137 laid down that in return for benefit, youths aged under 21 years who were out of work were liable for unpaid compulsory labour or attendance at vocational training courses; secondly, according to paragraph 74, apprentices were not required to pay insurance contributions until six months before their training ended, and no benefits were due if the apprenticeship was terminated before that date.[37]

These restrictions contradicted in practice the principle of legal entitlement to benefit without means testing on which AVAVG was based. The position of young people was also compromised in the emergency aid scheme when it was decreed at the same time (paragraph 91 of AVAVG) that youths under 21 years of age were liable to compulsory labour when in receipt of assistance. Worse was to come when the Müller government ran into fiscal and budgetary difficulties. As an economy measure, it was decreed on 29 June 1929 that the unemployed aged under 21 years with entitlement to family support were to be excluded altogether from emergency aid. Moreover, in further changes to AVAVG on 12 October 1929, the waiting period before payment of benefit could be made to under-21-year-old recipients was extended from seven to 14 days.[38] Thus, before the onset of the Depression, the position of the young unemployed in the state unemployment relief schemes was already severely disadvantaged as a prelude to its total destruction in the early 1930s.

The state's response to the plight of the young unemployed in the 1920s also extended to the provision of a diversified range of other measures which established a pattern and framework for coping with the more substantial pressures in this sphere during the Depression.[39] These measures of relief had a common set of objectives, which became more organised once the *Reichsanstalt*, set up by AVAVG in 1927, could co-ordinate with the Reich Labour Ministry: they were designed to make the period of unemployment as constructive as possible, so that by giving the unemployed something worthwhile to do their work skills and attitudes to work would be maintained in a positive fashion. The measures also aimed to thwart the danger of unemployed youth becoming wayward, criminally-minded or psychologically demoralised (*Jugendverwahrlosung*) and, simultaneously, just as important from the state's viewpoint, to keep them within the parameters of the existing democratic order: rebelliousness and proclivities towards political authoritarian extremism had to be quashed. To this extent, there was an element of what might loosely be termed 'social control' by the Republic, but within the highly unstable context of Weimar politics it was surely a benign exercise. Indeed, the Republic has often been criticised for not taking more steps to secure the democratic system before the successful totalitarian challenge from Left and Right in the early 1930s. Who could argue that it was in any sense pernicious or malevolent that the unemployed youth of Germany should be kept off the streets, encouraged to retain their self-respect and regard for the wider community, and to be kept out of the reach of the National Socialists and Communists for as long as was possible? None the less, it must also be said that, although youth unemployment in the 1920s was kept within certain bounds and did not threaten, at least until 1928/9, to assume the proportions of the Depression, the state's relief measures constantly fell somewhat short of what was required, or what would fairly have been considered satisfactory. The primary reason for this inadequacy was simply the relative lack of funds at the state's disposal to deal with a problem which had to accept a lower priority *vis-à-vis* a large number of other social issues confronting the Weimar Republic.[40]

In the early 1920s relief measures centred around state-sponsored *Jugendpflege* activities, including the provision of sports and recreational facilities, but from the middle of the decade, as a consequence of the relatively high youth unemployment in 1923/4 and 1925/6, a series of more specialised projects were initiated. These included the creation of *Werkheime* which, as day centres, provided limited opportunities for technical training and free meals. The first was set up in 1926 by Walter Friedländer's youth office in Berlin's Prenzlauer Berg and by the end of the year that depressed neighbourhood had five *Werkheime* catering for 220 unemployed youths.[41] The practice was established of having separate male and female centres, though in most there was a genuine and sometimes successful attempt made by staff, many of whom had a background in the youth movement or socialist organisations, to create a community spirit. In some centres, however, the reality was quite different, as a former teacher in a Berlin centre in 1926, Albert Lamm, has shown.[42] He describes a rather miserable picture of spartan facilities, ill-feeling among the youths, vandalism and a general atmosphere of violence and intimidation. This does not seem to have deterred many from using the centres, for in January 1927 a substantial majority of Berlin's 5000 unemployed (registered) youths were in attendance, and in Prussia as a whole this pattern was widely repeated.[43]

Running parallel with the *Werkheime* were the first attempts to create structured leisure time for jobless youth. The prototype so-called *Freizeitsheim* appeared in Saxony in 1926 and before the end of the 1920s others had sprung up across the country. Their main function, of course, was to keep these youths out of mischief; addressing the fundamental problems of unemployment as such was not within their area of competence.[44] The provision of vocational and broadly educational courses in technical colleges and Continuation Schools (*Fortbildungsschulen*) represented a more determined attempt by the state to prevent atrophy of work skills and discipline. However these courses increasingly carried with them an unobtrusive ideological–political purpose, namely, to give instruction on the merits of respectable citizenship within a parliamentary democracy.[45] In Hanover, all unemployed youths aged 21 years and under were required from 1926/7 to attend such courses at Continuation School or run the risk of forfeiting unemployment benefit. Other cities, including Berlin, took a more flexible approach.[46]

The Reich Labour Ministry, mindful of the perennial shortage of labour in agriculture and related industries, and convinced of the physical and moral merits of this type of work,[47] encouraged the unemployed youth of the towns and cities to consider a temporary transfer to the countryside. Retraining subsidies for this purpose were provided by central government, but the response was, perhaps understandably, minimal. Besides, the rural population tended to be somewhat suspicious of these outsiders and a harmonious working relationship was a rarity.[48] In addition to some emergency public works schemes in which a limited number of the young unemployed could find short-term and poorly-paid employment, and concessions such as free use of civic amenities in some areas, the state's final initiative was both controversial and wholly unsuccessful. This was the notion of introducing a compulsory ninth school year which the Prussian government mooted in early 1924. Support was attracted from the SPD, trade unions and the progressive educational movement, who appreciated efforts to extend the education of the working class, but vehement opposition was engendered from many parents and employers, both of whom, for different reasons, feared the proposal's implications for the labour market. The Prussian government, for its part, believed a ninth year would ease the pressure on youth unemployment by keeping the leaving class of Easter 1924 off the market for a year. But, unable to furnish the necessary funding and alarmed by the strength of opposition to it, the authorities abandoned the scheme. They had been taken aback by the employer's insistence that a ninth year was devoid of educational merit because primary schools were turning out pupils who were too frequently unfit intellectually to pursue a career in industry or commerce. There were many complaints from employers that a sizable proportion of each year's release had not even mastered the basic three 'Rs', and that what was really needed was a wholesale reform of the curriculum and teaching methods in primary schools in a way which would produce personnel more suited to the requirements of the economy.[49] The Prussian government was thus given plenty to ponder.

The general efficacy of the state's entire package of relief measures was without doubt highly questionable. The ability and willingness of youth to work was not maintained to a desirable degree, and some of the feared physical, psychological and moral implications of unemployment did materialise, particularly among the unskilled working-class youth of the cities. The fact was that the normal processes of socialisation through work were denied youth by unemployment and these measures were no substitute. But, on the other hand, the motives and intentions of government in respect of these measures of relief were sound and wholesome, and consistent therefore with the ethos of Weimar's *Sozialpolitik*. However, in the 1920s, some evidence of a trend emerged, which was to be accentuated during the Depression, relating to a tightening of the state's mechanism of attempted control over unemployed youth. The appearance of *Pflichtarbeit* in the unemployment benefit schemes, some examples of compulsory attendance at vocational training centres and more attention being accorded what might loosely be referred to as political–ideological indoctrination, suggest a particular direction, perhaps, in which the state's role was moving. But there was no well-conceived or co-ordinated planning involved in this. There was little possibility of this kind of strategem emerging from the shifting sands that constituted Weimar cabinet government in the 1920s; the political framework did not permit such rationality or consistency of policy because government held together precariously as an alliance of fundamentally divergent philosophies and interests. There is, therefore, no substantive case for saying that the minor manifestations of attempted control by the state in dealing with youth unemployment formed the basis of the overtly strong-handed, authoritarian direction of this issue by the non-parliamentary governments from Brüning to Schleicher. In the 1920s, after all, the state was a parliamentary democracy, however imperfect, with an admirable record of commitment and achievement in the social welfare field in which its overriding objective was the amelioration of the material situation of the least advantaged sections of German society. The authoritarian regimes of the early 1930s were motivated by an altogether different set of imperatives: the Weimar Republic of the 1920s was not the Weimar Republic of the 1930s.

If the life of unemployed youth was an unhappy one, it cannot be asserted that the situation of many who were in work was entirely satisfactory. Indeed the dividing line between the employed and unemployed youth was not always as sharp as has been made out. The material lot of working youth showed clear inadequacies despite the broader thrust of the Republic's welfare policy. One important reason for this state of affairs was the failure of the state significantly to extend the protective legislation for industrial working youth to which a modest beginning had been made before 1914. At the end of the war, that legislation for youths aged under 16 years and women which had been suspended for the duration of the conflict was reinstated, but despite much discussion involving government and other interested parties nothing of a fundamental nature was added to it in the 1920s. A good deal of what did exist was ignored or only partially implemented by employers and, of course, the 16–18-year-olds were hardly covered at all.[50] *Jugendpflege* provision in factories was ill-developed until the mid-1920s in virtually all parts of the Reich.[51] Working youth had every right to expect after 1918 that the Republic's social policy would deal specifically with their situation, whereas instead it was facilely and, as it transpired, erroneously assumed by government and a somewhat apathetic socialist and labour movement that national legislation on behalf of the working population would somehow percolate down to younger workers. This was particularly disappointing in view of the very positive attitude towards the Republic displayed by many of the younger proletariat, particularly in the early 1920s.[52] Only an updated and still imperfect Child Protection Act (*Kinderschutzgesetz*) appeared in 1925.[53] Violations of the 1903 legislation had been widespread, as the authorities knew very well,[54] and efforts to tighten up matters in the early 1920s had proved fruitless.[55] But even after 1925 child labour persisted[56] and, ironically, it was not until the Third Reich introduced more meaningful legislation, the Youth Protection Act (*Jugendschutzgesetz*), on 30 April 1938 that the practice was effectively stamped out.[57] Otherwise, relatively modest regulations for specific industries which were passed from time to time were all that the Republic could muster in this sphere.[58]

The youth movement was the most vigorous advocate of improved protection for youth and its disenchantment with the Republic's record was aired by the *Reichskonferenz der arbeitenden Jugend* in December 1926. Its statement called for the abolition of individual master–apprentice contracts and their replacement by a general regulation, a fixed minimum wage, abolition of night shifts for youths, paid overtime, improved provision for the unemployed, a ban on the dismissal of apprentices on completion of their training – as so often happened in times of recession – and their employment for at least a further six months on regular tariff-agreed wages. A plea was also made for the rescinding of paragraph 127a of the Commercial Code governing masters' quasi-parental prerogatives over their charges and the outlawing of corporal punishment.[59] Nothing came of all this, unfortunately, nor of the demands for a comprehensive *Jugendarbeitsschutzgesetz* made by the *Reichsausschuss der deutschen Jugendverbände* the same year.[60] In early 1927 the Socialist Youth Movement (SAJ) added its voice to the rising chorus of disapproval at the lack of progress when it complained:

> As we entered 1926 we were full of hope for an improvement in the situation of proletarian youth. In this, however, we were bit-

terly disappointed . . . Large parts of proletarian youth have already sunk into a feeling of hopelessness and lead a life devoid of content and belief in the future.[61]

Communist youth was the most outspoken critic of the Republic's performance, not unexpectedly, and campaigned throughout the 1920s against the alleged capitalist exploitation of young workers in industry.[62] The worst conditions for youth, however, were in agriculture, especially in the backward eastern provinces where feudalistic attitudes were largely allowed to persist without official interference throughout the Weimar era.[63]

The paucity of protective legislation inevitably meant that the working environment of apprentices and unskilled young workers contained much that was unpleasant.[64] The need to improve the situation of apprentices, in particular, had been acknowledged by the state from the early 1920s, and the question of their contract had been at the centre of discussion.[65] Apprenticeships, which were regulated according to a contract – in the early 1920s it was usually unwritten – agreed to by the master and the parents concerned,[66] numbered 986 567 in mid-1925 scattered throughout the economy but concentrated in the craft industries. Over 850 000 of these apprenticeships were held by males, and in an average year some 350 000 were available. In 1925 about 40 per cent of all 14–18-year-old males were apprentices. Because of demographic factors and the Depression, the number of apprentices had fallen by 1933 to 535 074 males and 72 171 females in industry and crafts, and a further 141 923 male and 131 293 female sales and clerical apprentices.[67] They worked long hours, received a pittance as a weekly allowance, had few if any statutory holidays, and were very much at the mercy of their masters.[68] They could be dismissed without notice and ran the risk of physical maltreatment, which was still quite common during the Weimar period.[69] Moreover an apprentice frequently lacked suitable accommodation if his master had not supplied him with a room during the years of training.[70] Employers generally opposed fundamental changes in these conditions. They were convinced that the system gave youths a good sense of discipline and purpose and themselves a ready supply of very cheap labour.[71] But the trade unions were also unwilling to interfere too much because they feared being caught in the middle between their duty to look after the rights of masters, who were invariably union members, and young people. As in so many of their other attitudes and activities, the unions were decisively geared to defending adult workers. Consequently, throughout the Weimar era, apprentices remained a vulnerable section of the young proletariat, especially in times of economic crisis. The situation of the unskilled young industrial worker in employment was slightly superior in some respects, though it would be misleading to overemphasise the differences. Skilled work had a higher status and attracted, in general, job security and enhanced pay rates after qualification, though wage differentials were in decline. Whether a youth on leaving school at 14 years took up an apprenticeship or unskilled employment depended on many factors such as the personality and capability of the individual, family circumstances, parental guidance and local availability of apprenticeships. The unskilled young worker received more pay than apprentices because his wages were covered by union-negotiated collective agreements and he enjoyed more mobility and freedom to change jobs, at least when the economy was stable, since he was not tied down by either a written or verbal contract. But his life-style was more likely to be irregular and insecure, and he would tend to live for the moment, without formulating any medium- or long-term plans. Unskilled jobs, too, were often mechanical and boring. Once the unskilled youngster passed the age of 18 or 19 years, when his contemporaries might be completing apprenticeships and he himself might be getting married with the ensuing financial burdens, his position was much less favourable. The years when he was 14–18 were probably the best of the unskilled worker's life, when he was free of school, had money in his pocket to spend on visits to dance halls, cafés and cinemas, and was unencumbered by responsibility.[72]

Like apprentices, unskilled youth were able after 1918 to join a union, though only a small number did so: in 1921, for example, only 10 per cent of under-18-year-olds in employment, or 252 197, were unionised, while in 1925 the figure had dropped to under 3 per cent, or 119 524 of a total union membership of 4 156 451. In 1929 a similar percentage still prevailed, accounting for only 229 561 of a total of 4 906 228.[73] Their poor representation in the unions partly accounts for the neglect of young workers' interests, while the unions, for their part, did little to encourage young people to become members.[74] The statements of support for young workers and apprentices made at the inaugural conference of the Socialist trade union movement (ADGB) at Nuremberg in 1919, and subsequently, were mere rhetoric, as developments clearly revealed later in the 1920s.

In a broad and reasonably representative survey of 134 217 young workers conducted by Mewes in the mid-1920s, a detailed picture of working conditions for the young was provided.[75] He found that 37 per cent worked more than 48 hours per week, including a sizable number whose weekly total was over 60 hours; 12–13 per cent of the sample still worked on Sundays. In addition to time actually spent working, account has also to be taken of travel time to and from work, cleaning-up time, meal-times and time spent on vocational courses, all of which left the young worker with little free time to himself, allowing for variations according to trade, location, city/countryside, and male/female.[76] Rates of pay were low by any standard, with 77 per cent of males earning between one and 10 marks per week. Mewes also ascertained that 23 per cent of his sample received no statutory holidays, 16 per cent were allowed up to three days off in the year, 8 per cent four to five days, 38 per cent six to eight days, 4 per cent nine to 10 days, and only 4 per cent a full fortnight. Altogether, only half were paid for their holiday. By comparison with their counterparts in Austria, where since 1919 a young worker who had completed six months' work and had the necessary medical clearance was entitled to four weeks' holiday, with the chance of spending it in a pleasant holiday complex (*Ferienheim*), the Germans were poorly rewarded. There were cases where a mere application for holiday leave resulted in the loss of a job or apprenticeship, particularly in smaller factories or family businesses.[77] In February 1925 the *Reichsausschuss der deutschen Jugendverbände* submitted a plan to government for the regulation of holidays, including three weeks' paid leave for under-16s and two weeks' paid leave for 16–18-year-olds. The *Reichsausschuss*, which had 108 holiday centres with 4760 beds at this time, was prepared to assist with the practical arrangements, but was rebuffed.[78] The problem was that the upper hand lay with the employers who adopted an intransigent attitude, arguing that holidays on the scale suggested would result in higher wage costs which in turn would reduce profits and discourage investment – in fact, the line of argument taken by employers in the mid- and late 1920s towards all aspects of social policy. In the even tougher climate of the Depression employers easily brushed aside this issue which, in any case, had assumed much less importance in the eyes of labour. Those fortunate enough to be in work did not wish to jeopardise it by agitating for holidays and inviting dismissal. Even parents, who in the 1920s had taken a prominent part in demanding statutory holidays, backed off in the early 1930s.[79]

Special mention might also be made of the young female worker who fared no better than her male colleagues and, indeed, in some ways was worse off. To miserable working conditions in the factory or in agriculture had to be added those domestic duties which were common in working-class families: cleaning, shopping, looking after younger children and mending, which all but eliminated her free time.[80] A life of gloomy drudgery was only beginning to be somewhat enlivened, at least in the large cities, by the development of the mass leisure and entertainment industry and popular trends in fashion.

An important area in which for a time the state did make a determined effort to advance matters lay in the provision for vocational training and the career guidance service for young people in the 1920s. With encouragement from both sides of industry,[81] the Reich Labour Ministry aimed to improve the range and quality of vocational training so that the apprenticeship system would provide adequate numbers of skilled manpower for the expected expansion of the economy after 1923/4. Unskilled young workers were included in the new plans, not only to enhance their technical ability, but also to help make them solid and dependable citizens, which was a perfectly sound proposition. In any event, the Weimar Constitution laid down that further part-time education should be made available for everyone of post-school age for a period of three years in a Continuation School, though this stipulation was not observed uniformly throughout the Reich.[82]

A body of opinion arose in the early 1920s in favour of a Compulsory Vocational School Act (*Berufsschulpflichtgesetz*)[83] but it ran into acrimonious controversy because of the conflicting views of unions and employers, funding shortages, and the inevitable political machinations. Similarly, a proposed Vocational Training Act (*Berufsausbildungsgesetz*) reached draft form in 1927 and after further review by cabinet was introduced into the Reichstag in December 1929. Then referred to committee, it failed to reappear from the maze of irreconcilable differences between unions and employers.[84] Each federal state, meanwhile, was free to devise its own vocational schooling system. Many introduced a compulsory scheme for young workers up to the age of 17 years,[85] but almost always the results proved unsatisfactory because unions and employers could not agree on a united plan of development. Disagreement arose over which categories of youth were to attend classes and about how attendance at these schools was to be regulated. Was the time for taking classes to be included in the overall working time of youth, or was it to be taken separately and classes attended in the evenings? Were those attending to be paid by their employers or not? The Working Hours decree (*Arbeitszeitverordnung*) of 21 December 1923 had allowed for a maximum of six hours' attendance at vocational school each week to be held outside normal working hours.[86] By the mid-1920s, however, the practice had become fairly standard where classes were held during working hours with the somewhat reluctant consent of employers. The argument over the pay issue in relation to attendance was not resolved until the Reich Labour Ministry inserted a clause in the draft of the law on vocational training in 1929 which prohibited employers from making deductions from the pay of those taking classes.

The unpropitious circumstances in which vocational schooling was introduced certainly limited its development. The census of 1925 revealed that 75 per cent of over-14-year-olds were in employment but that only half of them had vocational training in a practical skill.[87] In 1929/30 there were still 25 per cent of 14–18-year-olds who did not attend vocational school, most of them females and rural-based youth.[88] Prussia as a whole lacked an efficiently organised and widely available system.[89] But, even for the majority enrolled in courses, the situation was not entirely what had been intended. Truancy remained a serious problem throughout the 1920s, especially among unskilled male youth, and in class there was a good deal of disruptive behaviour from youths who resented having to be there in the first place, and who would no doubt have reacted negatively to any educational system because of a lack of inherent ability and motivation for study. The original objectives of enhancing work aptitude and moulding reliable citizens were consequently realised in only a very limited number of cases.

Closely allied to the issue of vocational training was that of career guidance services. Until 1918 this sphere was dominated by private agencies, including the few centres catering exclusively for youth.[90] Here youths could call for general information and advice about choice of career and problems that arose in a particular job, as well as personal and family worries. Few youths, however, took advantage of this facility. A *Zentralstelle für Lehrstellenvermittlung* had been established in Berlin in 1912 and similar offices sprang up later in other major cities, but it was not until the end of the First World War that developments assumed substantial proportions. The federal state governments were keen to promote the service, and Bavaria in December 1917, Prussia in March 1919, Saxony in April 1919 and Württemberg in February 1920 led the way.[91] Hamburg created a

Zentrale für Berufsberatung und Lehrstellenvermittlung in early 1919, and Bavaria appointed a federal careers adviser in October of the following year.[92] The first national regulations for a unified, public career guidance service were issued as part of the Labour Exchanges Act of 1922 and later, and definitively, with the new unemployment insurance scheme in 1927. In September 1922 some 21 regional labour exchanges incorporated nearly 600 public career guidance offices which handled an increasing number of enquiries – by 1924/5 over 306 000. Two years later, the number of enquiries had risen to 426 000.[93] Regional development of the service was patchy: Hamburg and Wurttemberg were well served, whereas most rural, small town areas and a few cities, mainly in southern and eastern Germany, were not.[94] Despite expansion, the service at the end of the 1920s was still not consulted by a majority of youths, and in the Depression it sharply declined because of cutbacks in funding and also because young people could no longer be selective in their choice of a career.[95]

There were some harsh penalties within and outside the labour market for many working-class youths in the 1920s which, coupled with the greyness and frequent material disadvantages of their urban family background, added up to a rather prosaic and poor life-style. Education offered little prospect of release because the financial exigencies of their situation precluded the possibility of more than a few progressing to superior employment opportunities through this channel. Only 5.4 per cent of male and 3.4 per cent of female pupils attending Prussian secondary schools in 1927 were working-class. In higher education, working-class students at universities and other institutes of advanced learning in summer semester 1928 constituted a mere 1.9 per cent of the total, 2.2 per cent in winter semester 1928/9 and 2.7 per cent in summer semester 1929.[96] It is little wonder that psychologists detected feelings of inadequacy or inferiority among many working-class youths.[97] Their lives were heavily circumscribed in material and intellectual terms, thus underlining the distance, for one thing, that Weimar's social welfare policy still had to travel substantially to alleviate the grass-roots elements of this predicament. A small number sought immediate liberation in emigration: 44 900 male and female youth aged 14–21 years left Germany between 1925 and 1933, the vast majority departing before the onset of the Depression.[98] For the very great majority of proletarian youth who remained, there were few secure points of orientation in life, few realistic avenues of advance in the future.[99] This rather dispiriting ambience was bound to produce, to some extent at least, a lack of understanding and sympathy between the young industrial proletariat and the Republic, which could only be accentuated in the turbulent times that lay ahead. The failure of the SPD and unions to attend seriously to the interests of working youth, the growing conflict between capital and labour, the unevenness of economic development, the parsimony of government funding in a number of areas vital to youth, and the state's failure to push through national legislation for the workplace all contributed to the less than satisfactory position of working-class youth in 1929 – a state of affairs which the Depression could only exacerbate.

6 Youth Unemployment in the Great Depression, 1929–1933

The impact of the Depression on the German labour market was catastrophic, but both in relative and absolute terms the younger generation, particularly 18–25-years-olds, was one of the major casualties in the community.[1] Their situation as workers was compounded by a series of ostensibly conflicting demographic trends. The years 1929–31 saw the entry into an already overstretched labour pool of the last of the fertile pre-war birth cohorts which immediately put further strain on the job market as the Depression deepened. The significance of this demographic influence, however, declined in 1931/2 in response to the comparatively low birth rates of the war and early postwar period, resulting in youth forming a smaller proportion of the Reich population: while, for example, 14–18-year-old were 8.4 per cent of the population as a whole in 1925, they were only 4.5 per cent in 1933, and their overall numbers fell from 4 068 000 in 1931 to 3 101 000 in 1933, a drop of 24 per cent. Moreover, between 1925 and 1933 the 14–20-year-old group fell from 12.9 to 8.1 per cent and the 20–25-year-olds from 10.1 to 9.8 per cent of the total population. Youth's place in the working population correspondingly underwent noticeable change: while the workforce (*Erwerbstätige*) increased from 32 million in 1925 to 32.3 million in 1933, the proportion of 14–20-year-olds fell from 5.95 to 3.82 million.[2] But these statistical movements, which might normally have been expected to ease youth's search for work, had no beneficial repercussions because of the continuing restraints of developments dating from the mid-1920s, including, most notably, the shake-out of labour occasioned by industrial rationalisation and the expansion of younger female groups in employment. A host of other adverse economic factors emanating from the Depression also intervened collectively to further depress job opportunities for the young. The number of openings available could not match the size of the younger labour pool in 1931–33.

It is not possible to present a totally precise analysis of the extent of youth unemployment in the early 1930s because the recorded statistics were still incomplete in some respects despite the undoubted improvements in data collection since the establishment in 1927 of the *Reichsanstalt*. As with certain categories of adult unemployed, not all the young jobless showed up in the officially recorded unemployment figures. As the Depression deepened and the welfare benefits system collapsed, many young workers were systematically excluded from registers by the frequent alterations to the rules of entitlement, and large numbers became part of the 'invisible' unemployed in 1932/3. School-leavers who had at no time held a job were invariably denied benefit and did not appear in official compilations. Young people were not included in the unemployment information drawn up by the trade unions unless they had found at least short-term employment on leaving school and had taken the chance to join a union.[3] The existence of a much diminished 'black economy' of casual employment further complicated the labour market position of the young. Even the comprehensive Population and Occupational Census of 16 June 1933 (*Volks-, Berufs-und Betriebszählung*), which Hertha Siemering used as the basis of her valuable statistical survey of youth, fails to fill all the gaps because, for example, it did not fully differentiate between groups of unemployed. Setting aside these obvious shortcomings, however, a reasonably well-defined picture of youth unemployment in the Depression which adequately conveys what a tragedy it was for the young may be constructed.

The first year of the Depression saw a substantial and accelerating increase in the unemployment of 14–25-year-olds, which set the scene for a trend destined to continue until after the collapse of the Republic itself. This unemployment was principally a working-class phenomenon, but middle-class academic youth in higher education and those who had elected for employment at any time between 14 and 19 years of age comprised a small percentage of those affected. University graduates joined the 'academic proletariat', while 300 000 white collar workers, of which up to 18 per cent were under 21 years of age, went on the dole.[4]

On 31 March 1930 there were 284 059 unemployed 14–21-year-olds in receipt of unemployment benefit (*Hauptunterstützungsempfänger*), representing 13.8 per cent of the total official jobless figure in the Reich of 2 053 380; on 31 May 1930 that percentage had risen to 14.9, and by December to 15 per cent, or 326 363 of the total.[5] Seasonal factors did not have much effect on youth unemployment during the winter months, as it did on adults, and throughout 1931 the situation deteriorated markedly. On 28 February 1931 there were 403 979 aged 14–21 years officially out of work, or 15.6 per cent of the total, rising

Youth Unemployment in the Great Depression, 1929–1933

Table 6.1 Youth unemployment (officially registered), 30 July 1932

Age	Male	Female	Total
14–17	79 323	70 751	150 074
18–20	339 837	142 313	482 150
21–25	617 536	207 094	824 630
14–25	1 036 696	420 158	1 456 854

on 31 March to 712 000 out of 4 743 000, or over 16 per cent.[6] This meant that a larger proportion of the under-25s in the employable population was out of a job than the proportion of adult workers, a trend which intensified in 1932. By the turn of the year in 1931 there were 840 000 aged 14–21 years registered as unemployed, and as the Depression edged towards its nadir in summer 1932 against a background of Brüning's severe deflationary policies, the plight of the young worsened. Youth unemployment numbers reached staggering heights: the one million mark was attained in April 1932, representing 24.1 and 38.5 per cent of the total male and female unemployed, respectively, and rose even further during the following months.[7] Figures released on 30 July 1932 by the *Reichsanstalt* revealed 1 456 854 male and female 14–25 year olds out of work at a time when the total for the Reich stood at nearly 5.5 million. Table 6.1 provides the details of this appalling situation.[8] These figures demonstrate that by mid-1932 younger workers were a far larger percentage of the total unemployed than had been the case before the Depression: for example, the jobless 14–18-year-olds formed a mere 2.6 per cent on average of the total registered unemployed in 1925–7.[9]

When allowance is made for the various categories of unemployed youth not revealed in official statistics, it might well have been the case that the real level of unemployment among 14–25-year-olds in mid-1932 was 2.5–3.0 million. During the last six months of that year and the first half of the following year the situation remained critical, as the Census of June 1933 showed: of a total registered unemployment figure of 4 712 432 males and 1 142 586 females, the youth constituency was as displayed in Table 6.2.[10] The male total represented 22.2 per cent of the total male population of that age in the Reich, while a much lower rate of unemployment was recorded among females of the same age group. Altogether, the Census

Table 6.2 Youth unemployment (officially registered), June 1933

Age	Male	Female	Total
14–18	90 624	57 462	148 086
18–20	265 526	107 618	373 144
20–25	900 752	293 222	1 193 974
14–25	1 256 902	458 302	1 715 204

intimated that there were 11 231 309 males and females aged 14–25 years in virtually equal proportion, with 50 per cent being 20–25 years of age. One-third of males aged 14–25 years were unemployed, constituting 26.6 per cent of the total male jobless, with the older youths (20–25 years) by far the major component.[11] Throughout the 1929–33 period, 18–25-year-old males were the group most severely hit by unemployment; their numbers were greater than any other single group and in relative terms also they were the most vulnerable, that is, relative to their proportion in the age structure of the working population. In 1932, 24.6 per cent of the male unemployed were aged 18–25 years, when they formed only 19.4 per cent of the working population.[12] In contrast, the comparative mildness of unemployment among 14–18-year-olds may be explained by the fact that they were a cheap source of labour as unskilled or irregular workers and an even cheaper source as apprentices. Competition for jobs among 14–18-year olds was not as intense because of the fall in the 1914–20 birth rate and cohorts of school-leavers were smaller than before. Furthermore certain types of poorly-paid, unskilled jobs traditionally taken by male youths aged under 18 years, including errand-running, newspaper-selling, and low-grade service posts, were still in reasonable supply in the early 1930s.

The social composition of the young unemployed and their place in the economy may be defined with some precision. Since about 75 per cent of employable youths aged 14–25 years in Germany were classified as 'workers' (*Arbeiter*) in 1933, with 43 per cent of them in industry and crafts, 33.5 per cent in agriculture and related industries, 12.6 per cent in commerce and transport, 3.6 per cent in public service and private business, and 6.9 per cent in domestic service, it is clear that what was in question was predominantly working-class unemployment. The sectors of highest job losses for young males were in heavy industry, above all, construction, machine-making and metal trades, in which the rate of youth unemployment in 1932 averaged around 50 per cent. The 1933 Census showed that the percentage of jobless 18–25-year-old males in the iron and metal trades was 46.2, in iron/steel/metal manufacture 47.8, in machine-making 52.6 and in electricity 49.6; chemicals and textiles were among the least affected, with corresponding rates of 26.1 and 20.7, respectively. Female youth unemployment lay mostly in the clothing and textile industries.[13]

The Depression created a new phenomenon in the German labour market: a substantial group of long-term youth unemployed.[14] As early as November 1930 the youth welfare authorities in Hamburg identified this new category in their city,[15] and officials in other principal cities were soon making the same observation. In Cologne it was reckoned that a significant though unspecified percentage of the 8869 registered under-21-year-old jobless in January 1931 had been in that predicament for a lengthy period of time,[16] as the Württemberg authorities estimated of their young unemployed.[17] A large number of these long-term jobless were apprentices who had been dismissed in the late 1920s. Unable to secure another position before the Depression struck they faced the early 1930s with virtually no prospects.[18] Also another category was composed of those apprentices who were not hired on completion of their training because they were too expensive in a period of plentiful and cheap unskilled labour.[19] Many of them did not find a suitable opening until after 1933 and in the intervening time accepted anything that was available in order to earn some money at least. The disillusionment and frustration they experienced was acute, leaving them with a feeling that long years of arduous training on a pittance had been a sheer waste of time.[20]

School-leavers formed another prominent component of the young long-term umemployed. Those leaving education in spring 1930 were particularly unfortunate for not only were many of them unable to find a job but they had also been born and brought up amidst the stringent conditions of wartime and the early 1920s. A good number of them were apparently physically weak and below the expected intellectual standard, thus adding considerably to their already extremely difficult task of finding employment. Employers were scathing in their criticism of them.[21] In 1930 there were some 793 000 school-leavers for only 200 000 apprenticeships, and the situation worsened: in 1931, the figures were 717 000 and 160 000 and in 1932, 624 000 and 120 000, respectively.[22] Even if more and more young people were reluctant to take on a demanding training because of the likelihood of there being no appropriate job at the end of it, this cohort inevitably contained many bitterly disappointed youths, obliged to occupy the very bottom rungs of the economic and social ladder. In Chemnitz in 1932 less than half the school-leavers found a job[23] and in other cities the position was no better. The Depression threw up, therefore, another new category of unemployed: 14–18-year-olds who had never worked.

A third major element in youth unemployment was the unskilled worker. Despite a growing tendency in the early 1930s for employers to recruit unskilled rather than skilled labour there were not sufficient opportunities available, of course, and tens of thousands of this most expendable of all groups in the labour market were cut adrift not only from work, but also, in many instances, from the mainstream of society as a whole. Marginalised in depressed inner city proletarian ghettos they were a principal social casualty of the Depression.

Wide regional variations appeared in youth unemployment, but a broad pattern became clear by 1931 which did not basically alter over the following few years. While in 1930/1 small and medium-sized towns of 25–50 000 inhabitants were the worst hit, by 1931 youth unemployment was concentrated in large cities and urban centres as well as heavily industrialised areas. Westphalia, parts of Hesse and the Rhineland, the Ruhr, Berlin-Brandenburg, Saxony and Upper Silesia were the blackest spots; rural and agrarian districts such as East Prussia, Pomerania and Mecklenburg were least affected.[24] The major cities had chronic levels and none more conspicuously than Berlin. In June 1933 there were 24 150 males and 19 850 females aged 14–20 years out of work, representing 38 per cent of the city's working male population of that age group, and 28 per cent of the corresponding female population.[25] Most of the male jobless were in industry and crafts, as was the case throughout the Reich. When the 20–25-year-old unemployed are added to the statistics the outcome in Berlin was 96 815 male unemployed aged 14–25 years in June 1933, a rate of 63.4 per cent of that total age group in the city. A few other cities had even higher rates: Gelsenkirchen recorded 84.6 per cent, Duisburg-Hamborn and Oberhausen 82.2 per cent, Dortmund 76.3 per cent, Breslau 72.0 per cent and Essen 67.2 per cent. Corresponding female unemployment in Prussia was the highest in Hindenburg, Breslau, Beuthen, Harburg-Wilhelmsburg and Berlin (33.0 per cent).[26] In Hamburg, the 14–25-year-olds constituted approximately one-quarter of the city's unemployment total of 136 112 in July 1932.[27]

The scale of youth unemployment in the early 1930s confronted the Republic with a line of demanding questions to which, it soon became obvious, it had no adequate answers. The magnitude of the social and political upheaval experienced by Germany would have stretched the resources of any governmental system, however stable, to the uppermost limits and would ultimately have engulfed most. The besieged Weimar Republic could not afford to take a less serious view of youth unemployment than it did of the adult variety because of the high profile enjoyed by the younger generation since the advent of the *Wandervogel* and nurtured in the 1920's by the Republic itself. But by 1930/1 it was clear that the humanitarian impulse which had lain at the heart of Weimar's social welfare programme for youth could no longer be sustained amidst the general disintegration of *Sozialpolitik*. The welfare state was overtaken and destroyed by the economic crisis and the allied retrenchment policy of government. Young people could not be spared and, indeed, arguably were to suffer more than most other sections of the community. One of the most striking and in many ways most damaging manifestations of the failure of the welfare net in respect of youth's situation was the wholesale erosion of the unemployment benefit system.

The difficulties and discrimination experienced by younger workers in this system throughout the 1920s were merely a foretaste of worse to come in the Depression when a series of drastic measures introduced by emergency decree worked to their severe disadvantage. The total result was a tightening of the rules of eligibility, partly with the aim of preventing abuses, an exclusion of many categories of unemployed youth from receiving benefit and a consequent saddling of their families with responsibility for their maintenance. The level of benefit, when continued to be paid at all, was reduced to derisory proportions, thereby forcing large numbers of youth onto the means-tested poor or welfare relief administered by local authorities, or out of the benefits system altogether. In essence, as the numbers of young unemployed rose, the number of them in receipt of any kind of public support fell. Material deprivation and frequently abject destitution on a massive scale inevitably followed, especially for those in large cities.

This particular path to comprehensive misery for the young unemployed was set in place in the first instance by Chancellor Brüning's emergency decree of 26 July 1930 which contained a section relating to changes in the unemployment insurance scheme (AVAVG). It stipulated that youths under 17 years of age were to continue receiving benefit only if they could no longer be adequately supported by their family or responsible relatives (*unterhaltspflichtige Familienangehöriger*).[28] Unemployed youth's legal entitlement to benefit under AVAVG was now abrogated by making it conditional upon a means test applied to their parents' or guardians' income. An underlying assumption was that they did not in any case need much money. More seriously, the aim of shifting responsibility for the young jobless from the state to families was unjustified, not least because working-class families were usually ill-equipped for this task, less so as the Depression worsened. Brüning's decree was followed by another on 1 December 1930 reducing the age at which unemployed youths could be given benefit from 17 to 16 years, and in the draconian emergency legislation of 5 June 1931 it was enunciated that all under-21-year-old unemployed would continue to receive benefit from AVAVG only if they could not be maintained by their family.[29] Rubbing salt into the wounds, this decree also broadened the scope for the exercise of *Pflichtarbeit* to over-21-year-old jobless, in certain circumstances; in practice, however, they were not commonly obliged to perform compulsory labour.[30] This was a source of only minor solace in the face of Chancellor von Papen's decree of 14 June 1932 whereby unemployment benefit was to be paid to under-21-year-olds provided they were demonstrably destitute, and even then, the imposition of further restrictions made payment less than certain.[31] By 1932 therefore, no one could deny that the state had decisively violated the fundamental principle of legal entitlement of the properly insured to benefit which was embodied in AVAVG. At the same time, both the emergency aid and poor relief schemes had been drastically reduced in scope, including the exclusion from the former on 11 October 1930 of all unemployed aged 21 years and under.[32]

The strains on working-class family life caused by these cutbacks are not to be underestimated. Because many families depended on all members over the school-leaving age of 14 receiving some kind of income to assist the household budget – and in the Depression very few could afford to carry a non-earning adult – the effect of the curtailment of the young unemployed rights to public benefit was to drive many of them from home and onto the roads. An alternative was to challenge the welfare system by breaking the rules and obtaining benefit by fraud, and working-class children and youths developed an intimate knowledge of the way the system operated, but the risk of being caught by welfare officials or police had to be carefully calculated. This type of surreptitious activity helped to inform the development of petty criminal attitudes among younger people in these years.[33]

For those on the other side of the employed/unemployed divide in the Depression conditions were not markedly better as employers gained the initiative in capital–labour relations more and more emphatically.[34] From around the country came reports of poverty wages being paid to youth, longer hours being worked without overtime payment, further restrictions on holidays and the increasing irrelevance of the state's protective legislation in the factories. While there were always exceptions, such as Württemberg's glass industry, where protective measures for young workers were introduced in 1930 and 1932,[35] the supervisory machinery dating from the more tranquil situation of the mid-1920s was powerless to prevent the spread of abuses.[36] The continuing maltreatment of industrial and craft apprentices was a public scandal which the Left and proletarian youth movement tried to expose fully, but without effect on government.[37] Unemployment was a tragic intrusion into the lives of many young Germans but it was patently more pressing than ever before to have sweeping reform of the conditions in which a majority still worked.

The era of mass unemployment exacerbated existing social problems and created new ones. The savage reductions in youth welfare expenditure after 1929/30[38] contributed to a decline in health standards, especially among the young working class of large urban and industrial areas, as government was eventually compelled to admit.[39] In Hamburg, the authorities spoke of 'an important deterioration' in child health, and rickets, a sure sign of poor-quality dieting, reappeared on a large scale in proletarian districts.[40] In many other cities the incidence of certain diseases, including tuberculosis, scurvy and nervous disorders, noticeably increased. Hard-pressed welfare officials had to curtail drastically the provision of holidays for deprived and jobless children and youth; Hamburg was forced to cancel its holiday programme for unemployed youth in 1931, owing to a lack of funds.[41] Child street-begging, which had been a common sight in the early postwar years, but which had disappeared in better times, and teenage vagabondage re-emerged on an expanded scale. In 1930 there were no fewer than 19 185 vagrant youths in Berlin and over 11 000 in Frankfurt, while Hamburg, Nuremberg, Wiesbaden and Karlsruhe also had large numbers. By the end of 1931 alone there were an estimated 400 000 youths on the roads (*Wanderburschen*) and tens of thousands more young Germans wandering around Europe.[42] A year later the problem was much worse, with as many as one million under way.[43] Local authorities were overwhelmed by these additional demands on scanty resources, especially as petty criminal behaviour was often an allied problem.[44] If vagrant youth was one of the most distressing products of the collapse of Germany's social fabric in the Depression, no less unpalatable was the considerable rise in juvenile prostitution of both sexes,[45] and the soaring suicide rate among young people. Even for a country with traditionally one of the highest suicide rates in the world, the statistics were alarming. In 1930/1 some 6000 youths took their own lives in a 12-month period,[46] and in Berlin in 1932 an average of ten or eleven suicide attempts by young people took place every day.[47]

The dire straits of younger children of the working-class unemployed, particularly of the long-term kind, were described by a large number of contemporary observers, including sociologists, doctors, psychologists and welfare workers, but none more graphically than by Ruth Weiland and the independent Communist writers Ruth Fischer and Franz Heimann.[48] Their living standards often fell below the poverty line, they were very vulnerable to physical and mental ailments, their educational opportunities were further retarded in badly equipped, run down city schools and their self-confidence and appreciation of moral values were destroyed. Expectations for the future ceased to exist for these children. The inability of parents to cope was reflected in the large increase in cases of child neglect and abuse.[49] Only limited assistance of an elementary type was usually available from the school medical and dental services which, after the impressive growth of the mid-1920s, fell into serious decline, particularly in Prussia.[50]

Government was not short of advice on how to tackle youth unemployment and its social consequences. The churches, welfare bodies, professional experts, the trade unions and the youth movement – perhaps the most outspoken – were all eager to contribute to the discussion. The *Reichsausschuss der deutschen Jugendverbände* offered well-meaning, constructive but rather limited proposals for work schemes and progressive welfare legislation, as illustrated by its statement on unemployment in October 1931 and, more notably, its '*Umbau-Nicht Abbau*' programme issued in January of the following year.[51] Individual youth organisations also joined in, including those of the extremist parties who were determined to exploit the unhappy circumstances for political advantage. In 1930 the Hitler Youth, which had developed a strong anti-capitalist, social revolutionary character and had founded vocational training schools in Berlin and other major cities for the many unemployed young workers and apprentices among its membership, advanced a comprehensive plan for a National Youth Law (*Reichsjugendgesetz*) aimed specifically at the needs of proletarian youth in the factories. Fair regulation of wages, holidays, working hours, relief for the unemployed, and apprentices' contracts were its main concern.[52] The KJVD issued strident demands for more caring consideration of the jobless by the state at regular intervals and in a draft law, *Gesetz zum Schutz der Jugend gegen soziale Verelendung* (Law for the Protection of Youth from Social Immiseration), which was defeated in the Reichstag in January 1931. A few months later, it set out a work creation scheme, '*Arbeitsbeschaffungsprogramm für die werktätige Jugend*'.[53] But all these demands by the youth movement fell on deaf ears because they exerted no influence on government policy.

Pseudo-moralistic exhortations from certain Christian groups for unemployed youth to grin and bear their discomfiture, and admonitions against youth becoming entrapped in vulgar materialism from the youth wing of the ADGB,[54] were distinctly unhelpful, of course, while the SPD's response, as the major party of the working class, was disgracefully belated and unremarkable. This was perhaps to be expected in view of the considerable lack of understanding that had arisen between a party unable for some time to make much of an appeal to the idealism of Weimar's younger generation as a whole, and unwilling to embrace the radical temper of many younger proletarians in particular. The SPD's toleration of Brüning's deflationary policies and of the ensuing dismemberment of the welfare system (to which it actively contributed at the local and regional level, especially in Prussia), coupled with the material want of the working class, could only serve to accentuate the alienation of a large number of youth from the party. Having conspicuously failed to produce any worthwhile ideas for combating mass unemployment and even hostile to trade union initiatives such as the WTB-Plan in 1932, all that the SPD came up with was the creation in August 1932 of the grandiosely-titled *Reichsarbeitsgemeinschaft Sozialer Dienst – Hilfswerk der Arbeiterschaft für die erwerbslose Jugend*, a body whose primary function was merely to co-ordinate with the government's voluntary labour service (*Freiwilliger Arbeitsdienst* – FAD).[55]

In the first years of the Depression, the state's role *vis-à-vis* the young, and particularly its many unemployed members, was principally motivated by the humanitarian concern which had characterised its youth welfare provision in the 1920s, especially as it was acutely aware that the generation undergoing the suffering had already been through the terrible ordeals of the war and hyperinflation. It was officially acknowledged that the plight of the young represented 'a danger to Volk and Fatherland'.[56] Hence efforts were made to devise various relief measures and to prepare youth for a return to work through vocational training courses and short-term employment schemes. The state also sought a judicious application of *Jugendpflege* and sought to lay down guidelines for co-ordination throughout the country.[57] Before long, however, all government endeavours were restricted by Brüning's austere public expenditure programme. Intentions, however well-meant and sincere, did not translate into successful practice, and the growing disparity between concept and reality was shattering for unemployed youth. Some of them, in any case, had refused to co-operate with any of the government's schemes through a chain of evasive actions. As the government's failure became increasingly apparent in the face of diminishing resources and escalating social problems during the first half of 1931, its overall approach to the young unemployed changed to some extent. While the humanitarian impulse did not disappear, it was mixed somewhat with a concern that had to do with maintaining order, keeping youth out of harm's way and, above all, minimising youth's vulnerability to moral collapse and predilection for radical politics. In short, a trend already noticeable before the Depression in the state's handling of youth unemployment (*Pflichtarbeit*, compulsory attendance at some vocational courses, political instruction) resurfaced in a much more assertive and unequivocal manner. The young unemployed were now to be brought more under the influence of disciplinary mechanisms through state direction, thus to fill the gap opened up by the decline in influence of traditional agencies of adult supervision, including parents, families, employers, schools and churches.[58] There was no consistently ordered rationale behind this limited exercise in social control, just as there was not in so many other spheres of government activity in 1930–2 because very little was capable of being precisely formulated amidst the upheaval. None the less, a situation emerged in Germany in 1931/2 which bore a certain, partial resemblance, in respect of the state's attitude to working-class youth, to the policies of the authoritarian Kaiserreich, particularly those relating to the Reich Law of Association (1908) and the campaign centred around the establishment of the loyalist *Jungdeutschlandbund*.

The state's relief provision in 1930/1 largely followed the familiar pattern established in the 1920s, albeit on an expanded scale. Its aim of devoting additional resources to vocational training and other educational courses was intimated in September 1930 by Dr Friedrich Syrup, President of the *Reichsanstalt*, and appropriate measures were announced three months later.[59] Efforts by the Prussian government and other authorities to enforce attendance in 1931[60] were ineffective, however, and during that year only a total of 330 835 young unemployed became involved.[61] Subsequent changes which made the courses less specialised and of shorter duration did little to improve the truancy rate.[62] The state encouraged the setting up of day centres (*Tagesheime*) where some work training, recreational facilities and meals were provided for unemployed youth who chose to attend, but by mid-1931 many of them had to close because of a lack of funding.[63] Work centres (*Werkheime*) and special centres for the long-term unemployed (*Erwerbslosenheime*) were useful but relatively few in number, while emergency labour schemes (*Notstandarbeit*) which involved hard manual work on municipal projects for a short period on very low wages were also tried without much success. The latter were designed for youths excluded from receiving unemployment benefit because they had not worked long enough previously to qualify for paying the necessary insurance contributions. Official attempts to structure the long idle hours of the unemployed in leisure centres (*Freizeitsheime*) were constantly hampered by the customary funding problems.[64] The scheme to transfer the unemployed to agriculture met with a decidedly muted response – only 18 500 under-21-year-olds were involved in 1930 – and was abandoned in 1932 because of growing rural unemployment.[65]

The purpose of all these centrally-directed initiatives was to strengthen youth's willingness to work, encourage good working habits and maintain morale, with a view to their return to the employed sector when the economic crisis had passed. A basic difficulty as far as youth was concerned, however, was that, since there was little prospect of securing a job in the foreseeable future, learning a skill carried little attraction. Moreover employers were tending to take on semi-skilled and unskilled labour because it was cheaper. From another, equally important perspective, the government's relief measures also failed: only a relatively small percentage of unemployed youth were affected by them, and then invariably for short periods,[66] thus in some contrast to its generally successful encouragement of sports and other outdoor activities.

A final government manoeuvre of a slightly different kind in the sphere of unemployment relief related to the old question of introducing a ninth compulsory school year which came up for discussion yet again in 1930/1 following an initiative by the Prussian federal authorities.[67] The reason behind the proposal to raise the school-leaving age to 15 years had nothing to do with positive educational criteria and all to do with the aim of providing short-term relief for the young labour market. It was estimated that in Prussia at Easter 1931 some 150 000 14-year-olds would be involved and a total of 250 000 in the Reich.[68] Funding for the proposal, which formed part of a broader package deal for unemployment, was refused the Prussian government by the Reich[69] and, in any event, provoked formidable opposition from employers anxious to maintain plentiful supplies of cheap labour, and from many working class parents for basically financial considerations.[70] In consequence, a much watered-down scheme, devoid of adequate funding and only voluntary, was introduced in Prussia in February 1931: it was a resounding failure.[71]

At a local and regional level youth welfare authorities could hardly be expected to cope with the implications of unemployment as well as address ordinary *Jugendpflege* activities as their resources dwindled. As early as 1930, officials in the Rhineland and Hesse were complaining loudly about their impossible burden, which only increased in response to the deepening Depression.[27] Even authorities with a generally progressive and resourceful reputation were constantly forced to reduce their provision. In Hamburg, a special committee for unemployed youth (*Arbeitsausschuss zur Fürsorge für jugendliche Erwerbslose*) set up in 1931 was gravely hampered by inadequate funding – the youth welfare budget having been reduced by 10 per cent in 1931/2 – and did not make much of an impact on the problem, much to the disappointment of officials who were especially alert to the moral dangers threatening the unemployed.[73] Despite the problems of youth welfare funding in the Rhineland as a whole, Cologne was probably unique in maintaining its traditional high and expensive standard of service, until plunged into total bankruptcy in 1932.[74] By the second half of that year at the latest, most authorities readily acknowledged that their meagre resources allowed them to reach only a small proportion of youth, including the unemployed.[75] The failure of the Reich Interior Ministry to obtain a larger slice of the government's public funds for youth in winter 1931/2 was a decisive turning-point, marking symbolically at least the virtual end of conventional relief measures for the young unemployed.[76] Unable to ignore the vast scale of *Jugendverwahrlosung*, the state's involvement took on a more negative character which may be said to have been inaugurated on 5 June 1931 when Brüning, prompted also by the *Brauns-Kommission* on unemployment, introduced the voluntary labour service scheme (FAD) as his government's principal initiative on youth unemployment.

FAD cannot be understood as just another relief measure for the unemployed youth of Germany. It was certainly designed to take as many of them as possible off the streets and into honest toil. But more was involved than this. FAD has to be seen in the broader context of Weimar's political struggle if its significance and nature are to be fully appreciated. It was by no means a novel concept because, since the early days of the Republic, the *Freikorps*, the extreme nationalist paramilitary formations of former soldiers, and also a number of predominantly right-wing groups of the middle-class youth movement (*Bündische* Youth), including the *völkisch Artamanen* organisation, had founded labour camps for their members in which a nationalist ideology was propagated.[77] By the early 1930s, interest groups and politicians of the Right, drawing on this tradition, were increasingly vociferous in their demands for the introduction of compulsory labour service not only as a means of fighting unemployment but also as a way of instilling a sense of discipline and patriotism among what was perceived as a rather wayward younger proletariat. It was felt that a spell of good, hard work would rid them of radical ideas and bring them into line with orderly modes of social conduct.[78] Several nationalist groups, among them the *Stahlhelm. Bund der Frontsoldaten*, which had set up their own labour camps with support from the DNVP and NSDAP, grouped under an umbrella association, the *Reichsarbeitsgemeinschaft für Deutsche Arbeitsdienstpflicht (RADA)*, to co-ordinate their campaign.[79] Against this background, the introduction of FAD was something of a sop on the basis of compromise: it was a distortion of the purest *Bündische* concept of labour service as practised by moderate groups such as the *Deutsche Freischar*, and it stopped well short of what the Right had been demanding, which Brüning justifiably rejected as neither politically nor financially expedient. Largely because the Right had been thwarted, both the SPD and ADGB gave their approval to FAD in 1932. On the other hand, the Communists continued to be strongly hostile to the entire concept, denouncing it as yet another trick of capitalist exploitation and fascist indoctrination of the downtrodden proletariat. The slogan adopted by the KJVD amply conveyed the essence of this rejectionist view:[80]

> Heute mit dem Spaten für Graf und Baron,
> Morgen in den Krieg gegen die Sowjetunion.

Without FAD being necessarily an instrument of outright political repression, as has been claimed by some historians,[81] it may be legitimately regarded as a significant step towards the compulsory scheme brought in by the National Socialists in 1935 (*Reichsarbeitsdienstpflicht*). FAD was to a certain degree an embryonic stage in the broader, progressively more intensive efforts by the state to politicise and even militarise working-class youth, in particular, in a rightward direction. There was no overt political pressure exerted on unemployed youth to join FAD, but the poor material situation in which many languished in 1931/2 brought a very real economic pressure to bear. In this way, the 'voluntary' principle of the scheme was undoubtedly undermined.[82] Especially under the more anti-democratic, authoritarian administrations of Chancellors Papen and Schleicher, FAD was used, within limits, to exert a disciplinary, controlling influence over a proletarian youth cut loose from normal processes of socialisation and supervision as a result of their unemployment.[83]

The scheme itself provided short-term (maximum of 20 weeks, later extended by Papen to 40 weeks) manual work of a mainly agricultural type, free board and accommodation in spartan camps for 18–25-year-old male unemployed, in the main. FAD was not really intended for females, though a small number of projects were established for them.[84] Throughout, private, mostly right-wing organisations, were heavily involved alongside the public authorities. In line with the manner in which the scheme developed after mid-1932, a decree issued by Papen on 16 July effectively stripped all statutory and legal safeguards pertaining to working conditions from the 'volunteers'. They were placed outside the legal framework governing pay and other aspects, which rendered them more vulnerable again to disciplinary influence.[85] The camps then became more militaristic in character and organisation as the Right and even the *Reichswehr* intensified their interest in FAD's longer-term potential.[86] As far as relieving unemployment as such, which was its ostensible *raison d' être* in 1931, FAD turned out to be yet another modest enterprise. Some 17 months after its inception, on 30 November 1932, it had only 285 000 enrolled,[87] a mere drop in the ocean of mass youth unemployment which then stood, officially, at 1.45 million and unofficially at twice that number.

For those unemployed youths compelled by economic necessity to apply to join FAD but who were rejected because they had not fulfilled the qualifying criteria for the unemployment benefit schemes, and also to cater for those who had exhausted their entitlement to service in FAD and had returned to the streets, the Schleicher government offered in December 1932 what was in some ways an extension of FAD, the *Notwerk der deutschen Jugend* (Emergency Programme for German Youth).[88] It provided, with the help of limited state funding, vocational training courses in conjunction with various types of youth and welfare bodies, recreational facilities and hot meals. Fulfilling a supervisory function akin to that of FAD, the *Notwerk* organised its modest membership in voluntary *Kamaradschaften*.[89]

The trend towards supervision and political/militaristic manipulation of unemployed working-class youth was most vividly exemplified by the creation of another allied scheme on 13 September 1932 by government. The *Reichskuratorium für Jugendertüchtigung* (National Board for Youth Training) was organised by the Reich Interior Ministry and led by a strict disciplinarian, General Edwin von Stulpnägel. It laid on short courses on a voluntary basis for unemployed aged 18–25 years in paramilitary exercises and games (*Wehrsport*) and small-calibre shooting. The wider framework within which this latest venture was constructed was unmistakably informed by a chauvinistic ideology. The reaction of working-class youth organisations and the radical Left was predictably sour.[90]

The gulf between government's relief measures and the bitter reality of youth unemployment grew more pronounced as resources fell further behind needs and as the political authority of the Republic weakened. Youth, especially the long-term unemployed aged 18–25 years, reacted in a far from uniform manner. A welter of often conflicting and contradictory responses to their material and psychological anguish emerged: despair, desperation, pessimism, hopelessness and frustration could link up with a feeling of bitterness, outrage and resentment against an economic and political system seemingly impotent to help, to produce an explosive mixture of emotions. The whole range of established authority, parents, the older generation, politicians, police, social workers, welfare and reform institutions, became targets for youth's hatred and repudiation. On other occasions and in different situations, however, these emotions could merely lead to a mood of sullen resignation and apathy, a loss of confidence and self-respect; youths would withdraw into themselves, become unstable, be unable to concentrate and allow their personal relationships to suffer. This may have been a futile attempt to shut out reality, but it ultimately produced a feeling of disorientation.[91]

Their profound disillusionment effectively removed many of these youths from the mainstream of Weimar society. They retreated to become pariahs and rebels on the periphery. Such was their widely perceived alienation and demoralisation that they were spoken of as 'a lost generation', destroyed by prolonged unemployment and its ineluctable socio-psychological implications. Highly placed government officials, like Dr Gertrud Bäumer of the Reich Interior Ministry, shared this pessimistic view. She informed a meeting in spring 1932 that 'never has the task of protecting and helping an endangered generation been so pressing as it is today . . . We are in danger of losing an entire generation of youth'.[92]

Of all the manifestations of the younger generation's alarming decline, two aspects were especially disturbing for ordinary contemporaries and authorities alike: the breakdown of morality in the widest sense and the affiliated issue of juvenile crime and delinquency, and the susceptibility of the young to political radicalism. Both were inextricably but neither simplistically nor exclusively connected with mass unemployment in the Depression.

7 Juvenile Crime, Delinquency and Correctional Education, 1918–1933

The conceptual framework within which juvenile criminality was treated by the law was fundamentally altered by the national legislation of 1922/3 (RJWG, JGG). These incorporated defined criteria regarding what was unacceptable in juvenile behaviour, and codes of practice for dealing with transgressors. Inevitably, within the scope of a parliamentary democratic State, the criteria reflected established 'bourgeois' assumptions of good order and conduct but, less pejoratively, they sought to lay a civilised foundation for the development of social relations in the community. Deviance and delinquency were measured against prescribed standards, with which many sections of the working class also readily identified; the lower unskilled and lumpenproletariat could not and did not, and thus became those groups most obviously in perennial conflict with the law. As with other important advances under the auspices of *Sozialpolitik*, however, it remained to be seen how far the humane ideas behind the new progressive legislation would be translated into practice. The stakes were of the highest, for as government and other official spokesmen stressed repeatedly after 1918, German youth had to be protected from moral danger of every description because the future of the Reich lay with them.

Any assessment of juvenile criminality is confronted by a series of problems relating to its exact measurement and significance. Officially recorded crime statistics in the Weimar era did not necessarily reflect the true level of misdemeanour, just as the registered number of unemployed did not represent the real extent of unemployment. It could be the case that increased rates of conviction were attributable not to a larger number of crimes being committed but rather to superior, more efficient detection methods, better co-operation between police and the general public, and more successful prosecutions in the courts. At the juvenile level, it has to be emphasised that a good deal of petty, everyday crime might well have gone unreported to the police and, therefore, there would be no subsequent prosecution and conviction. Parents might be informed by neighbours of their child committing an offence, but the matter would go no further than that. There was inevitably, in consequence, a certain amount of 'hidden' crime by juveniles during this period. Indeed, the highly disturbed conditions in Weimar society may have facilitated this type of crime. Moreover many minor juvenile crimes would doubtless go undetected, but even when they were uncovered and reported a prosecution would not automatically follow because of the inconvenience, expense or embarrassment to parents or the juvenile involved: one expert estimated that only one in every hundred cases of juvenile illegal activity proceeded to full litigation.[1] Crime rates, therefore, are composed of arrests, prosecutions and convictions, which might well not bear relation to the actual volume of criminality. Official crime figures, in any event, were compiled in the Weimar Republic by various organisations, including the police, youth welfare authorities, the Reich Statistical Office, and the German Association for Juvenile Courts, and they tended to reflect the particular area of crime interest of the monitoring agency. This meant in practice that some offences were stressed more than others at different times, which could easily result in distortion of trends because with a changing emphasis the rates of certain offences might be seen to fluctuate wildly when in fact their incidence might have been developing at a steady pace. Conviction rates might simply result from greater awareness on the part of the police or public of certain types of crimes at different times.

Global crime rates are not by themselves necessarily very meaningful, except to intimate general trends, unless they are measured against proportionate demographic developments: a drop in recorded crime statistics might not reflect a decline in criminality among juveniles if the number of juveniles of the same age group fell absolutely and in relation to the population at large as a result of natural influences, such as low birth rates, as happened in the latter years of the Republic. Finally, base crime figures may not be informative of the deeper characteristics of criminality, including the social composition and background of culprits, the ratio of petty to serious crime, and others. The broad figures have to be broken down into their constituent parts if a properly differentiated and detailed picture is to emerge.

A wide consensus developed among criminologists, psychologists and social-educational reformers in the 1920s that the cause of juvenile crime and delinquency was associated with political, social and economic factors, particularly those emanating from periods of profound instability, as occurred in Germany in 1918–23 and 1929–33. The traditional view which accentuated the inherent criminal nature of the offender was decisively repudiated. The new approach and interpretation shaped the RJWG and JGG, which were both principally concerned to deal with the problem of working-class deviance of one kind or another. The frequency as well as the types of offences were henceforth linked to socioeconomic and political phenomena, which encompassed material want, poverty, disturbed family life, absence of adequate educational opportunity and substandard housing and residential environment.[2]

The First World War had created for the first time in German history a serious problem of juvenile criminality in a situation of severe economic hardship and social dislocation, and by 1917 no less than 27 per cent of all convictions for offences were of juveniles (14–18 years of age). The longer the war dragged on the higher the crime rates for all sections of the community, but especially for the younger generation, who were involved on a large scale in offences against property (males) and offences of sexual immorality (females). The end of the fighting brought little respite. Juvenile crime figures remained at a high level throughout the early 1920s as the Republic plunged from one crisis to another. In 1918 the number of juvenile convictions reached 99 498, and continued at a proportionately serious rate until 1923, which saw the culmination of this veritable crime wave, as Table 7.1 makes clear.[3] A high proportion of those convicted had been unemployed at the time of offending, especially in 1923, when Berlin starkly exemplified this relationship.[4] The most common offence by far remained petty theft,[5] but there were also signs of a worrying trend towards new categories of juvenile crime, notably politically-inspired transgression, serious assault and murder, as well as sexual immorality in the shape of male and female prostitution.[6] The ample evidence for rising juvenile crime added further to the reformist contention that the traditional penal prescriptions in dealing with the problem were no longer valid, not least as an effective deterrent, and that an updated legal code which incorporated humane concepts of assessment and treatment was mandatory. The JGG, in particular, was expressive of the liberal approach by underlining the needs of the individual and the desirability of educational-rehabilitative measures in place of outright penal strictures. Juveniles were now recognised as legal subjects in their own right.

Table 7.1 Juvenile crime figures, 1918–23

Year	Total no. juvenile convictions	Delinquency rate per 100 000 of young persons of juvenile court age	Juvenile crimes as percentage of the total no. of crimes
1918	99 498 (84 845)	n.a.	29.2
1919	64 619 (55 447)	803	18.5
1920	91 171 (78 622)	1 137	12.5
1921	76 932 (63 134)	956	9.7
1922	72 124 (61 642)	906	9.5
1923	86 040 (76 280)	1 082	10.7

Note: Figures in brackets indicate number of males.

Although the implementation of JGG after 1924 was accompanied by some reservations from lawyers and youth welfare officials, there was broad agreement that taken as a whole the legislation was an important step forward. This optimism appeared to be vindicated within a remarkably short time as JGG, in conjunction with other factors, such as the relative economic stability of the mid-1920s, the new youth welfare programmes and the greater involvement of youth in sports activities and the organised youth movement, had an immediate and major impact on the recorded juvenile crime rate, if not on the degree of criminality as determined by the ratio of convictions against the size of the juvenile population. None the less, it was generally accepted that for the first time in a decade juvenile delinquency had become a problem of manageable proportions. The decline in the number of convictions owed something directly to the operation of JGG because it limited responsibility and restricted the age of those who could be prosecuted, as well as introducing more flexibility in proceeding with prosecutions and encouraging more use of educational measures instead of punishments. In consequence, the rate of juvenile convictions in 1928 was less than a third of the 1923 figure, as shown in Table 7.2.[7] An overwhelming majority of offenders were 16–18-year-old males; in 1927 only 0.47 per cent and in 1928 0.54 per cent of the 14–18-year-old population of the Reich was convicted of a felony.[8] The overall decrease in conviction rates for juveniles extended throughout the country and even notorious blackspots showed distinct improvement. In Berlin in 1928, for instance, 1 per cent of the 276 000 youths aged 14–18 years were convicted – most of them male, working-class and often from broken homes.

Table 7.2 Juvenile crime figures, 1925–9

Year	Total no. juvenile convictions	Delinquency rate per 100 000 of young persons of juvenile court age	Juvenile crimes as percentage of the total no. of crimes
1925	24 771 (21 018)	469	4.3
1926	24 066 (20 634)	463	4.0
1927	24 119 (20 564)	469	3.9
1928	27 104 n.a.	n.a.	n.a.
1929	25 673 n.a.	n.a.	n.a.

Note: Figures in brackets indicate number of males.

Unskilled manual workers and apprentices were the most numerous offenders, with petty theft the most common crime; only 10.4 per cent were out of work when they offended. Although Berlin's juvenile crime rate was still approximately twice the national average, it had been much higher in previous years.[9]

By 1929 the state could justifiably claim a measure of success in the field of juvenile crime: the problem was responding to the progressive ethos, whose influence was brought to bear in small ways as well. Thus, in a number of federal states at least, instructions were given to the police to interrogate suspected juvenile offenders in a sympathetic manner[10] – a virtually unthinkable occurrence before JGG and RJWG. This record of modestly successful and enlightened development was shattered, however, by the rude impact of the Depression, which paved the way, in turn, for totally different approaches after 1933.

During the early 1930s, the number of juvenile convictions did actually fall from 26 409 in 1930, to 22 844 in 1931 and to 21 539 in 1932; the male component of these figures was, respectively, 22 906, 20 062 and 19 071. Juvenile convictions as a percentage of the total number of convictions in the Reich also showed a drop, from 4.4 in 1930, to 4.0 in 1931 and to 3.8 in 1932.[11] The decline also extended to many of the most heavily populated cities, including Berlin, Leipzig, Essen and Dresden,[12] though Hamburg recorded an increase from 711 convictions in 1930, to 732 in 1931, and to 989 in 1932,[13] as did Cologne, from 420 in 1930 to 485 in 1932.[14] In smaller towns in industrial parts of the country notable decreases were registered: in the coal–mining town of Oberhausen, which was situated in the heart of the Rhenish–Westphalian industrial belt with a population of 195 000, a 33 per cent drop between 1930 and 1933 occurred.[15] In the smaller judicial district of Pössneck a substantial drop was also observed.[16]

These conviction rates seemed to contradict much contemporary opinion which expressed fears of an explosion in juvenile crime against the backdrop of the miseries of the Depression. Indeed so widespread was the public alarm that in an effort to play down the issue the Reich government reached an agreement with the press in August 1930 by which the latter undertook not to report cases of juvenile crime in a sensationalist manner. The Prussian government even established a special committee to facilitate liaison between the press and its Ministry of Welfare in matters of youth care.[17] But the feared scale of juvenile crime did not materialise for a variety of reasons. In the first place, demographic factors, particularly the low birth rates of the war and early postwar years, reduced the size of the 14–18-year-old age group by 1930/1 to the order of 600 000;[18] in Hamburg, to cite a major city as an illustration of this trend, this age group fell in number from 71 719 in 1925 to 35 107 in 1933.[19] A good deal of petty juvenile crime went unreported to the authorities in the general breakdown of normal patterns of social behaviour and response in the Depression. In any case, a hard-pressed police could not devote sufficient time and resources to detection, apprehension and prosecution of these crimes because of their growing involvement in coping with politically-motivated crime and street violence, as well as with a wave of adult crime. Furthermore a considerable amount of youthful energy was directed into the youth organisations and political movements, which served to partially remove the temptation of ordinary crime; these organisations helped to give youth a sense of purpose and discipline and in this way keep them out of trouble. On the other hand, many youngsters, especially the long-term jobless, became apathetic about nearly everything and were uninterested in any form of activity, including crime. The endeavours of youth welfare bodies in 1930/1, when they still commanded some resources, must also have helped divert youth from crime. At the same time, it may be argued that some sections of adult society in general took a more lenient view of youth because of their conspicuous plight in the era of mass unemployment and were as a result more reluctant than usual to see them land in further trouble with the law.

But the conviction rates, encouraging as they were, did not form an accurate measurement of the incidence of crime, which really showed a sharp rise in the early 1930s. Juvenile delinquency, while not attaining the levels of 1918–23 or fulfilling the worst fears of society in the Depression, none the less became once again a major problem[20] – a fact seized upon by the political Right, including the NSDAP, in their campaign for law and order and a 'get tough' attitude towards criminals of all types and ages. The true indication of the extent of juvenile crime is provided by determining the number of convicted youths as a percentage of the total number of youths aged 14–18 years or 18–21 years in the Reich population: applying this method it is revealed that the delinquency rate per 100 000 of 14–18-year-olds was 566 in 1930 but 623 in 1932,[21] an increase of approximately 10 per cent which, in view of the demographic factors already cited, represents a very substantial increase. When the other relevant points relating to non-reporting of petty crime, the strained resources of the police, a more flexible attitude by adults, and so on are further taken into account, it is patently clear that there was a serious crime wave among juveniles at that time.

There was no shortage of explanations adduced to account for the crisis. Emphasis was laid on factors such as alcoholism, the wayward example set by adults, including parents, the need for some youths to show off and commit a crime as an act of bravado, the lure of excitement offered by law-breaking, the revenge motive of a demoralised younger generation, and political instability. The various emergency decrees issued by the Brüning and Papen administrations had also put certain types of behaviour outside the law, while existing laws on public order were tightened and more vigorously enforced.[22] All of these influences undoubtedly had a bearing on the problem. Different influences operated to a different degree according to local or regional conditions. A majority of those professionally active in the field, however, believed that the most important and constant factor behind juvenile crime was mass unemployment and its sociopsychological consequences, even if 14–18-year-olds were not as badly affected by these matters as older groups of German youth. While it was accepted that the connection between unemployment and delinquency was neither as straightforward nor as simplistic as might appear at first sight and, further, that it was impossible to be absolutely precise, this consensus remained firm in the belief that the symbiotic relationship existed. In support of this view an extensive if not wholly conclusive body of interpretative and documentary evi-

Table 7.3 Juvenile criminals and unemployment in German cities, 1930-1

City	No. of unemployed juvenile criminals male and female		Unemployed juveniles as a percentage of the total no. of juvenile criminals (14–18 years)	
	1930	1931	1930	1931
Berlin	417	524	18.1	28.5
Hamburg	254	255	35.7	34.9
Cologne	224	255	53.4	48.3
Duisburg-Hamborn	157	156	41.4	45.5
Düsseldorf	59	119	19.6	57.0

dence from different parts of the Reich was produced. The Reich government, for one, was convinced of the significance of the two interacting phenomena.[23]

Unemployment, especially when long-term, frequently bred in the youth of the urban industrial proletariat a feeling of hopelessness and pessimism which, in association with dire economic want, forced them into criminal or semi-criminal activity. In their estrangement from the mainstream of Weimar society, many of those whose spirit had not been crushed were tempted to vent their frustration and anger against what they perceived with justification as a failed social and economic system.[24] Ehrhardt, in a more discerning analysis, contended that unemployment worked essentially in two ways in respect of juvenile criminality: it created either passivity and occasional outbursts of temper, or it led to a slow inner process of dissolution which ultimately produced what he termed 'a psychic demoralisation', which was instrumental in causing criminal activity.[25] This proclivity was promoted, above all, in a situation where the normal institutions of influence and supervision over youth, such as the family unit and work-place, were themselves victims of the galloping disarray and confusion in society at that particular time. Youth's behaviour was too often destined to be crucially undermined in these circumstances; divested of all important constraints, their vulnerability to law-breaking had rarely been so exposed.

The connection between unemployment and juvenile criminality may be statistically illustrated on the basis of official reports of both a local and national provenance. Table 7.3 relating to several of Germany's largest cities for 1930/1 conveys something of the re-

Table 7.4 Number of convicted juveniles who were unemployed at the time of their offence, 1932–3

City	Male 1932	Male 1933	Female 1932	Female 1933	Total 1932	Total 1933	Percentage 1932	Percentage 1933
Berlin	673	409	80	50	753	459	46.1	41.8
Hamburg	389	220	41	21	430	241	43.5	36.6
Cologne	234	189	21	19	255	208	52.5	58.8
Leipzig	122	37	16	3	138	40	40.7	17.8
Essen	140	76	14	13	154	89	38.8	35.0
Dresden	85	n.a.	3	n.a.	88	n.a.	65.2	n.a.
Breslau	174	118	23	13	194	131	25.4	21.0
Frankfurt/M	n.a.	55	n.a.	n.a.	n.a.	55	n.a.	40.7
Dortmund	124	103	13	11	137	114	50.5	43.5
Düsseldorf	44	n.a.	n.a.	n.a.	44	n.a.	28.1	n.a.
Hanover	69	37	10	8	79	45	29.1	22.6
Duisburg-Hamborn	181	66	9	3	190	69	63.0	44.5
Nuremberg	90	46	8	4	98	50	33.7	27.0
Stuttgart	83	38	8	2	91	40	31.9	20.4
Bochum	26	10	1	n.a.	27	10	49.1	33.3
Magdeburg	31	37	5	5	36	42	24.2	27.1
Mannheim	57	31	9	3	66	34	33.4	17.3
Stettin	19	11	2	1	21	12	13.6	9.8
Kiel	39	23	8	2	47	25	21.5	n.a.
Danzig	34	40	3	7	37	47	25.0	26.7
Halle	63	37	7	1	70	78	30.4	27.3
Total	2 677	1 606	281	173	2 958	1 779	36.6	31.3

lationship.[26] In 1931 the proportion of the unemployed among juvenile offenders was over 30 per cent also in Dresden, Dortmund and Bochum, and the average of the Reich's largest cities in 1930 was 20.3 per cent, but 27.2 per cent the following year. These figures are all the more startling when it is recalled that the corresponding statistics for 1927 were 9.4 per cent and for 1928 11.7 per cent.[27] As youth unemployment increased in the late 1920s and further in the early 1930s, the percentage of unemployed among juvenile criminals rose at an ever accelerating rate, culminating in 1932, when the Reich average reached 36.6 per cent; the largest cities showed the strongest correlation between the two aspects.[28] In towns of a population between 50 and 200 000, 29.2 per cent was recorded for that year, while smaller towns had a slightly reduced percentage.[29] The details for the largest cities in 1932, with the 1933 figures for comparative purposes, are shown in Table 7.4.[30]

The preponderance of working-class youth in these crime statistics was well-recognised and documented by contemporary observers. In Pössneck they constituted over 78 per cent of juvenile criminals on average throughout 1923–35.[31] In Oberhausen the average for 1928–38 was 75 per cent,[32] and even in Munich, which was not a major industrial centre with a large proletariat, the figure in 1932 was 78 per cent.[33] In Hamburg, a large majority of offenders came from the poorest districts of the city: Hammerbrook, St Pauli, Eimsbüttel and the central area around St Georg.[34] Supporting these figures were a number of investigations of convicted youths' family background. Schweizer noted how important the occupation of the father was for the development of the child/youth since it determined his place in society, invariably his type of job and attitude to work as a whole. Of the 320 juvenile delinquents studied by him in Württemberg, Schweizer found that 41 per cent had fathers who were unskilled manual labourers.[35] A similar analysis by Stury of juvenile inmates at the Niederschönfeld detention centre in Bavaria revealed that 74 per cent came from working-class families. He argued that the precariousness of the father's economic and social position created a hostility towards society among his children that subsequently manifested itself in criminal behaviour.[36] But, while there is no denying this proletarian dominance of juvenile crime statistics, it must also be stressed that the conviction rates once again do not present a complete account of the class nature of crime. Working-class youth were more likely to be arrested and prosecuted than their bourgeois counterparts from respectable homes in residential neighbourhoods, where wrong-doing of a comparatively trivial type was unlikely to encourage police intervention. At the same time, however, it was material to the situation that middle-class youth were probably still under the guidance and supervision of the family, school or church authorities, including the period of the Depression, which created an important blocking mechanism to crime.

The male constituent of juvenile delinquency may be more precisely defined. In 1930 and 1931 the largest single group of offenders was unskilled young workers, many of whom were unemployed. In Berlin they made up 51.1 per cent of juvenile offenders in 1930 and 48.8 per cent the following year, while the next most numerous group of lawbreakers, apprentices, were 21.8 per cent and 26.1 per cent, respectively. The cities of Hamburg, Cologne, Leipzig, Essen and Dresden had the same overall pattern at that time, as did most medium- and small-sized towns.[37] Apprentices and unskilled younger workers were undoubtedly the hardest hit among the young by the Depression, so that it is not unexpected that they should occupy a prominent position in the crime figures. In 1932 also they were by a wide margin the largest offending groups in all sizes of towns and cities;[38] in some places apprentices were the larger of the two, as in Munich where they were 42 per cent of the total,[39] and in others unskilled workers were the more conspicuous. Commercial and shop trade apprentices (*Kaufmannslehrling*), bakers' apprentices and craft industry apprentices (*Handwerkslehrling*) were the most frequent offenders.[40] The high profile in crime of apprentices generally may be explained by their extensive unemployment and, for those in work, their very low pay, greater opportunities for petty theft, the bad example set by adult workers and masters, and dissatisfaction with their training, especially if they considered themselves ill-suited to their apprenticeship. As for unskilled labourers, their life-style was often disjointed and without forward planning, which may have linked up with material deprivation to make them prone to small-time criminal activity. The group least affected by asocial conduct was school pupils aged over 14 years of age, almost all of whom were middle-class in the early 1930s. Their superior material situation, stronger family ties and the presence of supervisory agencies combined to give them more personal stability, contentment and aspirations for the future. In Oberhausen in 1932, for example, a mere 5 per cent of this group were among the juvenile criminals, which was approximately the average for the rest of the Reich.[41]

While male outnumbered female juvenile offenders in 1930–33 by a ratio of 7:1,[42] the 16–18-year-old group accounted for 67–69 per cent of juvenile crimes during that period, 15–16 year olds almost 24 per cent and the remainder were perpetrated by the youngest criminally responsible group.[43] In 1932, 22.7 per cent of convicted offenders were aged 14–15 years and 77.3 per cent aged 16–18 years.[44] A significant number of juvenile offenders came from broken homes. The absence of a father was often crucial, though divorce or separation of parents, illegitimacy, orphaning and other disruptive influences were also much in evidence. In Oberhausen in 1928, 18.6 per cent came from a broken home but the Depression made matters a lot worse, resulting in corresponding figures for 1930 of 20.7 per cent and for 1932 of 29.8 per cent.[45] In Schweizer's Württemberg sample, 60 per cent of male juvenile offenders and 72.2 per cent of female offenders came from an unsettled family background,[46] while in Hamburg the figures for male and female offenders combined were

39.5 per cent in 1930 and 32.5 per cent two years later; within these statistics for Hamburg, 10.5 per cent in 1930 and 10.2 per cent in 1932 were offenders who were illegitimate.[47] In Pössneck the average figure for juvenile offenders from broken homes in the early 1930s was 27.9 per cent.[48] The Reich average in the largest cities in 1932 was 23.8 per cent, whereas for medium-sized towns it was 30.3 per cent.[49] Accordingly, an unambiguous profile (including social background, class and occupation, age and gender) of juvenile offenders, particularly during the Depression, emerged.

The incidence of all types of juvenile crime grew during the Depression, but petty theft still remained the most common offence by far and was related, of course, to economic hardship. Theft of small sums of money was particularly widespread. One expert claimed that errant youth saw money 'as a kind of panacea [*Wundermittel*] with which to satisfy his numerous desires and dreams'.[50] Juvenile crimes were frequently associated with particular occupations: commercial apprentices falsified accounts and peculated, locksmith apprentices went in for burglary, messenger boys for pilfering and apprentice mechanics for car theft. Crimes of violence and aggression were often committed by youths whose work involved considerable physical strength, butchers, for instance, while waiters were linked to moral transgressions.[51] There was a disturbing trend in serious juvenile crime after 1930, involving a total of eight murders, 10 cases of manslaughter and 200 rapes in 1932 compared with five, four and 141, respectively, the previous year.[52] The bulk of this crime was the responsibility of unemployed, unskilled young workers and juveniles from broken homes.[53]

Equally perturbing was accumulating evidence that the new prescription of '*Erziehung statt Strafe*' was meeting in practice with patchy success, with distinct regional variation. The *Jugendgerichtshilfe*, which RJWG had put under the supervision of local youth welfare offices, often submitted reports on the juvenile accused to the courts in order to allow the judge the widest possible information on which to give a verdict. The practice developed in many parts of the Reich where the advice of the auxiliary body was quite influential, and in general that advice was to impose educational measures, or at least a combination of educational and punitive measures.[54] The educational means at the discretion of the courts included cautioning, which was often used, probation, which was also common and frequently employed together with a caution or a suspended prison sentence. The latter was in substantial use because it was widely believed that it combined the best of both educational and punitive measures: the threat of prison, even if for only a maximum of three months, which was the standard time, was employed in a sense to scare offenders into good conduct. Fines were not favoured by many authorities because they appreciated the probable inability of convicted juveniles to pay, in the circumstances of the Depression in particular.

Between 10 and 12 per cent of convicted juveniles in the Reich during 1924–33 received probation. Referral to *Fürsorgeerziehung* (FE), another educational measure, at least in concept, was applied in only the most serious cases because it was clearly more drastic than the other measures; only 4.7 per cent of convicted juveniles nationwide were referred in 1925 and a mere 3 per cent in 1932.[55] In Oberhausen on average during 1928–33, 41.2 per cent of convicted juveniles were given educational measures,[56] a pattern repeated in enlightened Hamburg, at least until 1932 when a trend in sentencing back towards punishment in reaction to the rising juvenile crime rate became apparent.[57] In conservative Bavaria, where the progressive ethos was not welcomed, some 55 per cent of convicted 14–18-year-olds in 1932 were jailed and a large number of the remainder fined.[58] In the Reich as a whole in 1924–33, about 50 per cent of juveniles convicted were sent to prison, but in 1932 the figure had risen to 57.4 per cent.[59] Reformist circles could not have been pleased either with increasing rates of recidivism among juveniles, which inevitably impugned the validity of the educational approach: the rate went up from 11.6 per cent in 1929 to 11.9 in 1930, 12.1 in 1931, and 14.1 in 1932.[60] Evidence of this kind was grist to the mill of the political Right in their campaign for more emphasis on old-fashioned discipline.[61] But the real tragedy of rising juvenile criminality after 1930 was that more and more offenders could no longer recognise that they had broken the law; their moral and ethical values had been so corrupted by prolonged unemployment and want that they simply failed to distinguish between what was right and what was wrong.[62]

This distressing dimension of juvenile criminality was manifested in many of the street gangs which re-emerged in some force during the Depression in Berlin and other major cities. These so-called '*Wilde Cliquen*' adopted a comprehensively anti-authoritarian, independent and anti-social outlook, and recruited overwhelmingly from déclassé, unemployed and unskilled male proletarian youth aged 16–25 years. Many were from broken homes and had become part of the army of homeless vagrants in the cities; a large number were also either former inmates of or fugitives from the correctional education system. Cast adrift from conventional society, these youths were doubtless searching for some kind of purpose and identity, comradeship and self-respect, as a means of surviving the chaos around them in the poverty-stricken working-class ghettos of Berlin, Hamburg and other cities, which were their strongholds.[63] But a contemporary sympathiser who stressed that gang members were bound by 'a romantic yearning for friendship' misrepresented the character of this milieu.[64]

The genesis of the gangs may be traced back to winter 1916/17 when some sections of undernourished proletarian youths arose in protest in Berlin against their harsh economic conditions and soon formed themselves into irregular, poorly disciplined variants of the bourgeois *Wandervogel*, which they bitterly derided.[65] None the less they adopted and adapted several of the *Wandervogel*'s principal activities, such as hiking, and took to wearing colourful, if not rather outrageous, outfits, which were partly designed to shock and repel despised middle-class society. From the earliest days, the gangs developed an exaggerated form of aggressive masculinity and were shrouded in an ambience of violence and promiscuous sexuality. For these reasons they attracted more than their fair share of drop-outs, thugs and hooligans whose existence cannot be wholly explained by adverse social and economic conditions: they constituted the perennial underclass of the urban proletariat. Enjoying only an intermittent development in the mid-1920s, the gangs came into public view in 1928/9 following a number of celebrated court cases involving some of their leaders.

The Depression gave the gangs a new lease of life, and reports began to circulate of entire neighbourhoods in Berlin being terrorised by the likes of the *Modderkrebs* (Rotten Cancers), *Tartarenblut* (Blood of the Tartars), *Eierschlamm* (Slimy Balls) and others with similarly offensive names; the best-known and most widely feared was the *Dreckstiebel* (Dirty Boots), whose favourite haunts were the depressed districts of Neukölln, Kreuzberg and Wedding.[66] Around 600 gangs with a total membership of perhaps 15 000 and each led by a *Cliquenbulle* roamed the streets of the capital.[67] Although only a minority were actively criminal, a larger proportion of the gangs walked a narrow tightrope between the law and petty crime. Their vandalism, penchant for petty theft and generally rowdy behaviour were invariably visited upon fellow unfortunates among Berlin's indigent working class, but caused scandal among a wider public. Crime may have been for some of the gangs a means of venting their frustration and demonstrating their hostility towards society, but this cannot excuse the degree of unadulterated viciousness and hooliganism that also lay behind their conduct. In 1932 the gangs were implicated in some of the most serious and reprehensible juvenile offences.[68] Lacking a sense of class solidarity and behaving as a law unto themselves, some of them espoused a nebulous anti-Fascism and maintained loose links with the KPD and its youth organisations which, in style and social composition, shared common ground. The Communist movement took up the gangs' cause and sought to recruit from their ranks,[69] thus confirming in the eyes of the political Right that they were symptoms of a hopelessly wayward proletarian youth that needed to be brought to heel,[70] in line with developing authoritarian trends in FAD, the *Notwerk der deutschen Jugend* and other government initiatives in the youth sphere in 1932. From a more understanding perspective, it may be said that the gangs, despite their considerable unsavoury elements, were ultimately products of material and moral deprivation, particularly in 1929–33. They were yet one more disturbing and dramatic manifestation of the extent of demoralisation among unemployed lower working-class youth who had been pushed into a posture of rebellion against a bankrupt society and political system.

The most intractable cases of juvenile delinquents could be referred to the correctional education system (FE), whose purpose, as laid down in the RJWG, was 'the prevention or elimination of waywardness.' Referral to FE was regarded as a last resort when all other educational measures had failed to produce positive results, and was invoked when it was felt by the appropriate authorities that there was serious but not irreversible delinquency whose educational rehabilitation had a reasonable chance of success. FE was the means by which the state, in its protective capacity as intimated in the Weimar Constitution, sought to make good the perceived deficiencies in the socialisation process of youth that conventionally involved family, parents, school and other agencies, through reformist educational methods. These deficiencies were identified following the enunciation of legal and pedagogical definitions of *Jugendverwahrlosung*.[71] Repudiating the genetic factor in the calculation of delinquency, which traditionalists emphasised, the progressive pedagogy was based on the essential assumption that there was good in everyone, including serious criminal offenders, and that everyone was able to be positively influenced by 'correct' educational practices within a properly constructed social and economic environment. The essence of the liberal ethos was to civilise, to bring wayward youth back into respectable society as reliable, constructive and clean-living members.[72] In this way it might be argued that FE was devised to impose conformity with established bourgeois concepts of law and order, good behaviour and a decent life-style, but in fact these were attitudes which were supported by broad sections of the secure working classes as well. At the same time, against the background of mounting public concern about youth's waywardness in Weimar society,[73] FE could be seen in a less flattering light as more of a means for controlling and disciplining certain elements of working-class youth. Herein lay the seeds of the acrimonious controversy which dogged the development of FE for much of the Weimar period.

Borrowing heavily from Prussian practice, the RJWG defined the circumstances in which referral to institutional care could take place, and extended the scope of FE, including the raising of the age limit for referral from 18 to 20 years, though the former was the usual cut-off point. It could be applied from the earliest age, though in general practice most of those referred were at least 14 years of age. Offences such as street-begging, vagrancy, immorality and criminal offences could all warrant the invocation of FE, which could be of indefinite duration up to the age of 21 years: on attaining that age, a youth had to be released into the community. Referred youth could either be sent to a reformatory (*Fürsorgeerziehungsanstalt*) or placed in the care of a suitable family, depending on his/her needs and broader circumstances. Families selected to care for these youths were those who 'could guarantee good, moral and religious education and satisfactory welfare provision. The families must enjoy a sound reputation, and be free of infectious diseases'.[74] Supervision was co-ordinated through the local *Jugendamt*. During the 1920s about 52 per cent of referrals on average were found a place with a family and in the early 1930s, in the face of severe expenditure cuts in reformatories, that figure increased to 55 per cent.

The clientele of FE was mostly male and drawn from the unskilled and poorly educated industrial working class from the major cities,[75] the group already identified as being heavily implicated in juvenile crime and the street gangs. A substantial majority came from broken or irregular family backgrounds. In one authoritative survey it was discovered that only 21 per cent of FE inmates (*FE-Zöglinge*) had enjoyed a stable family relationship.[76] A relatively large minority were mentally below average. At the *Staatserziehungsanstalt* Wasserburg in Bavaria in 1919–21 an overwhelming majority of the approximately 55–60 inmates were found to be psychiatrically subnormal. An investigation of 550 FE inmates (male and female) in Thuringian reformatories in 1922 revealed that 84, or 14.2 per cent, were subnormal in this respect, while another 14 had serious difficulties.[77] For a majority of these youths throughout the Reich, the conceptual and operational basis of institutional care had little meaning, and the chasm progressively widened; for them, FE was just another alien imposition by a hated state apparatus, which in their view was shaped to oppress the working class. The *Hamburger Volkszeitung* expressed a widely held opinion when it denounced FE's 'reactionary–military educational methods, including beatings of inmates, who are proletarian victims of a middle-class coercive education [*Zwangserziehung*]'.[78]

The poor public image of FE in the early postwar years, of which its officials were acutely aware, was a legacy of the Wilhelmine period, and its reform was acknowledged by most interested observers to be urgent,[79] particularly as juvenile crime soared in the early 1920s: the system was wilting under the strain.[80] The reformist path had already been pioneered by the likes of Karl Wilker's Lindenhof reformatory in Berlin from 1917–20.[81] He endeavoured to break down the tense structures of authoritarian supervision by creating a more informal relationship between staff and youths, devising more interesting work schedules and, above all, by abolishing corporal punishment (*körperliche Züchtigung*), which was the one feature perceived by the public to epitomise the worst side of FE (*Prügelerziehung*).[82] Inevitably, the Lindenhof experiment aroused the profound distrust of conservatives, who were tenacious in their adherence, even after the promulgation of RJWG and JGG, to the traditional, Christian-based ethos of authoritarian control in many of the reformatories; here punishment and methods designed to strengthen moral character were administered within the framework of a harsh discipline (*Disziplinpädagogik*).

From the mid-1920s the numbers of convicted juveniles referred to FE declined in response to the more flexible criteria introduced by the national legislation of 1922/3, and also to the downward trend in juvenile criminality. This decline continued into the Depression years when, more importantly, demographic movements making for a smaller 14–18-year-old segment of the population, and cuts in public funding which resulted in authorities being less willing than before to commit youths to institutional care, were influential. In the Reich, the numbers of FE inmates fell from 97 561 in March 1928 to 77 846 in March 1932; the male component therein went down from 54 416 to 44 689 and the female from 41 155 to 34 757.[83] In Prussia, a postwar high war reached in 1925 with 64 384 inmates; thereafter the numbers declined to 54 081 in 1929, to 44 663 in 1931, and finally to 34 084 in 1932, a fall during that period of 44 per cent. The male segment in Prussia was 58.5 per cent in 1925 and 56.1 per cent in 1932.[84]

Despite these encouraging trends, which might at first sight have suggested that the progressive ethos had been successfully applied,[85] the sad truth was that the new pedagogy was largely confined to the small minority of reformatories administered by the state and hardly penetrated the remainder which were run by the conservative-minded churches, Catholic and Protestant, and some private bodies. Of 776 reformatories in 1926, only 97 were state-controlled, while the Protestant churches had 420 and the Catholic 240.[86] In Bavaria and the provinces east of the Elbe the conservative ideology and practices remained intact. Committed liberal reformers in youth welfare, such as Dr Wilhelm Hertz of Hamburg and Dr Hartmann in Hanover, privately expressed their despair at an early date.[87] Several institutions, including, most notably, *Landeserziehungsanstalt* Bräunsdorf in Saxony under Rudolf Schlosser from 1928, and the *Fürsorgeerziehungsheim* Egendorf in Thuringia led by Walter Herrmann after 1924, earned a reputation for liberal thinking, though their practical achievements were somewhat limited.[88] The intransigence of conservative ideology lay at the root of the serious crisis in FE at the end of the 1920s,[89] for it spawned a series of damaging interrelated conditions.

Relative underfunding of FE in the 1920s produced poor material conditions in the reformatories, outdated facilities, and an inadequately trained and equipped staff, whose remuneration was also very low.[90] Too frequently, staff exhibited an unsympathetic attitude towards their young charges who were subjected in most reformatories outside direct state control to harsh working conditions[91] and authoritarian, even brutal discipline, which could easily degenerate into excessive corporal punishment. Although the apprenticeship scheme in the reformatories experienced problems with established trades interests on the outside,[92] within the reformatories themselves the training could simply become a squalid means of exploiting young labour.[93] The related question of inmates' pay or pocket money for work undertaken became a serious bone of contention, particularly as working-class families invariably needed every source of revenue available to maintain an adequate standard of living: the non-payment or confiscation of pay, a frequent occurrence, could only have further embittered the relationship between staff and inmates and their families.[94] Although as early as April 1926 the Prussian government decreed that corporal punishment was to be administered in reformatories only in exceptional circumstances and as a last resort – this was repeated in January 1929 – and in July 1929 ordered its cessation for all female inmates and certain categories of males,[95] most institutions took no notice and retained corporal punishment as a central feature of their administration.[96] Only in state-run reformatories and those under the control of enlightened authorities, as in Hamburg, was there evidence of more humane methods of supervision being employed on a large scale.[97] Above all, the intrinsic failure of the FE system lay in its longer-term effect on inmates because a comparatively large percentage of them returned to the system more than once as a result of committing further offences on release, while many more joined up with criminalised street gangs.[98] It is not surprising that the exposé of conditions in the reformatories by a former staff member at the Struveshof institution near Berlin, Peter Martin Lampel, in 1929, caused a public uproar.[99] The barbarism of the system which he described in vivid detail was seen by many as a crushing indictment of the *Sozialpolitik* ethos in practice. Widely publicised revolts by inmates, particularly those at the reformatories in Scheuen, Ricklingen and Rastenburg, East Prussia, which had a notorious reputation for inhuman discipline, served to fuel the growing controversy, while court cases of corrupt FE officials from reformatories in the early 1930s meant that the scandal retained a high profile among press and public alike.[100] Almost every day there seemed to be a sensational incident: a daring escape, of which there were plenty, or another suicide of an inmate.[101]

The progressive lobby and its allies on the Left acknowledged the crisis and sought to redress the situation. But the middle-class *Arbeitskreis zur Reform der Fürsorgeerziehung*, which was set up with some optimism,[102] made little headway in a political atmosphere increasingly inimical to liberalism in any guise. The SPD and its major welfare organisation, the *Arbeiterwohlfahrt*, demanded a complete overhaul of the FE system, including its incorporation into a wholly public-administered network, but even its strong base in Prussia did not allow the party to bring about change.[103] The most vehement critic of FE among the political parties, however, was the

KPD, which regarded the inmates as kindred spirits – victims of a rapacious capitalist order.[104] Despite party political activity being expressly forbidden to inmates and staff in the reformatories, Communist propaganda reached far into the system and the KPD was frequently held responsible for fomenting disorder and riots.[105] The party helped sponsor the *Reichsverband für dissidentische Fürsorge*, but like other pressure groups in this sphere it achieved nothing but a degree of publicity.[106] The most meaningful response on paper from government came in June 1931 when the Prussian Ministry of Welfare issued new guidelines on the administration and inspection of reformatories,[107] but the repeated demands made in 1931/2 by both the Prussian and Reich authorities for further cuts and economies in public expenditure – often with particular emphasis on FE – made it impossible for any reforms to be satisfactorily implemented.[108] In any case, there have to be serious doubts about the good intentions of government at that time as it was moving more and more towards a policy not of ameliorative reform in youth care but rather control and disciplined supervision. It is no coincidence that in early 1931 the Prussian government, while ostensibly preoccupied with the issue of FE reform, saw fit to issue instructions that discipline was to be tightened in reformatories.[109] The priorities had not changed at all, it seemed.

On the eve of the Depression, the FE reformatory system had few, if any defenders. It had lost the confidence of just about every interested body: inmates, their families, staff, youth welfare officials, the political Left, a substantial part of public opinion, and even many progressive educationalists. Anger and despair were present in equally voluminous measure. The system no longer offered anything that was positive, neither care, welfare nor effective remedial treatment. All that remained was an arid regime of punishment and control. In these pessimistic conditions, which were exacerbated by further policies of retrenchment in public expenditure, right-wing opinions were strengthened, thus plunging FE into deeper crisis.

As the liberal ethos of Weimar's *Sozialpolitik* floundered on all fronts after 1931, the sternly authoritarian imperatives that were being brought increasingly to bear in the youth sphere as a whole included, specifically for FE, elements of racist–biological thought. Under pressure from the Right, together with the implications of the government's financial problems, the crisis in FE crystallised in 1932 around the question of the so-called 'incorrigibles', that minority of inmates deemed to be beyond the scope of educational rehabilitation because of their severe mental or psychic retardation.[110] A considerable debate opened up about how best to treat these ineducable delinquents, with right-wing opinion demanding the application of strict criteria and solutions to the problem. The concept of ineducability (*Unerziehbarkeit*) was naturally anathema to the progressive lobby and the radical Left, but they proved ineffective in impeding the right-wing advance, especially in the Papen era.[111]

Awareness of the link between the constant need for economies and the question of excluding from FE those judged to be ineducable had become apparent in government thinking as early as autumn 1931. The Reich Interior Ministry and the Prussian Ministry of Welfare both produced drafts on future FE development in September of that year which substantially influenced Papen's notorious decrees of November 1932.[112] Heavy emphasis was laid on the difficulties of dealing with 18–20-year-olds in FE; they resented being tied down to house rules and regarded their stay in institutional care as a prison sentence. In consequence, they were susceptible to radical political influence and were at the forefront of disorders and riots; their attitudes and conduct disrupted the educational process for everyone in care, especially younger inmates. Thus their removal from FE would allow the educational programme to proceed more smoothly, and simultaneously save costs. These recommendations were met with horror by liberals and the Left,[113] but this did nothing to prevent them being adopted by Papen.

The concept of ineducability informed the basis of the decree of 4 November 1932,[114] which constituted the most decisive repudiation of the progressive ethos in Weimar's sphere of youth care. The selective principles now introduced were essentially conditioned by financial expediency, but they were also linked to some extent to crude social darwinist theories of racism and racial hygiene, thus foreshadowing the criteria that came to dominate the development of FE under the National Socialists. Under Papen's decree, the ineducables were to be prematurely released into the community from the reformatories, and FE provision as a whole was to end on attainment of the nineteenth year. Moreover the rules governing referral were altered to allow fewer delinquents to be sent to FE. A supplementary decree of 28 November allowed the authorities to postpone the release of over-aged and ineducable inmates until March 1933[115] and, in practice, the numbers excluded from the system were very small. A certain number of reformatories became redundant and were closed.[116]

Papen's legislation superficially appeared to be incompatible with simultaneous attempts by the state through FAD, the *Notwerk der deutschen Jugend* and other initiatives to exercise more control over working-class youth, particularly those who were unemployed and seen as a threat to good order. Why would the state deliberately release this type of youth from its direct sphere of influence? The answer seems to be that, while the authoritarian Papen regime was giving up with the ineducables, it was in a vague sense consigning them to a racially inferior status which subsequent National Socialist practice made explicit.[117] In other words, the decree of 4 November might be seen as actually the first step towards a more radical supervision of working-class youth that was based not on any recognisable pedagogical criteria but rather on the distorted notions of racial hegemony.[118] The atrocities of euthanasia, murder of the mentally defective, gypsies and other marginal groups conceivably had their legislative genesis in this decree.[119]

From an immediate socio-political perspective, this final crisis of FE provided conclusive proof, if any more was required by late 1932, that a substantial section of the unskilled, unemployed and criminal younger industrial proletariat was irrevocably alienated from the Weimar Republic and the entire system of parliamentary democracy. For them, FE was just one more failure in a discredited spectrum which included the police, courts, welfare office and politicians: all of these were dismissed as brothers-in-arms of an anti-working class animus in the state apparatus. The comprehensive disillusionment of the principal losers, these younger proletarians, had to find some form of political expression.

8 Conclusion: The Political Dimension

In their relentless campaign to destroy the Weimar Republic the antidemocratic, totalitarian movements of National Socialism and Communism both successfully styled themselves as 'parties of youth'. They appealed in their different ways to a sense of heroic idealism, militancy, excitement and novelty as well as to German youth's longing for a feeling of belonging and purpose behind a cause; they both aggressively sought to act out the much discussed, dramatic theme of a 'mission of youth' (*Sendung der jungen Generation*), which had resurfaced in vigorous form at the beginning of the Depression.[1] Chauvinistic nationalism on the one side, and proletarian internationalism on the other, supplied the often irrational commitment of the young to the NSDAP and KPD. The National Socialist slogan, '*Nationalsozialismus ist organisierter Jugendwille*' (National Socialism represents the organised will of youth), and Gregor Strasser's strident appeal for the gerontocracy of Weimar politics to step aside,[2] struck a deep responsive chord in a younger generation – or at least its middle-class component – which by 1932 had displayed a comprehensive disenchantment not only with the Republic's social and political system but also with the entire concept of parliamentary democracy. The KPD also ruthlessly exploited the reality of generational conflict among the younger proletariat to its considerable political advantage.[3] The failure of the German State Party, which was established with important backing from Artur Mahraum's *Jungdeutsche Orden* in 1930, was a stark warning of youth's lack of belief in democratic politics at that early date of Weimar's final crisis. The paramilitary formations of the NSDAP and KPD, in particular, quickly exerted a powerful attraction for the young in respect of their demands for discipline, self-sacrifice and comradeship in the struggle against the ubiquitous enemy.[4]

Middle- and working-class youth had displayed signs of dissatisfaction with the Republic in varying degrees even before the Depression descended. Bourgeois youth had, like adults of this class, generally failed to come to terms with the parliamentary system of government, Germany's diminished international status and the advance of the Left, and had identified strongly with right-wing values and organisations from the early 1920s as a matter of natural choice. The experience of the Depression served to fortify their rejectionist stance towards the Republic and then to accentuate their predilection for radical right-wing politics. Their support in 1930–2 for the NSDAP in terms of their large-scale membership of the party and its ancillary organisations and electoral backing was crucial to Hitler's success.[5] The younger bourgeoisie's adherence to the National Socialist cause in the early 1930s, and beyond, was thus the product of a longer-term development which simply culminated in the radicalised context of the Depression. The sharp rightward turn of *Bündische* Youth after 1930 was symptomatic of a broader movement of vehement protest among middle-class youth.[6]

The younger working class had rather less reason to be unsettled by the Republic's performance by 1929. The enhanced profile of the working class in politics, the guarantees and protection for labour embodied in the Weimar Constitution, and the undeniable achievements of *Sozialpolitik* had laid the foundations for a meaningful relationship. A notable minority of the working class, it is true, had never felt this was enough and looked for the type of radical socialist policies which only the KPD could furnish, and that party's modest but remarkably constant electoral constituency in 1924–30 was clear evidence that the Republic enjoyed considerably less than unanimous support from the proletariat.[7] As the 1920s unfolded, the SPD's followers became defined as mainly the employed skilled and semi-skilled industrial workers, while the KPD drew its backers from the unskilled, irregular and unemployed workers of the cities and larger towns: the SPD was the 'respectable' and the KPD the 'rough' end of the proletarian spectrum. By 1929 the development of the position of the young working class had revealed certain limitations. Alongside the material and legal benefits conferred by the RJWG and JGG, which in any case were subject to marked regional diversity in their implementation, young workers were more vulnerable than most other groups to unemployment in times of upheaval and recession, while the relief measures devised by the state were well-intentioned but not wholly efficacious. Moreover protective legislation at the work-place for the young was hardly extended in the 1920s, the unemployment benefit system discriminated against them in respect of qualifying criteria, level of benefit payable and of the imposition of compulsory labour (*Pflichtarbeit*), working conditions generally still involved long hours, low pay and few statutory holidays, apprentices often continued to suffer abusive treatment from masters, the prog-

Conclusion: The Political Dimension

rammes for vocational training and career guidance were fairly rudimentary, and the FE system was in practice severe and unenlightened. Yet, clearly, imperfections could not all be eradicated overnight, and it could be argued that the Republic had actually done rather well in view of its prodigious difficulties in 1918–23. The lot of the younger working class undoubtedly needed to be improved, but from the perspective of the immediate pre-Depression period there appeared to be no obvious reason why, despite certain disappointing features, the situation could not develop beneficially in the longer term, given normality. The Depression, however, and in particular, the experience of mass unemployment and its multifarious socio-psychological implications, abruptly and decisively terminated that optimism for the future, and brought the younger proletariat face to face with political reality in a way that was hardly conceivable only a short time previously. In other words, it cannot be affirmed that the mass of these young people possessed an inherent affinity with political radicalism throughout the 1920s which merely came to a head after 1929/30; only a small minority of them had been attracted to Communism or anarcho-syndicalism prior to the Depression. What they were subjected to thereafter, and which was material to their progressive alienation from the democratic Republic, was the fundamental undermining of the basic humanitarianism which had informed the state's approach to youth welfare provision and its replacement by initiatives designed to supervise and discipline them within a continuing authoritarian ethos.

It is a well-established fact of Weimar's electoral sociology that after 1930 the unemployed masses did not vote in significant numbers for the NSDAP, while the unemployed industrial working class of the major towns and cities gave substantial support to the KPD. In 1932 the NSDAP polled below their national average vote in areas where there was a higher than average rate of unemployment, and especially in large cities and heavily industrialised districts. Conversely, the party's principal sources of support lay in those parts of the Reich where unemployment was not such a serious problem. There was, therefore, a negative statistical correlation between the NSDAP's electoral success and levels of unemployment. It performed well in Protestant small-town and rural/agrarian areas where unemployment was below national average levels. The NSDAP received some backing from the relatively small numbers of white-collar unemployed, but this must be considered very marginal to its growth as the major German political movement. Indeed, in global terms, the party benefited appreciably only in an indirect way from unemployment in that it gained support from the fear induced by the threat rather than the reality of unemployment among those from a conservative, right-wing political background who had lost confidence in the likes of the DNVP.[8] In contrast, the KPD made a strenuous effort to attract the poorest, most deprived and unemployed groups of the urban working class, adult and young, and emerged the major beneficiary of the largely proletarian mass unemployment of the Depression era.[9]

Unemployment and its consequent material deprivation on a massive scale brought about the decisive alienation of the younger proletariat from the Republic. Their rude treatment in the various unemployment benefit schemes and the virtual collapse of the welfare system by 1932 left many of them marginalised and destitute. Vagabondage, increased suicide rates, falling health standards, malnutrition and much reduced educational opportunities were added to the catalogue of perverse social ills to which they were subjected. Out of work, they were estranged from the influence and point of reference provided by the factory work-place, as well as from other normal supportive agencies, including very often the family unit, and thus drifted out of the supervisory reach of just about everyone and everything. This became a generation in revolt against all forms of established authority: adults, police, courts, welfare officials and the FE system. Some expressed their hostility through engagement in crime, whose incidence rose after 1930, and through membership of a rowdy or criminalised street gang. Others, despite being equally upset, were no doubt caught up in the Marienthal syndrome whereby prolonged unemployment and material want produced a mood of apathy and resignation.[10] But even in these cases the disillusionment with the political system which had failed to prevent or to alleviate their misfortune must have been extensive. The inability of the SPD and trade unions to offer constructive help to them added to the sense of betrayal and rejection felt by young workers. In any event, the SPD had never captured the imagination of proletarian youth and as the 'party of state' was most directly compromised by the Republic's failures. The party tolerated Brüning's deflationary measures and failed to defend the welfare system it had been primarily responsible for constructing in the first place. Where the young did not actually desert the SPD, they remained within the socialist fold out of a sense of habitual loyalty rather than conviction. Their trust in the SPD was badly shaken and by 1932 widespread pessimism and hopelessness enveloped their ranks.[11] For their part, the trade unions had traditionally placed the highest priority on protecting the interests of their adult members, and in the Depression were less likely than before to pay serious attention to the plight of working-class youth. In turn, unemployed youth were not in a position to be influenced ideologically or politically by either the SPD or trade unions; their education in socialism grossly deficient, they were, therefore, wide open to more radical influence.

The significant support given to the KPD before 1933 by unemployed proletarian youth in the cities was prompted less by genuine ideological commitment than by the stark reality that this party was identified as the main vehicle of youthful, working-class protest against society and the whole Weimar 'system'. That their support was intrinsically non-ideological is surely confirmed by their obvious lack of schooling in Marxism at any level, apart from the few who may have been taught at home, and by the extraordinary turnover in membership of the KPD and KJVD in the early 1930s. As Conan Fischer has rightly observed, 'new recruits were not convinced Communists, and were about as ready to leave the party as they were to join'.[12] Their adherence was not to a sacred cause to which they were fundamentally and intellectually devoted. Instead, an intensely aggressive emotional rather than ideological radicalism compelled the direction of their political allegiance – a radicalism born of the profound deterioration in the material, spiritual and socio-psychological well-being of proletarian youth in the Depression. Moreover, even if there was only a slight movement in voters between the KPD and NSDAP, the ease with which some working-class youth, especially in the larger cities in 1932, were able to change sides hardly suggests a principled commitment of any type. In this process of drift from one side to the other, the NSDAP came off best, and continued to do so more obviously after 1933.

The political involvement of the younger, invariably unemployed working class of urban, industrial Germany in 1930–2 is best understood as that of the fundamentally disillusioned, despairing and angry, who were seeking the most effective means of demonstrating their repudiation of the Republic's failed economic and social system. It was a revolt motivated by the material and socio-psychological poverty occasioned by unemployment and not by the dictates of political ideology. These youths were ideologically and politically unattached. Lacking a considered commitment to either Communism or to National Socialism, they were simply against the grotesque catastrophe that was the parliamentary democracy of the Weimar

Republic in 1931/2. Alienated, disoriented, they were attracted by the politics of activism, violence and neo-authoritarianism. For them, politics had nothing to do with debate and reasoned argument and everything to do with the imperatives of the strong. Matters would be resolved by force and force alone. Deprived of the normal processes of socialisation – many of them from childhood – these youths saw nothing untoward in the brutality of radical, all-or-nothing political engagement. Their acceptance of the KPD/NSDAP alternatives was another manifestation of a society whose values and perspectives had been deracinated and distorted by permanent crisis.

Against this scenario of extraordinary instability, which reached a climax in 1932, the younger proletariat, particularly the unemployed, were bound, in view of their shattered material situation and ideologically non-committed radical temper, to be susceptible to the sophisticated blandishments of the ultimate winners of Weimar's political power game, the NSDAP. It cannot be credibly maintained that, in Daniel Horn's words, 'it stands to reason that working-class boys should not identify with National Socialism' after 1933.[13] After all, the NSDAP did attract a sizable working-class constituency by 1932, as did the Storm troopers (SA) and Hitler Youth, two of its leading ancillary organisations,[14] thus making it more of a genuine *Volkspartei* than a mere bourgeois *Sammlungsbewegung*. The workers who followed Hitler were certainly atypical in that they represented a motley association of formerly middle-class people who had fallen in occupation and status, nationalist workers who used to vote for the DNVP, domestic and non-unionised workers who were not severely affected by the Depression and others from an agrarian, non-socialist background, but they added up to a relatively significant proletarian group of supporters.[15] Included also were at least two categories of working-class youth: apprentices who had been dismissed as an economy measure before their training had been completed or who had been unable to find employment consistent with their qualifications when the period of training had been successfully negotiated; and school-leavers who had never been able to secure a job and who had remained outside the influence of the socialist and labour movements.[16] Furthermore it is highly relevant to this hypothesis that already before 1933 the younger working class had been prepared in an indirect way, and to an admittedly limited degree, for National Socialism through their exposure to authoritarian trends in the state's latter policy towards them: the development of certain coercive elements of FAD, the *Notwerk der deutschen Jugend*, the

Reichskuratorium, and the treatment of the ineducable minority in the FE system all pointed in the direction of the Third Reich's approach to youth policy.

Despite the absence of an objective natural affinity between the younger proletariat and National Socialism, least of all on class and politico-ideological grounds, such was the extent of their material and broadly spiritual collapse that once Hitler was in power he was able to win over many of them in support of his regime. This occurred not because they suddenly became committed National Socialists, but rather because Hitler was in a position to extend to them prospects for at least a partial restoration of their material situation through the elimination of mass unemployment, and a reconstitution of their self-respect through the seductive propaganda concerning the notions of *Volksgemeinschaft* and the dignity of labour. Their political emasculation and enslavement to a nefarious system of racial and militaristic fanaticism was the heavy price paid by this youth. Ironically their suffering during the Depression, which had brought about their approximation to National Socialism, was modest compared with what lay in store for them during 1933–45.

From a broader perspective, and setting aside the highly problematical dimensions of generational theory, a case may be made for regarding the generation caught up in Weimar's many-faceted turbulence and later in the sinister dénouement of the Third Reich as a 'lost generation'. For those born around 1910 childhood, adolescence and young adulthood meant the privations of a world war, revolution, political anarchy and economic disaster – all before Hitler! The long-term psychological consequences for this youth were damaging in the extreme.[17] But traumatic as their experience had become by the end of the Second World War, it would be misleading to insinuate that the generation in Germany so affected was uniquely unfortunate.[18] There was no German '*Sonderweg*' in this sense, for the comparable generations of other European countries went through just as much and, arguably in some cases, even more that was destructive of all notions of normality. To take a glaring example: the life history of any Pole born just before the First World War would include harsh occupation and subjugation by major foreign powers, a desperate struggle against the odds to achieve and then to retain independent nationhood, particularly in the face of implacable German and Soviet hatred and anti-statist minorities within Poland's own border, and then the incomparable rapacity of National Socialist occupation after 1939, followed by the ultimate irony, 'liberation' by the Red Army and the imposition of a Communist dictatorship totally lacking a popular mandate. In short, the German experience may have been deeply unpleasant, as intimated, but it formed only a segment of a larger European canvas marked by chaos, displacement and genocide.

Notes

1 Introduction

1. Franz Josef Krafeld, *Geschichte der Jugendarbeit. Von den Anfängen bis zur Gegenwart* (Weinheim/Basel, 1984); Christa Hasenclever, *Jugendhilfe und Jugendgesetzgebung seit 1900* (Göttingen, 1978).
2. Anthony Esler (ed.), *The Youth Revolution. The Conflict of Generations in Modern History* (Lexington, Mass., 1974); John R. Gillis, *Youth and History. Tradition and Change in European Age Relations 1770–Present* (New York, 1981); Dieter Dowe (ed.), *Jugendprotest und Generationskonflikt in Europa im 20. Jahrhundert* (Düsseldorf, 1986).
3. Detlev J. K. Peukert, *Grenzen der Sozialdisziplinierung. Aufstieg und Krise der deutschen Jugendfürsorge 1878 bis 1932* (Cologne, 1986).
4. Christoph Sachsse and Florian Tennstedt, *Geschichte der Armenfürsorge in Deutschland. Vom Spätmittelalter bis zum 1. Weltkrieg* (Stuttgart, Berlin, 1980); Sachsse and Tennstedt (eds), *Soziale Sicherheit und soziale Disziplinierung. Beiträge zu einer historischen Theorie der Sozialpolitik* (Frankfurt/M, 1986); Florian Tennstedt, *Sozialgeschichte der Sozialpolitik in Deutschland. Vom 18. Jahrhundert bis zum Ersten Weltkrieg* (Göttingen, 1981).
5. *Peukert, Grenzen*, p. 23.
6. Detlev J. K. Peukert, *Grenzen der Sozialdisziplinierung-Jugendfürsorge und Jugendsubkulturen, 1878–1932* (University of Essen, 1983).
7. Detlev J. K. Peukert, *Jugend zwischen Krieg und Krise. Lebenswelten von Arbeiterjungen in der Weimarer Republik* (Cologne, 1987).
8. Elizabeth Ruth Harvey, *Youth and the State in the Weimar Republic. A Study of Public Policies Towards Working-Class Adolescents in Hamburg, 1918–1933* (D.Phil., University of Oxford, 1987).
9. Ibid., quoted from Abstract.
10. Martina Naujoks, *Mädchen in der Arbeiterbewegung* (Hamburg, 1984); Rosemarie Schade, *The Leading Edge. Women in the German Youth Movement, 1905–1933* (Doctoral Diss., University of York, 1985).

2 The Younger Generation in the Kaiserreich

1. Jürgen Tampke, 'Bismarck's Social Legislation: A Genuine Breakthrough?', in Wolfgang J. Mommsen and Wolfgang Mock (eds), *The Emergence of the Welfare State in Britain and Germany* (London, 1981) pp. 71–83, argues that there was nothing intrinsically new about this legislation, which really was more a continuation of Prussian tradition.
2. Volker Hentschel, *Geschichte der deutschen Sozialpolitik (1800–1980). Soziale Sicherung und kollektives Arbeitsrecht* (Frankfurt, 1983) pp. 9–28; Gerhard A. Ritter, *Social Welfare in Germany and Britain* (Leamington Spa, 1986) pp. 17ff, 28, 33ff, 48, 131.

3. Wolfgang Scheibe, *Die Reformpädagogische Bewegung 1900–1932. Eine einführende Darstellung* (Weinheim/Basel, 1974, 4th edn) pp. 25ff, 51ff, 61ff.
4. Jürgen Reulecke, 'Bürgerliche Sozialreformer und Arbeiterjugend im Kaiserreich', *Archiv für Sozialgeschichte*, (AfS) XXII, 1982, pp. 299–329, here p. 313. See also Margarete Flecken, *Arbeiterkinder im 19. Jahrhundert. Eine sozialgeschichtliche Untersuchung ihrer Lebenswelt* (Weinheim/Basel, 1981).
5. Clemens Schultz, *Die Halbstarken* (Leipzig, 1912).
6. The terminology applied to youth in late nineteenth-century Germany is discussed by Ulrich Herrmann, 'Der "Jüngling" und der "Jugendliche". Männliche Jugend im Spiegel polarisierender Wahrnehmungsmuster an der Wende vom 19. zum 20. Jahrhundert in Deutschland', *Geschichte und Gesellschaft*, 11, 1985, pp. 205–16; and Lutz Roth, *Der sogenannte Jugendliche. Jünglinge und Jugendliche in Deutschland 1750 bis 1920* (Munich, 1983).
7. Klaus Saul, 'Der Kampf um die Jugend zwischen Volksschule und Kaserne. Ein Beitrag zur "Jugendpflege" im Wilhelminischen Reich 1890–1914', *Militärgeschichtliche Mitteilungen*, 10, 1971, pp. 97–143.
8. Klaus Tenfelde, 'Grossstadtjugend in Deutschland vor 1914. Eine historisch-demographische Annäherung', *Vierteljahrschrift für Sozial- und Wirtschaftsgeschichte*, 69, 1982, pp. 182–218, here 182–90.
9. Reinhard Spree, *Health and Social Class in Imperial Germany. A Social History of Mortality, Morbidity and Inequality* (Oxford, 1988) pp. 48–9, 55–102. Also, Hallie J. Kintner, *The Determinants of Infant Mortality in Germany from 1871 to 1933* (Ph.D., University of Michigan, 1982).
10. Klaus Tenfelde, 'Jugend und Gewerkschaften in historischer Perspektive', *Gewerkschaftliche Monatshefte*, 32, 1981, Nr. 3/4, pp. 129–43, here p. 131.
11. Ibid., p. 133; Peukert, *Grenzen der Sozialdisziplinierung*, p. 59.
12. Tenfelde, 'Grossstadtjugend', pp. 197ff, 207ff.
13. Toni Pierenkemper, 'Jugendliche im Arbeitsmarkt: Deutschland seit dem Ende des 19. Jahrhunderts', in Dowe (ed.) *Jugendprotest und Generationskonflikt in Europa im 20. Jahrhundert* (Düsseldorf, 1986) pp. 49–73, here p. 57f.
14. Peukert, *Grenzen*, p. 59.
15. See Fritz Stern *The Politics of Cultural Despair. A Study in the Rise of the Germanic Ideology* (New York, 1965); Walter Struve, *Elites Against Democracy. Leadership Ideals in Bourgeois Political Thought in Germany, 1890–1933* (Princeton, New Jersey, 1973), Part Two; Klaus Vondung (ed.), *Das wilhelminische Bildungsbürgertum. Zur Sozialgeschichte seiner Ideen* (Göttingen, 1976); Corona Hepp, *Avantgarde. Moderne Kunst, Kulturkritik und Reformbewegungen nach der Jahrhundertwende* (Munich, 1987).
16. Frank Trommler, 'Mission ohne Ziel. Über den Kult der Jugend im modernen Deutschland', in Thomas Koebner, Rolf-Peter Janz, Frank Trommler (eds), *'Mit uns zieht die neue Zeit': Der Mythos Jugend* (Frankfurt, 1985) pp. 14–49.
17. Walter Rüegg (ed.), *Kulturkritik und Jugendkult* (Frankfurt, 1974). See

contributions by Hans Bohnenkamp, pp. 23–38; Karol Szemkus, pp. 47–60; Thomas Nipperdey, pp. 87–114.
18. cf. Werner Kindt (ed.), *Die Wandervogelzeit. Quellenschriften zur deutschen Jugendbewegung, 1896–1919* (Düsseldorf, 1968); Jakob Müller, *Die Jugendbewegung als deutsche Hauptrichtung neukonservativer Reform* (Zurich, 1971); Walter Z. Laqueur, *Young Germany. A History of the German Youth Movement* (London, 1962); Ulrich Aufmuth, *Die deutsche Wandervogelbewegung unter soziologischem Aspekt* (Göttingen, 1979); Peter D. Stachura, *The German Youth Movement 1900–1945. An Interpretative and Documentary History* (London, 1981).
19. Paul de Lagarde, 'Über die Klage, dass der Jugend der Idealismus fehle', in *Deutsche Schriften* (Göttingen, 1892) p. 381.
20. August Messer, 'Die freideutsche Jugendbewegung', *Pädagogisches Magazin*, Heft 597, 1915, p. 9.
21. James C. Albisetti, *Secondary School Reform in Imperial Germany* (Princeton, New Jersey, 1983) p. 171f.
22. Ibid., pp. 6, 182, 283ff.
23. Heinz S. Rosenbusch, *Die deutsche Jugendbewegung in ihren pädagogischen Wirkungen und Formen* (Frankfurt, 1973) pp. 19–38; Scheibe, *Reformpädagogische Bewegung*, p. 51ff; Wilhelm Roessler, *Jugend im Erziehungsfeld* (Düsseldorf, 1957); Lenz Kriss-Rettenbeck and Max Liedtke (eds), *Regionale Schulentwicklung im 19. und 20. Jahrhundert* (Bad Heilbrunn, 1984), especially Heinz S. Rosenbusch, 'Wechselwirkungen zwischen Schule und eigentlicher Jugendbewegung, 1896–1923', pp. 183–95; Ulrich Herrmann, 'Die Jugendkulturbewegung. Der Kampf um die höhere Schule', Koebner et al. (eds), *'Mit uns zieht die neue Zeit'*, pp. 224–44, here pp. 224ff.
24. Helga Grebing, *The History of the German Labour Movement. A Survey* (Leamington Spa, 1985) p. 64.
25. Ritter, *Social Welfare*, p. 84.
26. Karl Erich Born, *Wirtschafts-und Sozialgeschichte des Deutschen Kaiserreichs (1867/71–1914)* (Stuttgart, 1985).
27. Christoph Sachsse and Florian Tennstedt, *Geschichte der Armenfürsorge in Deutschland. Vom Spätmittelalter bis zum 1. Weltkrieg* (Stuttgart, 1980).
28. From the large volume of literature relating to the working class before 1914 the following may be noted: Florian Tennstedt, *Vom Proleten zum Industriearbeiter. Arbeiterbewegung und Sozialpolitik in Deutschland 1880 bis 1914* (Cologne, 1983); Klaus Saul, Jens Flemming, Dirk Stegmann, Peter-Christian Witt (eds), *Arbeiterfamilien im Kaiserreich. Materialien zur Sozialgeschichte in Deutschland 1871–1914* (Königstein/ Ts., 1982); Nicholas Bullock and James Read, *The Movement for Housing Reform in Germany and France 1840–1914* (Cambridge, 1985); James S. Roberts, *Drink, Temperance and the Working Class in Nineteenth Century Germany* (London, 1984).
29. A comprehensive survey of these organisations is provided by Hertha Siemering, *Die deutschen Jugendpflegeverbände. Ihre Ziele, Geschichte und Organisation. Ein Handbuch* (Berlin, 1918), especially pp. 222–75, 377–438. See also Hermann Giesecke, *Vom Wandervogel bis zur Hitler-*

jugend. *Jugendarbeit zwischen Politik und Pädagogik* (Munich, 1981) p. 59ff.
30. Gerhard A. Ritter, *Staat, Arbeiterschaft und Arbeiterbewegung in Deutschland. Vom Vormärz bis zum Ende der Weimarer Republik* (Berlin/ Bonn, 1980) pp. 60f.
31. Walter Friedländer and Earl D. Myers, *Child Welfare in Germany Before and After Nazism* (Chicago, 1940) p. 166.
32. Landeshauptarchiv Koblenz (LHAK), 467/1268, *Verordnung vom 13.7.1900,* 'Die Beschäftigung . . . Motorbetriebe'.
33. For the record in Hamburg and the Rhineland, LHAK: 467/1267. *Abschrift der Minister für Handel und Gewerbe*, Berlin, 11.6.1906; 467/ 1269, *Minister der geistlichen und Unterrichts-Angelegenheiten*, Berlin, 7.7.1911.
34. LHAK: 618/2190, *Minister für Handel und Gewerbe*, Berlin, 25.5.1903; Hessisches Hauptstaatsarchiv Wiesbaden (HHStAW): 417/71, *memorandum of Preuss. Minister für Handel und Gewerbe*, Berlin, 22.8.1924. In 1907, 277 052 children aged under 14 years who had left school were in legal employment in the Reich, two-thirds of them in agriculture and related industries. Only 52 713 were employed in industry and the crafts sector (Siegfried Quandt (ed.), *Kinderarbeit und Kinderschutz in Deutschland 1783–1976. Quellen und Anmerkungen* (Paderborn, 1978) p. 110, Dok. No. 52).
35. LHAK: 441/23197 for the full text of the decree, which used the term '*Jugendpflege*' for the first time.
36. Ibid., 441/17338, press report of 4.2.1912.
37. Ibid., 441/17338, cf. *Der Kreuzzeitung*, 23.5.1911, Nr. 240.
38. The 1869 Commercial Code (Paragraph 127) regarded masters as being *in loco parentis*, entitling them to exercise firm guardianship (*väterliche Züchtigungsrecht*). In any dispute, the master's authority was invariably given full support by the law.
39. Richard J. Evans, ' "Red Wednesday" in Hamburg: Social Democrats, Police, and Lumpenproletariat in the Suffrage Disturbances of 17 January 1906', *Social History*, 4, 1979, pp.1–31.
40. cf. Johannes Schult, *Aufbruch einer Jugend. Der Weg der deutschen Arbeiterjugendbewegung* (Bonn, 1956)pp. 23–106; Erich Eberts, *Arbeiterjugend 1904–1945. Sozialistische Erziehungsgemeinschaft-Politische Organisation* (Frankfurt, 1980)pp. 25–52; Karl-Heinz Jahnke *et al.*, *Geschichte der deutschen Arbeiterjugendbewegung 1904–1945* (Dortmund, 1973); Heinrich Eppe, *Selbsthilfe und Interessenvertretung. Die sozial-und jugendpolitischen Bestrebungen der sozialdemokratischen Arbeiterjugendorganisation 1904–1933* (Bonn, 1983).
41. Alfred Noll, 'Die Arbeiterjugend unter dem Reichsvereinsgesetz von 1908', *Deutschlands Junge Garde. 50 Jahre Arbeiterjugendbewegung* (East Berlin, 1954)pp. 53ff.
42. A supplementary decree in April 1913 extended the same provisions to female youth. See Dr Becker and Regierungsdirektor Gildemeister, *Förderung der Jugendpflege durch Reich, Länder, Gemeinden und Gemeindeverbände* (Eberswalde-Berlin, 1932)p. 6.

43. LHAK: 441/17338, *Kölnische Zeitung*, 24.3.1912.
44. LHAK: 441/23197.
45. LHAK: 441/17349, *memorandum of Preuss. Minister des Innern*, Berlin, 26.2.1914. For details of how the funds were finally distributed see ibid., letter of 8.5.1914 from *Oberbürgermeister* Coblenz to *Regierungs-Präsident Coblenz*.
46. LHAK: 441/17338, *press report* 13.7.1912.
47. LHAK: 441/17333, various reports from lower Rhineland, 1913/14.
48. LHAK: 441/17347, *Bericht vom 16. Dez. 1911 über der Jugendpflege im Regierungsbezirk Coblenz*; ibid., 441/24249, '*Die Jugendpflege in Bromberg*', 1914; ibid., 442/10339, *Bericht über den Stand der Jugendpflege bis zum 1. Okt. 1924 im Regierungsbezirk Trier*, Trier, 18.12.1924. Also, Heinz Schröder, *Die Geschichte der Hamburgischen Jugendfürsorge 1863 bis 1924* (Doctoral Dissertation, University of Hamburg, 1966), *Hauptteil* B.
49. LHAK: 441/17347, *Bericht über die Verhandlungen in der I. Sitzung des Bezirksausschusses für Jugendpflege*, Coblenz, 25.4.1912.
50. Ibid., statement by Professor Deipser.
51. Ibid., *Verzeichnis der Mitglieder des Kreisausschusses für Jugendpflege*, 1913, and *Bericht des Preuss. Minister der geistlichen-und Unterrichts-Angelegenheiten*, Berlin, 11.3.1913.
52. Ibid., *Bericht der Bezirksausschusses für Jugendpflege*, Coblenz, 15.7.1913. Official satisfaction at progress in *Jugendpflege* before 1914 is expressed in HHStAW: 460/789, *Erlass der Preuss. Staatsministerium, 17.6.1924 betr. Pflege der schulentlass. Jugend*.
53. Justus Ehrhardt, 'Amtliche Jugendpflege und ihre Grenzen', *Das Junge Deutschland*, XXIV, 1930, Nr. 2, p. 97.
54. Reulecke, 'Bürgerliche Sozialreformer', p. 324; Hans-Peter Brüchhäuser and Antonius Lipsmeier (eds), *Quellen und Dokumente zur schulischen Berufsbildung 1869–1918* (Cologne, Vienna, 1985).
55. Karl Seidelmann, *Die Pfadfinder in der deutschen Jugendgeschichte, Teil I, Darstellung* (Hanover 1977) passim.
56. Saul, 'Kampf um die Jugend'; Reulecke, 'Bürgerliche Sozialreformer', p. 327. For a critical Catholic reaction to the setting up of the *Jungdeutschlandbund*, LHAK: 441/17338, *Kolpingsblatt*, 26.11.1911.
57. Howard Becker, *German Youth. Bond or Free* (London, 1946) p. 106.
58. Ritter, *Social Reform*, pp. 180–5. See also Hans Mommsen and Winfried Schulz (eds), *Vom Elend der Handarbeit. Probleme historischer Unterschichtenforschung* (Stuttgart, 1981).
59. Rose Ahlheim *et al.*, *Gefesselte Jugend. Fürsorgeerziehung im Kapitalismus* (Frankfurt, 1978, 5th edn) pp. 43ff.
60. Hans Scherpner, *Geschichte der Jugendfürsorge* (Göttingen, 1979, 2nd edn) p. 176.
61. Herbert Ruscheweyh, *Die Entwicklung des deutschen Jugendgerichts* (Weimar, 1918) pp. 13ff.
62. Gillis, *Youth and History*, p. 176.
63. Eric A. Johnson and Vincent E. McHale, 'Socioeconomic Aspects of the Delinquency Rate in Imperial Germany, 1882–1914', *Journal of Social*

History, 13, 1979/80, Spring, pp. 384–402, here pp. 387ff., 394ff. A contemporary view in support of this hypothesis in August Brandt, *Gefesselte Jugend in der Zwangs-Fürsorgeerziehung* (Berlin, 1929).
64. See Albert Gregor and Else Voigtländer, *Die Verwahrlosung. Ihre klinish-psychologische Bewertung und ihre Bekämpfung* (Berlin, 1918); Herbert Francke, *Jugendverwahrlosung und ihre Bekämpfung* (Berlin, 1926).
65. Felix P. Aschrott, *Die Behandlung der verwahrlosten und verbrecherischen Jugend und Vorschläge für Reform* (Berlin, 1892); H. Appelius, *Die Behandlung jugendlicher Verbrecher und verwahrloster Kinder* (Berlin, 1892).
66. Peukert, *Grenzen*, pp. 73, 83f, 86ff.
67. Rusheweyh, *deut. Jugendgerichts*, p. 102.
68. Staatsarchiv Hamburg (StAH): *Jugendbehörde* I, 487, Band 1, 'Das neue Jugendgericht' (Dr Hertz).
69. This replaced the 1878 *Zwangserziehungsgesetz* which had restricted the custodial process to under-12-year-olds. See also StAH: *Jugendbehörde* I, 232, Band 2, article by Herbert Francke: 'Die Neuordnung der Fürsorgeerziehung vom November 1932 in rechtsgeschichtliche Beleuchtung', *Sonderdruck, Zeitschrift für Kinderforschung*, 41, 1933, Heft 1, pp. 162–71. The law, which came into effect on 1 April 1901, also officially established the more propitious term *'Jugendfürsorge'* in place of *'Zwangserziehung'*.
70. Peukert, *Grenzen*, pp. 146f, 152ff. See also p. 328, Tables 12 and 14.
71. Ibid., p. 149.
72. Christa Hasenclever, *Jugendhilfe und Jugendgesetzgebung seit 1900* (Göttingen, 1978) p. 22.
73. Scherpner, *Jugendfürsorge*, p. 163.
74. Wilhelm Polligkeit, *Strafrechtsreform und Jugendfürsorge* (Langensalza, 1905).
75. Eric J. Leed, *No Man's Land. Combat and Identity in World War I* (Cambridge, 1979).
76. Robert Wohl, *The Generation of 1914* (London, 1980); Hans Jaeger, 'Generationen in die Geschichte. Überlegungen zu einer umstrittenen Konzeption', *Geschichte und Gesellschaft*, 3, 1977, pp. 429–52.
77. Newspaper stories abounded in the early period of the war of factory girls buying expensive items in luxury shops: LHAK: 441/17338, 'Die Verwahrlosung der Arbeiterjugend und die Jugendpflege', 19.8.1918.
78. Elizabeth Domansky and Ulrich Heinemann, 'Jugend als Generationserfahrung: Das Beispiel der Weimarer Republik', *Sozialwissenschaftliche Informationen für Unterricht und Studium*, 13, 1984, Heft 1, pp. 15–16; Jürgen Kocka, *Klassengesellschaft im Krieg. Deutsche Sozialgeschichte 1914–1918* (Göttingen, 1973) pp. 40–75.
79. Ludwig Preller, *Sozialpolitik in der Weimarer Republik* (Düsseldorf, 1978) p. 55.
80. Hentschel, *Sozialpolitik*, pp. 58–9; Hans-Ulrich Wehler, *The German Empire 1871–1918* (Leamington Spa, 1985) pp. 206–7; Hans-Joachim Bieber, *Gewerkschaften in Krieg und Revolution. Arbeiterbewegung, Industrie, Staat und Militär in Deutschland 1914–1920* (Hamburg, 1981) pp. 306–33.

81. Preller, *Sozialpolitik*, p. 41; Gillis, *Youth and History*, p. 162.
82. Volker Ullrich, 'Everyday Life and the German Working Class, 1914–1918', Roger Fletcher (ed.), *Bernstein to Brandt. A Short History of German Social Democracy* (London, 1987) pp. 55–64.
83. Historisches Archiv der Stadt Köln (HASK): *53/13, Jahresbericht 1914–1915 der Zentralstelle für Volkswohlfahrt*, Berlin, 1915; and 'Kriegszeit und Aufgaben der Jugendpflege', 1915.
84. LHAK: 441/44820, Preuss. *Minister von Trott zu Solz*, 12.9.1914 and 22.1.1915. For the concern of local authorities see ibid., 441/17349, *Landrat Kreuznach to Reg. Präsident Coblenz*, 19.7.1916; ibid., 442/10339, *Bericht über den Stand der Jugendpflege bis zum 1. Okt. 1924 im Regierungsbezirk Trier*, Trier 18.12.1924; ibid., 442/14283, *Landrat Saarbrücken to Reg. Präsident Trier*, 16.9.1919.
85. A total of 2.3 million German soldiers were killed and 2.7 million permanently disabled. The deceased were survived by 553 000 widows and 1 192 000 orphans. Fuller details in Robert W. Whalen, *Bitter Wounds. German Victims of the Great War, 1914–1939* (Ithaca, London, 1984). For expressions of official concern, StAH: *Jugendbehörde* I, 291, *Archiv Deutscher Berufsvormünder, Frankfurt, to Behörde für öffentliche Jugendfürsorge Hamburg*, August 1914.
86. LHAK: 441/17338, *Jugendfürsorgegesetz*, 13.7.1918. See also Hasenclever, *Jugendhilfe*, pp. 48–9; Scherpner, *Jugendfürsorge*, p. 178.
87. See Manfred Stadelmeier, *Zwischen Langemarck und Liebknecht. Arbeiterjugend und Politik im I. Weltkrieg* (Bonn, 1986).
88. LHAK: 442/10339, *Bericht der Kreisjugendpfleger*, Trier, 7.7.1919.
89. Kurt Wittig, *Der Einfluss des Krieges auf die Kriminalität der Jugendlichen und auf jugendliche Sträflinge* (Langensalza, 1916); Herbert Vornefeld, 'Die Jugendkriminalität im Weltkrieg: Erscheinungsformen und Ursachen', *Das Junge Deutschland*, 33, 1939, p. 497; A. Hellwig, *Der Krieg und die Kriminalität der Jugendlichen* (Halle, 1916).
90. Hauptstaatsarchiv Stuttgart (HStAS): J212/11, *Bericht*, 19.3.1918.
91. LHAK: 441/17338, 'Die Verwahrlosung der Arbeiterjugend und die Jugendpflege', 19.8.1918.
92. E. Roesner, 'Krieg und Kriminalität im Spiegel der Statistik', *Blätter für Gefängniskunde*, 71, 1940, p. 17.

3 The Weimar Sozialstaat

1. The role of the SPD in the November Revolution is best understood with reference to Susanne Miller, *Die Bürde der Macht. Die deutsche Sozialdemokratie 1918–1920* (Düsseldorf, 1978); Helga Grebing, *Geschichte der deutschen Arbeiterbewegung. Ein Überblick* (Munich, 1975, 6th edn) pp. 146–75; Heinrich August Winkler, *Von der Revolution zur Stabilisierung. Arbeiter und Arbeiterbewegung in der Weimarer Republik 1918 bis 1924* (Berlin, Bonn, 1984); Walter Euchner, 'Sozialdemokratie und Demokratie. Zum Demokratieverständnis der SPD in der Weimarer Republik', *A f S*, XXVI, 1986, pp. 125–78, here, pp. 139ff.
2. Herman Weber, Klaus Schönhoven and Klaus Tenfelde (eds), *Quellen zur Geschichte der deutschen Gewerkschaftsbewegung im 20. Jahrhun-*

dert. Band 1. 1. *Die Gewerkschaften in den Anfangsjahren der Republik 1919–1923* (Cologne, 1985) passim.
3. Gerhard A. Ritter, 'Entstehung und Entwicklung des Sozialstaats in vergleichender Perspektive', *Historische Zeitschrift* (HZ) 243, 1986, pp. 1–90; Gerald D. Feldman and Irmgard Steinisch, *Industrie und Gewerkschaften 1918–1924. Die überforderte Zentralarbeitsgemeinschaft* (Stuttgart, 1985); Preller, *Sozialpolitik*, pp. 249–82.
4. *RGBI*, 1923 i, Nr. 111, pp. 1042–5; Johannes W. Bähr, 'Sozialer Staat und Industrieller Konflikt. Das Schlichtungswesen zwischen Inflation und Weltwirtschaftskrise', in Werner Abelshauser (ed.), *Die Weimarer Republik als Wohlfahrtsstaat. Zum Verhältnis von Wirtschafts-und Sozialpolitik in der Industriegesellschaft* (Wiesbaden/Stuttgart, 1987) pp. 185–203, here pp. 185–7; Dieter Schiffmann, 'Der Staat als Arbeitgeber und Schlichter. Aspekte der Arbeitsbeziehungen im öffentlichen Dienst 1924–1930', ibid., pp. 204–25; Ursula Hüllbüsch, 'Koalitionsfreiheit und Zwangstarif. Die Stellungnahme des Allgemeinen Deutschen Gewerkschaftsbundes zu Tarifvertrag und Schlichtungswesen', in Ulrich Engelhardt, Volker Sellin and Horst Stuke (eds), *Soziale Bewegung und politische Verfassung. Beiträge zur Geschichte der modernen Welt* (Stuttgart, 1976) pp. 599ff.
5. See Gesine Asmus (ed.), *Hinterhof, Keller und Mansarde. Einblicke in Berliner Wohnungselend 1901–1920* (Reinbek, 1982).
6. Michael Ruck, 'Der Wohnungsbau – Schnittpunkt von Sozial – und Wirtschaftspolitik. Probleme der öffentlichen Wohnungspolitik in der Hauszinssteuerära 1924/5 – 1930/31', in Abelshauser (ed.), *Wohlfahrtsstaat*, pp. 91–123; Michael Drupp, 'Gemeinnützige Bauvereine im Wohnungswesen der Weimarer Republik', ibid., pp. 124–46; Peter-Christian Witt, 'Inflation, Wohnungszwangswirtschaft und Hauszinssteuer. Zur Regelung von Wohnungsbau und Wohnungsmarkt in der Weimarer Republik', in Lutz Niethammer (ed), *Wohnen im Wandel* (Wuppertal, 1979) pp. 385ff.
7. Werner Abelshauser, 'Die Weimarer Republik – Ein Wohlfahrtsstaat?', pp. 9–31.
8. Hentschel, *Sozialpolitik*, pp. 133ff.
9. Werner Abelshauser, 'Verelendung der Handarbeit? Zur sozialen Lage der deutschen Arbeiter in der grossen Inflation der frühen zwanziger Jahre', in Mommsen and Schulze (eds), *Vom Elend der Handarbeit*, pp. 445–76; Carl-Ludwig Holtfrerich, *Die deutsche Inflation 1914–1923. Ursachen und Folgen in internationaler Perspektive* (Berlin, New York, 1980) pp. 241ff.; Günther Mai, '"Wenn der Mensch Hunger hat, hört alles auf". Wirtschaftliche und soziale Ausgangsbedingungen der Weimarer Republik (1914–1924)', in Abelshauser (ed.), *Wohlfahrtsstaat*, pp. 33–62; Merith Niehuss, *Arbeiterschaft in Krieg und Inflation. Soziale Schichtung und Lage der Arbeiter in Augsburg und Linz, 1910–1925* (Berlin, New York, 1985) pp. 100ff., who stresses the miserable living conditions of workers in 1923. Also on the impact of the inflation, a revisionist argument by Andreas Kunz, 'Inflation als Verteilungskampf. Eine Bilanz der Neueren Forschung', in Abelshauser (ed.), *Wohlfahrtsstaat*, pp. 171–84; Gerald D. Feldman, Carl-Ludwig Holtfrer-

ich, Gerhard A. Ritter and Peter-Christian Witt (eds), *Die Anpassung an die Inflation* (Berlin, 1986).
10. See Michael Prinz, *Vom neuen Mittelstand zum Volksgenossen. Die Entwicklung des sozialen Status der Angestellten von der Weimarer Republik bis zum Ende der NS-Zeit* (Munich, 1986); the pre-war situation of white-collar workers is analysed by Toni Pierenkemper, *Arbeitsmarkt und Angestellte im deutschen Kaiserreich 1880–1913* (Stuttgart, 1987); Heinz-Gerhard Haupt, 'Mittelstand und Kleinbürgertum in der Weimarer Republik. Zu Problemen und Perspektiven ihrer Forschung', *A f S*, XXVI, 1986, pp. 217–38.
11. Gerald D. Feldman, 'The Weimar Republic: A Problem of Modernization?', *A f S*, XXVI, 1986, pp. 11, 16.
12. Rosemarie Leuschen-Seppel, *Zwischen Staatsverantwortung und Klasseninteresse. Die Wirtschafts-und Finanzpolitik der SPD zur Zeit der Weimarer Republik unter besonderer Berücksichtigung der Mittelphase 1924–1928/29* (Bonn, 1981); Heinrich August Winkler, *Der Schein der Normalität. Arbeiter und Arbeiterbewegung in der Weimarer Republik 1924 bis 1930* (Berlin, Bonn, 1985); Wilhelm L. Guttsman, *The German Social Democratic Party, 1875–1933* (London, 1981) pp. 156ff, 227ff, 251ff.
13. Abelshauser, 'Die Weimarer Republik – Ein Wohlfahrtsstaat?', in Abelshauser (ed.), *Wohlfahrtsstaat*, p. 17; Harold James, 'Die Wahrungsstabilisierung 1923/24 in Internationaler Perspektive', ibid., pp. 63–79.
14. Harold James, *The German Slump. Politics and Economics 1924–1936* (Oxford, 1986) p. 39.
15. William C. McNeil, *American Money and The Weimar Republic. Economics and Politics on the Eve of the Great Depression* (New York, 1986) chapters 1–3.
16. James, *Slump*, p. 21.
17. Witt, 'Inflation, Wohnungszwangswirtschaft . . .', pp. 385ff.
18. Preller, *Sozialpolitik*, p. 483; Ronald Wiedenhoeft, *Berlin's Housing Revolution. German Reform in the 1920s* (Ann Arbor, 1985).
19. Klaus J. Bade, 'Arbeitsmarkt, Bevölkerung und Wanderung in der Weimarer Republik', in Michael Stürmer (ed.), *Die Weimarer Republik. Belagerte Civitas* (Königstein/Ts., 1985, 2nd edn) pp. 165ff.
20. *RGBl*, 1924, I, p. 765. See also Elizabeth von Harnack, 'Germany's New Public Welfare Law', *Social Service Review*, I, 1927, No. 3, pp. 406–13.
21. David Abraham, *The Collapse of the Weimar Republic. Political Economy and Crisis* (New York, 1986, 2nd edn) p. 233.
22. Bähr, 'Sozialer Staat', in Abelshauser (ed.), *Wohlfahrtsstaat*, p. 187ff.
23. See Horst-Albrecht Kukuck and Dieter Schiffmann (eds), *Die Gewerkschaften von der Stabilisierung bis zur Weltwirtschaftskrise, 1924–1930* (Cologne, 1986).
24. John A. Garraty, *Unemployment in History. Economic Thought and Public Policy* (New York, 1978) p. 9.
25. Frank Niess, *Geschichte der Arbeitslosigkeit. Ökonomische Ursachen und politische Kämpfe. Ein Kapital deutscher Sozialgeschichte* (Cologne, 1979) pp. 11–12.
26. Paul Berndt, *Die Arbeitslosigkeit. Ihre Bekämpfung und Statistik* (Halle,

1899) p. 33; John Schikowski, *Über Arbeitslosigkeit und Arbeitslosenstatistik* (Leipzig, 1894) pp. 20ff.
27. Anselm Faust, 'State and Unemployment in Germany, 1890–1918. Labour Exchanges, Job Creation and Unemployment Insurance', in Mommsen and Mock (eds), *The Emergence of the Welfare State*, pp. 156–7, quoting a figure of 11 500 in 1909–10.
28. Peter D. Stachura, 'The Development of Unemployment in Modern German History', in Peter D. Stachura (ed.), *Unemployment and The Great Depression in Weimar Germany* (London, 1986) p. 6.
29. Hans-Joachim Bieber. 'The Socialist Trade Unions in War and Revolution', in Fletcher (ed.), *Bernstein to Brandt*, pp. 74ff.
30. Dietmar Petzina, 'The Extent and Causes of Unemployment in the Weimar Republic', in Stachura (ed.), *Unemployment*, p. 30. See also for detailed coverage Anselm Faust, *Arbeitsmarktpolitik im Deutschen Kaiserreich. Arbeitsvermittlung, Arbeitsbeschaffung und Arbeitslosenunterstützung, 1890–1918* (Stuttgart, 1986).
31. *Kaiserliches Statistisches Amt: Die beschäftigungslosen Arbeitnehmer im Deutschen Reich* (Berlin, 1896). It was only from the date of this census that the term '*Arbeitslosigkeit*' became widely used in Germany to denote 'unemployment'.
32. Manuel Saitzew (ed.), *Die Arbeitslosigkeit der Gegenwart* (Munich, Leipzig, 1932) pp. 10–90, 92ff.
33. Petzina, 'Extent and Causes' in Stachura (ed.), *Unemployment*, p. 31, states that the average annual rate of unemployed trade unionists between 1908 and 1913 was 1.9–2.9 per cent; Hentschel, *Sozialpolitik*, p. 104, quotes for the same period a rate of 2.6 per cent. See the detailed unemployment table in Jürgen Kuczynski, *Die Geschichte der Lage der Arbeiter in Deutschland von 1800 bis in die Gegenwart* (East Berlin, 1947) Band I, p. 215.
34. Stachura, 'Development of Unemployment', in Stachura (ed.), *Unemployment*, p. 7; Niess, *Arbeitslosigkeit*, p. 32.
35. Gerhard Kessler, *Die Arbeitsnachweise der Arbeitgeberverbände* (Leipzig, 1911) pp. 78ff.
36. Linda A. Heilman, 'Industrial Unemployment in Germany: 1873–1913', *A f S*, XXVII, 1987, p. 38.
37. Ibid., p. 38.
38. Niess, *Arbeitslosigkeit*, pp. 78, 150ff.
39. Heilman, 'Industrial Unemployment', pp. 26–7 and in her doctoral thesis of the same title (University of California, 1982) pp. 217–84. For the differences between 'respectable' and 'rough' working class see Richard J. Evans (ed.), *The German Working Class 1888–1933. The Politics of Everyday Life* (London, 1982), especially Dick Geary, 'Identifying Militancy: The Assessment of Working-Class Attitudes Towards State and Society', pp. 220–46.
40. Niess, *Arbeitslosigkeit*, pp. 156ff, 166–76.
41. Hentschel, *Sozialpolitik*, p. 105.
42. Preller, *Sozialpolitik*, pp. 229ff; Wolfgang J. Mommsen (ed.), '*Die Organisierung des Friedens. Demobilmachung 1918–1920*', in *Geschichte und Gesellschaft*, 9, 1983, Heft 2.

43. Preller, *Sozialpolitik*, p. 164; Gerald D. Feldman, 'Saxony, the Reich, and the Problem of Unemployment in the German Inflation', *A f S*, XXVII, 1987, pp. 103–44.
44. *RGBl*, 1919, I, p. 1305.
45. Preller, *Sozialpolitik*, pp. 236, 246f.
46. Feldman, 'Saxony', p. 110.
47. Susanne Rouette, 'Die Erwerbslosenfürsorge für Frauen in Berlin nach 1918', *Internationale Wissenschaftliche Korrespondenz zur Geschichte der deutschen Arbeiterbewegung* (IWK) 21, 1985, pp. 295–308.
48. Helmut Druke et al., *Spaltung der Arbeiterbewegung und Faschismus. Sozialgeschichte der Weimarer Republik* (Hamburg, 1980) p. 85.
49. *Statistisches Jahrbuch für das Deutsche Reich 1924/25* (Berlin, 1925) p. 296.
50. Hermann Aubin and Wolfgang Zorn (eds), *Handbuch der deutschen Wirtschafts-und Sozialgeschichte. Band 2: Das 19. und 20. Jahrhundert* (Stuttgart, 1976) p. 804.
51. Petzina, 'Extent and Causes' in Stachura (ed.), *Unemployment*, p. 31.
52. Preller, *Sozialpolitik*, p. 164.
53. Ibid., pp. 276–82; Walter Bogs, *Die Sozialversicherung in der Weimarer Demokratie* (Munich, 1981) pp. 104ff; Michael T. Wermel and Roswitha Urban, *Arbeitslosenfürsorge und Arbeitslosenversicherung in Deutschland* (Munich, 1949) pp. 24ff; Frieda Wunderlich, *Die Bekämpfung der Arbeitslosigkeit in Deutschland seit Beendigung des Krieges* (Jena, 1925).
54. Petzina, 'Extent and Causes', p. 31.
55. Druke, *Spaltung*, p. 86. In 1928 it is reckoned that 6.5 per cent of the jobless were long-term (Saitzew, *Arbeitslosigkeit*, p. 122).
56. Fritz Blaich, *Die Wirtschaftskrise 1925/26 und die Reichsregierung. Von der Erwerbslosenfürsorge zur Konjunkturpolitik* (Kallmünz, 1977); Dieter Hertz-Eichenrode, *Wirtschaftskrise und Arbeitsbeschaffung. Konjunkturpolitik 1925/26 und die Grundlagen der Krisenpolitik Brünings* (Frankfurt, 1982); on rationalisation, Robert A. Brady, *The Rationalization Movement in German Industry* (Berkeley, California, 1933) passim; Eva C. Schöck, *Arbeitslosigkeit und Rationalisierung. Die Lage der Arbeiter und die kommunistische Gewerkschaftspolitik 1920–1928* (Frankfurt, 1977) pp. 75ff, 150ff, 170f.
57. Petzina, 'Extent and Causes', p. 31.
58. Gunna Stollberg, *Die Rationalisierungsdebatte 1908–33* (Frankfurt, 1981) pp. 140ff.
59. Bogs, *Sozialversicherung*, pp. 104ff, 110–22.
60. See speech in Reichstag on 27 February 1927 by Reich Labour Minister Brauns, *Verhandlungen des Reichstags. Stenographische Berichte*, Band 392, p. 9239; Preller, *Sozialpolitik*, pp. 363–76, 422–53.
61. Anselm Faust, 'Von der Fürsorge zur Arbeitsmarktpolitik. Die Errichtung der Arbeitslosenversicherung', in Abelshauser (ed.), *Wohlfahrtsstaat*, pp. 260–79.
62. The position of the younger generation is reviewed in Chapter 5.
63. Bernd Weisbrod, 'The Crisis of German Unemployment Insurance in 1928/29 and its Political Repercussions', in Mommsen and Mock (eds), *Welfare State*, p. 189.

64. The unsatisfactory way in which female workers fared under the new legislation is analysed by Karin Hausen, 'Unemployment also Hits Women: The New and the Old Woman on the Dark Side of the Golden Twenties in Germany', in Stachura (ed.), *Unemployment*, pp. 78–120.
65. Heidrun Homburg, 'Vom Arbeitslosen zum Zwangsarbeiter. Arbeitslosenpolitik und Fraktionierung der Arbeiterschaft in Deutschland 1930–1933 am Beispiel der Wohlfahrtserwerbslosen und der kommunalen Wohlfahrtshilfe', *A f S*, XXV, 1985, pp. 260f.
66. Ibid., pp. 264–94, and by the same author, 'From Unemployment Insurance to Compulsory Labour: The Transformation of the Benefit System in Germany 1927–33', in Richard J. Evans and Dick Geary (eds), *The German Unemployed. Experiences and Consequences of Mass Unemployment from the Weimar Republic to the Third Reich* (London, 1987) pp. 80ff, 91ff. Those concerned were not freed from the obligation to repay until legislation was passed in December 1936 (Homburg, 'Vom Arbeitslosen', p 278). In January 1929, the long-term jobless constituted 9.5 per cent of the total (Saitjew, *Arbeitslosigkeit*, p. 122).
67. Dietmar Petzina, Werner Abelshauser and Anselm Faust, *Sozialgeschichtliches Arbeitsbuch III. Materialien zur Statistik des Deutschen Reiches 1914–1945* (Munich, 1978) p. 119.
68. Petzina, 'Extent and Causes', p. 31; Preller, *Sozialpolitik*, p. 422.
69. Weisbrod, 'German Unemployment Insurance', pp. 193ff.
70. Knut Borchardt, 'Zwangslagen und Handlungsspielräume in der grossen Weltwirtschaftskrise der frühen dreissiger Jahre. Zur Revision des überlieferten Geschichtsbildes', in Knut Borchardt (ed.), *Wachstum, Krisen, Handlungsspielräume der Wirtschaftspolitik. Studien zur Wirtschaftsgeschichte des 19. und 20. Jahrhunderts* (Göttingen, 1982); James, *Slump*, pp. 39–109, 190–245; Bernt Weisbrod, *Schwerindustrie in der Weimarer Republik. Interessenpolitik zwischen Stabilisierung und Krise* (Wuppertal, 1978), pp. 295ff; Henry A. Turner, *German Big Business and The Rise of Hitler* (Oxford, 1985) pp. 37–46, 100ff.
71. Grebing, *deutschen Arbeiterbewegung*, pp. 180f.
72. Michael Schneider, *Unternehmer und Demokratie. Die freien Gewerkschaften in der unternehmerischen Ideologie der Jahre 1918 bis 1933* (Bonn, 1975) p. 76.
73. Ilse Maurer, *Reichsfinanzen und Grosse Koalition. Zur Geschichte des Reichskabinetts Müller (1928–1930)* (Frankfurt, 1973).
74. Helga Timm, *Die Deutsche Sozialpolitik und der Bruch der grossen Koalition im März 1930* (Düsseldorf, 1982, new edn).
75. See Fritz Blaich, *Der Schwarze Freitag. Inflation und Wirtschaftskrise* (Munich, 1985) for an up-to-date interpretation, especially pp. 58–116. Also Charles P. Kindleberger, *The World in Depression 1929–1939* (London, 1973) pp. 291ff.
76. Karl Erich Born, *Die deutsche Bankenkrise, 1931. Finanzen und Politik* (Munich, 1967).
77. Preller, *Sozialpolitik*, pp. 166–7.
78. Willi Hemmer, *Die 'unsichtbaren' Arbeitslosen. Statistische Methodensoziale Tatsachen* (Zeulenroda, 1935) pp. 114ff, 184f; Wilhelm M. Breuer, *Deutschland in der Weltwirtschaftskrise 1929/1932* (Cologne,

1974) p. 38, gives a figure of over two million; Preller, *Sozialpolitik*, p. 394 puts it at one million; Niess, *Arbeitslosigkeit*, p. 40 at two million; Druke, *Spaltung*, p. 88 at three or four million; the contemporary *Institut für Konjunkturforschung* at 1.7–1.8 million. The 'invisible' unemployed were those who had exhausted their rights to benefit in all three support systems, those ineligible on other grounds, those groups excluded by successive emergency decrees, and those who did not even apply (often married female workers). Younger and elderly workers were proportionately ov represented in the 'invisibles', who were more likely to be located in agrarian, rural areas than industrial regions. The 'wandering' unemployed are estimated at 400 000 in 1932 (Blaich, *Schwarze Freitag*, p. 60.
79. Preller, *Sozialpolitik*, pp. 166–7. In some industries, such as textiles, the figure was much higher (41.3 per cent; see Rüdiger Hachtmann, 'Arbeitsmarkt und Arbeitszeit in der deutschen Industrie 1929 bis 1939', *A f S*, XXVII, 1987, p. 184).
80. Preller, *Sozialpolitik*, pp. 399–495; Wladimir Woytinsky, *The Social Consequences of The Economic Depression* (Geneva, 1936), pp. 164ff; Michael Schneider, *Streit um Arbeitszeit. Geschichte des Kampfes um Arbeitszeitverkürzung in Deutschland* (Cologne, 1984). For much relevant detail, Heinrich August Winkler, *Der Weg in die Katastrophe. Arbeiter und Arbeiterbewegung in der Weimarer Republik 1930 bis 1933* (Berlin, Bonn, 1987) passim.
81. Woytinsky, *Social Consequences*, pp. 164f, 344.
82. Preller, *Sozialpolitik*, pp. 167–8.
83. Petzina, 'Extent and Causes', pp. 34ff.
84. Homburg, 'Vom Arbeitslosen', p. 257.
85. Petzina/Abelshauser/Faust, *Sozialgeschichtliches* p. 121.
86. Blaich, *Schwarze Freitag*, p. 61.
87. Ibid., p. 69; Wilhelm Treue (ed.), *Deutschland in der Weltwirtschaftskrise in Augenzeugenberichten* (Munich, 1976) pp. 138ff, 245ff, 336ff; Alf Lüdtke, 'Hunger in der Grossen Depression. Hungererfahrungen und Hungerpolitik am Ende der Weimarer Republik', *A f S*, XXVII, 1987, pp. 145–76; Rudolf Vierhaus, 'Auswirkungen der Krise um 1930 in Deutschland. Beiträge zu einer historisch- psychologischen Analyse', in Werner Conze and Hans Raupach (eds), *Die Staats-und Wirtschaftskrise des deutschen Reiches 1929–33* (Stuttgart, 1967) pp. 155–75.
88. H. R. Knickerbocker, *Deutschland so oder so?* (Berlin, 1932).
89. Graf Alexander Stenbock-Fermer, *Deutschland von unten. Reise durch die Proletarische Provinz* (Stuttgart, 1931) pp. 7, 9ff.
90. The controversy over the 'Borchardt Thesis' is analysed by Knut Borchardt, 'Noch Einmal: Alternativen zu Brünings Wirtschaftspolitik?', *HZ*, 237, 1983, pp. 67–83; Werner Conze: 'Zum Scheitern der Weimarer Republik. Neue Wirtschafts-und sozialgeschichtliches Antworten auf alte Kontroversen', *Vierteljahrschrift für Sozial-und Wirtschaftsgeschichte*, 70, 1983, pp. 215–21; Carl-Ludwig Holtfrerich, 'Alternativen zu Brünings Wirtschaftspolitik in der Weltwirtschaftskrise?', *HZ*, 235, 1982, pp. 605–31.
91. Martin Broszat, *Hitler and the Collapse of Weimar Germany* (Leaming-

ton Spa, 1987) pp. 104ff; Gotthard Jasper, *Die gescheiterte Zähmung. Wege zur Machtergreifung Hitlers 1930–1934* (Frankfurt/M, 1986) pp. 55–63.
92. Knut Borchardt, 'Das Gewicht der Inflationsangst in den wirtschaftspolitischen Entscheidungsprozessen während der Weltwirtschaftskrise', in Gerald D. Feldman (ed.) *Die Nachwirkungen der Inflation auf die deutsche Geschichte, 1924–1933* (Munich, 1985) pp. 233–60.
93. This included the emergency decree of 8 December 1931 which lowered all wages governed by collective agreement to their levels of January 1927 (Gerhard Bry, *Wages in Germany, 1871–1945*, Princeton, 1960, p. 43); the broader picture is amply conveyed in Ilse Maurer and Udo Wengst (eds), *Politik und Wirtschaft in der Krise, 1930–1932. Quellen zur Ära Brüning*, 2 vols (Düsseldorf, 1980).
94. Michael Schneider, *Das Arbeitsbeschaffungsprogramm des ADGB. Zur gewerkschaftlichen Politik in der Endphase der Weimarer Republik* (Bad Godesberg, 1975) pp. 105–40.
95. Hentschel, *Sozialpolitik*, p. 130.
96. Bogs, *Sozialversicherung*, pp. 89ff; Homburg, 'Vom Arbeitslosen', pp. 277ff.
97. *Reichsarbeitsblatt*, Berlin, 25 June 1932, pp. 102ff, 111ff. See also Ulrike Hörster-Philipps, *Konservative Politik in der Endphase der Weimarer Republik. Die Regierung Franz von Papen* (Cologne, 1982).
98. Henning Köhler, 'Sozialpolitik von Brüning bis Schleicher', *Vierteljahrshefte für Zeitgeschichte* (VfZG), 21, 1973, 146–150; Detlev J. K. Peukert, *Die Weimarer Republik. Krisenjahre der Klassischen Moderne* (Frankfurt/M, 1987) pp. 132–49.
99. Homburg, 'Vom Arbeitslosen', pp. 264–94.

4 The Younger Generation and Welfare, 1918–1929

1. Hans Wolf, 'Von Wandervögeln, Scouts und Pfadfindern', *Jahrbuch des Archivs der Deutschen Jugendbewegung* (JbADJB) 3, 1971, p. 38.
2. Jürgen Reulecke, 'Männerbund versus Familie. Bürgerliche Jugendbewegung und Familie in Deutschland im ersten Drittel des 20. Jahrhunderts', in Koebner *et al. Mit uns zieht die neue Zeit*, pp. 199ff.
3. Harry E. Pross, *Jugend. Eros. Politik Die Geschichte der deutschen Jugendverbände* (Berne, 1964) pp. 469–82; Karl O. Paetel, *Jugend in der Entscheidung 1913–1933–1945* (Bad Godesberg, 1963) *pp.* 86–7; Rudolf Kneip (ed.), *Jugend der Weimarer Zeit. Handbuch der Jugendverbände 1919–1938* (Frankfurt, 1974) pp. 39, 135 ff; Peter D. Stachura, *Nazi Youth in the Weimar Republic* (Santa Barbara, Oxford, 1975) pp. 5–16; Stachura, *German Youth Movement*, pp. 94–112.
4. Richard N. Hunt, *German Social Democracy 1918–1933* (Chicago, 1970) pp. 92–108, 143ff; Guttsman, *Social Democratic Party*, pp. 156ff, 227ff, 251ff.
5. The point was frequently emphasised in the socialist press: see *Volkszeitung* (Stuttgart), 18 March 1927, article 'Partei und Jugend'. See also Bodo Brücher and Günter Hartmann: 'Die Sozialistische Arbeiter-

jugend in der Weimarer Zeit. Ihr Verhältnis zur SPD und ihr Eintreten für die Republik', *JbADJB*, 13, 1981, pp. 35–50; Günter Hartmann and Heinrich Lienker, *Sozialistische Arbeiterjugendbewegung in der Weimarer Republik* (Bielefeld, 1982); Helmuth Hägel; 'Die Stellung der sozialdemokratischen Jugendorganisationen zu Staat und Partei in den Anfangsjahren der Weimarer Republik', *IWK*, 12, 1976, pp. 166–216.
6. Hanno Drechsler, *Die Sozialistische Arbeiterpartei Deutschlands (SAPD). Ein Beitrag zur Geschichte der deutschen Arbeiterbewegung am Endle der Weimarer Republik* (Meisenheim, 1965).
7. E. Heimerich, *Jugendwohlfahrt und Sozialistische Weltanschauung* (Kiel, 1927); M. P. Liebrandt, *Jugendfürsorge und Jugendpflege* (Berlin, 1929).
8. Detlev Prinz and Manfred Rexin (eds), *Gewerkschaftsjugend im Weimarer Staat. Eine Dokumentation über die Arbeit der Gewerkschaftsjugend des ADGB in Berlin* (Cologne, 1983); Rotraud Tilsner-Gröll, *Jugendarbeit der SPD von den Anfängen bis zum Ende der Weimarer Republik* (Münster, 1978); and by same author, *Die Jugendbildungsarbeit in den freien Gewerkschaften von 1919–1933* (Frankfurt, 1982); Udo Wichert, 'Gewerkschaften und Jugend in der Weimarer Republik', *Gewerkschaftliche Monatshefte*, 32, 1981, Nr. 3/4 pp. 144–56.
9. The most prominent organisation was the *Deutsche Zentrale für Jugendfürsorge*, which changed its name to *Deutsche Zentrale für freie Jugendwohlfahrt* in June 1923. There was also the *Deutsche Kinderhilfe* and confessional groups, such as the *Arbeitsgemeinschaft für evangelischer Kinderpflege* (1922), reorganised in 1928 as the *Reichskonferenz für evangelische Kinderpflege*.
10. Scheibe, *Reformpädagogische Bewegung*, pp. 323ff.
11. Felix Raabe, *Die Bündische Jugend. Ein Beitrag zur Geschichte der Weimarer Republik* (Stuttgart, 1961); for membership figures pp. 43ff; Müller, *Die Jugendbewegung als deutsche Hauptrichtung*, pp. 164f, 389f, gives a membership of 110 000 in 1925, which appears too high; Stachura, *German Youth Movement*, p. 45ff.
12. Eberts, *Arbeiterjugend*, pp. 82ff; Gerhard Roger, *Die pädagogische Bedeutung der proletarischen Jugendbewegung Deutschlands* (Frankfurt, 1971).
13. Ulrich Linse, *Die Kommune der deutschen Jugendbewegung. Ein Versuch des Überwindung des Klassenkampfes aus dem Geiste der bürgerlichen Utopie. Die 'Kommunistische Siedlung Blankenburg' bei Donauwörth 1919/1920* (Munich, 1973); and by the same author (ed.), *Zurück, o Mensch, zur Mutter Erde. Landkommunen in Deutschland 1890–1933* (Munich, 1983).
14. Werner Kindt (ed.), *Die deutsche Jugendbewegung, 1920 bis 1933. Die Bündische Zeit. Quellenschriften* (Düsseldorf, 1974) pp. 1409–47.
15. Ibid., pp. 1477–1520. The *Gildenschaft Soziale Arbeit* was set up in Mecklenburg in 1925 by former *Bündische* members, including Justus Ehrhardt and Werner Kindt himself, to help in a small way to implement the Republic's new youth welfare legislation of 1922–4. The group had 300 members in 1927. For the *Zugscharen* see Friedrich G. Lennhoff, *Sozialarbeit in der Zeitgeschichte. Die Zugscharen. Eine*

Jugendhilfe-Organisation 1919–1937 (Munich, Basel, 1983). Further, Erich Stern, *Jugendpflege, Jugendbewegung, Jugendfürsorge* (Dortmund, 1925) and Manfred Zwerschke, *Jugendverbände und Sozialpolitik. Die Entwicklung des sozialpolitischen Willens in den deutschen Jugendverbänden* (Munich, 1963) pp. 111–30. The *Soziale Arbeitsgemeinschaft Berlin-Ost* is usefully discussed in Rolf Lindner, 'Bandenwesen und Klubwesen im wilhelminischen Reich und in der Weimarer Republik', *Geschichte und Gesellschaft*, 10, 1984, pp. 358ff, 363–8.
16. LHAK: 442/10339, *Landesbeirat für Jugendpflege*, 9.12.25.
17. The original central supervisory body for youth welfare, the *Zentralstelle für Volkswohlfahrt*, was replaced in 1919 by the *Ausschuss der deutschen Jugendverbände* which, in turn, was renamed the *Reichsausschuss der deutschen Jugendverbände* in 1927. In November 1932, the latter had 4 750 000 members from 117 groups. The athletics, sports, confessional and vocational organisations were the largest; about one-third of members were female. (Kindt, *Bündische Zeit*, pp. 1613–14; Kneip, *Jugend der Weimarer Zeit*, pp. 204–5.)
18. Ehrhardt, 'Amtliche Jugendpflege', pp.97–8.
19. *Die Verfassung des Deutschen Reichs vom 11. August 1919*, *RGBI*, 1919, II, Nr. 152, p. 1406; Rudolf Schuster (ed.), *Deutsche Verfassungen* (Munich, 1979, 11th edn) p. 120. Article 121 prescribed the rights of illegitimate children.
20. LHAK: 442/10328, *memorandum of Prussian Minister for Welfare*, 12.3.1920. Responsibility for youth welfare was transferred in 1919 from the Reich Education Ministry to the newly created Reich Ministry for Public Welfare (*Volkswohlfahrt*). See Josef Beeking, *Grundriss der Kinder-und Jugendfürsorge* (Freiburg i.B, 1929); L. Clostermann, T. Heller and P. Stephani, *Enzyklopädisches Handbuch des Kinderschutzes und der Jugendfürsorge* (Leipzig, 1930).
21. LHAK, 441/25704, booklet by Dr Teleky: 'Die Freizeit als Gesundheitsschutz der Jugendlichen'.
22. LHAK: 442/10327, *Preuss. Ministerium für Wissenschaft, Kunst und Volksbildung*, memorandum, Dec. 1918.
23. LHAK: 403/13202, Prussian Minister of Welfare, 22.11.1919; *Rhenisch-Westfälisches Wirtschaftsarchiv* (RWWA): 20/574/10. See here also 'Grundlegende Erlasse betreffend Förderung der Jugendpflege in Preussen', 1920.
24. LHAK: 403/13202, *Abschrift, meeting of Prussian Minister of Welfare*, Berlin, 18/19.12.1919.
25. LHAK: 441/44820, *Prussian Minister of Welfare*, 25.1.1920.
26. LHAK: 403/13202, *Regierungspräsident Coblenz to Prussian Minister of Welfare*, 10.5.1921. To be excluded from *Jugendpflege* activities were Communist youth groups whose applications for financial support at this time were invariably rejected by local authorities (see LHAK: 403/13202, *Regierungspräsident Trier to Communist Youth*, Trier, 5.4.1922).
27. LHAK: 403/13202, *Adenauer*, Cologne, 20.4.1921.
28. RWWA: 20/574/10, *Duisburger Sport-Club Preussen e.V.*, 29.3.1919;

Hauptstaatsarchiv Stuttgart (HStAS), E 151i/I/123, *Sportzeitung*, 12.4.1920.
29. LHAK: 442/10339, *Bezirksjugendpfleger Busch.* Trier, 15.1.1923.
30. Becker and Gildemeister, *Förderung der Jugendpflege*, p. 10.
31. Karl Hartung, *Richard Schirrmann und Wilhelm Münker, Die Gründer und Gestalter der deutschen Jugendherbergen* (Hagen, 1953).
32. LHAK: 442/10334 contains details of expenditure by government on *Jugendpflege* training, including *'Übersicht'*, Trier, April 1921; and HHStAW: 405/3813, *memorandum of Prussian Minister of Welfare*, Berlin, 14.6.1922; HASK: 903/160, *Beschäftigung von Junglehrern als Jugendpfleger.*
33. LHAK: 442/10328, *Mitteilungen der Beratungsstelle für Jugendpflege im Regierungsbezirk Cassel*, Nr. 1, June 1920, 'Neue Aufgaben der Jugendführung'.
34. HStAS: E 151i/I/123, *Protokoll vom Februar 1919*, 'Die Wohlfahrtspflege und Jugendarbeit in Württemberg. Ein Reformvorschlag'; ibid., 131/110 for *Jugendamtgesetz*, which became effective on 1.4.1920. Nine urban and 25 rural *Jugendämter* were established. For a detailed statement on the nature, form and function of these offices see ibid., E 151i/I/105, memorandum of 16.6.1920. By July 1922, Württemberg had 55 *Jugendämter*, ibid., Stuttgart, 27.7.1922, 'Die Durchführung des württ. Jugendamtgesetzes'.
35. HStAS: E 130a/356, *Württ. Innenminister*, 18.7.1919.
36. HHStAW: 460/789, *Erlass der Preuss. Staatsministerium, betr. Pflege der schulentlassene Jugend* 17.6.1923.
37. HStAS: E 151i/I/105, *Erlass des Ministeriums des Innern an die Oberämter betr. die Bekämpfung der Tuberkulose*, 21.1.1922.
38. StAH: *Sozialbehörde: GF51.02. Bericht der Behörde für das Gewerbe- und Fortbildungswesen*, Hamburg, 8.3.1922.
39. Ibid., *Auszug aus der Niederschrift über die 4. Sitzung des Ausschusses für Gesundheitsfürsorge am 11.5.1922.*
40. StAH: *Medizinalkollegium, II M8*, letter of 9.4.1920 from the *Deutscher Handwerk-und Gewerbekammertag.*
41. StAH: *Medizinalkollegium, IK6, Band 5, Jahresbericht 1922*, Hamburg, 21.4.1923 (Dr Bulle).
42. StAH: *Jugendbehörde: 338, Behörde für öffent. Jugendfürsorge*, Hamburg, 13.11.1922; ibid., *Gesundheits-und Pflegeamt der Polizeibehörde*, Hamburg, Oktober 1919 and *Besprechung am 17. Januar 1920 im Stadthaus*; ibid., *Bericht von Karl Otto (Jugendpfleger)*, Hamburg, 1.11.1921; ibid., *Jugendbehörde*: 65: *Tätigkeitsberichte Karl Otto to Behörde für öffentliche Jugendfürsorge*, Hamburg, 10.8.1920, November 1921, December 1921.
43. LHAK: 403/13208, *Landesjugendamt der Rheinprovinz*, April 1927.
44. LHAK: 441/25704, *Prussian Ministry of Welfare, Jahresbericht 1923.*
45. HASK: 903/317, 'Die Jugendpflege in Köln' in *Stadt-Anzeiger*, 27.7.1923.
46. HStAS: E 151i/I/105, *Bädischer Beobachter*, 10.3.1923. 'Uber das Elend der deutschen Kinder', and *Volksstimme* (Mannheim) 14.3.1923.

47. Württemberg's progressive and relatively generous approach was widely acknowledged – see HStAS: E 130b/1191, *Denkschrift des Württ. Ärzteverbands*, 1922.
48. LHAK: 441/17349, *Brief des Oberpräsident der Rheinprovinz, Coblenz*, 2.4.1919, intimates only 14 000 marks for the Rhineland in 1918/19.
49. LHAK: 441/17349, *Caritasverband Trier to Oberpräsident der Rheinprovinz*, 11.9.1920; ibid., 441/17350, *Oberpräsident der Rheinprovinz to Oberbürgermeister Coblenz*, 21.7.1922; *Prussian Minister of Welfare to the latter*, 22.2.1921.
50. LHAK: 442/10328, *Prussian Minister of Welfare*, 29.4.1921.
51. LHAK: 403/13202, statement of 5.3.1923; ibid., 442/10336, statement of 2.3.1923.
52. Fritz K. Ringer (ed.), *The German Inflation of 1923* (London, New York, 1969) pp. 112–18, speech by Deputy Franz Bumm, 20.2.1923; HASK: 903/317, 'Kinderelend in Köln' (press reports 1923–4), *Berliner Tageblatt*, 22.1 1924; LHAK: 403/13204, *Regierungspräsident Trier, betr.* 'Verwahrlosung der Jugend', 15.1.1924; ibid., 442/10339, *Tätigkeitsbericht des Bezirksjugendpflegers für das Jahr 1923*, 1.3.1924.
53. HHStAW: 405/3813, *Prussian Minister of Welfare*, 16.1.1923. The full title of the new body was *Landesbeirat für Jugendpflege, Jugendbewegung und Leibesübungen*.
54. LHAK: 442/15921, *Denkschrift des Preuss. Minister für Volkswohlfahrt*, Berlin, 14.5.1923.
55. LHAK: 442/10341, *Jahresbericht der Kreisjugendpflegerin Huberta v. Hatzfeld*, and ibid., 442/10339, *Tätigkeitsbericht des Bezirksjugendpfleger für das Jahr 1923*, Trier, 1.3.1924.
56. HHStAW: 405/3813, *Prussian Minister of Welfare*, 27.6.1923 and 14.7.1923; LHAK: 403/13204.
57. StAH: *Berufsschulbehörde, B 703, Jahresberichte 1915–1924*, of 13.7.1926.
58. LHAK: 442/15921, *Denkschrift*, Berlin, 14.5.1923.
59. HHStAW: 405/3813, *Prussian Minister of Welfare*, 26.9.1923, and of 15.2.1924.
60. StAH: *Medizinalkollegium*, III W 13, *Der Bürobeamte*, Nr. 5, 10.3.1927. There were altogether 14 338 suicides in Germany in 1924 (ibid., *Sonderabdruck des Deutsche Medizinische Wochenschrift*, Nr. 17, 1925).
61. HHStAW: 405/3813, *Prussian Minister of Welfare*, 15.2.1924 and *Prussian Minister of Education*, 11.3.1924. The total failure of the idea of a voluntary extension of the school year at Easter 1924 was blamed by the Prussian government on parental opposition, but its refusal to provide financial backing for the scheme and to appeal to private bodies for assistance was the fundamental reason. See LHAK: 403/13202, *Landesarbeits- und Berufsamt der Rheinprovinz*, Cologne, 21.12.1924.
62. LHAK: 403/13202, *Prussian Minister of Welfare*, 22.4.1924. The budget at his disposal in 1924 was 1.85 million marks (quoted in *Arbeiter-Jugend*, XXIV, 1932, Heft 4, pp. 99f).
63. HStAS: E 151/I/123, *Deutscher Verein für Armenpflege und Wohltätigkeit to Minister Lindemann*, Stuttgart, 25.3.1919, intimating the Reich

Government's intention to devise a *'Reichsjugendgesetz'*.
64. StAH: *Jugendbehörde*, 487, Band 1. The draft, which was officially dated 26.2.1920, is given in full here; and ibid., *Jugendbehörde*, 229, Band 2, for further detail of the background; see also *Hamburger Echo*, 4.3.1920 *(Abendausgabe)*.
65. LHAK: 441/44820, Prussian Welfare Minister, 25.1.1920.
66. StAH: *Jugendbehörde*, 229, Band 2, *Reich Finance Minister to Reich Interior Minister*, Berlin, February 1920.
67. LHAK: 442/16122, *Landrat Kreis Berncastel to Regierungspräsident Trier*, 20.3.1920. Indeed, a plan to establish a Reich Ministry for Youth was abandoned in 1921 because of the projected costs.
68. StAH: *Jugendbehörde*, 487, Band 1, *Behörde für öffentliche Jugendfürsorge*, Hamburg, to Dr Nöldeke, adviser to the Hamburg Senate, 3.3.1920; HStAS: E 130b/ 2946, *Abschrift, Reich Minister of Interior*, Berlin, 9.4.1920, and *Abschrift, Reich Finance Minister*, Berlin, 8.3.1920; the reaction of local bureaucrats in HStAS: E 151i/I/88, *Beamtenbeirat der Mittleren Justizbeamter to Württ. Interior Minister*, 22.6.1920.
69. StAH: *Jugendbehörde*, 229, Band 2, *Reich Minister of Justice*, February 1920.
70. HStAS: E 130b/2946, sundry memoranda, 1920–1.
71. HStAS: E 130b/2946, *Bay. Staatsregierung*, 17.3.1920; ibid., E 151i/I/ 88, 'Bemerkungen und Anträge Bayerns zum Entwurf eines RJWG', 17.3.1920. The submissions of the Hamburg and Baden governments are contained in this folder. For further detail on the Bavarian position, Bayerisches Hauptstaatsarchiv (Bay.HStA): *Staatsministerium des Äussern*, 100305, *Abschrift, Bayer. Ministerratssitzung vom 19 June 1922*, and ibid., *Staatsmin. d. Innern an das Staatsmin. d. Äussern*, Munich, 22.5.1922.
72. StAH: *Jugendbehörde*, 229, Band 2, article by Riebesell in *Der Aufbau. Wochenschrift für Erziehung*, 2, 1920, Nr. 16, 17.4.1920; ibid., *Jugendbehörde*, 487, Band 1, Riebesell's paper to a meeting of the *Deutsche Zentrale für Jugendfürsorge*, Berlin, 9.6.1920.
73. StAH: *Jugendbehörde*, 487, Band 1, *Hertz to Deutsche Zentrale für Jugendfürsorge*, Hamburg, 29.1.1920.
74. Ibid. See herein his memorandum entitled *'Das neue Jugendgericht'*.
75. Ibid., Dr Riebesell, *'Jugendgerichtsgesetz und Jugendwohlfahrtsgesetz'*, 14.10.1920.
76. Ibid. Full text of draft here. For additional relevant correspondence see HHStAW: 461/11051.
77. StAH: *Jugendbehörde*, 487, Band 1, memorandum *'Entschliessung'* of 1.12.1922. The revised draft of 2.11.1922 is provided here.
78. HStAS: E 151i/I/88, the *Vereinigung Deutscher Schul-und Fürsorgeärzte to Württ. Landtag*, Berlin, 29.7.1921.
79. LHAK: 442/10327, memorandum, Berlin, 22.3.1921; and ibid., 442/ 16122. The committee sat from 15 April 1921 to 1 February 1922 before returning to the Reichstag with the final draft. See HStAS: E 151i/I/88, *Bericht des 29. Ausschusses über den Entwurf eines RJWG, Reichstag, I, 1920–1922*, Drucksache Nr. 3959.

80. LHAK: 442/16122, *Wohlfahrtsschule der Stadt Köln to Wohlfahrtsstelle der Regierung in Trier*, 9.7.1921 and 16.12.1921; ibid., *Bezirksjugendpfleger Merseburg to Regierung in Trier*, 19.10.1922; StAH: *Jugendbehörde*, 229, Band 5.
81. HStAS: E 151i/I/88, Dr Karl Bürckert, *Fürsorgeamt*, Stuttgart, 23.7.1921.
82. HStAS: E 151i/I/88, the words of Centre Party Deputy, Frau Neuhaus, 13.6.1922.
83. Ibid.
84. StAH: *Jugendbehörde*, 229, Band 5, *Bericht, Reichstagssitzung vom 13/14.6.1922*.
85. Ibid. The similarity between this unjustifiably destructive and ideologically biased KPD line and Peukert's discussion of the law in *Grenzen der Sozialdisziplinierung*, pp. 137ff, 195ff, is striking.
86. HStAS: E 151i/I/88.
87. StAH: *Jugendbehörde*, 229, Band 5, Professor J. Klumker, 'Reichsjugendwohlfahrtsgesetz. Ein Wort in letzter Stunde', in *Sonderdruck aus der Kommunalen Praxis*, Nr. 20, 13.5.1922.
88. Ehrhardt; 'Amtliche Jugendpflege', 1930, pp. 99–100.
89. *Reichsgesetz für Jugendwohlfahrt vom 9. Juli 1922, RGBI*, 1922, I, Nr. 54, pp. 633–47; E. Friedeberg (= Wilhelm Polligkeit), *Das Reichsgesetz für Jugendwohlfahrt. Kommentar* (Berlin, 1930, 2nd edn).
90. The emphasis on individualism was precisely why the RJWG was denounced by the Third Reich, which stressed its incompatibility with the spirit of the *Volksgemeinschaft*. See *Jugend und Recht*, 11, 1937, p. 86; Günter Kaufmann, *Das kommende Deutschland. Die Erziehung der Jugend im Reich Adolf Hitlers* (Berlin, 1940, 2nd edn), pp. 13–14.
91. *Verordnung über das Inkrafttreten des RJWG vom 14. Februar 1924. RGBI*, 1924, I, Nr. 12, p. 110. At one stage the acute financial problems of the Reich government threatened to abort the entire enterprise: see HStAS: E 130b/2948, *Reich Interior Ministry to Reich Finance Minister*, Berlin, 19.11.1923.
92. *Jugendfürsorge* is the subject of later chapters.
93. Hasenclever, *Jugendhilfe und Jugendgesetzgebung*, pp. 52–58, 62ff.
94. LHAK: 442/14286, *Reichsverordnung*, 14.2.1924; StAH: *Jugendbehörde*, 329, report in *Soziale Praxis und Archiv für Volkswohlfahrt*, Nr. 29, 17.7.1924, of meeting in Berlin of the *Deutscher Archiv für Jugendwohlfahrt* (paper by Dr Hertz (Hamburg)). The latter took charge of Hamburg's youth welfare service in 1923; a *Jugendamt* replaced the *Behörde für öffentliche Jugendfürsorge* in January 1924 (StAH: *Jugendbehörde*, 428, Rundschreiben, Hamburg, 24.1.1924).
95. LHAK: 441/44820, report in *Volkswohlfahrt*, 5, 1924, p. 186.
96. HStAS: E 130b/2948, Reich Interior Ministry, 4.1.1924. By contrast see funding details as intimated in early 1923 in ibid., E 130b/2947, *Reich Interior Ministry*, 10.3.1923, and *Reich Finance Ministry*, 7.3.1923.
97. HStAS: E 151i/I91, *Reich Interior Minister to Länderregierungen*, 9.7.1924; ibid., E 130b/2948, *Abschrift*, Reich Interior Ministry meeting with Länderregierungen, 22.3.1924; ibid., E 151i/I/98, *Württ. Landesfürsorgebehörde betr. Beteilung der Gemeinden an den Kosten*, Stuttgart,

13.4.1927, and *Ministerialabteilung für Bezirks-und Körperschafts-Verwaltung*, Stuttgart, 4.4.1927.
98. HStAS: E 130b/2948, *Abschrift, Reich Interior Ministry*, 30.1.1925; LHAK: 442/14284, diverse; for details of personal applications for posts in the *Jugendämter* and discussion relating to their creation, see HStAS: E 151i/I/101. The *Jugendämter* were grouped into 13 *Landesjugendämter*. See also Hasenclever, *Jugendhilfe und Jugendgesetzgebung*, pp. 73ff.
99. HStAS: E 151i/I/90, for details of *Ausführungsgesetze* in Baden, 19.3.1925; Prussia, 29.5.1924; Bavaria, 26.5.1925; and Franz Fichtl (ed.), *Reichsgesetz für Jugendwohlfahrt mit den Ausführungsgesetzen sämtlicher Länder* (Munich, 1926). For Bavaria's attitude to RJWG, Bay.HSt.A: *Staatsministerium des Äussern, 106307, Abschrift, Staatsmin. d. Finanzen an der Staatsmin. d. Innern*, Munich, 12.12.1925.
100. LHAK: 442/14284, *Chairman of Kreiswohlfahrtsamt in Baumholder to Regierungspräsident Trier*, 23.6.1925; HStAS: E 151i/I/91, *Prussian Welfare Minister to Reich Interior Minister*, Berlin, 8.6.1925.
101. StAH: *Jugendbehörde*, 230, *Reich Interior Minister to Jugendamt*, Hamburg, 9.7.1925. Interpretation of Paragraph 28 of the RJWG relating to arrangements for foster-children was another major problem.
102. StAH: *Medizinalkollegium: II S 14, Niederschrift über eine Besprechung*, Hamburg, 7.2.1928 (health, youth and welfare departments). The Hamburg *Jugendamt* was criticised by the Left as early as 1925 for failing to bring an authentic 'social spirit' to its activity, despite the fact that it was committed to the original 1922 version of the RJWG and not its somewhat attenuated final version. (StAH: *Jugendbehörde*, I, 8, Band 5, report in *Hamburger Volkszeitung*, 17.11.1925).
103. HStAS: E 151i/I/178, provides full details of the Reichstag debate on the law, which came into force on 1.7.1923. See *RGBI*, 1923, I, Nr. 14, pp. 135–41; Hasenclever, *Jugendhilfe und Jugendgesetzgebung*, pp. 88ff.
104. Herbert Francke, *Das Jugendgerichtsgesetz (Kommentar)* (Berlin, 1926, 2nd edn.) p. 13; Walter Friedländer, *Jugendrecht und Jugendwohlfahrt. Lehrbuch der Wohlfahrtspflege* (Berlin, 1930, 2nd edn); Karl Peters, *Jugendgerichtsgesetz vom 16. Februar 1923, mit ergänzenden Gesetzen, Verordnungen und Verwaltungsvorschriften auf dem Gebiete des Jugendstrafrechts* (Berlin, 1942); and HStAS: E 151i/I/179, *Bericht der Reichsregierung vom 20. Januar 1930 betr. 'Organisation und Arbeit der Jugendgerichtshilfe in Deutschland'*.
105. HHStAW: *460/893, Amtsgericht*, Bad Homburg 20.12.1924, and miscellaneous correspondence and memoranda 1925–9.
106. Ibid., *Oberlandesgerichtspräsident*, Celle, 26.8.1924; also ibid., 461/11050, betr. *'Jugendgericht' from Der Erste Amtsanwalt*, Frankfurt/Main, 20.12.1924.
107. Ibid., *460/11052, Der Jugendrichter to Herr Oberstaatsanwalt*, Frankfurt/Main, 8.4.1932, and reply of 30.4.1932.
108. Ibid., 461/11050, betr. *'Jugendgericht' from the Oberstaatsanwalt*, Frankfurt/Main, 8.1.1925; StAH: *Jugendbehörde*, 487, Band 2, for expressions of support for the law.

109. StAH: *Jugendbehörde*, 487, Band 1, Dr Hertz 'Zum neuen Jugendgerichtsgesetz', 13.2.1923.
110. LHAK: 442/10336, *Erlass of Prussian Minister of Welfare*, 19.4.1924; StAH: *Jugendbehörde*, 487, Band 3, *Vorsitzende of Jugendgericht Hamburg to Jugendamt Hamburg*, 17.9.1923; report on 'Das Jugendgerichtsgesetz in der Praxis des Hamburger Jugendgerichts' by Herr Müller, May 1924. Further discussion of the JGG in the wider context of juvenile criminality is in Chapter 7.
111. Ferdinand Brandecker, 'Notizen zur Sozialisation des Arbeiterkindes in der Weimarer Republik', in Manfred Heinemann (ed.), *Sozialisation und Bildungswesen in der Weimarer Republik* (Stuttgart, 1976) p. 45.
112. LHAK: 403/13202, *Regierungspräsident Coblenz to Prussian Minister of Welfare*, 10.5.1921; and similar from *Regierungspräsident Aachen*, 1.6.1921.
113. Ibid., *Regierungspräsident Köln to Prussian Minister of Welfare*, 4.6.1921.
114. Ibid., *Regierungspräsident Trier to Oberpräsident der Rheinprovinz*, 14.1.1921; ibid., 442/10328, *Oberbürgermeister Trier to Regierungspräsident Trier*, 1.2.1921.
115. HHStAW: 405/3813, *memorandum, Kreisjugendpfleger*, 18.1.1921.
116. Ibid., *Magistrat, Ortsausschuss für Jugendpflege*, Wiesbaden, 11.2.1921.
117. HStAS: E 151i/I/193, *Abschrift*, Berlin, 17.8.1920.
118. HHStAW: 405/3813, *Prussian Minister of Welfare*, Berlin, 20.11.1920.
119. LHAK: 442/10327, *Prussian Minister of Welfare, 'Massnahmen zur Bekämpfung . . . '*, November 1920.
120. LHAK: 442/10328, *Prussian Minister of Welfare to Regierungs-und Oberpräsidenten*, 20.11.1920.
121. LHAK: 441/44820, quoted in *Volkswohlfahrt*, 1926, p. 41; Heinrich Hirtsiefer (ed.), *Jugendpflege in Preussen* (Eberswalde, 1930).
122. HStAS: E 130b/2951; on the perceived moral danger of the cinema in particular, see LHAK: 403/13205, *Kreisjugendpfleger* in M. Gladbach, 23/24.10.1925 and StAH: *Jugendbehörde*, 487, Band 2, *Oberbürgermeister Mülheim a. d. Ruhr to Regierungspräsident Düsseldorf*, 17.11.1923; on the Lichtspielgesetz, Bay.HStA: *Staatsministerium des Innern*, 66558, *Reich Interior Minister to Bayer. Minist. d. Äussern, Berlin, 28.11.1919 betr. Entwurf*. The Left continued to agitate against the law of 12 May 1920 throughout the 1920s.
123. LHAK: 403/13202, *Prussian Minister of Welfare*, 8.2.1923 and *Reich Chancellor*, 16.1.1923.
124. The draft was presented to the Reichstag on 3 May 1924, rejected by the Reichsrat in 1927 and a further draft introduced to the Reichstag in March 1929 disappeared in the machinery somewhere. The Württemberg government tried unsuccessfully to revive the scheme in July 1932. (HStAS: E 130b/2951, Reich Interior Ministry, Berlin, 21.4.1923 and 5.6.1925; report on Reichsrat meeting of 25.5.1927; ibid., E 151i/III/1435, *Auszug aus der Beilage 127-134 des Württ. Landtags vom 1. August 1932*.)

125. HHStAW: 405/3252, 'Bekämpfung der Schmutz in Schrift und Bild', 28.9.1925.
126. RGBI, 1926, I, p. 505; Else Matz and Ernst Seeger (eds), *Gesetz zur Bewahrung der Jugend vor Schund-und Schmutzschriften. Text und Kommentar* (Berlin, 1927); Hermann Popert, *Hamburg und der Schundkampf* (Hamburg, 1926); Rudolf Schenda, 'Schundliteratur und Kriegsliteratur', in R. Schenda (ed.), *Die Lesestoffe der Kleinen Leute* (Munich, 1976) pp. 78–104. The '*Schundkampf*' was aimed at 'penny dreadfuls' (*Groschenhefte*) and the '*Schmutzkampf*' against sexually erotic publications.
127. HStAS: E 151i/I/440, *Frankfurter Zeitung*, 15.6.1927.
128. Domansky and Heinemann, 'Jugend als Generationserfahrung', p. 19.
129. Peukert, *Grenzen*, pp. 175–89. Both the argument and the language used to express it are extravagant.
130. HStAS: E 130b/2711, *Reich Interior Ministry to Staatsregierungen*, 7.4.1933; *Württ. Staatsregierung to Württ. Interior and Cultural Ministries*, 15.6.1927; *Abschrift. Reich Interior Ministry*, 28.4.1927; *Abschrift*, III, 2766/20.5. The rather vexatious attitude of the Bavarian authorities towards the composition of the *Oberprüfstelle* is conveyed in Bay.HSt.A: *Staatsmin. d. Äussern, 100311, Bayer. Staatsmin. d. Innern a.d. Reichsmin. d. Innern*, Munich, 12.12.1927.
131. *Frankfurter Zeitung*, 15.6.1927.
132. Bay.HStA: *Staatsmin d. Innern, 66551, Prussian Welfare Minister to LJA betr. Nachrichtendienst*, Berlin, 1.2.1929; LHAK: 442/10344, 'Richtlinien zur Bekämpfung der Schundliteratur im Regierungsbezirk Trier', undated.
133. LHAK: 403/13208, LJA, *Niederschrift*, 30.6.1926 and 27.4.1927; ibid., 441/25704, *Die gesetzlichen Unterlagen zur Bekämpfung von Schund-und Schmutzschriften*, undated; ibid., 442/16 136, LJA. *Niederschrift*, 19.10.1928; ibid., 441/25 702, LJA, *Niederschrift*, 29.5.1929. A booklet to give guidance to those involved in the campaign was also supplied by the LJA: Hans Wingender, *Erfahrungen im Kampfe gegen Schund-und Schmutzschriften* (Düsseldorf, 1929). The KPD tried to have the law repealed in the Reichstag in 1928 (HStAS: E 151i/I/440).
134. LHAK: 441/23003, LJA, *Niederschrift*, 22.6.1931. Only 8000 marks was available for the campaign in the Rhineland in 1931 compared with 40 000 in 1929/30. Hamburg, an energetic campaigner also, suffered a similar experience – St.AH: *Sozialbehörde, AF 70.01, Bericht des Hamburger Jugendausschusses für die Zeit April 1929–May 1932*, pp. 8–9; further detail in Bay.HStA: *Staatsmin. d. Innern*, 66547–50.
135. HStAS: E 151i/I/440, Ludwig Carrière: 'Die Wirkung des Schund-und Schmutzgesetzes', Sept. 1928.
136. Ibid., press reports of 23.2.1928; Bay.HSt.A: Staatsmin. d. Innern, 73811, *Abschrift zu Nr. 2536 b 24 Der Bayerische Landtag*, 26.4.1928.
137. Peukert, *Grenzen*, p. 394, notes 6 and 18.
138. Elizabeth Harvey, 'Sozialdemokratische Jugendhilfereform in der Praxis: Walter Friedländer und das Bezirksjugendamt Berlin Prenzlauer Berg in der Weimarer Republik', *Theorie und Praxis der Sozialenarbeit*, 36, 1985, Part 6, pp. 216–29.

139. LHAK: 403/132(2, *Prussian Minister of Welfare*, 22.4.1924; *Arbeiter-Jugend*, 24, 1932 Heft 4, p. 99.
140. HASK: 610/1, *Verwaltungsberichte 1927–29*, here of October 1928; ibid., 903/171, *Jahresbericht, 1, April 1925 bis 31. März 1926 der Jugendamt Köln*, and same cf 1. April 1927–31. March 1928.
141. LHAK: 441/25702, *Niederschrift*, LJA, 29.5.1929; ibid., 442/10336, *Niederschrift*, LJA, 12.5.1926; ibid., 442/16138, indicating a LJA budget of 4 280 000 marks for 1928. See also Becker and Gildemeister, *Förderung der Jugendpflege*, pp. 107ff.
142. HHStAW: 405/3266, *Abschrift, Regierungspräsident*, Wiesbaden, 31.10.1928.
143. HStAS: E 130b'1191, *Staatspräsident to Württ. Finanzministerium*, 27.3.1925; ibid., *Regierungsblatt für Württemberg*, Nr. 8, 18.4.1928; ibid., E 151i/I/103o, *Niederschrift, Jugendamt*, Stuttgart, 25.6.1928.
144. Bay.HSt.A: *Staatsmin. d. Äussern, 100308, Staatsmin. d. Finanzen a. d. Staatsmin. d. Innern*, Munich, 3.7.1927, and Ministerratssitzung vom 2. Juli 1927. See a.so ibid., *Bekanntmachung*, 27.1.1928 (Staatsmin. d. Innern). The financial provision for 1925 is given in *Deutsche Zeitschrift für Wohlfahrtspflege*, 6, 1931, Nr. 10, p. 586; Bernhard Mewes, *Die Erwerbstätige Jugend. Eine Statistische Untersuchung* (Berlin, Leipzig, 1929) p. 108. Details of individual city and town provision on pp. 120ff, 134ff.
145. StAH: *Jugendbehörde, 98, Nordwestdeutschen Wohlfahrtsstatistik für Januar 1927*; *Direktor, LJA Hamburg to Senator Eisenbarth*, 21.3.1927; *Report, Jugendamt* Hamburg, 2.11.1927.
146. StAH: *Jugendbehörde*, 99, *Jugendamt to Senat*, 28.1.1928; and *Jugendamt to Finanzdeputation*, 1.8.1928; *Finanzdeputation to Jugendamt betr. Sparmassnahmen*, 12.5.1930. One very worthwhile item of expenditure was the *Jugendamt's* publication (in conjunction with the *Wohlfahrtsamt*) from December 1924 of a monthly journal, *Jugend-und Volkswohl. Hamburgische Blätter für Wohlfahrtspflege und Jugendhilfe*. A number of other progressive youth welfare authorities in Germany also started similar journals.
147. HHStAW: 405/3252, *Prussian Minister of Welfare*, Berlin, 26.5.1925.
148. StAH: *Medizinalkollegium*, II S 3, Band 2, *Hamburger Anzeiger*, Nr. 293, 16.12.1926; ibid., II S 7, Band 6, Dr Meyer, 16.10.1919; ibid., II S 7b, *Jahresversammlung des deut. Vereins für Schulgesund.*, Bonn, 10/11.9.1925; HStAS: E 151K/191, *Jahresbericht für Stadtkreis Stuttgart*, 1925.
149. Brandecker; 'Notizen', pp. 41f, 47–53; by same author: 'Erziehung durch die Klasse für die Klasse. Zur Pädagogik der Kinderfreundebewegung in Deutschland 1919–1933', in Heinemann (ed.), *Sozialisation und Bildungswesen*, pp. 167–86; Günter Dehn, *Grossstadtjugend. Beobachtungen und Erfahrungen aus der Welt der grossstädtischen Arbeiterjugend* (Berlin, 1919); and by same author, *Proletarischer Jugend. Ihre Lebensgestaltung und Gedankenwelt* (Berlin, 1929); Günter Krolzig, *Der Jugendliche in der Grossstadtfamilie. Auf Grund von Niederschriften Berliner Berufsschüler und-schülerinnen* (Berlin, 1930); Hildegard Hetzer, *Kindheit und Armut* (Leipzig, 1937); Otto

Rühle, *Das proletarische Kind. Eine Monographie* (Munich, 1922); a more optimistic but not entirely convincing portrait (because of methodological inconsistencies) of working-class youth life drawn by Robert Dinse, *Das Freizeitleben der Grossstadtjugend. 5000 Jungen und Mädchen berichten* (Eberswalde, 1932), especially pp. 12ff, 70ff, 85ff. See a corresponding study of the working class in 1929/30 in Erich Fromm, *Arbeiter und Angestellte am Vorabend des Dritten Reiches. Eine sozialpsychologische Untersuchung* (Stuttgart, 1980), English version: *The Working Class in Weimar Germany. A Psychological and Sociological Study* (Leamington Spa, 1984).

150. LHAK: 441/25704, *LJA der Rheinprovinz, Abschrift*, 20.10.1925; *Niederschrift*, 18.5.1927; ibid., 403/13208, LJA 27.4.1927; ibid., 442/10337, for LJA budget of 1926/27; StAH: *Sozialbehörde*, GF 51.02, *Nachrichtendienst*, Nr. 6, June 1928.
151. StAH: *Sozialbehörde*, GF 51.02, *Hamburgischer Landesverband für Volksgesundheitspflege*, e.V. to *Wohlfahrtsbehörde Hamburg*, 13.9.1928; ibid., *Medizinalkollegium*, II S 4, Band 2, *Erholungsfürsorge der staatlichen Schulen*, Hamburg 1929; ibid., *Sozialbehörde*, GF 51.05, 'Die Entwicklung der Heil-und Erholungsfürsorge . . .', 1927; ibid., GF 51.03, 'Erholungsfürsorge für Schulkinder . . .', 1928. Also, Ursula Büttner, *Hamburg in der Staats-und Wirtschaftskrise 1928–1931* (Hamburg, 1982) pp. 28ff, 180ff.
152. StAH: *Sozialbehörde*, GF 51.02, report to *Rechnungsamt*, Hamburg, 3.3.1927; ibid., 'Richtlinien für die Entsendung von Jugendlichen in Schul-und Ferienheime', 21.11.1927. A most informative study of the welfare holiday programme at this time is Marie Baum, *Beiträge zur planmässigen Ausgestaltung der Erholungsfürsorge für Kinder und Jugendliche*, published by the *Deutscher Archiv für Jugendwohlfahrt*, Berlin, 1928.
153. StAH: *Sozialbehörde*, GF 51.06, *Prussian Welfare Ministry to Jugendamt Hamburg*, 17.5.1929.
154. StAH: *Medizinalkollegium*, I B 38, Band 3, *Senatskommission to Gesundheitsbehörde*, Hamburg, 18.2.1927, and *Gesundheitsamt to Gesellschaft der Freunde des vaterländ. Schul-und Erziehungswesen*, 30.5.1927. In January 1920 there had been only 16 School doctors in Hamburg (ibid., II S 7, Band 6, Medizinalamt, Hamburg, 17.1.1920).
155. LHAK: 441/25702, *Niederschrift, Sitzung des Fachausschuss II des LJA*, 16.3.1928; ibid., 442/14285, *Niederschrift*, LJA Sitzung, 16.3.1928; StAH: *Medizinalkollegium*, II S 7, Band 3, *Schulzahnpflege*, Hamburg, 2.2.1928, and *Niederschrift*, 'Schulzahnärztliche Versorgung', Hamburg, 24.10.1928. On the socialisation issue, Michael H. Kater, 'Physicians in Crisis at the End of the Weimar Republic', in Stachura (ed.), *Unemployment*, pp. 49–77.
156. HHStAW: 405/3266, *Prussian Minister of Welfare*, Berlin, 3.3.1927.
157. Ibid., *Prussian Minister of Welfare to Regierungspräsident*, Berlin, 24.10.1929. Sensitivity on the flag issue is also revealed in Hamburg's schools – see StAH: *Medizinalkollegium*, II S 3, Band 2, *Oberschulbehörde to Schul-und Ferienheimeleiter*, 20.11.1928.
158. StAH: *Medizinalkollegium*, I K 27a, Band 3, *Dr Hermann, Schulärzt-*

11.4.1927; ibid., I K 27a, Band 4, *Dr Fleischer, Schulärztlicher Bericht 1928/29*, 8.5.1929; ibid., I B 38, Band 3, *Gesundheitsamt Hamburg to Gesellschaft . . . Erziehungswesen*, 30.5.1927. In 1928 only 14.8 per cent of Prussian schoolchildren were officially described as undernourished compared with 23 per cent in 1923 and 21.8 per cent in 1924. The figure for 1929 dropped further to 12.4 per cent (Hertha Siemering, *Deutschlands Jugend in Bevölkerung und Wirtschaft. Eine statistische Untersuchung*, Berlin 1937, p. 43).
159. StAH: *Sozialbehörde*, GF 51.05, *Dr Erichsen to Gesundheitsamt Hamburg*, 27.1.1929.
160. Siemering, *Deutschlands Jugend*, pp. 60f; StAH: *Medizinalkollegium*, I B 38, Band 3, *Herr Hell to Gesundheitsamt Hamburg*, 23.4.1929. Public concern about sexual diseases increased rapidly in the mid-1920s, creating pressure for legislation – the *Gesetz zur Bekämpfung der Geschlechtskrankheiten* of 18.2.1927. Some 19 130, mainly male adults, were afflicted in Prussia alone in December 1927 (StAH: *Medizinalkollegium*, III H 4d press reports 10.6.1928).
161. In 1930 there were in Germany 1 788 600 children and youths in foster-homes and other care institutions (Wilhelm Schickenberg, 'Pflegekinderfürsorge', *Soziale Praxis*, LXVI, 1937, p. 1074). There was constant scrutiny of the RJWG and amendments were made later in the 1920s to a number of its provisions, for example, relating to handicapped minors, in 1927 (HStAS: E 151i/III/800, *Entwurf eines Gesetzes zur Änderung des Reichsgesetzes für Jugendwohlfahrt*, 18.3.1927).
162. Anne Marie Niemeyer, *Zur Struktur der Familie. Statistische Materialien* (Berlin, 1931) p. 68.
163. StAH: *Sozialbehörde*, EF 60.13, *Nachrichtendienst*, Nr. 55, November 1924; 'Hamburger Massnahmen für ortsfremde . . . Jugendliche', *Wohlfahrtsamt*, Hamburg, February 1925; and *39. Deutscher Fürsorgetag: Leitsätze*, undated (1926).
164. Wilhelm Münker, *Das deutsche Jugendherbergswerk. Seine Entstehung und Entwicklung bis 1933* (Bielefeld, 1944) p. 88.
165. Gert Gröning and Joachim Wolschke, 'Soziale Praxis statt ökologischer Ethik. Zum Gesellschafts-und Naturverständnis der Arbeiterjugendbewegung', *JbADJB*, 15, 1984/85, pp. 216–17; *Metallarbeiter-Jugend*, 1929, Nr. 33, p. 226.
166. Thomas Lange, 'Der "Steglitzer Schülermordprozess" 1928', in Koebner *et al.* (eds), *'Mit uns . . . '*, pp. 412–37.
167. Herman Nohl, 'Die Jugend und der Alltag. Ein Beitrag zur Lebenskunde der Jugendlichen', *Die Erziehung*, 3, 1928, p. 215. Compare with his views in Nohl, *Die Jugendwohlfahrt. Sozialpädagogische Vorträge* (Leipzig, 1927). Official views are most authentically recorded in the minutes of the annual conferences of the federal states on the theme of youth welfare. Full details in Bay.HStA: *Staatsmin. d. Innern*, 73807, for example, of the fifth conference in the Reich Interior Ministry, Berlin, 7/8 June 1929. Records of earlier annual conferences in ibid., *Staatsmin. d. Äussern*, 100309.
168. Bernhard Mewes, 'Die Sterblichkeit der Jugendlichen in Preussen', *Das Junge Deutschland*, XXV, 1931, p. 202.

5 Youth in the Labour Market, 1918–1929

1. StAH: *Jugendbehörde* I, 427, Band 2, *Rundschreiben from the Reich Labour Minister to Staatsregierungen*, 1.9.1925, stressing the need for a reserve of skilled labour.
2. Wolfgang Köllmann, 'Bevölkerungsentwicklung in der Weimarer Republik', in Hans Mommsen, Dietmar Petzina, Bernd Weisbrod (eds), *Industrielles System und Politische Entwicklung in der Weimarer Republik* (Düsseldorf, 1977) Band 1, pp. 77f.
3. Siemering, *Deutschlands Jugend*, pp. 70f, 101ff.
4. Bernhard Mewes, 'Die berufliche Gliederung der deutschen Jugend', *Das Junge Deutschland*, XXIII, 1929, pp. 381ff; Siemering, *Deutschlands Jugend*, p. 10; Mewes, *Die Erwerbstätige Jugend*, p. 6.
5. Erwin Niffka, 'Die berufliche Lage der Jugend in der Gegenwart unter besonderer Berücksichtigung der männlichen Jugendlichen im Alter von 14 bis 21 Jahren', in Kurt Richter (ed.), *Handbuch der Jugendpflege*. *Heft 1, I Teil: Der jugendliche Mensch (männliche Jugend)* (Eberswalde, 1932) p. 70; Erwin Niffka and Hertha Siemering, *Jugend in Wirtschaft und Beruf* (Berlin, 1930) p. 29.
6. Niffka, 'Die berufliche Lage', p.70.
7. Peukert, *Jugend zwischen Krieg und Krise*, pp. 34ff.
8. LHAK: 441/44820, ministerial statement of 5.11.1918 entitled, 'Förderung der Jugend beim Übergang vom Kriege zur Friedenswirtschaft',
9. RWWA: *Akten der Industrie – und Handelskammer Münster*: 5/24/13, 14, 16 and 17 for details covering 1918–21.
10. StAH: *Jugendbehörde* I, 427, Band 2, report in *Hamburger Echo*, 20.2.1926 on 'Die Berufsberatung', in *Hamburger Anzeiger*, 19.5.1926 on 'Lehrling oder ungelernter Arbeit?', and in *Hamburger Fremdenblatt*, 4.11.1926 on 'Jugend, Wirtschaft, Berufsberatung'.
11. LHAK: 442/10339, meeting in Rhine Labour Office, report, Düsseldorf, 4.2.1924; HStAS: E 130b/2941, brochure *'Fürsorge für erwerbslosen Jugendliche'*, published by the *Deutsches Archiv für Jugendwohlfahrt*, Berlin, 1924.
12. Ernst Herrnstadt, *Die Lage der arbeitslosen Jugend in Deutschland* (Berlin, 1927) pp. 5ff.
13. Hans Staudinger, 'Die Erwerbslosigkeit der Jugendlichen, ihre wirtschaftlichen Folgen und deren Bekämpfung', *Arbeiterwohlfahrt*, 6, 1931, Heft 6, pp.161–2.
14. LHAK: 441/24041, *Wohlfahrtsamt Neuwied to Regierungspräsident Coblenz*, 16.9.1924, describing the labour market for youth in the Koblenz area as 'very bad', especially for 16–18-year-olds who were unskilled. A similar story is told in a report from the *Arbeitsnachweis Coblenz*, 20.10.1924.
15. Mewes, *Die Erwerbstätige Jugend*, p. 10; Schöck, *Arbeitslosigkeit und Rationalisierung*, pp. 151ff, 171; Niess; *Geschichte der Arbeitslosigkeit*, pp. 35ff.
16. Wolfgang Emmerich (ed.), *Proletarische Lebensläufe. Autobiographische Dokumente zur Entstehung der zweiten Kultur in Deutschland* (Reinbek/Hamburg, 1974) Band 2, pp.. 253f.
17. Niffka, 'Die berufliche Lage' p. 77.

18. Herrnstadt, *Die Lage*, pp. 26f.
19. Mewes, *Die Erwerbstätige Jugend*, pp. 12ff; Niffka and Siemering, *Jugend*, pp. 61ff.
20. Antoinette Schärer and Petra Wagner, *Jugendarbeitslosigkeit in Berlin während der Zeit der Weimarer Republik* (Diploma-Arbeit, Pädagogische Hochshule Berlin, 1976) pp. 35ff.
21. LHAK: 441/44820, report in *Volkswohlfahrt*, 1926, p. 975.
22. Niffka, 'Die berufliche Lage', p. 77; Herrnstadt, *Die Lage*, p. 7.
23. Fritz Gräsing, 'Erziehungsarbeit am Erwerbslosen Jugendlichen', in Carl Mennicke (ed.), *Erfahrungen der Jugendlichen* (Potsdam, 1930) pp. 41–42. By 1928 Berlin was sheltering 10 363 wandering youths (*Wanderburschen*) and Frankfurt/Main some 8000 (John W. Taylor, *Youth Welfare in Germany*, Nashville, Tenn., 1936, p.120)
24. Herrnstadt, *Die Lage*, p. 5. The Rhineland was one of the regions where youth unemployment persisted at high levels until at least the early spring of 1927 (LHAK: 441/24041, report of *Landesarbeits-und Berufsamt der Rheinprovinz*, Düsseldorf, 24.12.1926; and ibid.: *Kreisarbeitsnachweis Mayen to Regierungspräsident Coblenz*, 23.2.1927, and *Landesarbeits-und Berufsamt der Rheinprovinz to Preussische Minister für Volkswohlfahrt*, 28.3.1927) By contrast, Hamburg was one of the areas able to overcome the problem at this time (StAH: *Sozialbehörde* I, AF 70.01, *Arbeitsamt to Wohlfahrtsamt Hamburg*, 29.11.1927).
25. Bernhard Mewes, 'Die Arbeitslosigkeit der Jugendlichen', *Das Junge Deutschland*, XXV, 1931, Heft 11, p. 554. There were possibilities for unemployed youth to find irregular work in the 'black economy' or in casual work in agriculture in the 1920s – options not readily available after 1929.
26. StAH: *Sozialbehörde* I, AW 00.71, *Jugendamt Hamburg to Wohlfahrtsbehörde*, 4.12.1929.
27. Mewes, 'Die Arbeitslosigkeit', p. 554; Niffka and Siemering, *Jugend*, p. 67.
28. For example, see LHAK: 441/24041, *Regierungspräsident Münster to Oberbürgermeister of the Rhineland*, 10.12.1926.
29. Ernst Lau and Mathilde Kelchner, 'Die jugendliche Arbeiterschaft und die Arbeitslosigkeit', in Richard Thurnwald (ed.), *Die neue Jugend* (Leipzig, 1927) pp. 321–40. This is based on a survey of Berlin unemployed youths in 1921/2. Another influential report was in Heinrich Többen, *Die Jugendverwahrlosung und ihre Bekämpfung* (Münster, 1927, 2nd edn).
30. HHStAW: 460/743, *Amtsgericht Frankfurt/Main*, 1.3.1929, and ibid.: 405/3813, 'Jugendpflege an erwerbslosen Jugendlichen', 1924.
31. StAH: *Jugendbehörde* I, 291, *Reich Labour Minister to Minister for Social Welfare (Soziale Fürsorge)*, 26.6.1920.
32. Herrnstadt, *Die Lage*, pp. 9–14; Preller, *Sozialpolitik*, p. 368.
33. Walter Friedländer, 'Relief Measures for the Young Unemployed', in *Children, Young People and Unemployment*, published by The Save The Children International Union (Geneva, 1933) pp. 60–62.
34. Harvey, *Youth and the State in the Weimar Republic* (Thesis) p. 127.
35. For bitter criticism of the system for the way it treated the young jobless

see HASK: 903/160, report in *Rheinischer Zeitung*, 7.12.1926; and LHAK: 441/44820, report in *Volkswohlfahrt*, 1926, p. 975.
36. Herrnstadt, *Die Lage*, pp. 9–14.
37. Carl Birkenholz, 'Der Lehrling in der Arbeitslosenversicherung', *Jugend und Beruf*, 6, 1931, Heft 5, pp. 97–100.
38. Preller, *Sozialpolitik*, p. 421.
39. Käte Gaebel, 'Die Erwerbslosigkeit der Jugendlichen', in Rotes Kreuz (ed.), *Deutsche Jugendwohlfahrt. Denkschrift zum Weltkongress für Kinderhilfe* (Geneva, 1925) pp. 73–77.
40. LHAK: 403/13202, *Landesarbeits-und Berufsamt der Rheinprovinz*, statement, 12.12.1924, on funding.
41. Harvey, '*Sozialdemokratische Jugendhilfereform*', p. 227.
42. Albert Lamm, *Betrogene Jugend. Aus einem Erwerbslosenheim* (Berlin, 1932) especially pp. 12, 82. See also Erna Magnus, *Werkheime für erwerbslose Jugendliche. Neue Fürsorgeformen aus der Arbeit von Berliner Jugendämtern* (Berlin, 1927), which takes a more positive view of the experiment.
43. Herrnstadt, *Die Lage*, pp. 18, 23.
44. LHAK: 441/25704, Erich Ollenhauer, 'Die Freizeitsbewegung der Jugend', *Tagung des Landesausschusses der rheinischen Jugendverbände*, 14/15 May 1927, Düsseldorf, *Vorträge*, pp. 11–18; Wilhelm Hertz, 'Freizeiten für Jugendliche Erwerbslose', *Zentralblatt für Jugendrecht und Jugendwohlfahrt* (ZBl), XXIII, 1931, Nr. 7, pp. 245–47.
45. LHAK: 441/44820, *Erlass, Preuss. Minister für Volkswohlfahrt*, 'Fortbildung und Umschulung von Erwerbslosen, insbesondere von Jugendlichen', 23.4.1926. See also Willi Gleitze, 'Fürsorge-und Arbeitsmarktpolitische Massnahmen für Erwerbslose Jugendliche', in Mennicke (ed.), *Erfahrungen*, pp. 17, 27ff; Herrnstadt, *Die Lage*, pp. 45ff. for details of the Prussian decree of 15.2.1924.
46. HStAS: E 130b/2941, 'Richtlinien für die Beschulung der erwerbslosen Jugendlichen von 14 bis 18 Jahren', 10.12.1923, Berlin; for Hanover, see Joachim Bartz and Dagmar Mor, 'Der Weg in die Jugendzwangsarbeit-Massnahmen gegen Jugendarbeitslosigkeit zwischen 1925 und 1935', in Gero Lenhardt (ed.), *Der hilflose Sozialstaat-Jugendarbeitslosigkeit und Politik* (Frankfurt/M, 1979) p. 46.
47. LHAK: 403/13202, *President of the Reichsamt für Arbeitsvermittlung*, Berlin, 30.5.1922, on the advantages of sending unemployed youth to the countryside.
48. LHAK: 442/10339, meeting of Rhine Labour Office, Düsseldorf, 4.2.1924, report by Dr Langenberg.
49. Wolfgang Muth, *Berufsausbildung in der Weimarer Republik* (Stuttgart, 1985, Beiheft 41, *Zeitschrift für Unternehmensgeschichte*) pp. 53ff, 65–70
50. HStAS: J 150I/133a/3, pamphlet published by the *Christlicher Metallarbeiterverband Deutschlands, Abteilung Jugendpflege*, entitled 'Jugend vor die Front!' (Duisburg, n.d.).
51. StAH: *Jugendbehörde* I, 329, memorandum by Ilse Redewald, 'Wiederbelebung der Fabrikpflege'; and *Arbeitsamt Hamburg to Herr Nordmeier*, 4.11.1925.
licher Bericht, 11.4.1925, and *Dr Schall to Gesundheitsamt Hamburg*,

52. *Arbeiter-Jugend*, Nr 1, 1920, p. 11; see also Reinhard Lüpke, *Zwischen Marx und Wandervogel. Die Jungsozialisten in der Weimarer Republik 1919–1931* (Marburg, 1984).
53. LHAK: 467/1269, *Gesetz betr. Kinderarbeit in gewerblichen Betrieben vom 31.7.1925* (RGBI, 1925, Nr. 36, p. 162).
54. HHStAW: 407/496, *Abschrift, Preussisches Gewerbeaufsichtsamt*, Frankfurt, 6.8.1920; and ibid., 407/498, *Preussisches Gewerbeaufsichtsamt*, Frankfurt, to *Polizeipräsidium*,Frankfurt, 15.12.1921, and 29.5.1922.
55. HHStAW: 423/1088, *Preuss. Minister für Wissenschaft, Kunst und Volksbildung*, 23.12.1924.
56. HHStAW: 417/71, *Regierungspräsident Wiesbaden*, memorandum, 21.12.1928.
57. Albert Müller, 'Der Weg zum Jugendschutzgesetz 1938', *Das Junge Deutschland*, 32, 1938, p. 247; Fritz Petrick, *Zur sozialen Lage der Arbeiterjugend in Deutschland 1933 bis 1939* (East Berlin, 1974) pp. 90ff.
58. HStAS: E 130b/3170, 'Verordnung über die Beschäftigung jugendlicher Arbeiter auf Steinkohlenbergwerken', 24.4.1925, 3.3.1927, 25.3.1929, as examples.
59. *Aus der Geschichte der deutschen Arbeiterjugendbewegung 1904–1945, Dokumente und Materialien*, Ed. Institut für Marxistische Studien und Forschungen (Frankfurt/Main, 1975), p. 110f.
60. Niffka and Siemering, *Jugend*, pp. 84ff; Zwerschke, *Jugendverbände und Sozialpolitik*, pp. 111–30. Report of a meeting of the *Reichsausschuss* in Kassel in October 1925 on the theme, 'Die Freizeit der Jugend', in LHAK: 442/10337.
61. LHAK: 403/13205, *Bezirkskonferenz der SAJ*, Trier, 12/13 Feb. 1927.
62. A draft Labour Protection Law, incorporating demands for young workers, failed in the Reichstag in 1926 and 1929 (Friedländer and Myers, *Child Welfare*, p.166; Preller, *Sozialpolitik* pp. 352–8).
63. LHAK: 442/16121, *Regierungspräsident Trier to Landräte*, 4.12.1926; Waltraut Forkel, 'Kinderarbeit auf dem Lande', *ZBl*, xxv, 1933, Nr. 8, pp. 238–43; Helene Simon, *Landwirtschaftliche Kinderarbeit* (Berlin, 1925).
64. HASK: 903/160, report '*Die Notlage der arbeitenden Jugend*', Cologne, 14.2.1926.
65. RWWA: *Akten der Industrie-und Handelskammer Duisburg*: 20/574/16, *memorandum of Deutscher Industrie-und Handelstag*, 5.12.1919.
66. For examples of apprentices' contracts that were written see RWWA: *Akten der Industrie-und Handelskammer Duisburg*: 20/588/7, *Lehrverträge*, 1920–23.
67. Muth, *Berufsausbildung*, pp. 248ff, 279; Niffka, 'Die berufliche Lage', p. 72; Siemering, *Deutschlands Jugend*, p. 408f.
68. Mewes, *Die Erwerbstätige Jugend*, pp. 37ff, and see below.
69. RWWA: *Akten der Industrie-und Handelskammer Duisburg*: 20/588/6, letter to *Handelskammer Duisburg* from manager of iron works, 28.4.1920, and reply, 4.5.1920, upholding the right of instant dismissal. On maltreatment. StAH, *Jugendbehörde I, 427, Band 2, Abschrift*, Hamburg, 16.7.1925.
70. LHAK: 441/25704, *Landesjugendamt der Rheinprovinz*, 28.4.1925.
71. Otto Leibrock, 'Zur Neuregelung des Lehrlingswesen', *Der Arbeitgeber*,

1921, Heft 3, p. 37f; and RWWA: *Akten der Industrie-und Handelskammer Duisburg*: 20/588/5, Handelskammer Duisburg to Polizei, Dinslaken, 29.8.1922.
72. Hermann Bues, *Die Stellung der Jugendlichen zum Beruf und zur Arbeit* (Bernau, 1926) pp. 76ff; Gertrud Staewen-Ordemann, *Menschen der Unordnung. Die proletarische Wirklichkeit im Arbeitsschicksale der ungelernten Grossstadtjugend* (Berlin, 1933) pp. 28–42.
73. Wickert, 'Gewerkschaften', pp. 145ff; Walter Maschke, 'Die Jugend in den Gewerkschaften', in Thurnwald (ed.), *Die neue Jugend*, pp. 220–30. He quotes (p. 228) for mid-1925 267 966 youths in the unions, or 6 per cent of the total, but he probably has included older age groups, 18–21 years or 18–25 years.
74. Tilsner-Gröll, *Jugendarbeit der SPD*, p. 109. The ADGB started to publish in 1926 a monthly periodical, *Jugend-Führer*, for young leaders in the unions, but other important initiatives for younger members were not forthcoming.
75. Mewes, *Die Erwerbstätige Jugend*, especially pp. 54ff, 59ff, 66ff, 74ff, 82ff. For comparative purposes see also the sample in Eppe, *Selbsthilfe*, pp. 190ff.
76. For regional details of working time, Agathe Schmidt, *Aus Arbeit und Leben der werktätige Jugend* (Berlin, 1925) on Kiel; LHAK: 441/25704, Dr Szajkowski, 'Die Freizeit der werktätigen Jugend unter besonderer Berücksichtigung der rheinischen Verhältnisse'. Further useful data in Paul F. Lazarsfeld (ed.), *Jugend und Beruf. Kritik und Material* (Jena, 1931) pp. 1ff.
77. StAH: *Sozialbehörde*, I, GF 51.03, 'Vor welchen Aufgaben stehen wir in der Kinder-und Erholungsfürsorge?', November 1926; and ibid., GF 51.02, 'Erholungsfürsorge für Jugendliche', in *Nachrichtendienst*, Nr. 6, June 1928.
78. LHAK: 403/13208, *Denkschrift der Reichsausschuss*, 24.2.1925.
79. StAH: *Sozialbehörde* I, GF 51.02, *Niederschrift über die Oberfürsorgeinnensitzung*, Hamburg, 19.5.1932.
80. Lisbeth Franzen-Hellersberg, *Die jugendliche Arbeiterin. Ihre Arbeitsweise und Lebensform* (Tübingen, 1932) pp. 46ff.
81. On employers' response, RWWA: *Akten der Industrie-und Handelskammer Duisburg*: 20/588/2, Deutsche Industrie-und Handelstag, 26.9.1923.
82. R. H. Samuel and R. Hinton-Thomas, *Education and Society in Modern Germany* (London, 1971) p. 38.
83. LHAK: 403/13205, *Tagung, Jugendpfleger der Rheinprovinz*, 23.10.1925; Bay.HStA: *Staatsministerium des Innern*, 73810, Reichsarbeitsminister to Reichswirtschaftsminister, betr. *Entwurf (Lehrlingsgesetz)*, Berlin, 20.7.1923. Bavarian objections given in ibid., *Staatsmin. für Unterricht und Kultur an das Staatsmin. für Soziale Fürsorge*, Munich, 13.9.1923.
84. Muth, *Berufsausbildung*, pp. 445ff, 481–580; Niffka and Siemering, *Jugend*, pp. 84–7 for contribution of the *Reichsausschuss der deutschen Jugendverbände*.
85. HHStAW: 405/3041, in Hessen, the *Gesetz betr. Die Erweiterung der Berufs-(Fortbildungsschule)pflicht*, 31.7.1923; StAH: *Berufsschulbehörde*, B703, *Gesetz über die Verwaltung des Berufsschulwesens vom 14. Juli 1922*.

86. *Arbeitszeitverordnung vom 21. Dezember 1923*, in *RGBl*, 1923, I, Nr 134, pp. 1249ff; on the conflicts of interest, StAH: *Berufsschulbehörde*, B 703, *Jahresbericht 1927*, Hamburg, 10.7.1928.
87. Muth, *Berufsausbildung*, p. 1.
88. Klaus Kümmel, 'Zur schulischen Berufserziehung im Nationalsozialismus. Gesetze und Erlasse', in Manfred Heinemann (ed.), *Erziehung und Schulung im Dritten Reich. Teil 1* (Stuttgart, 1980) p. 276.
89. StAH: *Berufsschulbehörde* I, B 703, *Jahresbericht 1927*, 10.7.1928; ibid., *Medizinalkollegium*, II S 76, *Bericht über die Jahresversammlung des deutschen Vereins für Schulgesundheitspflege*, Bonn, 10/11 September 1925. Official reports on vocational school provision in Bavaria 1922–30 were self-congratulatory – see Staatsarchiv München (StAM): *Regierung von Oberbayern*, 56683 and 56684, miscellaneous annual reports.
90. Hugo Sauer, *Jugendberatungsstellen* (Berlin, 1918).
91. Muth, *Berufsausbildung*, pp. 78ff, 116ff.
92. StAH: *Berufsschulbehörde*, B 703, and B 111, report by *Jugendausschuss der Hamburgisches Arbeitsamt*, 23.1.1919; StAM: *Regierung von Oberbayern*, 61759, *Bekanntmachung, Staatsministerium d. Innern*, 31.10.1920.
93. Muth, *Berufsausbildung*, pp. 88ff, 121, 129; Preller, *Sozialpolitik*, p. 453f; Rudolf Wiedwald, 'Berufsberatung und Wirtschaft', in *Jugend-und Volkswohl, Hamburgische Blätter für Wohlfahrtspflege und Jugendhilfe*, 2, 1927, Heft 9/10, pp. 73f.
94. StAH: *Jugendbehörde* I, 427, Band 2, various press reports in February, May, November 1926: *Jugend-und Volkswohl, Hamburgische Blätter für Wohlfahrtspflege und Jugendhilfe*, Heft 9/10, January 1927; also in StAH: *Jugendbehörde* I, 427, Band 2, 'Richtlinien für das Zusammenarbeiten von Jugendamt und Berufsberatungsstellen', 1.3.1927; For Württemberg, HStAS: E 151i/III/1582, '*Verzeichnis der Berufsberatungsstellen . . . nach dem Stande vom 6. November 1925*'; for Bavaria, StAM: *Regierung von Oberbayern*, 61759, various reports from localities 1919–21.
95. In his study of the factors influencing career choice among youth, Lazersfeld identified 'pleasure' as more important than parental influence, personality, family circumstances and others. Catholics tended to select traditional occupations, he found, while Protestants were more prepared to become involved in newer, capitalist jobs (Lazarsfeld (ed.), *Jugend und Beruf*, pp. 7–24).
96. Lazarsfeld (ed.), *Jugend und Beruf*, p. 53. On the broader school question interesting comment is provided by Reinhard Dithmar and Jörg Willer (eds), *Schule zwischen Kaiserreich und Faschismus. Zur Entwicklung des Schulwesens in der Weimarer Republik* (Darmstadt, 1981); Heinrich Küppers, 'Weimarer Schulpolitik in der Wirtschafts-und Staatskrise der Republik', *VfZG*, 28, 1980, Heft 1, pp. 20–46; Wolfgang W. Wittwer, *Die sozialdemokratische Schulpolitik in der Weimarer Republik* (Berlin, 1980); Peter Lundgreen, *Sozialgeschichte der deutschen Schule im Überblick* (Göttingen, 1981).
97. LHAK: 442/16079, Professor Behn, 'Pädagogische Psychologie der Jugend', Bonn, 17/22 June 1926.
98. Siemering, *Deutschlands Jugend*, p. 23.

99. Eduard Spranger, 'Männliche Jugend', in Kurt Richter (ed), *Handbuch der Jugendpflege, Heft 1, Der Jugendliche Mensch* (Eberswalde-Berlin, 1932) p. 33. See also Friedl. Fürnberg and Kurt Müller, *Die Lage der arbeitenden Jugend in den kapitalistischen Ländern* (Berlin, 1928).

6 Youth Unemployment in the Great Depression, 1929–1933

1. Niffka, 'Die berufliche Lage', p. 78.
2. Siemering, *Deutschlands Jugend*, pp. 10ff; see also Detlev J. K. Peukert, 'Die Erwerbslosigkeit junger Arbeiter in der Weltwirtschaftskrise in Deutschland 1929–1933', *Vierteljahrschrift für Sozial-und Wirtschaftsgeschichte*, 72, 1985, Heft 3, pp. 305ff.
3. Detlev Peukert, 'The Lost Generation: Youth Unemployment at the End of the Weimar Republic', in Evans and Geary (eds), *The German Unemployed*, p. 191, note 3.
4. Herbert Strauf, 'Die Berufslage der jungen Angestellten', in *Die Zwiespruch*, June 1931, pp. 280ff.
5. Mewes, 'Die Arbeitslosigkeit', pp. 553–4; Hermann Maass, 'Hilfe für die erwerbslose Jugend', *Das Junge Deutschland*, XXV, 1931, pp. 1–8, quotes a figure of 500 000 for 31 December 1930; the figures for mid-January 1931 are provided in Bruno Klopfer, 'Die jungen Arbeitslosen und der "freiwilliger Arbeitsdienst"', *Soziale Praxis*, 40, 1931, Heft 28, pp. 916–20.
6. Mewes, 'Die Arbeitslosigkeit', pp. 554ff.
7. Niffka, 'Die berufliche Lage', pp. 78–9; Staudinger, 'Die Erwerbslosigkeit', p. 161; Rudolf Wiedwald, 'Die Arbeitslosigkeit der Jugend in den Jahren 1932 bis 1934', *ZBI*, XXVI, 1934, Nr 8, pp. 231–2, quotes 915 576 jobless youths in spring 1932.
8. Kurt Richter, 'Massnahmen zur Betreuung der erwerbslosen Jugend', in Kurt Richter (ed.), *Handbuch der Jugendpflege*, Heft 14 (Eberswalde-Berlin, 1933) p. 18; *Reichsarbeitsblatt*, Teil II, September 1932, p. 383.
9. Herrnstadt, *Die Lage*, pp. 5f.
10. Siemering, *Deutschlands Jugend*, pp. 183, 354; Wiedwald, 'Die Arbeitslosigkeit', p. 232.
11. Siemering, *Deutschlands Jugend*, pp. 12, 122ff, 286f.
12. Wiedwald, 'Die Arbeitslosigkeit', p. 234.
13. Siemering, *Deutschlands Jugend*, pp. 138ff, 266ff. Niffka and Siemering, *Jugend*, pp. 43, 54.
14. As noted by Theodor Geiger, *Die soziale Schichtung des deutschen Volkes* (Stuttgart, 1932, new edn 1967) pp. 96f.
15. StAH: *Sozialbehörde* I, AW 00.77, memorandum from *Jugendamt* to *Wohlfahrtsbehörde, Abteilung Arbeitsfürsorge*, 6 11.1930.
16. HASK: 610/1, *Jugendamt to Dr Berndorff*, 20.1.1931.
17. HStAS: E 151i/I/56, *Württ. Innenministerium to Jugendämter*, 5.10.31, reply of *Jugendamt Stuttgart*, 16.11.1931.
18. *Arbeiter-Jugend*, 23, 1931, Heft 7, p. 150; Staudinger, 'Die Erwerbslosigkeit', p. 162.
19. HASK: 1187/K38, 'Gefährdung von Lehrverträge durch die Wirtschaftskrise?', in *Nachrichtendienst des Deut. Vereins für Öffentliche und Pri-*

vate *Fürsorge*, XIII, 1932, Nr 7, pp. 183ff, and ibid., 'Das Berufsschicksal von Handwerkslehrlingen nach Beendigung der Lehre', pp. 186ff.
20. *Arbeiter-Jugend*, 22, 1930, Heft 2, pp. 25–6, 'Arbeitslose Jugend'.
21. Ibid., p. 25; Carl Bensel, *Wirtschaftsnot-Arbeitslosenelend* (Mannheim, 1931) pp. 21ff.
22. Muth, *Berufsausbildung*, p. 133.
23. Dick Geary, 'Jugend, Arbeitslosigkeit und politischer Radikalismus am Ende der Weimarer Republik', *Gewerkschaftliche Monatshefte*, 34, May 1983, p. 307.
24. Mewes, 'Die Arbeitslosigkeit', pp. 556–7; Siemering, *Deutschlands Jugend*, pp. 247–62, 268ff; for the Rhineland, LHAK: 441/23003, *Abschrift*, LJA meeting, 22.6.1932; for Wiesbaden, HHStAW: 405/3041, *Regierungspräsident betr. 'Betreuung der erwerbslosen Jugend'*, 10.1.1931, and *Regierungspräsident to Preuss. Minister für Volkswohlfahrt*, 13.4.1931.
25. Siemering, *Deutschlands Jugend*, p. 294ff; Walter Schönstedt, *Kämpfende Jugend. Roman der arbeitenden Jugend* (Berlin, 1932) p. 132.
26. Siemering, *Deutschlands Jugend*, pp. 300ff, 310ff.
27. StAH: *Arbeitsbehörde* I, 16, *Sondererhebung über die Zahl der jugendlichen Arbeitslosen*, 30.7.1932.
28. *RGBI*, 1930, I, Nr. 31, p. 311; a full explanation in Rudolf Wiedwald, 'Fürsorgemassnahmen für jugendliche Arbeitslose vom Standpunkt der Arbeitsämter', *Arbeiterwohlfahrt*, 5, 1930, Heft 24, pp. 737–41.
29. *RGBI*, 1930, I, Nr. 47, p. 517; ibid., 1931, I, Nr. 22, p. 279.
30. Between October 1930 and December 1932 no more than 15 000 unemployed in any one month in the Reich were engaged in compulsory labour for that purpose (Homburg, 'Vom Arbeitslosen', p. 280, note 83).
31. *RGBI*, 1932, I, Nr. 35, p. 273.
32. Preller, *Sozialpolitik*, p. 435.
33. See next chapter.
34. Employers successfully blocked the introduction of protective measures for young workers in the Westphalian coal industry in early 1930, as one example of their power (HStAS: E 130b/3170, *memorandum of Ministerialrat Druck*, Berlin, 26.3.1930).
35. HStAS: E 130b/3170, *Verordnung vom 26.3.1930 and 21.3.1932*; and *Württ. Wirtschaftsministerium to Württ. Gesandschaft*, Stuttgart, 5.3.1932.
36. *Arbeiter-Jugend*, 23, 1931, Heft 11, p. 254, 'Jugendschutzarbeit in der Praxis'; HStAS: E 151i/I/56, *report of Württ. Landtag session*, 21.5.1931.
37. *Arbeiter-Jugend*, 24, 1932, Heft 3, pp. 69ff, article emotively entitled, 'Lehrlinge, wehrt euch gegen Prügel', and ibid., 22, 1930, Heft 9, pp. 194f., 'Lehrlingsmisshandlungen und Jugendausbeutung'; HStAS: J 150I/133a/4, KJVD pamphlet, 'Wir rufen euch zum Kampf!' (Berlin, 1932).
38. HHStAW: 405/3266, *Preuss. Minister für Volkswohlfahrt*, 16.12.1929, in the first of many warnings to reduce youth welfare budgets.
39. LHAK: 442/16121, *Rundschreiben des Reichsministeriums des Innern an die obersten Jugendwohlfahrtsbehörden der Länder*, Berlin, 29.3.1932.
40. StAH: *Sozialbehörde* I, AF 70.01, *Abschrift, Bericht über die ärztlichen*

Erfahrungen betr. den Gesundheitszustand der Kinder vom 1.11.31–
1.4.32, 27 April 1932.
41. StAH: Sozialbehörde I, AW 00.97, Niederschrift über die 4. Sitzung
des Ausschusses über Fürsorge für jugendliche Erwerbslose, 4.11.1931;
ibid., Arbeitsbehörde I, 152, Hertz to Notstandskommission des Senats,
2.4.1931.
42. StAH: Sozialbehörde I, EF 60.13, 'Bedrohliches Anwachsen der Zahl
der jugendlichen Wanderer infolge steigender Arbeitslosigkeit', October
1930, and April 1931; ibid., Jugendamt to Deut. Verein für Öffentliche
und Private Fürsorge, 28.11.30; Bay HStA: Staatsministerium des Innern, 73812, Landesfürsorgeverband Oberfranken an das Staatsmin. d.
Innern, Bayreuth, 4.10.1929; see further Treue (ed.), Deutschland in der
Weltwirtschaftskrise, pp. 251, 337.
43. Das Junge Deutschland, 32, 1938, p. 203.
44. HHStAW: 460/743, Abschrift, Amtsgericht, Bonn, 4.7.1932, betr. 'Strafrechtliche Behandlung minderjähriger Landstreicher'.
45. Bruno N. Haken, Stempelchronik. 261 Arbeitslosenschicksale (Hamburg, 1932) pp. 68ff, 72ff; Justus Ehrhardt, 'Männliche Prostitution und
Jugendverwahrlosung', ZBI, 22, 1930, Heft 7, pp. 217–23.
46. Jahnke, Geschichte d. deut. Arbeiterjugendbewegung, p. 395.
47. Ruth Weiland, Die Kinder der Arbeitslosen (Eberswalde-Berlin, 1933)
p. 37; Treue (ed.), Weltwirtschaftskrise, pp. 143f. 247, 253, 338.
48. Weiland, passim; an abridged English version was published as The
Effects of Unemployment on Children and Young People (Geneva,
1933); Ruth Fischer and Franz Heimann, Deutsche Kinderfibel (Berlin,
1933).
49. Siemering, Deutschlands Jugend, pp. 71–2.
50. For the difficulties of the school medical service in Hamburg see StAH:
Medizinalkollegium, I K 27a, Band 5, Dr Breyendorff, Schuljahr 1931/2,
undated report; for the dental provision in the Rhineland, LHAK:
441/23003, Sonderdruck, Deutsche Zahnärztliche Wochenschrift, Nr. 9,
12.5.1932, article by Dr Elizabeth Schenk; comment on Prussia in
Siemering, Deutschlands Jugend, p. 58.
51. StAH: Sozialbehörde I,AF 70.01, for full details of both; 'Umbau-Nicht
Abbau. Vorschläge des Reichsausschuss der deutschen Jugendverbände
für ein Notprogramm der Jugendhilfe'.
52. Stachura, Nazi Youth, pp. 56, 68 (note 27).
53. Staatsarchiv Bremen (StAB): 3–A. 18, Nr. 145.
54. Gewerkschaftsjugend, 11, 1930, Nr. 6.
55. Arbeiter-Jugend, 24, 1932, Heft 8, p. 250; Martin Martiny, 'Sozialdemokratie und junge Generation am Ende der Weimarer Republik', in
Wolfgang Luthardt (ed.), Sozialdemokratische Arbeiterbewegung und
Weimarer Republik (Frankfurt/Main, 1978), vol. II, pp. 56–117.
56. LHAK: 442/10344, Niederschrift über die Sitzung des Bezirksausschusses
für Jugendpflege am 15. April 1931, remarks by Regierungsdirektor Gildemeister.
57. LHAK: 441/44820, Reich Minister of Welfare, statement of 15.5.1930;
Erwin Niffka, 'Berufsausbildung und Erwerbslosenschulung', Arbeit und
Beruf, 10, 1931, Ausgabe A, Nr. 7, p. 100, for Prussian Minister of
Welfare's decree on Jugendpflege of 16.10.1930.

58. A different emphasis in a broadly similar argument is given by Elizabeth Harvey, 'Youth Unemployment and the State: Public Policies towards Unemployed Youth in Hamburg during the World Economic Crisis', in Evans and Geary (eds), *The German Unemployed* (London, 1987) pp. 142, 149.
59. StAB: 3-A, 18, Nr. 145, *Syrup to Landesarbeitsämter*, 20.12.1930; *Ministerialrat* Ziertmann, 'Über die Beschulung und Betreuung der erwerbslosen Jugend', *Arbeit und Beruf*, 10, 1931, Ausgabe A, Nr. 7, p. 95. See also Friedrich Syrup, *Der Arbeitseinsatz und die Arbeitslosenhilfe in Deutschland* (Berlin, 1936).
60. LHAK: 441/44820, *Erlass, Prussian Minister for Trade and Commerce*, 7.1.1931; Heinrich Troeger, 'Beschulung jugendlicher Erwerbsloser', *Arbeit und Beruf* 10, 1931, Nr. 11, pp. 161–3; for similar action taken shortly afterwards by the Hamburg authorities see StAH: *Sozialbehörde* I, AW 00.77, *Jugendbehörde to Senator Neumann*, 21.2.1931.
61. StAB: 3-A, 18, Nr. 145, *Präsident der Reichsanstalt*, 15.7.1932.
62. StAH: *Sozialbehörde* I, AW 00.97, *Abschrift, Ausschuss für erwerbslosen Jugend*, 9.3.1931; ibid., 'Junge Erwerbslose auf der Schulbank', in *Hamburger Echo*, 15.1.1932.
63. Walter Friedländer, 'Zur Frage der Tagesheim für jugendliche Erwerbslose', *ZBI*, XXIII 1931, pp. 322–4; *Die Zwiespruch*, Nr. 45, 7 November 1931.
64. Bundesarchiv Koblenz (BAK): R2/18881, *Reichsarbeitsministerium to Reichsfinanzministerium*, 21.7.1932.
65. StAH: *Arbeitsbehörde* I, 116, *Rundschreiben des Reichsanstalts*, 29.6.1932.
66. StAB: 3-A, 18, Nr. 145, report by Dr Syrup, 15.7.1932, and Syrup to Reich Labour Minister, 20.8.1931.
67. BAK: R2/18815, *Preuss. Minister für Handel und Gewerbe an den Preuss. Ministerpräsidenten betr. Massnahmen zur Minderung der Arbeitslosigkeit*, 16.10.1930.
68. StAH: *Sozialbehörde* I, AW 34.01, *Rundschreiben des Reichsarbeitsministerium betr. Verlängerung der Schulpflicht*, 22.11.1930 and 29.11.1930.
69. BAK: R2/18813, *Preuss. Ministerpräsident an Reichskanzlei*, 23.10.1930.
70. Ibid., *Reichsarbeitsminister an den Staatssekretär der Reichskanzlei*, 13.12.1930.
71. *Ministerialrat* Ziertmann, 'Zur Frage der Verlängerung der Schulpflicht', *Arbeit und Beruf*, 10, 1931, Ausgabe A, Nr. 5, pp. 59–63.
72. LHAK: 441/25702, *Abschrift, LJA meeting*, 28.10.1930, and 22.11.1930; see also 'Jugendpflegerische Erfassung der erwerbslosen Jugend' (no author cited), *ZBI*, XXII, 1930, pp. 245–8; HHStAW: 405/3266, *Regierungspräsident*, Wiesbaden, 7.1.1930.
73. StAH: *Jugendbehörde* I, 99, *Finanzdeputation to Jugendbehörde*, 23.5.1930; *Rechnungsamt to Jugendbehörde*, 12.5.1930 and reply of 2.8.1930; ibid., *Sozialbehörde* I, AF 70.01, *Bericht des Hamburger Jugendausschuss*, April 1929–March 1932; ibid., AW 00.77, *Jugendamt to Wohlfahrtsbehörde*, 6.11.1930; *Jugendbehörde to Senator Neumann*, 21.2.1931. For general background, Ursula Büttner and Werner Jochmann, *Hamburg auf dem Weg ins Dritte Reich. Entwicklungsjahre, 1931–1933* (Hamburg, 1983).

74. HASK: 610/13, 'Nachrichten aus dem Städtischen Amt für Jugendpflege und Leibesübungen', Cologne, 31.12.1932; James, *German Slump*, p. 102.
75. LHAK: 441/23003, *Abschrift*, LJA meeting, 19.4.1932 and 22.6.1932; Harvey, *Youth and the State* (thesis) p. 164.
76. LHAK: 442/16121, *Rundschreiben des Reichsministeriums des Innern an die obersten Jugendwohlfahrtsbehörden der Länder*, Berlin, 29.3.1932, on the need to enlist more private sponsorship for youth welfare; Harvey, *Youth*, p. 143.
77. Stachura, *The German Youth Movement*, pp. 52–3; Kindt (ed.), *Deutsche Jugendbewegung: Die Bündische Zeit*, pp. 1521ff; Peter Schmitz, *Die Artamanen. Landarbeit und Siedlung bündischer Jugend in Deutschland 1924–1935* (Bad Neustadt a.d. Saale, 1985).
78. For fears about youth's radicalism in government circles, StAB: 3–A, 18, Nr. 145, *Reich Labour Minister to Reichszentrale für Heimatdienst*, 22.12.1930; LHAK: 442/16121, *Rundschreiben des Reichsministeriums des Innern*, 29.3.1932; HStAS: E 151i/I/56, *Württ. Landesausschuss für Jugendpflege to Jugendpflegeverbände*, 10.11.1932; for an example of right-wing thinking on the subject, Karl Schöpke, *Deutsches Arbeitsdienstjahr statt Arbeitslosenwirrwarr* (Munich, 1930).
79. Henning Köhler, *Arbeitsdienst in Deutschland* (Berlin, 1967) p. 66; Wolfgang Benz, 'Vom freiwilliger Arbeitsdienst zur Arbeitsdienstpflicht', *VfZG*, 16, 1968, Heft 4, pp. 317–46; Konstantin Hierl, *Im Dienst für Deutschland, 1918–1945* (Heidelberg, 1954). But note the equivocal attitude towards the notion of a compulsory scheme displayed by employers, who feared not only its costs but also its political and psychological repercussions, as explained by Wilhelm Friedrich, 'Freiwilliger Arbeitsdienst oder Arbeitsdienstpflicht?', *Der Arbeitgeber*, 15 July 1932, pp. 314–19.
80. Jahnke, *Geschichte der deut. Arbeiterjugendbewegung*, p. 437; KJVD: *Arbeitsdienstpflicht. Faschistische Geissel für die werktätige Jugend* (Berlin, 1932).
81. Bartz and Mor, 'Der Weg in die Jugendzwangsarbeit', pp. 54–68, 77ff.
82. Hellmut Lessing and Manfred Liebel, 'Jungen vor dem Faschismus. Proletarische Jugendcliquen und Arbeitsdienst am Ende der Weimarer Republik', in Johannes Beck *et al.* (eds), *Terror und Hoffnung in Deutschland 1933–1945. Leben im Faschismus* (Reinbek/Hamburg, 1980) pp. 403f.
83. For general background, Helmut Marcon, *Arbeitsbeschaffungspolitik der Regierungen Papen und Schleicher* (Frankfurt/Main, 1974).
84. Olga Essig, 'Die weibliche Jugend im FAD', *Jugend-und Volkswohl*, 8, 1932, p. 80; and 'Der FAD für Mädchen' in *Arbeiterwohlfahrt*, 8, 1933, Heft 6.
85. *RGBl*, 1932, I, Nr. 45, p. 352.
86. Köhler, *Arbeitsdienst*, pp. 202f, 217f.
87. Ibid., p. 144; Friedrich Syrup, 'Der FAD für die männliche deutsche Jugend', *Reichsarbeitsblatt*, 1932, Teil II, Nr. 27, records that as late as August 1932 only 96 067 were enrolled. For the development of FAD in Hamburg see Harvey, 'Youth Unemployment' in Evans and Geary (eds), *The German Unemployed*, pp. 160ff.

88. StAB: 4, 65: 721/135, *proclamation by Reich President*, 24.12.1932; Rudolf Wiedwald: 'Das Notwerk der deutschen Jugend', *ZBl*, XXIV, 1932/33, Nr. 10; the positive response of the Württemberg government in HStAS: E 151i/I/56, *Württ. Wirtschaftsministerium to Präsident des Landesarbeitsamt*, 31.12.1932.
89. The projected membership of 500 000 was a fantasy of governmental imagination; as an example, only 16 000 youths joined in the entire Rhineland. (LHAK: 441/25705, *Koblenzer Lokalanzeiger*, 4.2.1933, and *Bezirksjugendpfleger Koblenz*, report, 14.2.1933.) On funding see BAK: R43II/519, *report to Reich Chancellor*, 17.10.1932; and ibid., R2/18537, *Aufzeichnungen des Reichsfinanzminister betr. Notwerk*, 16.12.1932.
90. *Arbeiter-Jugend*, 25, 1933, Heft 1, pp. 8f.
91. Maria Tippelmann, 'Über die Auswirkung der Arbeitslosigkeit auf Jugendliche. Eine psychologische Studie', *Freie Wohlfahrtspflege*, 6, 1931, Teil 1, Nr. 7, pp. 309–21; Teil 2, Nr. 8, pp. 364–77; Reinhold Weisser, 'Hannovers jugendliche Erwerbslose', *Wohlfahrtswoche*, 7, 1932, Nr. 9, pp. 67–9. Further insights are in Haken, *Stempelchronik*, pp. 45ff, 49ff and Staewen-Ordemann, *Menschen der Unordnung*, pp. 81–96.
92. StAH: *Sozialbehörde* I, AF 70.01, report in *Hamburger Echo*, Nr. 98, 21.4.1932.

7 Juvenile Crime, Delinquency and Correctional Education, 1918–1933

1. Karl Peters, 'Vorschläge zum Jugendstrafrecht', *ZBl*, XXVII, 1935, Heft 2, p. 37.
2. Eugen Schweizer, *Die Ursachen der Kriminalität und Verwahrlosung bei Kindern und Jugendlichen* (Langensalza, 1933) pp. 8–18.
3. Figures from Friedländer and Myers, *Child Welfare in Germany*, p. 144, and Herbert Graichen, *Die Kriminalität der Jugendlichen im Bezirk des Amtsgerichts Pössneck (1923–1935)* (Jena, 1937) p. 5.
4. HStAS: E 130b/2941, report 'Fürsorge für erwerbslose Jugendlichen', Berlin, 1924.
5. Stressing the influence of poverty on such crime is Michael Grüttner, 'Working-Class Crime and the Labour Movement: Pilfering in the Hamburg Docks, 1888–1923', in Evans (ed.), *The German Working Class*, pp. 54–9.
6. Elsa von Liszt: 'Die Kriminalität der Jugendlichen in Berlin in den Jahren 1928, 1929 und 1930', *Zeitschrift für die gesamte Strafrechtswissenschaft*, LII, 1932, p. 251.
7. Friedländer and Myers, *Child Welfare*, p. 144; Graichen, *Kriminalität*, p. 5.
8. Harald Poelchau, 'Kriminalstatistik der Jugendlichen in 1927 und 1928', *Zeitschrift für die gesamte Strafrechtswissenschaft*, L, 1930, p. 2 (*Sonderdruck*).
9. von Liszt, *Die Kriminalität der Jugendlichen*, pp. 253–8.
10. HStAS: E 151i/III/1445, *Richtlinien für die polizeiliche Vernehmung von Kindern und Jugendlichen vom 1. Mai 1929*.

11. Friedländer and Myers, *Child Welfare*, p. 144; Graichen, *Kriminalität*, p. 5; in 1930 there were 65 708 18–21-year-olds convicted and in 1932 the number had fallen to 64 720; in 1930 the number of convicted 21–25-year-olds was 108 869 (Siemering, *Deutschlands Jugend*, p. 76; *Statistisches Jahrbuch für das Deutsche Reich*, 51, 1932, p. 537).
12. Heinz Jacoby, 'Die Kriminalität der Jugendlichen in den Jahren 1930 und 1931', *Zeitschrift für die gesamte Strafrechtswissenschaft*, LIV, 1935, p. 87; details here also of the female component of these figures, which was rarely above 20 per cent for any one major city and more usually around 12–15 per cent: see also Justus Ehrhardt, 'Die Kriminalität der Jugendlichen in den Jahren 1932 und 1933', *Zeitschrift für die gesamte Strafrechtswissenschaft*, LIV, 1935, p. 667. The figures for Bavaria in 1932 are provided by Hans Otto Hofmann, 'Die Kriminalität in Bayern 1932 bis 1934', *Zeitschrift des bayerischen statistischen Landesamts*, 67, 1935, pp. 358–9.
13. Hans Kruse, 'Die Straffälligkeit der Jugend in den Jahren 1930–1936', *Monatsschrift für Kriminalbiologie und Strafrechtsreform*, 28, 1937, Heft 11, p. 497.
14. Ehrhardt, 'Kriminalität', 1935, pp. 667ff.
15. Helmut Asbeck, *Die Jugendkriminalität im Amtsgerichtsbezirk Oberhausen (Rhld.) (1928–1938)* (Düsseldorf, 1940) p. 4, and Rolf Schuster, *Die Erpressungskriminalität im Bezirk des Landgerichts Wuppertal in den Jahren 1927–1937* (Jena, 1940).
16. Graichen, *Kriminalität*, p. 1.
17. HStAS: E 151i/III/830, *Reichsministerium des Innern an den Obersten Landesjugendwohlfahrtsbehörden*, 7.2.1930; LHAK: 442/14287, *Preuss. Minister für Volkswohlfahrt an Oberpräsidenten und Regierungspräsidenten betr. Berichterstattung über Jugendkatastrophen*, 18.8.1930.
18. Jacoby, 'Kriminalität', p. 89ff.
19. Hans Kruse, 'Die Entwicklung der Jugendkriminalität in Hamburg in den Jahren 1933 und 1934', *Hamburger Lehrerzeitung*, 14, 31 August 1935, Nr. 31/32, p. 309.
20. Robert G. Waite, *Juvenile Delinquency in Nazi Germany, 1933–1945* (Doctoral Dissertation, State University of New York, 1980) pp. 12ff; BAK: R22/1157, *Reichsminister der Justiz betr. 'Entwicklung der Jugendkriminalität'*, Berlin, 13.11.1940.
21. Asbeck, 'Jugendkriminalität', p. 4; Friedländer and Myers, *Child Welfare in Germany*, p. 144.
22. For reaction to the emergency decree of 14 June 1932 and the effect the decree had on the legal status of youth, HStAS: E 151i/I/179, various documents relating to the legislation.
23. LHAK: 442/16121, *Rundschreiben des Reichsministeriums des Innern an die Obersten Jugendwohlfahrtsbehörden der Länder*, Berlin, 29.3.1932.
24. Otto Schürer von Waldheim, 'Jugendkriminalität und Beruf', *Blätter für Gefängniskunde*, 72, 1941/2, pp. 3–42, especially 7ff; Mathilde Kelchner, 'Motive jugendlicher Rechtsbrecher', *Deutsche Jugendhilfe*, 31, 1939, pp. 3f; E. Roesner, 'Kriminalität, Arbeitslosigkeit und Winterhilfswerk', *Blätter für Gefängniskunde*, 71, 1940, p. 269; Graichen,

Kriminalität, pp. 5, 7–10; Asbeck, 'Jugendkriminalität', p. 4ff; Kruse, 'Die Straffälligkeit', p. 497f.
25. Ehrhardt, 'Kriminalität', 1935, p. 671.
26. Jacoby, 'Kriminalität', pp. 95f. The statistics are of the registered unemployed.
27. Ibid., pp. 95–6; von Liszt, *Die Kriminalität der Jugendlichen*, pp. 251, 256.
28. Ehrhardt, 'Kriminalität', 1935, p. 670; and Asbeck, 'Jugendkriminalität', p. 44.
29. Full details in Jacoby, 'Kriminalität', pp. 88f; Ehrhardt, 'Kriminalität', 1935, p. 670.
30. Ehrhardt, 'Kriminalität', p. 670.
31. Graichen, *Kriminalität*, p. 25, on a sample of 304.
32. Asbeck, 'Jugendkriminalität', pp. 40f.
33. Klaus Seibert, *Die Jugendkriminalität Münchens in den Jahren 1932 und 1935* (Leipzig, 1937) p. 41. For a detailed discussion of his findings consult Peukert, *Jugend zwischen Krieg und Krise*, pp. 274f.
34. Kruse, 'Straffälligkeit', p. 502.
35. Schweizer, *Ursachen*, pp. 87ff.
36. Richard Stury, *Die äusseren Entwicklungsbedingungen junger Rechtsbrecher. Untersucht an den Insassen des Jugendgefängnisses Niederschönfeld* (Leipzig, 1938) pp. 26ff.
37. Jacoby, 'Kriminalität', p. 100.
38. Ehrhardt, 'Kriminalität', 1935, p. 685.
39. Seibert, *Die Jugendkriminalität*, pp. 33–4.
40. Jacoby, 'Kriminalität', pp. 98f.
41. Asbeck, 'Jugendkriminalität', p. 28.
42. Graichen, *Kriminalität*, pp. 20f.
43. Asbeck, 'Jugendkriminalität', p. 23; Graichen, *Kriminalität*, pp. 18ff.
44. 'Die Kriminalität der Jugendlichen im Jahre 1933' (unsigned), *ZBI*, XXVIII, 1936, Heft 1, p. 14.
45. Asbeck, 'Jugendkriminalität', pp. 36ff.
46. Schweizer, *Ursachen*, pp. 78ff.
47. Kruse, 'Straffälligkeit', pp. 503f.
48. Graichen, *Kriminalität*, p. 23.
49. Ehrhardt, 'Kriminalität', p. 688.
50. Graichen, *Kriminalität*, p. 11.
51. Schürer von Waldheim, 'Jugendkriminalität', p. 5; Kruse, 'Straffälligkeit', p. 507. Homosexual offences were not common before 1933 – at least not commonly prosecuted, though there was an upward trend. In 1931 a total of 89 youths were convicted, representing 2.3 per cent of 100 000 juvenile crimes, and in 1932 116 youths were convicted, or 3.3 per cent; cf. Wilhelm Knopp, *Kriminalität und Gefährdung der Jugend* (Berlin, 1941) p. 88.
52. 'Die Entwicklung der Kriminalität der Jugendlichen in den Jahren 1930–1933' (unsigned), *ZBI*, XXVI, 1934/35, pp. 126–7.
53. Haken, *Stempelchronik* (Hamburg, 1932) p. 73.
54. Poelchau, 'Kriminalstatistik', pp. 108ff.
55. Hubert Matthias, *Die Praxis der Jugendgerichte 1924–1933 an Hand der*

Reichskriminalstatistik (Doctoral Dissertation, University of Cologne, 1937) pp. 99f.
56. Asbeck, 'Jugendkriminalität', pp. 53ff.
57. Kruse, 'Die Entwicklung der Jugendkriminalität', p. 311; Harvey, *Youth and the State*, pp. 217ff.
58. Hofmann, 'Kriminalität in Bayern', p. 365.
59. Matthias, *Praxis*, pp. 25ff. In 1929 the number of juveniles sentenced to jail was 11 147, in 1930 it was 11 670 and in 1931 it fell to 10 718 ('Die Entwicklung der Kriminalität der Jugendlichen in den Jahren 1930–1933', *Praxis*, p. 126).
60. Matthias, *Praxis*, pp. 52–3; but see slightly lower figures quoted in Jacoby, 'Kriminalität', pp. 104f.
61. 'Fünf Jahre Kampf gegen Jugendkriminalität', (unsigned), *Das Junge Deutschland*, XXXII, 1938, p. 203; Ehrhardt, 'Kriminalität', 1935, pp. 665f. It is interesting to note that, despite being lambasted by the Right, including the NSDAP, the JGG remained in force after 1933 and was not fundamentally revamped until the promulgation of the *Reichsjugendgerichtsgesetz* of 6 November 1943: see Heinz Kummerlein, *Der Reichsjugendgerichtsgesetz vom 6. November 1943* (Munich, Berlin, 1944). Preparations for a new version of JGG in 1931 were abandoned (Bay. HStA: *Staatsministerium des Äussern, 100310, Reichsminister der Justiz an die Landesregierungen*, Berlin, 30.6.1931).
62. Haken, *Stempelchronik*, p. 75.
63. Hellmut Lessing and Manfred Liebel, *Wilde Cliquen. Szenen aus einer anderen Arbeiterjugendbewegung* (Bensheim, 1981) passim; Ernst Haffner, *Jugend auf der Landstrasse Berlin* (Berlin, 1932); Eberhard Giese, 'Kriminelle Jugendbanden und Mittel zur Milderung jugendlicher Erwerbslosigkeit', *Freie Wohlfahrtspflege*, 6, 1931, Heft 2, pp. 82–6.
64. Staewen-Ordemann, *Menschen der Unordnung*, p. 125.
65. Detlev J. K. Peukert, 'Die "Wilde Cliquen" der Zwanziger Jahre', in Wilfried Breyvogel (ed.), *Autonomie und Widerstand. Zur Theorie und Geschichte des Jugendprotestes* (Essen, 1983) pp. 56–77.
66. Otto Voss and Herbert Schön, 'Die Cliquen jugendlicher Verwahrloster als sozialpädagogisches Problem', in Mennicke (ed.), *Erfahrungen der Jugendlichen*, pp. 69–89, here p. 71.
67. Estimates of their membership vary considerably. Justus Ehrhardt, 'Cliquenwesen und Jugendverwahrlosung', *ZBl*, XXI, 1930, Heft 12, p. 414, gives 16 000 for 1930; Eve Rosenhaft, 'Organising the "Lumpenproletariat": Cliques and Communists in Berlin during the Weimar Republic', in Evans (ed.), *The German Working Class*, p. 183, gives 10 000; Staewen-Ordemann, *Menschen der Unordnung*, p. 124 puts the figure at 15 000.
68. Justus Ehrhardt, *Strassen ohne Ende* (Berlin, 1931) p. 28.
69. Eve Rosenhaft, *Beating the Fascists? The German Communists and Political Violence, 1929–1933* (London, 1983) pp. 27, 130–6; Peukert, *Jugend zwischen Krieg und Krise*, pp. 251–65.
70. E. Roesner, 'Der Nationalsozialismus als Überwinder der Kriminalität', *Monatsblätter für Gerichtshilfe, Gefangenen- und Entlassenenfürsorge*, 12, 1937, p. 78.

71. Manfred Heinemann, 'Normprobleme in der Fürsorgeerziehung', in Manfred Heinemann (ed.), *Sozialisation und Bildungswesen in der Weimarer Republik* (Stuttgart, 1976) pp. 131–50. For examples of youths taken into care and the reasons, consult the voluminous documentation in LHAK: 403/13207, *Landeshauptmann der Rheinprovinz*, correspondence, 1926.
72. St.AH: *Jugendbehörde* I, 493, *Erlass des Preuss. Minister für Volkswohlfahrt*, 1.4.1926 for the official view.
73. HStAS: E 151i/I/150, *memorandum from Landarmenbehörde (Neckarkreis)*, 22.11.1921.
74. Lina Ammon, 'Die Fürsorgeerziehung in Bayern', *Arbeiterwohlfahrt*, 5, 1930, Heft 18, p. 555.
75. *Arbeiter-Jugend*, 24, 1932, Heft 1, p. 16; for an emotive description of FE inmates from a SPD member of the Württemberg Landtag, HStAS: E 151i/I/105, *Württ. Landtagssitzung*, 6.2.1923; see also Peukert, *Grenzen*, pp. 208f.
76. Justus Ehrhardt, 'Straffällige Fürsorgezöglinge. Ein Beitrag zur Krise der Fürsorgeerziehung', *ZBI*, XX, 1928, Heft 6, p. 144; in April 1925, for further example, 23 per cent of inmates in Cologne's FE reformatories were orphans, from a total of 5854, given in HASK: 903/171, *Jahres-Bericht, 1. April 1925 bis 31. März 1926, der Jugendamt der Stadt Köln*. See also more evidence of broken home background in LHAK: 403/13206, *Landeshauptmann der Rheinprovinz*, 26.2.1925.
77. StAM: *Regierung von Oberbayern*, 60127, *Berichte über das Ergebnis der psychiat. Untersuchungen, 1919–1921*; HStAS: E 151i/I/88, *Thür. Wirtschaftsministerium, Abteilung Arbeit und Wohlfahrt, to Reichsministerium des Innern*, Weimar, 7.4.1922.
78. StAH: *Jugendbehörde* I, 8, Band 5, *Hamburger Volkszeitung*, 19.1.1923.
79. HHStAW: 403/1263, *Landeshauptmann der Rheinprovinz*, Düsseldorf, 3.8.1926; Heinrich Webler, *Jugendfürsorge im Dritten Reich. Einführung in Wesen und Aufgabe der Jugendfürsorge und das neue Reichsjugendwohlfahrtsgesetz* (Freiburg i. Br., 1923).
80. HHStAW: 460/743, *Landgericht to Landgerichtspräsidenten*, 16.1.1920.
81. Karl Wilker, *Der Lindenhof. Werden und Wollen* (Heilbronn, 1921); Curt Bondy, *Pädagogische Probleme im Jugendstrafvollzug* (Mannheim, 1925).
82. Rudolf Schlosser, 'Die Formen der Disziplin in Erziehungsanstalten', *Arbeiterwohlfahrt*, 3, 1928, Heft 6, pp. 186–90; LHAK: 441/24870, *Jugendamt Bad Kreuznach an Regierungspräsident Coblenz*, 25.10.1924, 'Die FE wird als Straferziehung und die FE-Anstalten als Strafanstalten angesehen'.
83. Friedländer and Myers, *Child Welfare in Germany*, p. 137; Siemering, *Deutschlands Jugend*, p. 72; Annaliese Ohland, 'Die Fürsorgeerziehung in Deutschland', *ZBI*, XXV, 1933, pp. 304–17.
84. LHAK: 442/16140, *Statistik über die Fürsorgeerziehung in Preussen für das Rechnungsjahr 1931 (1. April 1931 bis 31. Marz 1932)*, issued by the *Preuss. Statistischen Landesamt*.
85. Erich Weniger, 'Das Erziehungsideal in der Jugendfürsorge', *ZBI*, XX, 1928, Heft 6, pp. 155–7.

86. Walter Friedländer, 'Fürsorgeerziehungsanstalten', *Arbeiterwohlfahrt*, 2, 1927, pp. 48f. The churches received substantial funding from the state for this service. For the situation in Bavaria, Bay. HStA: *Staatsministerium des Innern, 73811, FE-Anstalten in Bayern*, and ibid., 73808, *Verzeichnis der bayerischen FE-Anstalten*, Munich, May 1929.
87. St.AH: *Jugendbehörde* I, 493, *Hartmann to Hertz*, 29.11.1927; for FE development in Hamburg before the implementation of the progressive approach see Heinz Schröder, *Die Geschichte der Hamburgischen Jugendfürsorge 1863 bis 1924* (Doctoral Dissertation, University of Hamburg, 1966) pp. 198ff, 203ff.
88. Helmut Wiese, *Der Fürsorgezögling. Eine erziehungswissenschaftliche Untersuchung* (Halle, 1928); Lothar Frede, 'The Educational System in the Penal Institutions of Thuringia', *Mental Hygiene*, XIV, 1930, July, pp. 610–27.
89. Justus Ehrhardt, 'Kritik an der Fürsorgeerziehung', *Das Junge Deutschland*, XX, 1929, Heft 3, pp. 264ff.
90. HStAS: E 151i/III/1315, *Württ. Kulturministerium to Württ. Innenministerium*, Stuttgart, 12.12.1929; St.AH: *Jugendbehörde* I, 99, *Finanzdeputation to Hamburger Jugendbehörde*, 23.5.1930; HHStAW: 403/1263, *Der Landeshauptmann, Wiesbaden, to Landesausschuss*, 27.5.1925; Bay. HStA: *Staatsministerium des Innern, 73807, Bay. LJA betr. Kosten der FE*, Munich, 27.6.1929, and *Bay. Staatsmin. der Finanzen an das Staatsmin. d. Innern*, Munich, 20.7.1929.
91. Every single activity in the reformatories from work to clothes to be worn were set out in pedantic detail by a mass of regulations; cf. HHStAW: 403/1267, *Der Landeshauptmann der Provinz Westfalen*, Münster, 20.6.1930. For an informative account of the daily routine in *Erziehungsanstalt* Ohlsdorf in Hamburg, St.AH: *Jugendbehörde* I, 493, *Hausordnung*, 15.3.1928.
92. HStAS: E 151i/III/1295, *Erziehungsanstalt St. Konradlhaus to Württ. Landesfürsorgebehörde*, 22.1.1926, and ibid., 'Lehrwerkstätten in Fürsorgeerziehungsanstalten', 10.5.1926. On the placement of FE inmates in apprenticeships, StAH: *Jugendbehörde* I, 427, Band 2, *LJA Hamburg to Arbeitsamt Hamburg*, 15.5.1924, and ibid., *Arbeitsamt Hamburg to Senatsreferenten*, 6.2.1926.
93. StAH: *Jugendbehörde* I, 428, *Bericht*, 19.10.1923.
94. HStAS: E 151i/III/1257, *Zentralleitung für Wohltätigkeit to Württ. Innenministerium*, Stuttgart, 29.1.1931; Rudolf Schlosser, 'Die Lohnfrage in der Fürsorgeerziehungsanstalt', *Arbeiterwohlfahrt*, 5, 1930, Heft 6, pp. 161–7.
95. HStAS: E 151i/III/1256, *Preuss. Minister für Volkswohlfahrt, Erlass*, 1.4.1926, *Erlass*, 12.7.1929; StAH: *Jugendbehörde* I, 493, *Erlass*, 15.1.1929.
96. HStAS: E 151i/III/1256, *Württ. Ministerium des Innern to Heil – und Pflegeanstalt Stetten*, Stuttgart, 2.12.1932; for a defence of the use of corporal punishment, ibid., 'Körperliche Züchtigung in den Anstalten', by *Landesverband d. Katholischer Erziehungsanstalten*, 25.4.1929.
97. Hertz's liberal approach was expressed in his draft memorandum, 'Strafen und besondere Massnahmen in den Erziehungsanstalten',

26.1.1928, in St.AH: *Jugendbehörde* I, 493, *Jugendamt Hamburg*. The draft was slightly modified and adopted on 4 April 1930 under the title, 'Disziplinarmassnahmen in den Erziehungsanstalten', StAH: *Jugendbehörde* I, 488a.
98. Justus Ehrhardt, 'Die Kriminalität der Fürsorgezöglinge', *Freie Wohlfahrtspflege*, 5, 1931, pp. 489–98.
99. Peter Martin Lampel (ed.), *Jungen in Not. Berichte von Fürsorgezöglingen* (Berlin, 1929); by the same author, *Revolte im Erziehungshaus. Schauspiel der Gegenwart in drei Akten* (Berlin, 1929), and *Verratene Jugend. Lebensgeschichten aus der Weimarer Republik. Roman* (Bensheim, 1979). See also Brandt, *Gefesselte Jugend*; Hedwig Wachenheim, 'Revolte im Erziehungshaus', *Arbeiterwohlfahrt*, 4, 1929, Heft 2, pp. 37–40.
100. Curt Bondy, *Scheuen. Pädagogische und psychologische Betrachtungen zum Lüneberger Fürsorgeerziehungsprozess* (Berlin, 1931); Justus Ehrhardt, 'Krise der Jugendfürsorge – und was nun?', *Wille und Werk. Pressedienst der deutschen Jugendbewegung*, Ausgabe A, Nr. 26, 1931, 2 July 1931; Heinrich Webler, 'Jugendfürsorge im Chaos', *ZBI*, XXIV, 1931, Heft 1, pp. 16ff; Heinrich Webler, 'Das Berliner Landerziehungsheim in Scheuen', *ZBI*, XXIII, 1931, pp. 201–10; *Arbeiter-Jugend*, 24, 1932, Heft 1, pp. 15f, and ibid., Heft 4, pp. 120f; HASK: 903/171, *Rheinische Zeitung*, 15.3.1930, and 18.2.1932; ibid., *Stadt-Anzeiger zu Köln*, 17.3.1930; Herbert Francke, 'Reform der Aufsicht über die Erziehungsanstalten. Lehren des ersten Scheuen-Prozesses', *ZBI*, XXII, 1930, pp. 381–3; Hedwig Wachenheim, 'Scheuen', *Arbeiterwohlfahrt*, 6, 1931, Heft 16, pp. 481–9.
101. The high death rate of inmates could not be ignored. In Prussia in 1928 a total of 183 died in care, though the numbers declined, in conjunction with demographic and other influences, until reaching 116 in 1931; details in LHAK: 442/16140, *Statistik über die Fürsorgeerziehung in Preussen für das Rechnungsjahr 1931* (1. April 1931 bis 31. März 1932), issued by *Preuss. Statistischen Landesamt*.
102. Ahlheim, *Gefesselte Jugend*, p. 53; Kindt (ed.), *Deutsche Jugendbewegung: Die Bündische Zeit*, p. 1482.
103. Walter Friedländer, 'Richtlinien zur Umgestaltung der Fürsorgeerziehung', *Arbeiterwohlfahrt*, 4, 1929, Heft 10, pp. 289–319; a motion for reform was put forward by the SPD, Centre Party and German State Party in the Prussian Landtag on 18.12.1930, StAH: *Jugendbehörde* I, 493, *Antrag*.
104. KJVD: *Fürsorgehöllen* (Berlin, 1930).
105. HStAS: E 151i/III/1258, *Auszug aus der Niederschrift über die Sitzung des Ausschusses des Jugendamts vom 6.2.1931*, and ibid., *Zentralleitung für Wohltätigkeit to Württ. Ministerium des Innern*, Stuttgart, 19.8.1931; Hedwig Wachenheim, 'KPD und FE, *Arbeiterwohlfahrt*, 5, 1930, Heft 7, pp. 202–6.
106. Ahlheim, *Gefesselte Jugend*, pp. 263, 274.
107. StAH: *Jugendbehörde* I, 493, *Runderlass betr. Fürsorgeerziehung*, 20.6.1931.
108. BAK: R36/1976, *Preuss. Ministerium für Volkswohlfahrt an den Ober-*

präsidenten betr. FE-Kosten, 26.2.1931; StAH *Jugendbehörde* I, 232, Band 1, *Preuss. Minister für Volkswohlfahrt to Reichsminister des Innern*, 18.9.1931. Expenditure on FE in Prussia fell from 40.1 million marks in 1927 to 32.6 million in 1931, which was for a smaller number of inmates. Expenditure per inmate in Prussia fell from 688 marks in 1928 to 613 in 1932 – LHAK: 442/16140, *Statistik über die Fürsorgeerziehung in Preussen für das Rechnungsjahr 1931* (1. April 1931 bis 31. Marz 1932), issued by *Preuss. Statistischen Landesamt*. In the Rhineland, the FE budget was reduced by 38.8 per cent between 1931 and 1932 (LHAK: 442/16136, *Abschrift, LJA der Rheinprovinz, Sitzung*, 19.4.1932). The situation in Bavaria was even more unpromising (Bay.HStA: *Staatsministerium des Innern*, 73807, *Staatsmin. d. Finanzen an das Staatsmin. d. Innern*, Munich, 8.5.1931, and the latter to *die Regierungen: Kammern d. Innern*, Munich 18.8.1931).
109. BAK: R36/1982, *Landeshauptmann der Provinz Westfalen, Anweisung betr. Verschärfung der Strafmassnahmen in der FE in besonderen Fällen*, 17.3.1931.
110. In 1931, 58.9 per cent of FE inmates in Prussia were deemed mentally sound, a further 20.3 per cent 'limited', 6.1 per cent 'weak' and 14.6 per cent 'psychopathic', LHAK: 442/16140, *Statistik über die Fürsorgeerziehung in Preussen für das Rechnungsjahr 1931* (1. April 1931 bis 31. Marz 1932), issued by *Preuss. Statistischen Landesamt*. The same percentage of psychopathic inmates was ascertained in Prussia in 1932, ibid., *Statistik über die Fürsorgeerziehung in Preussen für das Rechnungsjahr 1932* (1. April 1932 bis 31. Marz 1933).
111. Peukert, *Grenzen*, pp. 248–52; Harvey, *Youth and the State*, pp. 269–81.
112. St.AH: *Jugendbehörde* I, 232, Band 1, *Preuss. Minister für Volkswohlfahrt to Reichsminister des Innern*, 18.9.1931, and ibid., *Staatssekretär in der Reichskanzlei to Reich Ministers*, 11.9.1931; HStAS: E 151i/III/800, *Entwurf des Reichsminister des Innern betr. 'Notverordnung über die Fürsorgeerziehung'*, Berlin, 14.1.1932.
113. StAH: *Jugendbehörde* I, 232, Band 1, *Denkschrift, LJA Hamburg*, 2.10.1931, *Hamburger Anzeiger*, 21.10.1931 on 'Abbau der Fürsorgeerziehung?'; ibid., Wilhelm Hertz, *Vorbericht für die Tagung des Wohlfahrtskomitee der deutscher Städtetag*, Berlin, 13.11.1931, who argued that exclusion of the ineducables would threaten public order and health, and also reflect badly on the authority of the state. But there is evidence, paradoxically provided by Hertz himself, of this category of inmate being prematurely released from FE from late 1931, thus a full year before Papen's legislation, see ibid., *Jugendbehörde Hamburg to Reichsminister des Innern*, 15.9.1931, and *Hertz to Finanzdeputation Hamburg*, 13.1.1932; an interesting *Denkschrift* by *Die Arbeitsgemeinschaft Münchener Lehrlingsheime*, November 1931, warning of the political implications of FE cuts is in Bay. HStA: *Staatsministerium des Innern*, 73807; see also, Walter Friedländer, 'Abbau der Fürsorgeerziehung durch Notverordnung?', *Arbeiterwohlfahrt*, 6, 1931, Heft 21.
114. *RGBl*, 1932, I, Nr. 74, pp. 522–3.
115. *RGBl*, 1932, I, Nr. 77, p. 531.
116. Local reaction to the decrees can be gauged by referring to LHAK:

442/16136, *Übersicht über den Gesamtbestand der Fürsorgezöglinge in Rheinprovinz*, 1.4.1932-31.3.1933; ibid., 442/16140, *Landeshauptmann der Rheinprovinz*, Düsseldorf, 31.12.1932, betr. *'Einführung einer neuen Erziehungsliste'*; HStAS: E 151i/III/800, *Württ. Landesfürsorgebehörde to Württ. Innenministerium*, 18.1.1933, intimating the release of 100 inmates; StAH: *Jugendbehörde I, 232, Band 2, Niederschrift aus die Sitzung des LJA und Jugendamt*, 15.12.1932. 99 inmates were released and two reformatories closed in Hamburg, ibid., *Jugendamt to Finanzdeputation*, 30.5.1933.
117. Heinz Vagt, 'Die Bedeutung des nationalsozialistischen Erziehungsgedankens für die Praxis der Fürsorgeerziehung', *ZBl*, XXV, 1933, Heft 1, pp. 290–303, especially 297.
118. Peukert, *Grenzen*, pp. 253–60, does not fully address this question of where 'social control' ended and where movement towards racial criteria began.
119. Herbert Francke, 'Die Neuordnung der Fürsorgeerziehung von November 1932 in rechtsgeschichtlicher Beleuchtung', *Zeitschrift für Kinderforschung*, XLI, *Sonderdruck*, 1933, Heft 1, pp. 162–71. A useful introductory synthesis of this question is provided by Robert N. Proctor, *Racial Hygiene. Medicine under the Nazis* (Cambridge, Mass., 1988).

8 Conclusion: The Political Dimension

1. E. Günther Gründel, *Die Sendung der jungen Generation. Versuch einer umfassenden revolutionären Sinndeutung der Krise* (Munich, 1932); Hans Zehrer, 'Achtung, junge Front! Draussenbleiben!', *Die Tat*, 21, I, 1929/30, pp. 25ff; Irmtraud Götz von Olenhusen, 'Die Krise der jungen Generation und der Aufstieg des Nationalsozialismus', *JbADJB*, 12, 1980, pp. 56–8; Joachim Radkau, 'Die singende und die tote Jugend. Der Umgang mit Jugendmythen im italienischen und deutschen Faschismus', in Koebner et al. (eds), *'Mit uns zieht die neue Zeit'*, pp. 104ff.
2. Gregor Strasser, *Kampf um Deutschland* (Munich, 1932), pp. 171ff, speech in the Reichstag, May 1927: *'Macht Platz, Ihr Alten! Eure Zeit ist abgelaufen!'*.
3. Michael H. Kater, 'Generationskonflikt als Entwicklungsfaktor in der NS-Bewegung vor 1933', *Geschichte und Gesellschaft*, 11, 1985, pp. 217–43; Hans Mommsen, 'Generationskonflikt und Jugendrevolte in der Weimarer Republik', in Koebner et al. (eds), *'Mit uns zieht die neue Zeit'*, pp. 50–67
4. Richard Bessel, *Political Violence and the Rise of Nazism. The Storm Troopers in Eastern Germany, 1925–1934* (New Haven, Conn., London, 1984); Conan Fischer, *Stormtroopers. A Social, Economic and Ideological Analysis, 1929–1935* (London, 1983); Mathilde Jamin, *Zwischen den Klassen. Zur Sozialstruktur der SA-Führerschaft* (Wuppertal, 1984); Peter H. Merkl, *The Making of a Stormtrooper* (Princeton, N.J., 1980); Eve Rosenhaft, *Beating the Fascists?* (London, 1983).
5. Good coverage in Thomas Childers, *The Nazi Voter. The Social Foundations of Fascism in Germany, 1919–1933* (Chapel Hill, 1983); Richard F.

Hamilton, *Who Voted For Hitler?* (Princeton, NJ, 1982); Michael H. Kater, *The Nazi Party. A Social Profile of Members and Leaders, 1919–1945* (Cambridge, Mass., 1983); Peter Manstein, *Die Mitglieder und Wähler der NSDAP 1919–1933. Untersuchungen zu ihrer schichtmässigen Zusammensetzung* (Frankfurt/M, 1988).
6. Peter D. Stachura, 'Deutsche Jugendbewegurg und Nationalsozialismus. Interpretationen und Perspektiven', *JbADJB*, 12, 1980, pp. 41ff, 45ff; Arno Klönne, 'Jugendbewegung und Faschismus', ibid., pp. 23–34.
7. Details of the KPD's Reichstag vote in Alfred Milatz, *Wähler und Wahlen in der Weimarer Republik* (Bonn, 1968. 2nd edn) p. 108.
8. Jürgen W. Falter et al. 'Arbeitslosigkeit und Nationalsozialismus. Eine empirische Analyse des Beitrags der Massenerwerbslosigkeit zu den Wahlerfolgen der NSDAP 1932 und 1933', *Kölner Zeitschrift für Soziologie und Sozialpsychologie*, 35, 1983, Heft 3, pp. 525–54 (*Sonderdruck*); Jürgen W. Falter and Dirk Hänisch, 'Die Anfälligkeit von Arbeitern gegenüber der NSDAP bei den Reichstagswahlen, 1928–1933', *A f S*, XXVI, 1986, pp. 179–216; Jürgen W. Falter, 'Unemployment and the Radicalisation of the German Electorate 1928–1933: An Aggregate Data Analysis with Special Emphasis on the Rise of National Socialism', in Stachura (ed.), *Unemployment and The Great Depression*, pp. 187–208; Jürgen W. Falter et al., *Wahlen und Abstimmungen in der Weimarer Republik. Materialien zum Wahlverhalten 1919–1933* (Munich, 1986). For a concise summary, Eberhard Kolb, *The Weimar Republic* (London, 1988) pp. 188ff.
9. Eve Rosenhaft, 'Working-class Life and Working-class Politics: Communists, Nazis and the State in the Battle for the Streets, Berlin 1928–1932', in Richard Bessel and E. J. Feuchtwanger (eds), *Social Change and Political Development in the Weimar Republic* (London, 1981), pp. 207–40; Rosenhaft, 'The Unemployed in the Neighbourhood: Social Dislocation and Political Mobilisation in Germany 1929–33', in Evans and Geary (eds), *The German Unemployed*, pp. 194–227; Geary, 'Jugend, Arbeitslosigkeit . . .', pp. 304ff.
10. Marie Jahoda, Paul F. Lazarsfeld and Hans Zeisel, *Die Arbeitslosen von Marienthal* (Berlin, 1933, new edn Bonn, 1960; English version published as: *Marienthal. The Sociology of an Unemployed Community* (London, 1974)). It must be doubted whether the findings of this study of a small Austrian village of 1486 people in autumn 1931–early 1932 are applicable to the situation of the young unemployed in Germany. Village life in Austria can hardly be compared to urban-industrial society in Germany where the bulk of unemployment was concentrated during the Depression; the findings were more differentiated than is now usually suggested by a number of historians, and the situation of the younger unemployed was not specifically investigated in any case. Marienthal was by any measurement an extreme case and not therefore necessarily applicable elsewhere; more important in determining attitudes than unemployment was the social and political environment in which the jobless lived. Finally, some other, lesser-known studies, even of other parts of Austria itself, come to quite opposite conclusions about the outlook of the unemployed: see, for example, Hans Safrian, '"Wir

ham die Zeit der Arbeitslosigkeit schon richtig genossen auch." Ein Versuch zur (über-) Lebensweise von Arbeitslosen in Wien zur Zeit der Weltwirtschaftskrise von 1930', in Gerhard Botz and Josef Weidenholzer (eds), *Mündliche Geschichte und Arbeiterbewegung* (Vienna, Cologne, 1984) pp. 293–331, which rejects the view that unemployed younger people in Vienna were apathetic.

11. Peter D. Stachura, 'The SPD and the Collapse of the Weimar Republic', in Fletcher (ed.), *Bernstein to Brandt*, pp. 162ff; Manfred Scharrer (ed.), *Kampflose Kapitulation. Arbeiterbewegung 1933* (Reinbek, 1984).
12. Conan J. Fischer, 'Unemployment and Left-Wing Radicalism in Weimar Germany, 1930–1933', in Stachura (ed.), *Unemployment and The Great Depression*, pp. 209–25, here, p. 221.
13. Daniel Horn, 'Youth Resistance in the Third Reich: A Social Portrait', *Journal of Social History*, 7, 1973, p. 32.
14. Fischer, *Stormtroopers*, pp. 25–81; Stachura, *Nazi Youth*, pp. 57–62. Also relevant is Volker Kratzenberg, *Arbeiter auf den Weg zu Hitler? Die Nationalsozialistische Betriebszellen-Organisation. Ihre Entstehung, ihre Programmatik, ihr Scheitern, 1927–1934* (Frankfurt/M, 1987).
15. Falter, see references in note 8; also Dick Geary, 'Unemployment and Working-Class Solidarity in Germany 1929–1933'. Paper delivered at University of East Anglia, July 1983 (copy kindly provided by author).
16. Wolfgang Uellenberg, *Die Auseinandersetzungen sozialdemokratischer Jugendorganisationen mit dem Nationalsozialismus* (Bonn, 1981) p. 63f.
17. Peter Loewenberg, 'The Psychohistorical Origins of the Nazi Youth Cohort', *American Historical Review*, 76, 1971, pp. 1457–1502, especially pp. 1458, 1501; Peter H. Merkl, *Political Violence Under the Swastika. 581 Early Nazis* (Princeton, N.J., 1975) Parts II, III, IV.
18. Peukert, *Jugend zwischen Krieg und Krise*, p. 308; Peukert, 'Die Erwerbslosigkeit junger Arbeiter', p. 326; Peukert, 'The Lost Generation: Youth Unemployment at the End of the Weimar Republic', in Evans and Geary (eds), *The German Unemployed*, p. 190.

Bibliography

1 Unpublished Archival Sources

i Archiv der Deutschen Jugendbewegung, Burg Ludwigstein

Akten 170/1–6: Jugendbewegung und Nationalsozialismus

ii Bayerisches Hauptstaatsarchiv, Munich

Staatsministerium des Innern
Staatsministerium des Äussern

iii Bundesarchiv, Koblenz

R   2 : Reichsfinanzministerium
R 11 : Reichswirtschaftskammer
R 18 : Reichsministerium des Innern
R 21 : Reichsministerium für Wissenschaft, Erziehung und Volksbildung
R 22 : Reichsjustizministerium
R 36 : Deutscher Gemeindetag
R 41 : Reichsarbeitsministerium
R 43 : Reichskanzlei
NS 28: Hitler-Jugend
NS 37: Hauptamt für Volkswohlfahrt der NSDAP/Reichsverwaltung der Nationalsozialistischen Volkswohlfahrt e. V.

iv Historisches Archiv der Stadt Köln

Bestand   53   : Fürsorge 1816–1933
Bestand   610   : Amt für Jugendpflege und Leibesübungen (1920–44)
Bestand   903   : Handakten Dr. Billstein
Bestand 1187   : Christine Teusch
Zeitgeschichtliche Sammlung.

v Hauptstaatsarchiv, Stuttgart

Bestand E 130a and 130b : Staatsministerium
Bestand E 131   : Pressestelle des Staatsministeriums
Bestand E 151i   : Ministerium des Innern: öffentliche Fürsorge, Wohlfahrtswesen, Jugendfürsorge
Bestand E 151 k   : Ministerium des Innern: Gesundheitswesen
Bestand J 150 I   : Flugschriftensammlung

Bestand J 212 : Zeitungsausschnittssammlung zur Geschichte der SPD und der Gewerkschaften in Württemberg

vi Hessisches Hauptstaatsarchiv, Wiesbaden

Abteilung 403 : Bezirksverband des Regierungsbezirks Wiesbaden
Abteilung 405 : Preussische Regierung Wiesbaden
Abteilung 407 : Polizeipräsidium Frankfurt
Abteilung 417 : Landratsamt Unterlahnstein
Abteilung 423 : Landratsamt Kreis Wetzlar
Abteilung 425 : Landratsamt Main-Taunus-Kreis
Abteilung 460 : Landgericht Frankfurt/Main
Abteilung 461 : Staatsanwaltschaft bei dem Landgericht Frankfurt/Main

vii Landeshauptarchiv Koblenz

Bestand 403 : Oberpräsidium der Rheinprovinz
Bestand 441 : Bezirksregierung Koblenz
Bestand 442 : Bezirksregierung Trier
Bestand 467 : Landratsamt Kreuznach und ehem. Landratsamt Meisenheim
Bestand 475 : Neuwied
Bestand 491 : Landratsamt Simmern
Bestand 618 : Stadt-und Bürgermeisterei, Verbands-Gemeinde Boppard.

viii Rheinisch-Westfälisches Wirtschaftsarchiv zu Köln

Akten der Industrie-und Handelskammer Duisburg
Akten der Industrie-und Handelskammer Münster
Akten der Industrie-und Handelskammer Wuppertal

ix Staatsarchiv Bremen

Bestand 4/65 : Nachrichtenstelle der Polizeidirektion Bremen
Bestandsgruppe 3 : Senatsregistratur; Quellen zur Geschichte der Arbeiterbewegung
Bestandsgruppe 4 : Behörden, Dienststellen und Gerichte des Landes und der Stadtgemeinde Bremen

x Staatsarchiv Hamburg

Medizinalkollegium
Jugendbehörde I
Sozialbehörde I
Arbeitsbehörde I
Berufsschulbehörde I

xi Staatsarchiv München

Regierung von Oberbayern
Amtsgericht München-Jugendgericht

2. Contemporary Publications

i Newspapers

Bädischer Beobachter
Berliner Tageblatt
Frankfurter Zeitung
Hamburger Anzeiger
Hamburger Echo
Hamburger Fremdenblatt
Hamburger Volkszeitung
Hamburger Lehrerzeitung
Koblenzer Lokalanzeiger
Kölnische Zeitung
Der Kreuzzeitung
Münchner Neueste Nachrichten
Rheinische Zeitung
Sportzeitung (Stuttgart)
Stadt-Anzeiger zu Köln
Volksstimme (Mannheim)
Volkszeitung (Stuttgart)
Vorwärts

ii Periodicals

Die Arbeit. Zeitschrift für Gewerkschaftspolitik und Wirtschaftskunde
Arbeit und Beruf. Monatsschrift für Fragen der Berufsberatung und verwandter Gebiete
Der Arbeitgeber. Zeitschrift der Vereinigung der Deutschen Arbeitgeber-Verbände
Arbeiter-Jugend. Monatsschrift der Sozialistischen Arbeiterjugend
Arbeiterwohlfahrt
Der Aufbau. Wochenschrift für Erziehung
Blätter des Deutschen Roten Kreuzes, Wohlfahrt und Sozialhygiene
Blätter für Gefängniskunde
Blätter für katholische Anstaltspädagogik
Blätter der Zentralleitung für Wohltätigkeit in Württemberg
Der Bürobeamte
Deutsche Jugendhilfe
Deutsche Medizinische Wochenschrift
Deutsche Zeitschrift für Wohlfahrtspflege
Die Erziehung
Der Fährmann. Monatsblätter für Jugendpflege, Jugendbewegung und Jugendwohlfahrt
Freie Wohlfahrtspflege
Der Führer. Monatsschrift für Führer und Helfer der Arbeiterjugendbewegung
Gesunde Jugend. Zeitschrift für die geistige und körperliche Ertüchtigung der Jugend
Gewerkschaftsjugend
Gewerkschafts-Zeitung. Organ des Allgemeinen Deutschen Gewerkschaftsbund

Jugend und Beruf. Monatsschrift zur Förderung der Berufsberatung und der beruflichen Ausbildung
Jugend und Recht
Jugend-und Volkswohl. Hamburgische Blätter für Wohlfahrtspflege und Jugendhilfe
Die Jugendfürsorge
Das Junge Deutschland. Amtliches Organ des Reichsausschuss der deutschen Jugendverbände
Mental Hygiene
Metallarbeiter-Jugend. Wochenblatt des deutschen Metallarbeiter-Verbandes
Monatsblätter für Gerichtshilfe, Gefangenen-und Entlassenenfürsorge
Monatsschrift für Kriminalbiologie und Strafrechtsreform
Nachrichtendienst des Deutschen Vereins für öffentliche und private Fürsorge
Pädagogisches Magazin
Social Science Review
Soziale Praxis. Zentralblatt für Sozialpolitik und Wohlfahrtspflege
Die Tat
Volkswohlfahrt. Amtsblatt der Preussischen Ministeriums für Volkswohlfahrt
Wille und Werk. Pressedienst der deutschen Jugendbewegung
Die Wohlfahrtspflege in der Rheinprovinz
Wohlfahrtswoche
Zeitschrift des bayerischen Statistischen Landesamts
Zeitschrift für die gesamte Strafrechtswissenschaft
Zeitschrift für Kinderforschung
Zentralblatt für Jugendrecht und Jugendwohlfahrt
Die Zwiespruch

iii Official Printed Sources

Gesetz-und Verordnungsblatt für den Freistaat Bayern, 1925–33
Hamburgisches Gesetz-und Verordnungsblatt, 1921–33
Kaiserliches Statistisches Amt: Die beschäftigungslosen Arbeitnehmer im Deutschen Reich, Berlin 1896
Preussischen Ministeriums für Volkswohlfahrt: Massnahmen zur Betreuung erwerbsloser Jugendlicher, Berlin 1930, Veröffentlichungen des Preussischen Ministeriums für Volkswohlfahrt, Band XIII
Preussische Statistischen Landesamt: Statistik über die Fürsorgeerziehung in Preussen für das Rechnungsjahr 1931 (1. April 1931 bis 31. März 1932)
Preussische Statistischen Landesamt: Statistik über die Fürsorgeerziehung in Preussen für das Rechnungsjahr 1932 (1. April 1932 bis 31. März 1933)
Reichsarbeitsblatt. Amtsblatt des Reichsarbeitsministeriums und des Reichsamts für Arbeitsvermittlung, 1921–33.

Reichsgesetzblatt, 1918–33
Reichsministerium des Innern: Reichsministerialblatt. Zentralblatt für das Deutsche Reich, 1920–32
Statistik des Hamburgischen Staates, 1918–28
Statistisches Amt der Stadt Berlin: Statistiches Jahrbuch der Stadt Berlin
Statistisches Jahrbuch für die freie und Hansestadt Hamburg, 1925–32/33
Statistisches Reichsamt: Statistik des deutschen Reiches
Statistisches Reichsamt: Statistisches Jahrbuch für das deutsche Reich, 1918–33.
Verhandlungen des Reichstags. Stenographische Berichte und Anlagen, 1920–32.

iv. Secondary Works

Aichhorn, August, *Verwahrloste Jugend. Die Psychoanalyse in der Fürsorgeerziehung* (Leipzig, Vienna, 1925).
Ammon, Lina, 'Die Fürsorgeerziehung in Bayern', *Arbeiterwohlfahrt*, 5, 1930, Heft 18, 553–7.
Appelius, H., *Die Behandlung jugendlicher Verbrecher und verwahrloster Kinder* (Berlin, 1892).
Asbeck, Helmut, *Die Jugendkriminalität im Amtsgerichtsbezirk Oberhausen (Rhld.) (1928–1938)* (Düsseldorf, 1940).
Aschrott, Felix P., *Die Behandlung der verwahrlosten und verbrecherischen Jugend und Vorschläge für Reform* (Berlin, 1892).
Baum, Marie, *Familienfürsorge* (Karlsruhe, 1927).
Baum, Marie, *Beiträge zur planmässigen Ausgestaltung der Erholungsfürsorge für Kinder und Jugendliche* (Berlin, 1928).
Bäumer, Gertrud, *Die Zusammenarbeit der öffentlichen und der freien Jugendhilfe in den Jugendämtern* (Berlin, 1926).
Becker, Dr and Gildemeister, Regierungsdirektor, *Förderung der Jugendpflege durch Reich, Länder, Gemeinden und Gemeindeverbände* (Eberswalde-Berlin, 1932).
Beeking, Josef, *Grundriss der Kinder-und Jugendfürsorge* (Freiburg i. Br., 1929).
Behm, Carl, *Erholungsfürsorge* (Leipzig, 1926).
Behrend, Franz, *Das Reichsgesetz für Jugendwohlfahrt. Kommentar* (Berlin, Munich, 1925).
Berndt, Paul, *Die Arbeitslosigkeit. Ihre Bekämpfung und Statistik* (Halle, 1899).
Birkenholz, Carl, 'Der Lehrling in der Arbeitslosenversicherung', *Jugend und Beruf*, 6, 1931, Heft 5, 97–100.
Bondy, Curt, *Die proletarische Jugendbewegung in Deutschland unter besonderer Berücksichtigung der Hamburger Verhältnisse* (Lauenburg, 1922).
Bondy, Curt, *Pädagogische Probleme im Jugendstrafvollzug* (Mannheim, 1925).
Bondy, Curt, *Scheuen. Pädagogische und Psychologische Betrachtungen zum Lüneberger Fürsorgeerziehungs-prozess* (Berlin, 1931).
Brandt, August, *Gefesselte Jugend in der Zwangs-Fürsorgeerziehung* (Berlin, 1929).

Bühler, Charlotte, *Das Seelenleben der Jugendlichen* (Jena, 1929, 5th edn).
Clostermann, Ludwig, Heller, Theodor, and Stephani, P., *Enzyklopädisches Handbuch des Kinderschutzes und der Jugendfürsorge* (Leipzig, 1930).
Damaschke, Adolf, *Die Arbeitslosigkeit und Ihre Überwindung. Briefe an einen jungen Staatsbürger* (Berlin, 1931).
Dehn, Günther, *Grossstadtjugend. Beobachtungen und Erfahrungen aus der Welt der grossstädtischen Arbeiterjugend* (Berlin, 1919).
Dehn, Günther, *Die religiöse Gedankenwelt der Proletarierjugend* (Berlin, 1924).
Dehn, Günther, *Proletarischer Jugend. Ihre Lebensgestaltung und Gedankenwelt* (Berlin, 1929).
Deutsches Archiv für Jugendwohlfahrt (ed.), *Fürsorge für erwerbslose Jugendliche* (Eberswalde-Berlin, 1924).
Deutsches Archiv für Jugendwohlfahrt (ed.), *Aus der Praxis der Erwerbslosenhilfe an Jugendlichen* (Eberswalde-Berlin, 1931).
Dinse, Robert, *Das Freizeitleben der Grossstadtjugend. 5000 Jungen und Mädchen berichten* (Eberswalde-Berlin, 1932).
Dünner, Julia, *Handwörterbuch der Wohlfahrtspflege* (Berlin, 1929).
Ehrhardt, Justus, 'Straffällige Fürsorgezöglinge. Ein Beitrag zur Krise der Fürsorgeerziehung', *ZBl* XX, 1928, Heft 6, 143–46.
Ehrhardt, Justus, 'Kritik an der Fürsorgeerziehung', *Das Junge Deutschland*, XXIII, 1929 Heft 3, 264ff.
Ehrhardt, Justus, 'Amtliche Jugendpflege und ihre Grenzen', *Das Junge Deutschland*, XXIV, 1930, Heft 2, 96–103.
Ehrhardt, Justus, 'Männliche Prostitution und Jugendverwahrlosung. Ein Beitrag zur Wandlung der Formen der Jugendverwahrlosung', *ZBl*, XXII, 1930, Heft 7, 217–23.
Ehrhardt, Justus, 'Die Kriminalität der Fürsorgezöglinge', *Freie Wohlfahrtspflege*, 5, 1931, 489–98.
Ehrhardt, Justus, 'Die Kriminalität der Fürsorgezöglinge', *Freie Wohlfahrt tspflege*, 5, 1931, 489–98.
Ehrhardt, Justus, 'Krise der Jugendfürsorge – und was nun?', *Wille und Werk, Pressedienst der deutschen Jugendbewegung*, 6, 1931, Nr. 26 (Juli).
Ehrhardt, Justus, *Strassen ohne Ende* (Berlin, 1931).
Ehrhardt, Justus, 'Die Kriminalität der Jugendlichen in den Jahren 1932 und 1933', *Zeitschrift für die gesamte Strafrechtswissenschaft*, 54, 1935, 665–91.
Eschbach, Walter, *Proletarisches Kinderelend* (Berlin, 1922).
Essig, Olga, 'Die Weibliche Jugend im FAD', *Jugend-und Volkswohl*, 8, 1932, 80ff.
Fichtl, Franz (ed.), *Reichsgesetz für Jugendwohlfahrt mit den Ausführungsgesetzen sämtlicher Länder* (Munich, 1926).
Fischer, Ruth and Heimann, Franz, *Deutsche Kinderfibel* (Berlin, 1933).
Forkel, Waltraut, 'Kinderarbeit auf dem Lande', *ZBI*, XXV, 1933, Heft 8, 238–43.
Francke, Herbert, *Jugendverwahrlosung und ihre Bekämpfung* (Berlin, 1926).
Francke, Herbert, *Das Jugendgerichtsgesetz (Kommentar)* (Berlin, 1926, 2nd edn).
Francke, Herbert, 'Reform der Aufsicht über die Erziehungsanstalten. Lehren des ersten Scheuen-Prozesses', *ZBI*, XXII, 1930, 381–3.

Francke, Herbert, 'Die Neuordnung der Fürsorgeerziehung von November 1932 in rechtsgeschichtlicher Beleuchtung', *Zeitschrift für Kinderforschung*, XLI, 1933, Heft 1, 162–71 (Sonderdruck).
Franzen-Hellersberg, Lisbeth, *Die jugendliche Arbeiterin. Ihre Arbeitsweise und Lebensform* (Tübingen, 1932).
Frede, Lothar, 'The Educational System in the Penal Institutions of Thuringia', *Mental Hygiene*, XIV, 1930, 610–27.
Friedeberg, E. (= Wilhelm Polligkeit), *Das Reichsgesetz für Jugendwohlfahrt. Kommentar* (Berlin, 1930, 2nd edn).
Friedländer, Walter, 'Fürsorgeerziehungsanstalten', *Arbeiterwohlfahrt*, 2, 1927, 48ff.
Friedländer, Walter, 'Richtlinien zur Umgestaltung der Fürsorgeerziehung', *Arbeiterwohlfahrt*, 4, 1929, 289–319.
Friedländer, Walter, *Jugendrecht und Jugendwohlfahrt. Lehrbuch der Wohlfahrtspflege* (Berlin, 1930, 2nd ed).
Friedländer, Walter, 'Zur Frage der Tagesheime für jugendliche Erwerbslose', *ZBl*, XXIII, 1931, 322–4.
Friedländer, Walter, 'Abbau der Fürsorgeerziehung durch Notverordnung?', *Arbeiterwohlfahrt*, 6, 1931, 542ff.
Friedländer, Walter, 'Relief Measures for the Young Unemployed', in *Children, Young People and Unemployment*, pub. by The Save The Children International Union (Geneva, 1933) pp. 57–64.
Friedländer, Walter and Myers, Earl D., *Child Welfare in Germany Before and After Nazism* (Chicago, 1940).
Friedrich, Theodor and Voigt, Wilhelm, *Berufswünsche und Zukunftspläne der Jugend* (Breslau, 1928).
Friedrich, Wilhelm, 'Freiwilliger Arbeitsdienst oder Arbeitsdienstpflicht?', *Der Arbeitgeber*, 15, 1932, 314–19.
Fürnberg, Friedhelm and Müller, Kurt, *Die Lage der arbeitenden Jugend in den kapitalistischen Ländern* (Berlin, 1928).
Fürth, Henriette, *Zur Sozialisierung der öffentlichen Wohlfahrtspflege* (Berlin, 1928).
Gaebel, Käte, 'Die Erwerbslosigkeit der Jugendlichen' in, Rotes Kreuz (ed.), *Deutsche Jugendwohlfahrt. Denkschrift zum Weltkongress für Kinderhilfe* (Geneva, 1925) 73–7.
Giese, Eberhard, 'Kriminelle Jugendbanden und Mittel zur Milderung jugendlicher Erwerbslosigkeit', *Freie Wohlfahrtspflege*, 6, 1931, Heft 2, 82–6.
Gleitze, Willi, 'Fürsorge-und Arbeitsmarktpolitische Massnahmen für Erwerbslose Jugendliche', in Mennicke (ed.), *Erfahrungen* (see below) 17–40.
Graichen, Herbert, *Die Kriminalität der Jugendlichen im Bezirk des Amtsgerichts Pössneck (1923–1935)* (Jena, 1937).
Gräsing, Fritz, 'Erziehungsarbeit am Erwerbslosen Jugendlichen', in Mennicke (see below) 41–68.
Gregor, Albert and Voigtländer, Else, *Die Verwahrlosung. Ihre klinisch-psychologische Bewertung und ihre Bekämpfung* (Berlin, 1918).
Gründel, E. Günther, *Die Sendung der jungen Generation. Versuch einer umfassenden revolutionären Sinndeutung der Krise* (Munich, 1932).
Haeckel, Heinrich, *Jugendgerichtshilfe* (Berlin, 1927).

Haeckel, Heinrich, *Jugendgerichtshilfe* (Berlin, 1927).
Haffner, Ernst, *Jugend auf der Landstrasse Berlin* (Berlin, 1932).
Haken, Bruno Nelissen, *Stempelchronik. 261 Arbeitslosenschicksale* (Hamburg, 1932).
Harnack, Elizabeth von, 'Germany's New Public Welfare Law', *Social Science Review*, I, 1927, No. 3, 406–13.
Heimerich, Erich, *Jugendwohlfahrt und sozialistische Weltanschauung* (Kiel, 1927).
Hellwig, A., *Der Krieg und die Kriminalität der Jugendlichen* (Halle, 1916).
Hemmer, Willi, *Die 'unsichtbaren' Arbeitslosen. Statistische Methoden-soziale Tatsachen* (Zeulenroda, 1935).
Herrnstadt, Ernst, *Die Lage der arbeitslosen Jugend in Deutschland* (Berlin, 1927).
Hertz, Wilhelm, 'Freizeiten für jugendliche Erwerbslose', *ZBI*, XXIII, 1931, Heft 7, 245–7.
Hetzer, Hildegard, *Kindheit und Armut* (Leipzig, 1937).
Hirtsiefer, Heinrich (ed.), *Jugendpflege in Preussen* (Eberswalde-Berlin, 1930).
Hodermann, Wolfram, *Das Neue Jugendwohlfahrtsrecht* (Berlin, 1928).
Hofmann, Hans Otto, 'Die Kriminalität in Bayern 1932 bis 1934', *Zeitschrift des bayerischen Statistischen Landesamts*, 67, 1935, 357–66.
Internationales Arbeitsamt (ed.), *Die Arbeitslosigkeit der Jugendlichen* (Geneva, 1935).
Jacoby, Heinz, 'Die Kriminalität der Jugendlichen in den Jahren 1930 und 1931', *Zeitschrift für die gesamte Strafrechtswissenschaft*, LIX, 1935, 85–117.
Jahoda, Marie, Lazarsfeld, Paul F., and Zeisel, Hans, *Die Arbeitslosen von Marienthal* (Berlin, 1933).
Jung, H., *Das Phantasieleben der männlichen werktätigen Jugend* (Münster, Westf., 1930).
Kaufmann, Günter, *Das kommende Deutschland. Die Erziehung der Jugend im Reich Adolf Hitlers* (Berlin, 1940, 2nd edn).
Kelchner, Mathilde, 'Motive jugendlicher Rechtsbrecher', *Deutsche Jugendhilfe*, 31, 1939, 3–10.
Kelchner, Mathilde and Lau, Ernst, *Die Berliner Jugend und die Kriminalliteratur. Eine Untersuchung auf Grund von Aufsätzen Jugendlicher* (Leipzig, 1928).
Kessler, Gerhard, *Die Arbeitsnachweise der Arbeitgeberverbände* (Leipzig, 1911).
Klopfer, Bruno, *Jugendpflege an erwerbslosen Jugendlichen. Erfahrungen und Vorschläge* (Berlin, 1926).
Klopfer, Bruno, 'Die jungen Arbeitslosen und der "freiwilliger" Arbeitsdienst', *Soziale Praxis*, 40, 1931, Heft 28, 916–20.
Knickerbocker, H. R., *Deutschland so oder so?* (Berlin, 1932).
Knopp, Wilhelm, *Kriminalität und Gefährdung der Jugend* (Berlin, 1941).
Kommunistischer Jugendverband Deutschlands, *Fürsorgehöllen* (Berlin, 1930).
Kommunistischer Jugendverband Deutschlands, *Arbeitsdienstpflicht. Faschistische Geissel für die werktätige Jugend* (Berlin, 1932).
Krebs, Otto, 'Die Schwererziehbaren in der Fürsorgeerziehung', *Arbeiterwohlfahrt*, 6, 1931, Heft 5, 129ff.

Krolzig, Günter, *Der Jugendliche in der Grossstadtfamilie. Auf Grund von Niederschriften Berliner Berufsschüler und-schülerinnen* (Berlin, 1930).
Kruse, Hans, 'Die Entwicklung der Jugendkriminalität in Hamburg in den Jahren 1933 und 1934', *Hamburger Lehrerzeitung*, 14, 1935, Nr. 31/32, 309–11.
Kruse, Hans, 'Die Straffälligkeit der Jugend in den Jahren 1930–1936' *Monatsschrift für Kriminalbiologie und Strafrechtsreform*, 28, 1937, Heft 11, 497–516.
Kummerlein, Heinz, *Der Reichsjugendgerichtsgesetz vom 6. November 1943* (Munich, Berlin, 1944).
Lagarde, Paul de, *Deutsche Schriften* (Göttingen, 1892).
Lamm, Albert, *Betrogene Jugend. Aus einem Erwerbslosenheim* (Berlin, 1932).
Lampel, Peter Martin (ed.), *Jungen in Not. Berichte von Fürsorgezöglingen* (Berlin, 1929).
Lampel, Peter Martin, *Revolte im Erziehungshaus. Schauspiel der Gegenwart in drei Akten* (Berlin, 1929).
Lau, Ernst and Kelchner, Mathilde, 'Die jugendliche Arbeiterschaft und die Arbeitslosigkeit', in Thurnwald (ed.), *Die Neue Jugend* (see below) pp. 321–40.
Lazarsfeld, Paul F. (ed.), *Jugend und Beruf. Kritik und Material* (Jena, 1931).
Leibrock, Otto, 'Zur Neuregelung des Lehrlingswesen', *Der Arbeitgeber*, 4, 1921, Heft 3, 37f.
Lemke, H., *Öffentliche Jugendhilfe in Hamburg* (Hamburg, 1925).
Liebrandt, M. P., *Jugendfürsorge und Jugendpflege* (Berlin, 1929).
Liszt, Elsa von, 'Die Kriminalität der Jugendlichen in Berlin in den Jahren 1928, 1929 und 1930', *Zeitschrift für die gesamte Strafrechtswissenschaft*, LII, 1932, 250–71.
Maass, Hermann, 'Hilfe für die erwerbslose Jugend', *Das Junge Deutschland*, XXV, 1931, 1–18.
Magnus, Erna, *Werkheime für erwerbslose Jugendliche. Neue Fürsorgeformen aus der Arbeit von Berliner Jugendämtern* (Berlin, 1927).
Maschke, Walter, 'Die Jugend in den Gewerkschaften', in Thurnwald (ed.), *Die neue Jugend* (see below), 220–30.
Matthias, Hubert, *Die Praxis der Jugendgerichte 1924–1933 an Hand der Reichskriminalstatistik* (Doctoral Dissertation, University of Cologne, 1937).
Matz, Else and Seeger, Ernst (eds), *Gesetz zur Bewahrung der Jugend vor Schund-und Schmutzschriften. Text und Kommentar* (Berlin, 1927).
Mennicke, Carl (ed.), *Erfahrungen der Jugendlichen* (Potsdam, 1930).
Messer, August, 'Die freideutsche Jugendbewegung', *Pädagogisches Magazin*, Heft 597, 1915, 9–12.
Mewes, Bernhard, *Die Erwerbstätige Jugend. Eine Statistische Untersuchung* (Berlin, Leipzig, 1929).
Mewes, Bernhard, 'Die berufliche Gliederung der deutschen Jugend', *Das Junge Deutschland*, XXIII, 1929, 381–7.
Mewes, Bernhard, 'Die Arbeitslosigkeit der Jugendlichen', *Das Junge Deutschland*, XXV, 1931, 553–8.
Mewes, Bernhard, 'Die Sterblichkeit der Jugendlichen in Preussen', *Das*

Junge Deutschland, XXV, 1931, 201–7.
Muchow, Martha and Muchow, Hans, *Der Lebensraum des Grossstadtkindes* (Hamburg, 1935).
Müller, Albert, 'Der Weg zum Jugendschutzgesetz 1938', *Das Junge Deutschland*, XXXII, 1938, 247–50.
Münker, Wilhelm, *Das deutsche Jugendherbergswerk. Seine Entstehung und Entwicklung bis 1933* (Bielefeld, 1944).
Niemeyer, Annemarie, *Zur Struktur der Familie. Statistische Materialien* (Berlin, 1931).
Niffka, Erwin, 'Berufsausbildung und Erwerbslosenschulung', *Arbeit und Beruf*, 10, 1931, Heft 7, 100–2.
Niffka, Erwin, 'Die berufliche Lage der Jugend in der Gegenwart unter besonderer Berücksichtigung der männlichen Jugendlichen im Alter von 14 bis 21 Jahren', in Richter (ed.), *Handbuch, Heft 1*, (see below), 65–91.
Niffka, Erwin and Siemering, Hertha, *Jugend in Wirtschaft und Beruf* (Berlin, 1930).
Nohl, Herman, *Die Jugendwohlfahrt. Sozialpädagogische Vorträge* (Leipzig, 1927).
Nohl, Herman, 'Die Jugend und der Alltag. Ein Beitrag zur Lebenskunde der Jugendlichen', *Die Erziehung*, 3, 1928, 215–17.
Ohland, Annaliese, 'Die Fürsorgeerziehung in Deutschland', *ZBl*, XXV, 1933, 304–17.
Peters, Karl, 'Vorschläge zum Jugendstrafrecht', *ZBl*, XXVII, 1935, 37–44.
Peters, Karl, *Jugendgerichtsgesetz vom 16. Februar 1923* (Berlin, 1942).
Poelchau, Harald, 'Kriminalstatistik der Jugendlichen in 1927 und 1928', *Zeitschrift für die gesamte Strafrechtswissenschaft*, L, 1930, 108–15 (Sonderdruck).
Polligkeit, Wilhelm, *Strafrechtsreform und Jugendfürsorge* (Langensalza, 1905).
Polligkeit, Wilhelm, *Landesrechtliche Ausführungsbestimmungen zum Reichsjugendwohlfahrtsgesetz* (Berlin, 1930).
Popert, Hermann, *Hamburg und der Schundkampf* (Hamburg, 1926).
Richter, Kurt (ed.), *Handbuch der Jugendpflege*. Heft 1, I Teil: *Der jugendliche Mensch (männliche Jugend)* (Eberswalde-Berlin, 1932).
Richter, Kurt, 'Massnahmen zur Betreuung der erwerblosen Jugend', in Kurt Richter (ed.), *Handbuch der Jugendpflege*, Heft 14 (Eberswalde-Berlin, 1933) 18–75.
Roesner, E., 'Der Nationalsozialismus als Überwinder der Kriminalität', *Monatsblätter für Gerichtshilfe, Gefangenen-und Entlassenenfürsorge*, 12, 1937, 73–8.
Roesner, E., 'Kriminalität, Arbeitslosigkeit und Winterhilfwerk', *Blätter für Gefängniskunde*, 71, 1940, 264–75.
Roesner, E., 'Krieg und Kriminalität im Spiegel der Statistik', *Blätter für Gefängniskunde*, 71, 1940, 17–24.
Rühle, Otto, *Das proletarische Kind. Eine Monographie* (Munich, 1922).
Ruscheweyh, Herbert, *Die Entwicklung des deutschen Jugendgerichts* (Weimar, 1918).
Saitzew, Manuel (ed.), *Die Arbeitslosigkeit der Gegenwart* (Munich, Leipzig, 1932).
Sauer, Hugo, *Jugendberatungsstellen* (Berlin, 1918).

Schickenberg, Wilhelm, 'Pflegekinderfürsorge', *Soziale Praxis*, LXVI, 1937, 1072–8.
Schikowski, John, *Über Arbeitslosigkeit und Arbeitslosenstatistik* (Leipzig, 1894).
Schlosser, Rudolf, 'Die Formen der Disziplin in Erziehungsanstalten', *Arbeiterwohlfahrt*, 3, 1928, Heft 6, 186–90.
Schlosser, Rudolf, 'Die Lohnfrage in der Fürsorgeerziehungsanstalt', *Arbeiterwohlfahrt*, 5, 1930, Heft 6, 161–7.
Schmidt, Agathe, *Aus Arbeit und Leben der werktätige Jugend* (Berlin, 1925).
Schönstedt, Walter, *Kämpfende Jugend. Roman der arbeitenden Jugend* (Berlin, 1932: new edn Berlin, 1971).
Schöpke, Karl, *Deutsches Arbeitsdienstjahr statt Arbeitslosenwirrwarr* (Munich, 1930).
Schultz, Clemens, *Die Halbstarken* (Leipzig, 1912).
Schürer von Waldheim, Otto, 'Jugendkriminalität und Beruf', *Blätter für Gefängniskunde*, 72, 1941/42, 3–42.
Schuster, Rolf, *Die Erpressungskriminalität im Bezirk des Landgerichts Wuppertal in den Jahren 1927–1937* (Jena, 1940).
Schweizer, Eugen, *Die Ursachen der Kriminalität und Verwahrlosung bei Kindern und Jugendlichen* (Langensalza, 1933).
Seibert, Klaus, *Die Jugendkriminalität Münchens in den Jahren 1932 und 1935* (Leipzig, 1937).
Siemering, Hertha (ed.), *Die Deutschen Jugendpflegeverbände. Ihre Ziele, Geschichte und Organisation. Ein Handbuch* (Berlin, 1918).
Siemering, Hertha, *Deutschlands Jugend im Bevölkerung und Wirtschaft. Eine statistische Untersuchung* (Berlin, 1937).
Simon, Helene, *Aufgaben und Ziele der neuzeitlichen Wohlfahrtspflege* (Stuttgart, Berlin, 1922).
Simon, Helene, *Landwirtschaftliche Kinderarbeit* (Berlin, 1925).
Spranger, Eduard, *Psychologie des Jugendalters* (Leipzig, 1927).
Spranger, Eduard, 'Männliche Jugend', in Richter (ed.), *Handbuch der Jugendpflege*, Heft 1 (see above) 1–61.
Staewen-Ordemann, Gertrud, *Menschen der Unordnung. Die proletarische Wirklichkeit im Arbeitsschicksal der ungelernten Grossstadtjugend* (Berlin, 1933).
Staudinger, Hans, 'Die Erwerbslosigkeit der Jugendlichen, ihre wirtschaftlichen Folgen und deren Bekämpfung', *Arbeiterwohlfahrt*, 6, 1931, Heft 6, 161–70.
Stenbock-Fermor, Graf Alexander, *Deutschland von unten. Reise durch die Proletarische Provinz* (Stuttgart, 1931).
Stern, Erich, *Jugendpflege, Jugendbewegung, Jugendfürsorge* (Dortmund, 1925).
Steuck, Gerhard, *Das Erziehungsideal in der Jugendfürsorge* (Berlin, 1927).
Strauf, Herbert, 'Die Berufslage der jungen Angestellten', *Die Zwiespruch*, 14 June 1931, 280ff.
Stury, Richard, *Die äusseren Entwicklungsbedingungen junger Rechtsbrecher. Untersucht an den Insassen des Jugendgefängnisses Niederschönfeld* (Leipzig, 1938).

Syrup, Friedrich, 'Der FAD für die männliche deutsche Jugend', *Reichsarbeitsblatt*, 1932, Teil II, Nr. 27.
Syrup, Friedrich, *Der Arbeitseinsatz und die Arbeitslosenhilfe in Deutschland* (Berlin, 1936).
Taylor, John W., *Youth Welfare in Germany* (Nashville, Tenn., 1936).
Thurnwald, Richard (ed.), *Die neue Jugend* (Leipzig, 1927).
Tippelmann, Maria, 'Über die Auswirkung der Arbeitslosigkeit auf Jugendliche. Eine psychologische Studie', *Freie Wohlfahrtspflege*, 6, 1931, Teil 1, Nr. 7, 309–21; Teil 2, Nr. 8, 364–77.
Többen, Heinrich, *Die Jugendverwahrlosung und ihre Bekämpfung* (Münster, 1927).
Troeger, Heinrich, 'Beschulung jugendlicher Erwerbsloser', *Arbeit und Beruf*, 10, 1931, Heft 11, 161–3.
Unsigned, 'Jugendpflegerische Erfassung der erwerbslosen Jugend', *ZBI*, XXII, 1930, 245–8.
Unsigned, 'Der FAD für Mädchen', *Arbeiterwohlfahrt*, 8, 1933, Heft 6, 178–80.
Unsigned, 'Die Entwicklung der Kriminalität der Jugendlichen in den Jahren 1930–1933', *ZBI*, XXVI, 1934/35, 124–8.
Unsigned, 'Die Kriminalität der Jugendlichen im Jahre 1933', *ZBI*, XXVIII, 1936, 14–15.
Unsigned, 'Fünf Jahre Kampf gegen Jugendkriminalität', *Das Junge Deutschland*, XXXII, 1938, 202–13.
Vagt, Heinz, 'Die Bedeutung des nationalsozialistischen Erziehungsgedankens für die Praxis der Fürsorgeerziehung', *ZBI*, XXV, 1933, 290–303.
Voss, Otto and Schön, Herbert, 'Die Cliquen jugendlicher Verwahrloster als sozialpädagogisches Problem', in Mennicke (ed.), *Erfahrungen* (see above) 69–89.
Vossen, Karl, *Die Fürsorgeerziehung in der Rheinprovinz* (Düsseldorf, 1928).
Wachenheim, Hedwig, *Republik und Wohlfahrtspflege* (Berlin, 1927).
Wachenheim, Hedwig, *Republik und Wohlfahrtspflege* (Berlin, 1927).
Wachenheim, Hedwig, 'Revolte im Erziehungshaus', *Arbeiterwohlfahrt*, 4, 1929, Heft 2, 37–40.
Wachenheim, Hedwig, 'KPD und FE', *Arbeiterwohlfahrt*, 5, 1930, Heft 7, 202–6.
Wachenheim, Hedwig, 'Scheuen', *Arbeiterwohlfahrt*, 6, 1931, Heft 16, 481–9.
Webler, Heinrich, *Jugendfürsorge im Deutschen Reich. Einführung in Wesen und Aufgabe der Jugendfürsorge und das neue Reichsjugendwohlfahrtsgesetz* (Freiburg i. Br., 1923).
Webler, Heinrich, 'Das Berliner Landerziehungsheim in Scheuen', *ZBI*, XXIII, 1931, 206–10.
Webler, Heinrich, 'Jugendfürsorge im Chaos', *ZBI*, XXIV, 1932, Heft 1, 16–20.
Weiland, Ruth, *Die Kinder der Arbeitslosen* (Eberswalde-Berlin, 1933).
Weiland, Ruth, *The Effects of Unemployment on Children and Young People* (Geneva, 1933).
Weisser, Reinhold, 'Hannovers jugendliche Erwerbslose', *Wohlfahrtswoche*, 7, 1932, Heft 9, 67–9.

Weniger, Erich, 'Das Erziehungsideal in der Jugendfürsorge', *ZBI*, XX, 1928, Heft 6, 155–7.
Werner, Ernst, *Die Organisation, Einrichtung und praktische Durchführung der Jugendpflege und Jugendfürsorge innerhalb und ausserhalb des RJWG* (Berlin, 1925).
Wiedwald, Rudolf, 'Berufsberatung und Wirtschaft', *Jugend-und Volkswohl*, 2, 1927, Heft 9/10, 73–7.
Wiedwald, Rudolf, 'Fürsorgemassnahmen für jugendliche Arbeitslose vom Standpunkt der Arbeitsämter', *Arbeiterwohlfahrt*, 5, 1930, Heft 24, 737–41.
Wiedwald, Rudolf, 'Das Notwerk der deutschen Jugend', *ZBI*, XXIV, 1932/33, Heft 10, 265–9.
Wiedwald, Rudolf, 'Die Arbeitslosigkeit der Jugend in den Jahren 1932 bis 1934', *ZBI*, XXVI, 1934, Heft 8, 231–4.
Wiese, Helmut, *Der Fürsorgezögling. Eine erziehungswissenschaftliche Untersuchung* (Halle, 1928).
Wilker, Karl, *Der Lindenhof, Werden und Wollen* (Heilbronn, 1921).
Wilker, Karl, *Fürsorgeerziehung als Lebensschulung. Ein Aufruf zur Tat* (Berlin, 1921).
Wingender, Hans, *Erfahrungen im Kampfe gegen Schund-und Schmutzschriften* (Düsseldorf, 1929).
Wittig, Kurt, *Der Einfluss des Krieges auf die Kriminalität der Jugendlichen und auf jugendliche Sträflinge* (Langensalza, 1916).
Woytinsky, Wladimir, *The Social Consequences of the Economic Depression* (Geneva, 1936).
Wunderlich, Frieda, *Die Bekämpfung der Arbeitslosigkeit in Deutschland seit Beendigung des Krieges* (Jena, 1925).
Zehrer, Hans, 'Achtung, junge Front! Draussenbleiben!', *Die Tat*, 21, I, 1929/30, 25–7.
Ziertmann, Ministerialrat, 'Zur Frage der Verlängerung der Schulpflicht', *Arbeit und Beruf*, 10, 1931, Heft 5, 59–63.
Ziertmann, Ministerialrat, 'Über die Beschulung und Betreuung der erwerbslosen Jugend', *Arbeit und Beruf*, 10, 1931, Heft 7, 94–8.
Zimmermann, Waldemar, *Die Lebens-und Arbeitsverhältnisse der erwerbstätigen Jugend in Deutschland* (Göttingen, 1926).

3. Secondary Literature – A Select List

Readers are referred to the notes to the main text for the full range of sources consulted. Contributors to edited anthologies are not as a general rule listed separately here, but details are also provided in the footnotes.

Abelshauser, Werner (ed.), *Die Weimarer Republik als Wohlfahrtsstaat. Zum Verhältnis von Wirtschafts-und Sozialpolitik in der Industriegesellschaft* (Wiesbaden, Stuttgart, 1987).
Abraham, David, *The Collapse of the Weimar Republic. Political Economy and Crisis* (New York, 1986, 2nd edn).
Ahlheim, Rose et al., *Gefesselte Jugend. Fürsorgeerziehung im Kapitalismus* (Frankfurt/M, 1978, 5th edn).

Albisetti, James C., *Secondary School Reform in Imperial Germany* (Princeton, N.J., 1983).
Aubin, Hermann and Zorn, Wolfgang (eds), *Handbuch der deutschen Wirtschafts-und Sozialgeschichte. Band 2, Das 19. und 20. Jahrhundert* (Stuttgart, 1976).
Aus der Geschichte der deutschen Arbeiterjugendbewegung 1904–1945. Dokumente und Materialien. Edited by Institut für Marxistische Studien und Forschungen (Frankfurt/M, 1975).
Bartz, Joachim and Mor, Dagmar, 'Der Weg in die Jugendzwangsarbeit-Massnahmen gegen Jugendarbeitslosigkeit zwischen 1925 und 1935', in Gero Lenhardt (ed.), *Der hilflose Sozialstaat-Jugendarbeitslosigkeit und Politik* (Frankfurt/M, 1979) 28–94.
Beck, Johannes et al. (eds), *Terror und Hoffnung in Deutschland 1933–1945. Leben im Faschismus* (Reinbek, 1980).
Blaich, Fritz, *Der Schwarze Freitag. Inflation und Wirtschaftskrise* (Munich, 1985).
Bogs, Walter, *Die Sozialversicherung in der Weimarer Demokratie* (Munich, 1981).
Borchardt, Knut (ed.), *Wachstum, Krisen, Handlungsspielräume der Wirtschaftspolitik* (Göttingen, 1982).
Broszat, Martin, *Hitler and The Collapse of Weimar Germany* (Leamington Spa, 1987).
Bruch, Rüdiger vom (ed.), *'Weder Kommunismus noch Kapitalismus.' Bürgeliche Sozialreform in Deutschland vom Vormärz bis zur Ära Adenauer* (Munich, 1985).
Brüchhäuser, Hans-Peter and Lipsmeier, Antonius (eds), *Quellen und Dokumente zur schulischen Berufsbildung 1869–1918* (Cologne, Vienna, 1985).
Büttner, Ursula, *Hamburg in der Staats-und Wirtschaftskrise 1928–1931* (Hamburg, 1982).
Büttner, Ursula and Jochmann, Werner, *Hamburg auf dem Weg ins Dritte Reich. Entwicklungsjahre 1931–1933* (Hamburg, 1983).
Conze, Werner and Raupach, Hans (eds), *Die Staats-und Wirtschaftskrise des Deutschen Reiches 1929/33* (Stuttgart, 1967).
Dobkowski, Michael N. and Wallimann, Isidor (eds), *Towards the Holocaust. The Social and Economic Collapse of the Weimar Republic* (Westport, Conn., 1983).
Domansky, Elizabeth and Heinemann, Ulrich, 'Jugend als Generationserfahrung: Das Beispiel der Weimarer Republik', *Sozialwissenschaftliche Informationen für Unterricht und Studium*, 13, 1984, Heft 1, 14–21, 50–8.
Dowe, Dieter (ed.), *Jugendprotest und Generationskonflikt in Europa im 20. Jahrhundert* (Düsseldorf, 1986).
Drüke, Helmut et al., *Spaltung der Arbeiterbewegung und Faschismus. Sozialgeschichte der Weimarer Republik* (Hamburg, 1980).
Eberts, Erich, *Arbeiterjugend 1904–1945. Sozialistische Erziehungsgemeinschaft-Politische Organisation* (Frankfurt, 1980).
Emmerich, Wolfgang (ed.), *Proletarische Lebensläufe. Autobiographische Dokumente zur Entstehung der Zweiten Kultur in Deutschland, Band 2: 1914 bis 1945* (Reinbek, 1975).

Bibliography

Eppe, Heinrich, *Selbsthilfe und Interessenvertretung. Die sozial-und jugendpolitischen Bestrebungen der sozialdemokratischen Arbeiterjugendorganisationen 1904–1933* (Bonn, 1983).
Esler, Anthony (ed.), *The Youth Revolution. The Conflict of Generations in Modern History* (Lexington, Mass., 1974).
Evans, Richard J. (ed.), *The German Working Class 1888–1933. The Politics of Everyday Life* (London, 1982).
Evans, Richard J. and Geary, Dick (eds), *The German Unemployed. Experiences and Consequences of Mass Unemployment from the Weimar Republic to the Third Reich* (London, 1987).
Falter, Jürgen W. and Hänisch, Dirk, 'Die Anfälligkeit von Arbeitern gegenüber der NSDAP bei den Reichstagswahlen 1928–1933', *Archiv für Sozialgeschichte*, XXVI, 1986, 179–216.
Faust, Anselm, *Arbeitsmarktpolitik im Deutschen Kaiserreich. Arbeitsvermittlung, Arbeitsbeschaffung und Arbeitslosenunterstützung, 1890–1918* (Stuttgart, 1986).
Feldman, Gerald D. (ed.), *Die Nachwirkungen der Inflation auf die deutsche Geschichte 1924–1933* (Munich, 1985).
Feldman, Gerald D., 'The Weimar Republic: A Problem of Modernization?' *Archiv für Sozialgeschichte*, XXVI, 1986, 1–26.
Feldman, Gerald D., 'Saxony, the Reich, and the Problem of Unemployment in the German Inflation', *Archiv für Sozialgeschichte*, XXVII, 1987, 103–44.
Feldman, Gerald D.; Holtfrerich, Carl-Ludwig; Ritter, Gerhard A. and Witt, Peter-Christian (eds), *Die Anpassung an die Inflation* (Berlin, 1986).
Flecken, Margarete, *Arbeiterkinder im 19. Jahrhundert. Eine sozialgeschichtliche Untersuchung ihrer Lebenswelt* (Weinheim, Basel, 1981).
Fletcher, Roger (ed.), *Bernstein to Brandt. A Short History of German Social Democracy* (London, 1987).
Garraty, John A., *Unemployment in History. Economic Thought and Public Policy* (New York, 1978).
Geary, Dick, 'Jugend, Arbeitslosigkeit und politischer Radikalismus am Ende der Weimarer Republik', *Gewerkschaftliche Monatshefte*, 34, May 1983, 304–9.
Geiger, Theodor, *Die soziale Schichtung des deutschen Volkes* (Stuttgart, 1967, new edn).
Giesecke, Hermann, *Vom Wandervogel bis zur Hitlerjugend. Jugendarbeit zwischen Politik und Pädagogik* (Munich, 1981).
Gillis, John, R., *Youth and History. Tradition and Change in European Age Relations 1770–Present* (New York, 1981).
Götz von Olenhusen, Irmtraud, 'Die Krise der jungen Generation und der Aufstieg des Nationalsozialismus', *JbADJB*, 12, 1980, 53–82.
Götz von Olenhusen, Irmtraud, *Jugendreich-Gottesreich-Deutsches Reich. Junge Generation, Religion und Politik 1928–1933* (Cologne, 1987).
Grebing, Helga, *Geschichte der deutschen Arbeiterbewegung* (Munich, 1975, 6th edn).
Greinert, Wolf-Dietrich, *Schule als Instrument sozialer Kontrolle und Objekt privater Interessen. Der Beitrag der Berufsschule zur politischen Erziehung der Unterschichten* (Hanover, 1975).
Guttsman, Wilhelm L., *The German Social Democratic Party, 1875–1933* (London, 1981).

Hartmann, Günter and Lienker, Heinrich, *Sozialistische Arbeiterjugendbewegung in der Weimarer Republik* (Bielefeld, 1982).
Harvey, Elizabeth, 'Sozialdemokratische Jugendhilfereform in der Praxis: Walter Friedländer und das Bezirksjugendamt Berlin Prenzlauer Berg in der Weimarer Republik', *Theorie und Praxis der Sozialarbeit*, 36, 1985, 6, 218–29.
Harvey, Elizabeth Ruth, *Youth and the State in the Weimar Republic. A Study of Public Policies Towards Working-Class Adolescents in Hamburg 1918–1933* (D.Phil., University of Oxford, 1987).
Hasenclever, Christa, *Jugendhilfe und Jugendgesetzgebung seit 1900* (Göttingen, 1978).
Heilman, Linda A., 'Industrial Unemployment in Germany: 1873–1913', *Archiv für Sozialgeschichte*, XXVII, 1987, 25–49.
Heinemann, Manfred (ed.), *Sozialisation und Bildungswesen in der Weimarer Republik* (Stuttgart, 1976).
Heinemann, Manfred (ed.), *Erziehung und Schulung im Dritten Reich. Teil I & II* (Stuttgart, 1980).
Hentschel, Volker, *Geschichte der deutschen Sozialpolitik (1800–1980). Soziale Sicherung und kollektives Arbeitsrecht* (Frankfurt/M, 1983).
Hepp, Corona, *Avantgarde. Moderne Kunst, Kulturkritik und Reformbewegungen nach der Jahrhundertwende* (Munich, 1987).
Herrmann, Ulrich, 'Der "Jüngling" und der "Jugendliche". Männliche Jugend im Spiegel polarisierender Wahrnehmungsmuster an der Wende vom 19. zum 20. Jahrhundert in Deutschland', *Geschichte und Gesellschaft*, 11, 1985, Heft 2, 205–216.
Herrmann, Ulrich; Renftle, Susanne; and Roth, Lutz, *Bibliographie zur Geschichte der Kindheit, Jugend und Familie* (Munich, 1980).
Homburg, Heidrun, 'Vom Arbeitslosen zum Zwangsarbeiter. Arbeitslosenpolitik und Fraktionierung der Arbeiterschaft in Deutschland 1930–1933 am Beispiel der Wohlfahrtserwerbslosen und der kommunalen Wohlfahrtshilfe', *Archiv für Sozialgeschichte*, XXV, 1985, 251–98.
Hörster-Philipps, Ulrike, *Konservative Politik in der Endphase der Weimarer Republik. Die Regierung Franz von Papen* (Cologne, 1982).
Jahnke, Karl-Heinz et al., *Geschichte der deutschen Arbeiterjugendbewegung 1904–1945* (Dortmund, 1973).
James, Harold, *The German Slump. Politics and Economics 1924–1936* (Oxford, 1986).
Jasper, Gotthard, *Die gescheiterte Zähmung. Wege zur Machtergreifung Hitlers 1930–1934* (Frankfurt/M, 1986).
Johnson, Eric A. and McHale, Vincent E., 'Socioeconomic Aspects of the Delinquency Rate in Imperial Germany, 1882–1914', *Journal of Social History*, 13, 1979/80, Spring, 384–402.
Kindt, Werner (ed.), *Die deutsche Jugendbewegung, 1920 bis 1933. Die Bündische Zeit. Quellenschriften* (Düsseldorf, 1974).
Kocka, Jürgen, *Klassengesellschaft im Krieg. Deutsche Sozialgeschichte 1914–1918* (Göttingen, 1973).
Koebner, Thomas; Janz, Rolf-Peter; and Trommler, Frank (eds), *'Mit uns zieht die neue Zeit'. Der Mythos Jugend* (Frankfurt/M, 1985).
Köhler, Henning, *Arbeitsdienst in Deutschland. Pläne und Verwicklichungs-*

formen bis zur Einführung der Arbeitsdienstpflicht im Jahre 1935 (Berlin, 1967).
Kolb, Eberhard, *The Weimar Republic* (London, 1988).
Krafeld, Franz Josef, *Geschichte der Jugendarbeit. Von den Anfängen bis zur Gegenwart* (Weinheim, Basel, 1984).
Lampel, Peter Martin, *Verratene Jugend. Lebensgeschichten aus der Weimarer Republik* (Bensheim, 1979).
Lennhoff, Friedrich Georg, *Sozialarbeit in der Zeitgeschichte. Die Zugscharen. Eine Jugendhilfe-Organisation 1919–1937* (Munich, Basel, 1983).
Lessing, Hellmut; Liebel, Manfred; and Schonig, Bruno, 'Jugend zwischen Perspektivlosigkeit und Faschismus', Introduction to Lampel, *Verratene Jugend* (see above) 7–36.
Lessing, Hellmut and Liebel, Manfred, *Wilde Cliquen. Szenen aus einer anderen Arbeiterjugendbewegung* (Bensheim, 1981).
Lindner, Rolf, 'Bandenwesen und Klubwesen im wilhelminischen Reich und in der Weimarer Republik', *Geschichte und Gesellschaft*, 10, 1984, 352–75.
Loewenberg, Peter, 'The Psychohistorical Origins of the Nazi Youth Cohort', *American Historical Review*, 76, 1971, 1457–1502.
Lüdtke, Alf, 'Hunger in der Grossen Depression. Hungererfahrungen und Hungerpolitik am Ende der Weimarer Republik', *Archiv für Sozialgeschichte*, XXVII, 1987, 145–76.
Martiny, Martin, 'Sozialdemokratie und junge Generation am Ende der Weimarer Republik', in Wolfgang Luthardt (ed.), *Sozialdemokratische Arbeiterbewegung und Weimarer Republik. Materialien zur gesellschaftlichen Entwicklung 1927–1933, Band II* (Frankfurt/M, 1978) 56–117.
Mitterauer, Michael, *Sozialgeschichte der Jugend* (Frankfurt/M, 1986).
Mommsen, Hans; Petzina, Dietmar; and Weisbrod, Bernd (eds), *Industrielles System und Politische Entwicklung in der Weimarer Republik* (Düsseldorf, 1977), 2 Vols.
Mommsen, Wolfgang J. (ed.), 'Die Organisierung des Friedens. Demobilmachung 1918–1920', in *Geschichte und Gesellschaft*, 9, 1983, Heft 2.
Mommsen, Wolfgang J. and Mock, Wolfgang (eds), *The Emergence of the Welfare State in Britain and Germany* (London, 1981).
Muth, Wolfgang, *Berufsausbildung in der Weimarer Republik* (Stuttgart, 1985).
Niess, Frank, *Geschichte der Arbeitslosigkeit. Ökonomische Ursachen und politische Kämpfe. Ein Kapitel deutscher Sozialgeschichte* (Cologne, 1979).
Petrick, Fritz, *Zur sozialen Lage der Arbeiterjugend in Deutschland 1933 bis 1939* (East Berlin, 1974).
Petzina, Dietmar; Abelshauser, Werner; and Faust, Anselm, *Sozialgeschichtliches Arbeitsbuch III. Materialien zur Statistik des Deutschen Reiches 1914–1945* (Munich, 1978).
Peukert, Detlev J. K., 'Die "Wilden Cliquen" der Zwanziger Jahre', in Wilfried Breyvogel (ed.), *Autonomie und Widerstand. Zur Theorie und Geschichte des Jugendprotestes* (Essen, 1983), 66–77.
Peukert, Detlev J. K., 'Die Erwerbslosigkeit junger Arbeiter in der Weltwirtschaftskrise in Deutschland 1929–1933', *Vierteljahrschrift für Sozial- und Wirtschaftsgeschichte*, 72, 1985, Heft 3, 305–28.
Peukert, Detlev J. K. *Grenzen der Sozialdisziplinierung. Aufstieg und Krise*

der deutschen Jugendfürsorge 1878 bis 1932 (Cologne,1986).
Peukert, Detlev J. K., Jugend zwischen Krieg und Krise. Lebenswelten von Arbeiterjungen in der Weimarer Republik (Cologne, 1987).
Peukert, Detlev J. K., Die Weimarer Republik. Krisenjahre der Klassicshen Moderne (Frankfurt/M,1987).
Preller, Ludwig, Sozialpolitik in der Weimarer Republik (Düsseldorf,1978, orig. 1949).
Prinz, Detlev and Rexin, Manfred (eds), Gewerkschaftsjugend im Weimarer Staat. Eine Dokumentation über die Arbeit der Gewerkschaftsjugend des ADGB in Berlin (Cologne,1983).
Reulecke, Jürgen, 'Bürgerliche Sozialreformer und Arbeiterjugend im Kaiserreich', Archiv für Sozialgeschichte, XXII, 1982, 299–329.
Ritter, Gerhard A., Social Welfare in Germany and Britain (Leamington Spa, 1986).
Ritter, Gerhard A., 'Entstehung und Entwicklung des Sozialstaats in vergleichender Perspektive', Historische Zeitschrift, 243, 1986, 1–90.
Rosenhaft, Eve, 'Working-class Life and Working-class Politics: Communists, Nazis and the State in the Battle for the Streets, Berlin 1928–1932', in Richard Bessel and E. J. Feuchtwanger (eds), Social Change and Political Development in the Weimar Republic (London, 1981) pp. 207–40.
Rosenhaft, Eve, Beating the Fascists? The German Communists and Political Violence, 1929–1933 (London, 1983).
Roth, Lutz, Der sogenannte Jugendliche. Jünglinge und Jugendliche in Deutschland 1750 bis 1920 (Munich, 1983).
Sachsse, Christoph and Tennstedt, Florian, Geschichte der Armenfürsorge in Deutschland. Vom Spätmittelalter bis zum 1. Weltkrieg (Stuttgart, Berlin, 1980).
Sachsse, Christoph and Tennstedt, Florian (eds), Soziale Sicherheit und soziale Disziplinierung. Beiträge zu einer historischen Theorie der Sozialpolitik (Frankfurt/M, 1986).
Saul, Klaus, 'Der Kampf um die Jugend zwischen Volksschule und Kaserne. Ein Beitrag zur 'Jugendpflege' im wilhelminischen Reich 1890–1914', Militärgeschichtliche Mitteilungen, 10, 1971, Heft 1, 97–143.
Saul, Klaus; Flemming, Jens; Stegmann, Dirk; and Witt, Peter-Christian (eds), Arbeiterfamilien im Kaiserreich. Materialien zur Sozialgeschichte in Deutschland 1871–1914 (Königstein, 1982).
Scheibe, Wolfgang, Die Reformpädagogische Bewegung 1900–1932. Eine einführende Darstellung (Weinheim, Basel, 1974, 4th edn).
Scherpner, Hans, Geschichte der Jugendfürsorge (Göttingen, 1979, 2nd edn).
Schröder, Heinz, Die Geschichte der Hamburgisches Jugendfürsorge 1863 bis 1924 (Doctoral Dissertation, University of Hamburg, 1966).
Schulze, Hagen, Weimar. Deutschland 1917–1933 (Berlin, 1982).
Spree, Reinhard, Health and Social Class in Imperial Germany. A Social History of Mortality, Morbidity and Inequality (Oxford, 1988).
Stachura, Peter D., The German Youth Movement 1900–1945. An Interpretative and Documentary History (London, 1981).
Stachura, Peter D. (ed.), Unemployment and The Great Depression in Weimar Germany (London, 1986).

Stürmer, Michael (ed.), *Die Weimarer Republik. Belagerte Civitas* (Königstein, 1985, 2nd edn).
Tenfelde, Kalus, 'Jugend und Gewerkschaften in historischer Perspektive', *Gewerkschaftliche Monatshefte*, 32, 1981, Heft 3/4, 129–43.
Tenfelde, Klaus, 'Grossstadtjugend in Deutschland vor 1914. Eine historisch–demographische Annäherung', *Vierteljahrschrift für Sozial-und Wirtschaftsgeschichte*, 69, 1982, Heft 2, 182–218.
Tennstedt, Florian, *Sozialgeschichte der Sozialpolitik in Deutschland. Vom 18. Jahrhundert bis zum Ersten Weltkrieg* (Göttingen, 1981).
Tilsner-Gröll, Rotraud, *Jugendarbeit der SPD von den Anfängen bis zum Ende der Weimarer Republik* (Münster, 1978).
Tilsner-Gröll, Rotraud, *Die Jugendbildungsarbeit in den freien Gewerkschaften von 1919–1933* (Frankfurt/M, 1982).
Treue, Wilhelm (ed.), *Deutschland in der Weltwirtschaftskrise in Augenzeugenberichten* (Munich, 1976).
Vondung, Klaus (ed.), *Das wilhelminische Bildungsbürgertum. Zur Sozialgeschichte seiner Ideen* (Göttingen, 1976).
Wehler, Hans-Ulrich, *The German Empire 1871–1918* (Leamington Spa, 1985).
Weisbrod, Bernd, *Schwerindustrie in der Weimarer Republik. Interessenpolitik zwischen Stabilisierung und Krise* (Wuppertal, 1978).
Wichert, Udo, 'Gewerkschaften und Jugend in der Weimarer Republik', *Gewerkschaftliche Monatshefte*, 32, 1981, Heft 3/4. 144–56.
Winkler, Heinrich August, *Von der Revolution zur Stabilisierung. Arbeiter und Arbeiterbewegung in der Weimarer Republik 1918 bis 1924* (Berlin, Bonn, 1984).
Winkler, Heinrich August, *Der Schein der Normalität. Arbeiter und Arbeiterbewegung in der Weimarer Republik 1924 bis 1930* (Berlin, Bonn, 1985).
Winkler, Heinrich August, *Der Weg in die Katastrophe. Arbeiter und Arbeiterbewegung in der Weimarer Republik 1930 bis 1933* (Berlin, Bonn, 1987).
Zwerschke, Manfred, *Jugendverbände und Sozialpolitik. Die Entwicklung des sozialpolitischen Willens in den deutschen Jugendverbänden* (Munich, 1963).

Index

Adenauer, Konrad, 42, 72
ADGB, *see* Trade unions
Anarcho-syndicalism, 157
Anti-semitism, 17
Anti-socialist legislation, 10
Appelius, H., 28
Apprentices, 4, 5, 8, 22, 23, 25, 26, 53, 69, 73, 96f, 98, 102, 107, 108f, 110, 111, 118, 119, 123, 125, 137, 142f, 144, 150, 156, 160, 205, n92
Apprentices' contracts, 8, 98, 107, 108, 109, 125, 192, n66
Arbeiterwohlfahrt, 88, 151
Arbeitsbeschaffungsprogramm f. d. werktätige Jugend, 125
Arbeitsgemeinschaft für evangelischer Kinderpflege, 177 n9
Arbeitsgemeinschaft für ländliche Jugendpflege, 75
Arbeitsgemeinschaft Münchener Lehrlingsheime, 207 n113
Arbeitskreis zur Reform der FE, 151
Arbitration system, 38, 39, 43, 56, 57
Artamanen movement, 129
Aschrott, Felix P., 28
Ausschuss der deutschen Jugendverbände, 173 n17
Austria, 110, 209, n10
AVAVG (Law on Unemployment Insurance), 45, 52ff, 57ff, 62, 100, 102f, 113, 121f

Baade, Fritz, 61
Bäumer, Dr Gertrud, 122
Bavaria, 6, 77, 80, 82, 80, 112, 113, 142, 145, 149, 150, 181 n71, 183 n99, 185 n130, 193 n83, 194 n89 & 94, 201 n12, 205 n86, 207 n108
Bayer, Maximilian, 26
Behörde für öffent. Jugendfürsorge, 182 n94
Berlin, 16, 23, 28, 46, 49, 60, 71, 75, 79, 89, 93, 99, 104, 112, 120, 123, 124, 125, 135, 136, 137, 140, 141, 142, 145, 146, 149, 151, 190 n23 & 29
Bildungsbürgertum, 15
Bismarck, Otto von, 10, 11, 15, 19, 45
Bismarckjugend, 66

'Borchardt Thesis', 175 n90
Boy Scout movement, 26
Bracher, Karl Dietrich, 41
Bräunsdorf (reformatory), 150
Brauns, Heinrich, 39, 43, 129, 173 n60
Brauns-Kommission, 129
Britain, 14, 19
Brüning, Heinrich, 61, 67, 106, 117, 121f, 125, 126, 129, 139, 158
Bund deutscher Jugendvereine, 21
Bündische Youth, 68f, 129, 156, 177 n11 & 15

Caritas, 20
Census (1895), 14, 46, 172 n31
Census (1925), 95, 112, 115
Census (1933), 116, 117ff, 120
Central Youth Commission, 24
Centre Party, 4, 36, 39, 65, 67, 71, 79, 80, 81, 87, 206 n103
Children's Protection Act, 22, 107
Christliche Verein junger Männer, 21
Churches, the, 5, 6, 10, 12, 16, 20f, 27, 32, 47, 71, 77, 79, 80, 84, 124, 126, 142, 150, 167 n56, 205 n86
Civil Legal Code, 29
Classen, Walter, 21
Cologne, 28, 42, 47, 72, 75, 79, 85, 89, 119, 128, 137, 140, 141, 142, 204 n76
Commercial Code, 21, 107, 166 n38
Communist youth, 107, 178 n26
   (*see also under* KJVD & *Rote Jungfront*)
Compulsory labour, 101, 102, 106, 122
   (*see also under* Working-class youth)
Compulsory Vocational School Act, 111
Continuation schools, 22, 26, 104, 111
Correctional education, 2, 9, 28ff, 145f, 147–54, 157, 158, 161, 204 ns71, 75, 76, 205 n87, 206 n103, 207 n108, 110, 113, 116
Country Boarding Schools, 19, 68
Criminal Code, 44

Dähnhardt, Dr Heinz, 80f
'*Das Jahrhundert des Kindes*', 11

230

Index

Dawes Plan, 42, 76, 98
Demobilisation, 48f, 51, 94, 96
Depression (1870s), 10, 45
Depression (1890s), 46
Depression, the (1929–33), 4, 7, 8, 43, 54, 55, 57, 58ff, 66, 67, 69, 70, 88, 92, 93, 94, 95, 98, 100, 102f, 106, 110, 113, 114, 115–32, 137ff, 140ff, 145ff, 149, 152, 155–61, 209 n10
Deutsche Freischar, 69, 129
Deutsche Kinderhilfe, 177 n9
Deutsche Zentrale für freie Jugendwohlfahrt, 177 n9
Deutsche Zentrale für Jugendfürsorge, 21, 27, 79, 177 n9
Deutscher Archiv für Jugendwohlfahrt, 182 n94
Deutscher Verein für Schulgesundheitspflege, 91
Deutsches Zentralkomitee für Zahnpflege, 91
'*Die Seele deines Kind*', 11
'*Die Seele des Kindes*', 12
Dreckstiebel gang, 146

Ebert, Friedrich, 24, 34, 35
Ebert–Groener Pact, 35
Economic democracy, concept of, 56
Educational reform movement, 12, 18f, 28ff, 68f, 78f, 81, 82ff, 105, 134f, 145, 147f, 149, 150, 151, 152ff, 205 n87, 97
Egendorf (reformatory), 150
Ehrhardt, Justus, 140, 177 n15
Eierschlamm gang, 146
Einstein, Albert, 15
Emergency aid (*Krisenfürsorge*), 52ff, 62, 102, 122
Emigration, 42, 113
Evangelischer Verband zur Pflege der weiblichen Jugend Deutschlands, 21

Factory Councils Act, 38
FAD (*Freiwilliger Arbeitsdienst*), *see* Voluntary labour service
Federal Republic of Germany, 6
Female youth, 5, 14, 73, 95, 98ff, 104, 108, 110f, 112, 113, 115, 117ff, 120, 130, 135, 143, 149, 150, 151, 166 n42, 168 n77, 174 n64, 178 n17, 201 n12
Feminist movement, 5, 16
First World War, 4, 7, 11, 14, 18, 22, 26, 27, 30ff, 36, 39, 40, 45, 48, 49, 50, 64, 65, 66, 69, 70, 71, 73, 75, 83, 85, 86, 90, 91, 94, 95, 96, 106, 112, 115, 119, 126, 135, 161, 168 n77, 169 n85, 171 n10
Fischer, Conan, 159
Fischer, Ruth, 124
Foster-children, 183 n101, 188 n161
France, 14
Freie Schulgemeinde Wickersdorf, 19
Freie Sozialistische Jugend, 66
Freikorps, 129
Freizeitsheim, 104, 127
Freud, Sigmund, 15
Freund, Dr Richard, 46
Fürsorgeerziehung (Fe), *see* Correctional education; Reformatories
Fürsorgeerziehungsgesetz, 29, 168 n69

Generational conflict, 1, 17, 30, 64, 155, 158, 161f
German Association for Juvenile Courts, 134
German Bookbinders' Association, 46
German Communism, 1, 35, 155, 157, 159
German Communist Party (KPD), 41, 53, 57, 66, 80, 87, 103, 129, 131, 147, 152, 155, 156, 157ff, 159ff, 182 n85, 185 n133, 209 n7
German Democratic Party (DDP), 36, 66
German National People's Party (DNVP), 66, 87, 129, 158, 160
German People's Party (DVP), 58, 66
German State Party, 155, 206 n103
German Youth Movement, 1, 4, 5, 7, 16–19, 25f, 30f, 66, 67, 69, 71, 80, 88, 89, 93, 103, 107, 124, 136, 177 n11 (*see also* Bündische Youth; Wandervogel; and Working-class youth)
Gesellschaft für Soziale Reform, 20
'*Gesetz zum Schutz der Jugend gegen soziale Verelendung*', 125
'*Gesetz zur Bekämpfung der Geschlechtskrankheiten*', 188 n160
Gildenschaft Soziale Arbeit, 69, 177 n15
'Golden Twenties', the, 41ff, 89ff, 93
Goltz, Freiherr von der, 26
Grand Coalition government, 57f, 92, 102
Gründerzeit, 10
Guardianship Court, 83
Gurlitt, Ludwig, 19

Index

Hamburg, 6, 12, 23, 49, 60, 73, 77, 78, 88, 89f, 91, 112, 113, 119, 120, 123, 128, 137, 138, 140, 141, 142, 143, 144, 145, 146, 150, 151, 181 n71, 183 n102, 185 n134, 186 n146, 187 n154, 157, 190 n24, 197 n50, 198 n60, 205 n87, 91, 208 n116
'Hamburger Volkszeitung', 149
Hartmann, Dr., 150
Harvey, Elizabeth, 5
Hauptausschuss der Arbeiterwohlfahrt, 37
Heimann, Franz, 124
Herrmann, Walter, 150
Hertz, Dr Wilhelm, 78, 88, 150, 182 n94, 205 n97, 207 n113
Hiertsiefer, Heinrich, 86
Hilfsverein für Jünglinge, 20
Hindenburg, Paul von (Reich President), 41
Hindenburg-Jugend, 66
Hinse, Dr, 75
Hitler, Adolf, 57, 63, 156, 160, 161
Hitler Youth, 66, 124f, 160
Horn, Daniel, 160
Hyper-inflation, 4, 36, 39, 40, 48, 49, 61, 74, 81, 82, 94, 97, 126, 170 n9

Independent Social Democratic Party (USPD), 35, 66, 79f
Industrialisation (in Germany), 10, 11, 14f, 16, 21, 22, 44, 45, 47, 64
Innere Mission, 20
Institut für Konjunkturforschung, 175 n78

Journeymen's Associations, 20
Juchacz, Marie, 80, 88
Jugendämter, 73, 76ff, 80, 82f, 89, 148, 179 n34, 182 n94, 183 n98, 102
Jugendamtsgesetz, 72, 179 n34
Jugendarbeitsschutzgesetz, 107
Jugendbund (NSDAP), 66
'Jugend-Führer', 193 n74
Jugendfürsorge, 2, 12, 21, 27ff, 80, 81, 145f, 147–54, 168 n69
Jugendgerichtsgesetz (JGG), 8, 78, 82ff, 133, 135ff, 149, 156, 177 n15, 181 n77, 183 n103, 108, 184 n110, 186 n146, 203 n61 (*see also* Juvenile crime)
Jugendgerichtshilfe, 144
Jugendpflege, 2, 6, 7, 8, 21ff, 24ff, 27, 30, 67–93, 103ff, 106ff, 123ff, 126ff, 136, 166 n35, 178 ns17, 20 and 26, 179 n32, 186 n144 (*see also* Working-class youth)
Jungdeutsche Orden, 155
Jungdeutschlandbund, 26, 126, 167 n56
Jung-Zentrum, 65
Juvenile crime at delinquency, 4ff, 8f, 13, 21, 23, 27ff, 32, 78f, 82ff, 100, 122f, 124, 132, 133–54, 158; before 1918, 7, 13, 21, 23, 27ff, 32, 135; in the 1920s, 135ff, 139, 141, 145, 149, 204 n76; in the Depression, 8, 132, 137ff, 140ff, 143ff, 149
and conviction rates, 7, 28f, 32, 134, 135, 136ff, 140ff, 142ff, 149, 150, 201 n11, 12, 202 n51, 203 n59
and 'ineducables', 152–4, 161, 207 n113
and Juvenile Courts Law (JGG), *see Jugendgerichtsgesetz*
and legal definition of, 29f, 133f, 147f, 201 n22
and liberal ethos, 8, 13, 27ff, 78f, 82f, 133ff, 136ff, 144ff, 147ff, 150ff, 205 n87, 97, 206 n103
and reasons for, 8, 28, 32, 135, 138, 139ff, 144, 145, 200 n5, 204 n76
and recidivism, 145, 203 n60
and sentences, 144f, 203 n59
social and class profile of, 4, 5, 13, 28, 32, 122, 134, 135, 136f, 138, 140ff, 142ff, 148, 202 n31, 204 n76
and street gangs, 9, 32, 145–7, 148, 151, 158, 203 n67
and types of crime, 32, 122f, 134f, 137f, 143f, 147, 202 n51
and unemployment, 8, 100, 135, 137, 138, 139ff, 142ff, 144ff, 202 n26
see also Correctional education; Reformatories

Kaiser Wilhelm 11, 11, 13, 18, 19, 23, 30, 34
Kapp Putsch, 38
Kelchner, Mathilde, 100
Key, Ellen, 11
Kindt, Werner, 177 n15
KJVD (*Kommunistische Jugendverband Deutschlands*), 66, 125, 130, 159 (*see also* Communist youth)
Köhler, Heinrich, 56
Kolping, Domvikar, 20
KPD, *see* German Communist Party
Krantz, Paul, 93
Kulturkritik, 14f, 16, 18, 19, 47

Index

Labour aristocracy, 47
Labour Courts Act, 42
Labour exchanges, 45, 46, 48, 50, 51, 54, 113
Labour Exchanges Act, 51, 54, 113
Labour law, 38
Labour offices, 54
Labour Protection Act (draft), 192 n62
Labour Service, 8, 125, 129–31 (*see also* Voluntary labour service)
Lagarde, Paul de, 15, 17
Lamm, Albert, 104
Lampel, Peter Martin, 151
Landesbeirat für Jugendpflege., 180 n53
Landesjugendamt (LJA), 88, 89, 183 n98, 186 n141
Landesjugendwohlfahrtsgesetz (Württemberg), 89
Langbehn, Julius, 15
Langemarck, Battle of, 30
Lau, Ernst, 100
Law against Trashy and Erotic Literature, 87ff
Lazarsfeld, Paul F., 194 n95
League of German Opposition to Smoking, 86
Lhotzky, Heinrich, 11
Lichtspielgesetz, 86, 184 n122
Liebknecht, Karl, 35
Lietz, Hermann, 19
Lindenhof (reformatory), 149
Litt, Theodor, 69
'Lost generation' (of youth), 9, 132, 161f
Lower middle class, 4, 16
Lumpenproletariat, 4, 47, 133, 146
Luxemburg, Rosa, 35

Mahraum, Artur, 155
Marienthal, 158, 209 n10
Marx, Wilhelm, 79
Marxism, 159
Meissner Formula, 17
Mewes, Bernhard, 110
Middle-class youth, 12, 16ff, 19, 21, 26, 30f, 68ff, 93, 116, 142, 143, 155f
Modderkrebs gang, 146
Müller, Hermann, 55, 58, 102

'*Nachrichtendienst*', 88
Nähring, Paul, 23
Naphtali, Fritz, 56
National Auxiliary Service Law, 31, 38, 48

National Factory Council, 38
National Labour Office, 48
National Office for Labour Exchange, 50
National Socialism, 1, 7, 9, 53, 57, 63, 66, 67, 103, 129, 130, 139, 153, 154, 155, 156, 157ff, 159ff, 203 n61
Nationalvereinigung Evangelischer Jünglingsbündnisse, 21
National Youth Law (1930), 125
National Youth Welfare Act, *see Reichsjugendwohlfahrtsgesetz* (RJWG)
Natorp, Paul, 69
Niederschönfeld (reformatory), 142
Nietzsche, Friedrich, 15
Nohl, Hermann, 69
Notwerk der deutschen Jugend, 131, 147, 154, 160, 200 n89
November Revolution, 32, 34ff, 40, 64, 65, 161, 169 n1
NSDAP, *see* National Socialism

Oberprüfstelle, 87f, 185 n130
Ohlsdorf (reformatory), 205 n91

Pan-Germanism, 17
Papen, Franz von, 3, 8, 39, 62, 122, 130, 139, 153, 154, 207 n113
Peukert, Detlev, 2ff, 182 n85
Poland, 161f
Polligkeit, Wilhelm, 29
Poor Law relief, 20, 47, 50, 54, 62, 121, 122
Population (Reich), 6, 13ff, 20, 27, 55, 58, 68, 90, 95ff, 115ff, 120, 134, 138, 139, 149
Prenzlauer Berg, 89, 104
Preyer, Wilhelm, 11
Prussia, 6, 7, 21, 22, 24–9, 32, 41, 46, 61, 69, 71, 74, 75, 82, 104, 105, 112, 113, 120, 124f, 127f, 138, 148, 150, 151, 163 n2.1, 180 n61, 183 n99, 188 n158, 160, 191 n45, 197 n50, 206 n101, 103, 207 n108, 110
Prussian Ministry of Welfare, 74–7, 86–8, 90, 91, 138, 151–3, 180 n62
'*Psychologie des Jugendalters*', 64
Public Welfare Act, 42

Rastenburg (reformatory), 151
Rationalisation (industrial), 43, 51f, 95, 98, 115
Red Army, 162

Index

Reformatories (in correctional education), 2, 5, 29. 148–54, 204 n71, 75 & 76, 205 n36, 91, 92, 96 & 97, 206 n101, 207 n108, 110, 113 & 116
Reich Finance Minister, 76, 82
Reich Law of Association, 23, 24, 126
Reich Ministry of Education, 178 n20
Reich Ministry of the Interior, 72, 76, 78, 82, 86, 88, 128, 131, 132, 153, 188 n167
Reich Ministry of Justice, 77, 78
Reich Ministry of Labour, 39, 43, 52, 56, 103, 104, 111, 112, 173 n60
Reich Ministry for Public Welfare, 178 n20
Reich Ministry for Youth, 181 n67
Reich Statistical Office, 134
Reichsanstalt für Arbeitsvermittlung und Arbeitslosenversicherung, 45, 54, 55, 97, 103, 116, 117, 127
'*Reichsarbeitsblatt*', 45
Reichsarbeitsgemeinschaft für Deutsche Arbeitsdienstpflicht, 129
Reichsarbeitsgemeinschaft für Jugenderholungs-und Heilfürsorge, 91
Reichsarbeitsgemeinschaft Sozialer Dienst, 125
Reichsausschuss der deutschen Jugendverbände, 69f, 80, 88, 107, 110, 124, 178 n17, 192 n60, 193 n84
Reichsbeirat für körperliche Erziehung, 72
Reichsflagge, 91
Reichsjugendgerichtsgesetz (1943), 203 n61
Reichsjugendgesetz, 181 n63
Reichsjugendwohlfahrtsgesetz (RJWG), 8, 76ff, 79ff, 82ff, 89, 90, 92, 93, 133, 135, 137, 144, 147ff, 156, 177 n15, 181 n64, 182 n90, 91, 183 n99, 101 & 102, 188 n161
Reichskonferenz der arbeitenden Jugend, 107
Reichskonferenz für evangelische Kinderpflege, 177 n5
Reichskuratorium für Jugendertüchtigung, 131, 161
Reichsverband der deutschen Industrie, 57
Reichsverband der deutsch-nationalen Parteijugendgruppen, 66
Reichsverband der deutschen Windthorstbünde, 65
Reichsverband deutscher demokratischer Jugendvereine, 66
Reichsverband für deutsche Jugendherbergen, 92
Reichsverband für dissidentische Fürsorge, 152
Reichsrat, 184 n124
Reichstag, 47, 48, 53, 74, 78, 79, 80, 82, 111, 173 n60, 181 n79, 183 n103, 184 n124, 185 n133, 192 n62, 208 n2
Reichstag Elections, 43, 56, 125, 157f, 209 n7
Reichswehr, 130
'*Rembrandt als Erzieher*', 15
Rhineland, 25, 60, 74, 86, 88, 89, 90, 120, 128, 180 n48, 185 n134, 190 n24, 197 n50, 200 n89, 207 n108
Ricklingen (reformatory), 151
Riebesell Dr P., 77, 78
Rote Jungfront, 66
Ruhr miners, 57
Ruhrlade, 57

Schacht, Hjalmar, 63
Scheuen (reformatory), 151
Schleicher, General Kurt von, 8, 62, 106, 130, 131
Schleunner, Oberstudiendirektor, 69
Schlosser, Rudolf, 150
'*Schmutzkampf*', 185 n126
Schultz, Clemens, 12, 21
'*Schundkampf*', 185 n126
Schweizer, Eugen, 142, 143
Second World War, 161
Secondary schools (*Gymnasia*), 18f, 113
Siegmund-Schultze, Friedrich, 69
Siemering, Hertha, 116
Sinzheimer, Hugo, 56
Social control, theory and practice of, 2ff, 7f, 26f, 30ff, 84, 87, 94, 103, 105f, 126, 130f, 148, 152, 154, 157, 159f, 208 n118
Social Democratic Party (SPD), 4, 10, 18, 19, 23, 24, 25, 34ff, 41, 42, 43, 44, 47, 48, 52, 55, 56, 58, 59, 61, 62, 65, 66, 67, 80, 81, 87, 88, 104, 105, 107, 114, 125, 129, 151, 156, 158, 159, 160, 169 n1, 204 n75, 206 n103
Social Reform Movement, 1, 2, 4, 6, 7, 11ff, 14, 19, 20, 27, 28ff, 36, 44, 51, 67f, 93, 134f, 145

Index

Socialist Workers' Party (SAPD), 67
Soviet Union, 161
Soziale Arbeitsgemeinschaft Berlin-Ost, 69, 178 n15
Sozialistische Proletarierjugend, 66
Sozialpolitik, 4ff, 8, 10f, 19ff, 24ff, 30ff, 36–63, 64–93, 94–114, 121ff, 125ff, 133, 151, 152f, 156f
Spartacists, 35
Spranger, Eduard, 64
Stahlhelm, 129
Stampfer, Friedrich, 41
Stegerwald, Adam, 71, 76
Stinnes–Legien Agreement, 37
Storm Troopers (SA), 160
Strasser, Gregor, 155
Stresemann, Gustav, 50, 58
Struveshof (reformatory), 151
Stulpnägel, General Edwin von, 131
Stury, Richard, 142
Syrup, Dr Friedrich, 127

Tagesheime, 127
Tarnow, Fritz, 56, 61
Tartarenblut gang, 146
Tenants' protection Act, 39
Third Reich, 107, 161, 182 n90
Trade unions, 1, 4, 11, 20, 23, 24, 31, 34f, 36ff, 40, 42f, 44ff, 50ff, 54ff, 57ff, 61, 63, 67, 90, 92, 97, 98, 105, 107, 108f, 111, 114, 116, 124, 125, 129, 158ff, 172 n33, 193 n74
Trott zu Solz, August von, 25

'Umbau–Nicht Abbau' programme, 124
Unemployment, adult, 43–55, 57–63, 97ff, 115–21, 125, 157f, 172 n31 & 33, 173 n55, 174 n66, 175 n78 & 79, 209 n10
  and unemployment benefit and relief measures, 38, 44–56, 57ff, 97, 98ff, 100ff, 113, 121ff, 133, 176 n93 (*see also* AVAVG)
Unemployment, youth, 6, 7, 8, 31, 69, 95–100, 103ff, 115–32, 135, 139ff, 145ff, 154, 156, 157–61, 190 n24, 25, 29 & 35, 191 n47, 195 n5 & 7, 196 n30, 209 n10
  and regional variation of, 120
  and social at psychological consequences of, 7, 8, 100ff, 103f, 105, 121ff, 123ff, 126ff, 131ff, 135, 139ff, 145ff, 157–61
  and social composition of, 118ff
  and unemployment benefit and relief measures for, 6, 8, 53, 97, 98–106, 107, 116, 121ff, 124–32, 156, 158, 190 n35, 191 n47
United States, 58

Verband der Arbeiterjugendvereine Deutschlands, 65
Verband der katholischer Jünglingsvereinigung Deutschlands, 21
Verband der Sozialistische Arbeiterjugend Deutschlands, 66, 68f
Verband deutscher Arbeitsnachweise, 46
Verein für Sozialpolitik, 20
Verordnung über Erwerbslosenfürsorge, 50, 101
Versailles, Treaty of, 36, 40, 94
Vocational Training Act, 111, 112
Volksgemeinschaft, 30, 161, 182 n90
Voluntary Labour Service (FAD), 8, 125, 129–31, 147, 154, 160f, 199 n79 & 87
'*Vorwärts*', 41

Wandervogel, 16–19, 23, 30f, 68, 69, 121, 146
Wasserburg (reformatory), 149
Weber, Max, 15
Weiland, Ruth, 91, 124
Weimar Constitution, 37ff, 70, 77, 81, 87, 94, 111, 147, 156, 178 n19
Welfare Insurance legislation, 10f, 19f, 40, 45ff, 75ff, 100–6, 121ff
Welfare relief, *see* Poor Law relief
Welfare State (*Sozialstaat*), 32, 34–63
'Welfare unemployed', 54, 62, 174 n66
Werkheime, 104, 127
Werksgemeinschaft, concept of, 56
Westphal, Max, 88
White-collar workers (*Angestellte*), 43, 50, 52, 54, 60, 99, 116, 157, 171 n10
Wilhelmine Reich (*Kaiserreich*), 2, 3, 5, 7, 10–33, 34, 44ff, 65, 67, 94, 126, 149
Wilker, Karl, 149
Windthorst, Ludwig, 65
Windthorstbünde, 65
Winterhilfekasse, 47
Wissell, Rudolf, 43, 56
Workers, in Germany, 2, 4, 10, 11, 13, 19, 20, 27, 34ff, 38ff, 43–63, 73, 78,

104, 122, 124, 125, 133, 148, 149, 156, 157f, 160, 170 n9, 172 n39, 175 n78, 187 n149
Working-class youth, in Germany
 and alcohol, 22, 84ff, 139
 and career guidance, 111ff, 157, 194 n95
 and compulsory labour, 101, 102, 106, 122, 126, 156, 196 n30
 and demographic change, 13f, 58, 95f, 108, 115ff, 134ff, 138f, 149, 206 n101
 and education, 19, 68f, 73ff, 78f, 80ff, 101, 105, 111, 113, 116, 124, 126, 128, 158, 180 n61, 194 n96
 and emigration, 113
 and erotic literature, 22, 85ff, 88ff, 185 n126
 and factory protection for, 8, 21f, 23, 31, 94, 96, 106f, 108ff, 114, 123, 125, 156, 192 n62, 196 n34
 and First World War, 31ff, 96, 106, 135, 146
 government attitude towards, 1–9, 11ff, 19ff, 22ff, 25ff, 29ff, 64–93, 94–114, 121ff, 125ff, 129ff, 133–54, 155–61
 and health of, 21, 71, 73ff, 79, 90ff, 123, 124, 158, 187 n154, 188 n158 & 160, 197 n50
 and holidays, 8, 90f, 108, 110, 123, 125, 156, 187 n152
 and the labour market, 5, 8, 94–114, 115–32, 158, 166 n34, 189 n14 (*see also* Unemployment, youth)
 and masters' brutality towards, 23, 107f, 123, 156, 192 n69 (*see also under* Apprentices' contracts)
 and morals, 23, 32, 75, 79, 84ff, 92, 97, 100, 124, 126, 128, 132, 133, 135, 148, 184 n122 & 124, 188 n160, 202 n51
 and National Socialism, 7, 9, 93, 155–61
 and numbers in population of, 13ff, 58, 95ff, 115ff, 120, 128, 134, 136, 138f
 and political radicalism, 1, 2, 7, 9, 13, 23, 24, 25ff, 30, 32f, 64, 66f, 103, 126, 129ff, 153, 154, 155ff, 159ff, 199 n78

 and suicide, 23, 75, 93, 124, 151, 158
 and trade unions, 109, 114, 193 n73
 and vagrancy, 73, 74f, 92, 99, 122, 123f, 145, 148, 158, 190 n23
 and vocational education, 73ff, 101f, 104, 106, 110ff, 125ff, 131, 157, 191 n45, 194 n89
 and welfare provision, 67–93, 106f, 121ff, 124–32, 156f, 158ff, 178 n17 & 20, 188 n167, 196 n38, 199 n76
Working-class youth movement, 1, 23ff, 26, 65f, 68, 73, 107f, 123, 131
Workers' and Soldiers' Councils, 35
Workmen's Protection Act, 19, 22
Working Hours legislation, 42, 112
Woytinsky, Wladimir, 61
WTB-Plan, 61, 125
Wulle, Reinhold, 64
Württemberg, 72, 73, 74, 89, 112, 113, 119, 123, 142, 143, 179 n34, 180 n47, 184 n124, 204 n75
Wyneken, Gustav, 17, 19

Youth Gangs (*Cliquen*), 9, 32, 145–7, 148, 151, 158, 203 n67
Younger generation, definition of, 5, 6
Youth Protection Act (1938), 107
Youth Welfare Decree (*Jugendpflegeerlass*, 1911), 7, 22f, 24ff
Youth welfare lobby, 4, 8, 22, 67, 70, 93, 100

ZAG (Joint Industrial Alliance), 37, 40
Zahn, Dr Von, 88
Zentralausschuss für Volks-und Jugendspiele, 72
Zentrale für Berufsberatung und Lehrstellenvermittlung, 113
Zentralstelle für Arbeiterwohlfahrt, 20
Zentralstelle für Lehrstellenvermittlung, 112
Zentralstelle für Volkswohlfahrt, 178 n17
Zentralverband katholischer Jungfrauenvereinigungen Deutschlands, 21
Zugscharen, Die, 69, 177 n15
Zwangserziehungsgesetz (1878), 27, 168 n69

DATE DUE

NOV 27 '90			
MAY 22 1999			
AUG - 3 1998			
	261-2500		Printed in USA